Modern App Development with Python and Flet

Second Edition

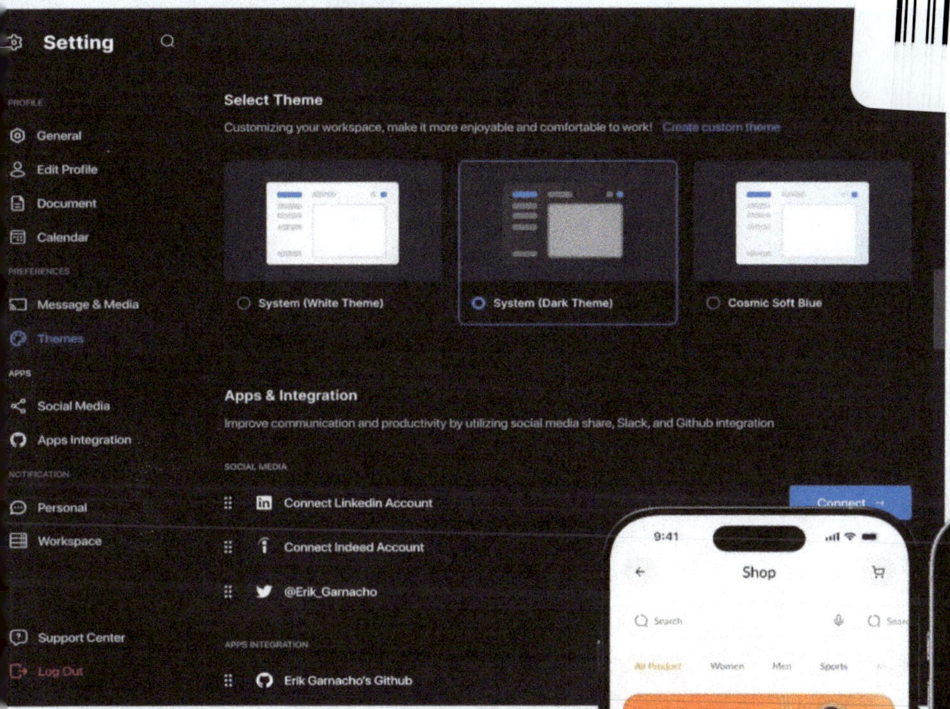

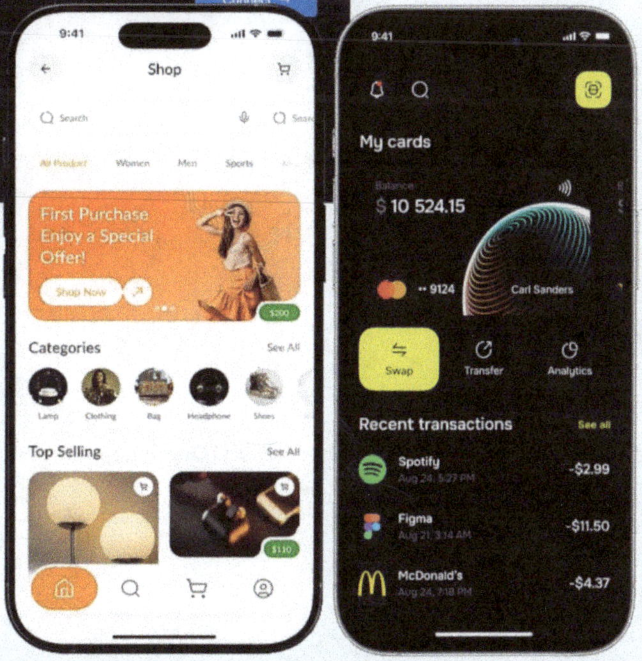

Build Cross-Platform Android, iOS, Web and Desktop Applications Quickly and Easily

Williams Asiedu

Quereila

Modern App Development with Python and Flet

Build Cross-Platform Android, iOS, Web and Desktop Applications Quickly and Easily

Second Edition

Williams Asiedu

Ouereila Publishing

Modern App Development with Python and Flet

Build Cross-Platform Android, iOS, Web and Desktop Applications Quickly and Easily

ENOP0013
ISBN: 979-8-2956-9029-7

Copyright © 2026 Ouereila Publishing

Ouereila Publishing

For permissions, inquiries, or licensing requests, please contact:
Email: ouereila@gmail.com

Table of Contents

Preface

Python is one of the most widely used programming languages in the world today. It plays a major role in fields such as Artificial Intelligence, Machine Learning, Web Development, Game Development, Data Science, Automation, Cybersecurity, Scientific Computing, Scripting, Cloud Computing, and DevOps. Its popularity continues to grow because of its simple syntax, readability, versatility, strong community support, vast ecosystem of libraries, cross-platform capability, and rapid development speed.

Despite its dominance across many domains, Python has historically seen limited use in mobile application development and modern desktop UI development. This is largely because Python has long been associated with backend systems, data processing, and scripting rather than user interface design. Over the years, several frameworks and toolkits have been developed to enable desktop application development with Python. However, many of them were restricted in flexibility, modern UI components, cross-platform consistency, or were limited primarily to desktop environments.

Meanwhile, frameworks like Google's **Flutter** revolutionized UI development with rich, responsive, and beautiful cross-platform interfaces. Python developers needed a solution that could combine Python's simplicity with Flutter's powerful UI engine.

That solution is **Flet**.

Flet bridges the gap by allowing developers to build modern mobile, desktop, and web applications using Python, while rendering the user interface through the Flutter SDK. It offers a rich collection of UI controls, strong structural design, cross-platform deployment, and growing community support. Its adoption is increasing rapidly as developers discover how easily they can build beautiful, production-ready applications using Python alone.

Flet represents a significant step forward in Python application development.

This book is designed to guide you through the Flet framework—from the very basics to advanced application development and deployment. By the end, you will be able to design, build, and package fully functional applications across multiple platforms.

Who This Book Is For

This book is written for anyone interested in developing applications for mobile, desktop, or web platforms—whether for personal projects, professional deployment, or publication on marketplaces such as the Google Play Store or the Apple App Store.

Prior Python experience is helpful but not mandatory. Beginners are encouraged to have a basic understanding of Python fundamentals before diving in. The explanations throughout the book are written in clear and simple English, with detailed definitions and practical examples to help you grow confidently as a developer.

Structure of the Book

The book is organized into four coherent chapters, each building upon the previous one:

Chapter 1 introduces graphical user interfaces and reviews existing Python frameworks.

Chapter 2 explores Flet in depth, including installation, tools, dependencies, and environment setup.

Chapter 3 focuses on Flet controls, properties, methods, layouts, and practical usage.

Chapter 4 explains how to package and deploy Flet applications as standalone builds ready for distribution.

Version Information

Flet is an actively evolving framework. As developers continue to improve and optimize it, certain syntax elements or control behaviors may change in future releases. Readers are encouraged to consult the official Flet documentation when necessary.

This book follows the redesigned architecture introduced in version 0.90 and later.

Code Snippets

Throughout this book, you will find highlighted code sections labeled under Python headings. These examples are practical and can be copied, modified, and tested to help you build your own applications step by step.

Images and Illustrations

Screenshots and visual illustrations are included to enhance understanding. Most images show application outputs on mobile or desktop platforms. These visuals are meant to simulate real development scenarios and improve comprehension—even if you are not actively coding while reading.

Notes to Readers

- 📌 Technology evolves quickly. While this edition reflects a stable version of Flet at the time of writing, APIs and features may change in future updates.
- 📌 Some properties and methods may appear repeatedly in different chapters. This repetition is intentional, as readers may not always read the book sequentially.
- 📌 When working with code examples, replace image files or media resources with your own where necessary.
- 📌 If you encounter difficulty understanding a concept, consult Python's official module documentation or refer to the official Flet documentation for additional clarification.

Chapter 1

Graphical User Interface

Learning Objectives

Upon completing this chapter, you will be able to:

- Define and explain the concept of a Graphical User Interface (GUI).
- Describe the role and responsibilities of the backend in application development.
- Explain the frontend and its role in user interaction.
- Understand how the frontend and backend communicate and interact within an application architecture.
- Identify and compare various Python GUI frameworks.

Graphical User Interface (GUI)

Application Software

At this stage, it is assumed that you have learned the fundamentals of Python programming and have built a solid foundation for application design and development. As a developer, you are expected to possess the ability to write programs and integrate frameworks to produce complete, functional software applications.

Every software project typically progresses through several stages, including **planning**, **prototyping**, **development**, **testing** and **evaluation**. Each stage contributes to shaping a reliable and efficient application.

Application software refers to a collection of computer programs designed to perform specific tasks or solve particular problems. It represents the logical implementation of ideas through source code, developed using programming languages and frameworks. The process of converting source code into a complete, usable software product is known as application **development**. This process involves both the backend (logic and processing) and the frontend (user interface and interaction).

Backend Phase

The **backend** of an application handles the logical operations, data management and core functionalities that ensure the system runs correctly. It is built using programming constructs such as classes, functions, variables and objects that work together to process data and perform operations unseen by the user.

Users interact indirectly with the backend through actions performed on the frontend. Each action triggers backend logic, which may include:

1. Executing a function or process.
2. Sending, retrieving or updating records in a database.
3. Managing application states and user sessions.
4. Performing calculations, data validation or file operations.

5. Communicating with external services through APIs.

These backend processes are crucial in maintaining the stability and functionality of the entire application. The backend ensures that user requests are processed and appropriate responses are generated efficiently.

Frontend Phase

The **frontend** is the visible and interactive part of an application—the environment where users issue commands and receive results. It consists of graphical or textual interfaces designed to make interaction intuitive and user-friendly.

Users communicate with the application by performing actions such as clicking, tapping, dragging, typing or scrolling. These actions generate events that send parameterized commands or signals to the backend for processing. Once the backend executes the corresponding logic, the result is displayed on the frontend through visual or textual updates.

The frontend and backend communicate continuously through a bidirectional data flow, ensuring seamless interaction between user inputs and system responses. In graphical applications, this communication is often implemented through **Graphical User Interfaces (GUIs)**—an area where frameworks like **Flet** excel by enabling developers to build interactive frontends using Python.

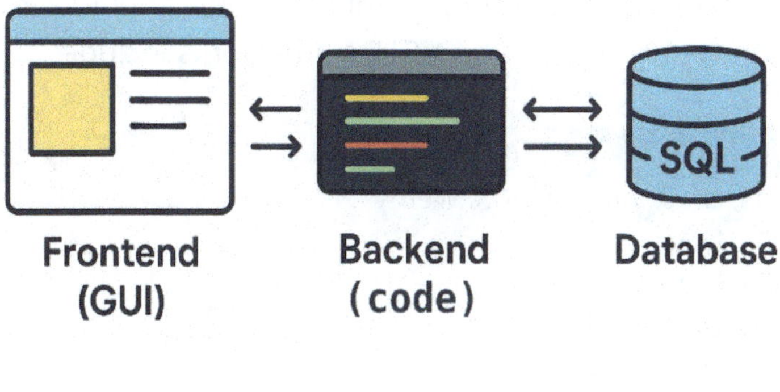

Figure 1.0 : Frontend and Backend Logic

Graphical User Interface (GUI)

A **Graphical User Interface (GUI)** connects the frontend and backend of an application, enabling communication between the user and the underlying program logic. It provides visual components that allow users to perform actions such as clicking, typing or selecting items to execute tasks defined in the backend.

A GUI makes programs easier to use by replacing complex commands with simple graphical interactions. Through GUI elements, users can initiate actions and view real-time results without needing to understand the underlying code.

A GUI consists of a collection of components, often called **widgets** or **controls**, such as buttons, text boxes, labels, editors, sliders, menus, images and other interactive elements. These widgets work together to perform a specific task or create a complete user interface.

GUI frameworks or toolkits are not part of the core programming language itself. Instead, they are external libraries or modules that must be installed and imported into a program. Each framework has its own syntax, structure and rules for building interfaces. Generally, GUI frameworks are designed for specific programming languages, meaning that a framework written for one language cannot be directly used in another without adaptation or binding support.

Python GUI Frameworks

Python provides several frameworks for building graphical applications across different platforms. The most commonly used Python GUI frameworks include:

Table 1.0

Framework	Supported Platforms
Flet	Windows, macOS, Linux, Android, iOS, Web
PyQt / PySide	Windows, macOS, Linux
Kivy / KivyMD	Windows, macOS, Linux android
Tkinter	Windows, macOS, Linux
wxPython	Windows, macOS, Linux
Dear PyGui	Windows, macOS, Linux
PySimpleGUI	Windows, macOS, Linux

Each of these frameworks has unique features and design patterns suited for particular types of applications. For example, Tkinter is Python's standard GUI library and is ideal for lightweight desktop tools, while PyQt and PySide are preferred for more advanced, feature-rich interfaces.

Flet Framework Overview

Although Python is widely used across major domains such as data science, automation and machine learning, it has traditionally had limited adoption in mobile and web development. The Flet framework addresses this limitation by enabling developers to create cross-platform applications that run on desktop, mobile and web environments from a single Python codebase.

Flet provides an extensive collection of modern widgets and layout tools that make it easier to design professional interfaces. It simplifies the development process by combining Python's backend power with responsive frontend elements, giving developers a unified platform for building interactive applications.

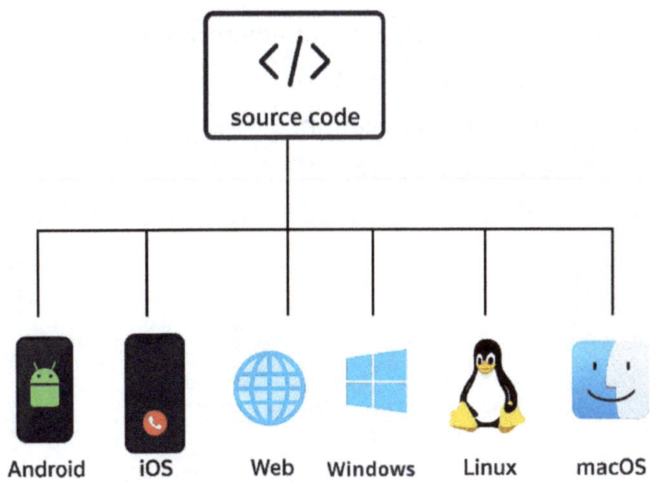

Figure 1.1 : Code once, deploy to many platforms

Chapter 2

Flet Framework

Learning Objectives

Upon completing this chapter, you will be able to:

- Explain the origin and evolution of the Flet framework.
- Describe the architecture and core principles of Flet.
- Identify the required tools and system prerequisites for working with Flet.
- Install and configure Flet in a development environment.
- Use the Flet Command-Line Interface (CLI).
- Develop and run your first Flet application.
- Understand the structure of a Flet project.
- Test and deploy Flet applications on mobile and desktop platforms.

Flet Framework

In traditional application development, one of the major challenges programmers faced was **platform dependency**. Desktop and mobile devices have vastly different underlying architectures, requiring developers to write separate code for each platform (Windows, Linux, macOS, Android and iOS). This approach was time-consuming, error-prone and difficult to maintain.

To address these constraints, Google introduced Flutter in 2017, a cross-platform framework that allows developers to write a single codebase and compile it for multiple platforms, including Windows, Linux, macOS, Android, iOS and the Web. Flutter provides a rich set of modern widgets and user interface elements, enabling high-quality applications with consistent look and feel across platforms. Flutter uses the Dart programming language and its integration with Python is limited.

In 2022, Feodor Fitsner created Flet, a Python-based framework inspired by Flutter's Material Design principles. Flet allows Python developers to create desktop, mobile and web applications using a single codebase, without learning a new programming language. Its rich collection of controls (widgets) and simple syntax make it easier to integrate into Python programs. Flet enables the creation of interactive and professional applications for multiple platforms from the same source code.

Supported Platforms and File Extensions

Table 2.0

Platform	File extension / Package
Windows	.exe (Executable)
macOS	.app (macOS Application)
Linux	.appImage, .deb, .tar.gz
Web	.html + JavaScript + server integration
Android	.apk (Android Application Package) / .aab (Android App Bundle)
iOS	.ipa (iOS App Store Package)

Insight

In this book, we focus on creating applications using Flet with a primary emphasis on mobile and desktop. However, the source code you develop can also be deployed to **web** without modification.

Why Choose Flet

Flet offers several advantages that make it an attractive choice for both beginners and professional developers:

- **Rich Set of Controls** – Provides a variety of ready-to-use UI elements such as buttons, text fields, sliders, tables and media components.
- **No External Dependencies** – Flet is self-contained and requires minimal installation setup, making deployment straightforward.
- **Write Once, Deploy Everywhere** – Applications can be developed once in Python and packaged for all major platforms without rewriting code.
- **Simple and Intuitive Syntax** – Designed to be easy to learn for Python developers, allowing fast development and fewer coding errors.
- **Fast and Easy to Debug** – Python's readability and Flet's structure simplify troubleshooting and application testing.
- **Cross-Platform Material Design** – Provides modern, consistent design standards across all platforms.
- **Supports Reactive Programming** – Enables dynamic UI updates in response to user actions without complex state management.
- **Integration with Existing Python Ecosystem** – Works seamlessly with Python libraries for databases, machine learning and data visualization.
- **Lightweight and Efficient** – Flet applications can run efficiently even on resource-constrained devices.

Prerequisite

Before installing and working with Flet, ensure your system meets the following requirements.

Python

Flet requires Python 3.10 or later. You can verify your Python version by running:

```
python --version
```

Visual Studio

Install **Visual Studio Code** (highly recommended) or any other preferred IDE.

Supported Platforms

macOS

Flet supports macOS 12 (Monterey) or later.

Windows

Flet supports 64-bit versions of Windows 10 and Windows 11.

Linux

Flet supports:

- Debian 10, 11 and 12
- Ubuntu 20.04, 22.04 and 24.04 LTS

Creating a Virtual Environment (venv)

Creating a virtual environment is optional but strongly recommended. A virtual environment allows you to install Flet and its dependencies in an isolated space, preventing conflicts with other Python projects or global packages.

Step 1: Create a Project Directory

```
mkdir my_app
```

Step 2: Create and Activate a Virtual Environment

Using Python's built-in venv module:

```
python -m venv .venv
source .venv/bin/activate
```

Installation

Flet does not require any additional libraries aside from the **Flet** module itself. To install Flet, open the Command Prompt or PowerShell on Windows or the Terminal on Linux or macOS and enter the following command:

```
pip install flet[all]
```

Note

Some platforms may encounter issues with the flet[all] syntax. If this occurs, use the alternative command: *pip install "flet[all]"*

Specifying a Version

If you need to install a specific version of Flet for compatibility reasons, you can specify the version number. For example, to install version 0.28:

```
pip install flet==0.28
```

As of the time of writing this book, the current version of Flet is **1.0 (Redesigned Architecture)**.

"flet[all]" command installs all the necessary components to create Flet applications. After installation, no additional libraries are required. The package also includes **flet-cli**, which allows developers to manage Flet projects from the command line.

Checking the Installed Version

To verify the installed Flet version on your device, use:

```
flet --version
```

or

```
flet -v
```

or

```
flet --doctor
```

or

```
flet -d
```

Upgrading Flet

Flet is actively maintained and new versions are released regularly with additional features and improvements. To upgrade to the latest version, use:

```
pip install 'flet[all]' --upgrade
```

Linux-Specific Requirements

Linux users should ensure that **GStreamer** libraries are installed, as they are required for Flet to run properly. Most Linux distributions include these libraries by default. However, if you encounter an error like the following:

```
Error while loading shared libraries: libgstapp-1.0.so.0: cannot open shared object file: No such file or directory
```

you need to install GStreamer manually. Use the following commands:

```
$ sudo apt-get update
$ sudo apt-get install libgstreamer1.0-dev libgstreamer-plugins-base1.0-dev \
libgstreamer-plugins-bad1.0-dev gstreamer1.0-plugins-base gstreamer1.0-plugins-good \
gstreamer1.0-plugins-bad gstreamer1.0-plugins-ugly gstreamer1.0-libav \
gstreamer1.0-doc gstreamer1.0-tools gstreamer1.0-x gstreamer1.0-alsa \
gstreamer1.0-gl gstreamer1.0-gtk3 gstreamer1.0-qt5 gstreamer1.0-pulseaudio
```

These commands ensure that all required libraries are installed for Flet to function correctly on Linux.

Getting Started with Flet

By this stage, you should be familiar with **Python** and its installation. Now, we will begin creating, testing and running Flet applications.

The Flet library includes many functions, classes and objects that allow you to build interactive applications. To take full advantage of Flet's features, it is recommended to use an **Integrated Development Environment (IDE)** with code completion and suggestions.

Recommended IDE

The best option is **Visual Studio Code**, which provides:

- ***Intellisense*** for Python, assisting with code completion and function suggestions.
- ***GitHub Copilot*** integration for AI-assisted coding.
- A built-in terminal or PowerShell, which can be used to run Flet commands directly.

> **Note**
>
> You can download Visual Studio Code from its official website:
> https://code.visualstudio.com/

Using an IDE like Visual Studio Code will allow you to write, test and debug Flet applications efficiently in a single environment.

Creating a Flet Application

Flet applications can be created using two main approaches, depending on the project type and target platforms. You can choose a method based on whether your application is for **desktop only** or **cross-platform deployment**.

Methods to Create a Flet Application

1. Running directly from a Python script
2. Creating a Flet project directory and running main.py

Choosing the Appropriate Method

Table 2.1

Factor	Method 1: Direct Python Script	Method 2: Flet Project Directory
Application Type	Desktop only	Desktop, Mobile and Web
Platform Testing	Desktop testing	Desktop and Mobile testing
Virtual Environment	Optional	Recommended

Method 1: Running Directly from a Python Script (Desktop Applications)

This method is ideal for **desktop applications** or for quickly testing ideas.

Steps:

1. Create a Python file, for example: myapp.py.
2. Import the Flet module and define a main function:

myapp.py

```python
import flet as ft

def main(page: ft.Page):
    pass  # Your widgets or controls will go here

ft.run(main)
```

3. Run the Python script using your IDE's **Run** button or from the terminal/command line:

```
python myapp
```

A blank desktop application window will open. You can now start adding widgets, layouts and functionality.

> 📖 **Note**
>
> This approach supports only **desktop applications**. Mobile or web deployment is not available when running directly from a script.

Method 2: Creating a Flet Project Directory (Cross-Platform Applications)

This method is recommended for projects that target multiple platforms, require a virtual environment or are intended for professional development.

Steps:

1. Open Visual Studio Code or another IDE.
2. Navigate to your working directory.
3. Ensure your device is connected to the internet.
4. Open the terminal (or Command Prompt on Windows).
5. Create a new Flet project using the command: ***flet create***

```
flet create <project_name>
```

Where <project_name> is the name for your project directory.

The command generates a structured project directory with necessary files for cross-platform development.

Default Project Directory Structure

<project_name> (Parent Directory)

```
📁
|
├──── src
|   ├── 📁 assets
|   |   ├──── icon.png
|   |   └──── splash_android.png
|   └──── main.py
|
├──── .gitignore
├──── pyproject.toml
├──── README.md
└──── 📁 storage
        ├── 📁 data
        ├── 📁 temp
```

Components Explained:

- **src/** – Contains the application source code and assets.
- **assets/** – Stores images, icons and other static resources.
- **main.py** – The entry point of the application where the main function is defined.
- **.gitignore** – Lists files and directories to be ignored by version control.
- **pyproject.toml** – Manages project dependencies and metadata.
- **README.md** – Provides a description and instructions for the project.

Note

The structure may change in future Flet versions. However, the purpose of each file and folder remains the same.

Project Directory Components

src (Source) Directory

The src directory is the most important folder in the Flet project. It contains the **main.py** file, which is the entry point for your application. All program execution begins in *main.py* and this file can also import and call other user-defined modules as needed.

The main.py file comes with a default template demonstrating a small working Flet application, which helps you understand the program structure.

Example template in main.py

Python

```
import flet as ft


def main(page: ft.Page):
    counter = ft.Text("0", size=50, data=0)

    def increment_click(e):
        counter.data += 1
        counter.value = str(counter.data)
        counter.update()

    page.floating_action_button = ft.FloatingActionButton(
        icon=ft.Icons.ADD, on_click=increment_click
    )
    page.add(
        ft.SafeArea(
            ft.Container(
                counter,
                alignment=ft.Alignment.CENTER,
            ),
            expand=True,
        )
    )


ft.run(main)
```

Running the Program

There are three main ways to run your Flet application:

1. **Using Flet CLI:**

```
flet run
```

or

```
flet run script_name
```

2. Using Visual Studio Code: Press the **Run** button to start the program.
3. Using the command line:

```
python main.py
```

Note

- When running from command line and your main.py is inside the src folder, ensure the correct path is specified: Eg: *python src/main.py*
- Testing on desktop is necessary before deploying or debugging on mobile devices.

Modifying Code

The default template in **main.py** often contains a simple counter program for demonstration purposes. For your project, you can replace it entirely with a new code structure:

Key Points:

1. ***import flet as ft*** – Imports the Flet library.
2. ***def main(page: ft.Page):*** – Defines the main function, which contains all logic and Flet controls.
3. ***ft.run(main)*** – Launches the application by executing the main() function.

For web applications, specify the view argument to open the app in a browser:

ft.run(main, view=ft.AppView.WEB_BROWSER)

assets Directory

The assets folder contains all media files (images, audio, video), documents, database files and any other resources used in the application. These files are bundled with the application during packaging.

By default, assets includes the **app icon** and **splash screen icon.** Replace these with your project's icon and splash screen for branding consistency.

.gitignore

GitHub is an online repository used for version control of your application. The .gitignore file specifies files and directories that should not be uploaded to GitHub. All other files are included in the repository.

pyproject.toml

The pyproject.toml file is critical for the Flet project. It manages:

- The Flet version for the project
- The dependencies and libraries required by the application
- The project metadata

Flet uses this file to create a virtual environment for the project without installing dependencies globally on your system.

Insight

The **pyproject.toml** file and its usage are thoroughly explained in Chapter 4 - **Publishing** at the end of this book.

Testing and Debugging Flet Applications

Testing and debugging are essential steps in the development process to ensure your Flet application works correctly across platforms. Flet supports testing on desktop, web and mobile devices.

Desktop and Web Applications

Testing or debugging on a desktop is straightforward. When a program is executed, it automatically opens a window application. This approach works for Windows, macOS and Linux.

You can run the application using:

1. Flet CLI: *flet run*

```
flet run
```

or

```
flet run script_name
```

2. IDE (e.g., Visual Studio Code): Press the Run button.
3. Command line:

```
python main.py
```

For web applications, specifying the view argument opens the app in a web browser, creating a server link that can be accessed locally or shared:

```
flet.run(main, view=flet.AppView.WEB_BROWSER)
```

Then run

```
flet  run --web
```

or

```
flet  run -w
```

The browser link can be copied and opened on other browsers or devices for testing.

Mobile Applications

Testing on a mobile device requires a slightly different approach, as desktop simulation does not fully reflect mobile behavior. Flet allows real-time testing on mobile devices using a server mode.

Steps to Test on Mobile:

1. Install the Flet mobile app:
   Download the Flet app from Google Play Store (Android) or App Store (iOS).

   Play Store
   https://play.google.com/store/search?q=flet&c=apps

   App Store
   https://apps.apple.com/us/app/flet/id1624979699

2. Establish Network Connection
   Connect your mobile device and computer to the **same network**. Options include:
   - Connect both devices to the same **Wi-Fi** network.
   - Use a **hotspot** from either the phone or computer.

3. Starting the Flet Development Server

   To run your Flet app and generate a QR code for mobile testing:

   1. Open your Terminal, PowerShell or CMD.
   2. Run your Flet app (for example):

   Android

```
flet run  --android
```

   Or

```
flet run --android script_name
```

   iOS

```
flet run --ios
```

   Or

```
flet run --ios script_name
```

This generates a **QR code** in the terminal.

4. Open the Scanner app on your Android or iOS device. Scan the QR code.
5. Tap the URL to automatically open the app in the Flet mobile app.

Adding the App Manually (Mobile)

If you prefer manual setup:

1. Open the Flet mobile app.
2. Tap the "+" button to connect to a server.
3. Enter the server address in the format:
   http://192.168.1.50:8550
4. Tap **Add** to connect.

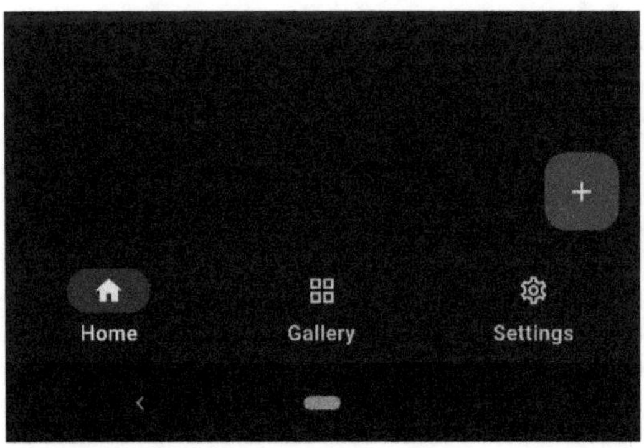

Replace the IP address and port with your machine's details.

Once connected, the app will load on your mobile device and reflect changes made in real time.

Hot Reload

Flet supports hot reload, which allows you to apply changes to your app while testing — without stopping and restarting the server.

You can use the following flags when running your app for hot reload:

- *flet run -d* or *flet run --directory*
- *flet run -r* or *flet run –recursive*

Chapter 3

Flet Controls

Learning Objectives

Upon completing this chapter, you will be able to:

- Define and explain Flet controls and their purpose.
- Identify common control properties and methods.
- Apply colors and styling within Flet applications.
- Understand the role of the Page object in application management.
- Customize application themes and visual appearance.
- Implement data storage and retrieval within applications.
- Explore and utilize various Flet controls, including their properties and methods.
- Design responsive layouts using Flet layout controls.
- Implement and configure button controls.
- Work with forms and input controls for data collection.
- Implement system notifications and user feedback mechanisms.
- Manage page navigation and application routing.
- Handle file operations and media playback.
- Create and manage tables.
- Use controls for graphics, animations, and data visualization.
- Implement charts for visual data representation.
- Utilize Flet services for enhanced application functionality.

Flet Controls

Controls

In Flet, widgets are called controls. Controls form the building blocks of a Flet application. Each control has **methods** and **properties**:

- Properties define the control's appearance, behavior, functionality and overall style.
- Some properties are unique to specific controls, while others are shared properties common to most or all Flet controls. Common properties use the same format across all controls, making them easier to learn and apply.

Insight

To explore all available Flet controls programmatically, use Python's **dir()** function:

```
>>> import flet
>>> controls_list = [x for x in dir(flet)]
>>> print(controls_list)
```

Common Shared Properties in Flet Controls

Below are some key shared properties, with explanations:

Table 3.0

Method/Property	Definition
adaptive	A boolean argument. When True, the control adapts to the platform's native design style (iOS android, Windows, macOS, Linux).
opacity	A float value (0.0 to 1.0) specifying the control's transparency. 0.0 is fully transparent and 1.0 is fully opaque.
rtl	Boolean property that sets **right-to-left layout** for text or content, commonly used in languages like Arabic or Hebrew.
key	Assigns a **unique identifier** to the control for references.

width / height	Sets and returns the control's width and height.
visible	When False, the control is hidden; default is True.
disabled	When True, the control is inactive and does not respond to user interactions such as taps, clicks, scroll or hover; default is False.
animate_offset	Animates movement from one offset to another.
animate_opacity	Animates changes in opacity.
animate_position	Animates control movement within layouts.
animate_rotation	Animates rotation transformations.
animate_scale	Animates scaling of the control.
animate_size	Animates changes in control size.
animate_alias	Boolean property to enable or disable smoothing of edges in drawings or controls.
aspect_ratio	Maintains a specified width-to-height ratio.
badge	Adds a **badge label** to a control, such as a notification count.
will_unmount	Called before the control is removed from the page.
update	Applies changes made to the control and refreshes the UI immediately.
uid	**uid** – Unique identifier for internal use.
top / bottom / left / right	Sets the control's position when using **Stack layout**.
expand	When True, the control fills all available space.
expand_loose	Fills available space but allows surrounding controls to influence layout.
data	Stores any associated data, including numbers, strings, lists, tuples, dictionaries, sets or bytes.
did_mount	Triggered after the control has been added to the page.
event_handlers	Stores references to the control's event listeners.
invoke_method / invoke_method_async	Calls a method on the control, synchronously or asynchronously.
is_isolated	Marks a control as isolated for specific rendering optimizations.
parent	Returns the parent control containing the current control.
page	Returns the page object to which the control belongs.
before_update	Called before a control is updated.
build / build_update_commands	Used internally to build and refresh the control structure.
clean	Resets the control state.
copy_attrs	Helper property for column layouts.
offset	Copies attributes from another control.
rotate	Rotates the control to a specific degree.
margin	Creates margin between the control and its environment.
scale	Increases the size of the control by a factor.

Insight

If a property is common, it can usually be applied to any control even if it is not explicitly documented for that control. This allows developers to reuse techniques consistently across different widgets.

For example,

Python

```
import flet as ft

def main(page: ft.Page):

    text = ft.Text(
        "Hello  Pythonist",
        key="greetings",
        offset= ft.Offset(0.3,0.6),
        rotate= 45,
        opacity=0.8,
        aspect_ratio=1.4,
        expand = True,
    )

    page.add(text)

ft.run(main)
```

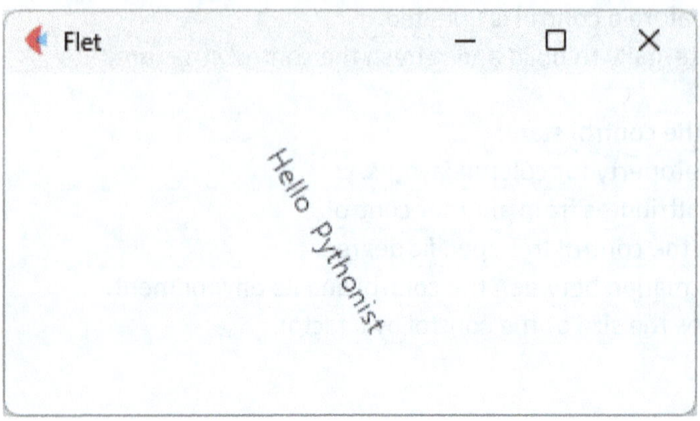

Color

The visual appeal of an application heavily depends on its color scheme. In Flet, most controls have color properties that allow you to style various parts of a control, such as:

- Background
- Foreground
- Font/text
- Borders
- Icons and other controls

Ways to Apply Color in Flet

There are three main ways to set colors in Flet controls:

1. Using Color Names

The simplest way to apply color is by using common color names as strings. Examples include:

• red	• green	• black	• orange	• pink
• blue	• yellow	• white	• purple	• grey

```
Python

ft.Text("Hello, Flet!", color= "red"),
```

2. Using Hexadecimal Values

Colors can also be specified using **hex codes**, which provide precise control over color selection. Hex codes must begin with #.

```
Python

ft.Container(bgcolor="#FF5733", width=200, height=100)
```

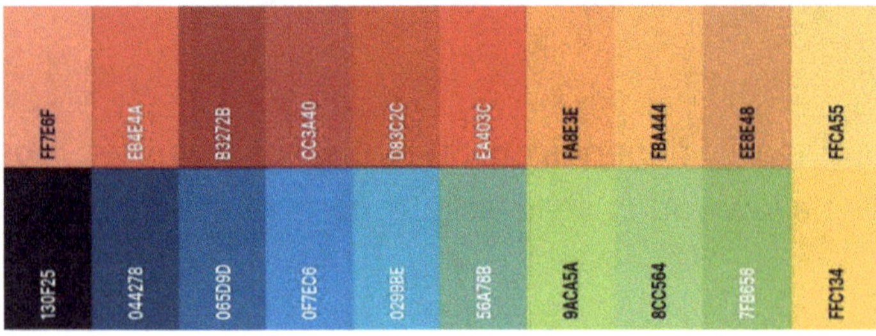

Figure 3.0 : Samples of hexadecimal color codes

3. Using Predefined Flet Colors

Flet provides a set of predefined colors that can be accessed using:

- flet.Colors.COLOR_NAME
- flet.ColorValue.COLOR_NAME

```python
ft.Text("Hello, Flet!", color= ft.Colors.GREEN),
ft.Text("Hello, Flet!", color= ft.ColorScheme.surface), #Theme colors
```

Figure 3.1 : Some predefined Flet Color values

Adjusting Transparency with Opacity

Flet allows colors to be semi-transparent or lighter by using the **with_opacity()** method. The opacity value ranges from **0.0** to **1.0**, where 0.0 is completely invisible and 1.0 is fully opaque.

Example - 50% transparent red,

Python

```
ft.Text("Hello", color=ft.Colors.with_opacity(0.5, "red")),
```

Insight

Transparency is especially useful for overlays, backgrounds, splash, tint and interactive effects.

Page

In Flet, every application is built around a Page.

A **Page** is a container with a layout that holds other controls. In the Flet program structure, the Page is the root control and all other controls are added to it. Pages can even contain other Pages (**Pagelete**) if needed.

By default, a Page uses a Column layout, so its child controls are arranged from top to bottom.

Note

The Page in Flet is the **central hub for your application**. Most UI logic, control arrangement and event handling revolve around it. Understanding its properties and methods is crucial for building robust and responsive applications.

Properties and Methods

Insight

To view the complete list of available methods and properties for the Page class, you can use the built-in **dir()** function on a Page object.

```
>>> import flet
>>> for method in dir(flet.Page):
...     print(method)
```

Adding Controls to a Page

Method/Property	Definition *Table 3.1*
add(control)	Adds a control to the page. Controls are added sequentially based on the page layout.
insert(index, control)	Inserts a control at a specific position in the page's control list.
remove (control)	Removes a specific control from the page.
remove_at (index)	Removes a control at the specified index.

add(control)

Python

```python
import flet as ft

def main(page: ft.Page):
    page.add(
        ft.Text("Hello, World"),
        ft.Text("This is my first App"),
    )

ft.run(main)
```

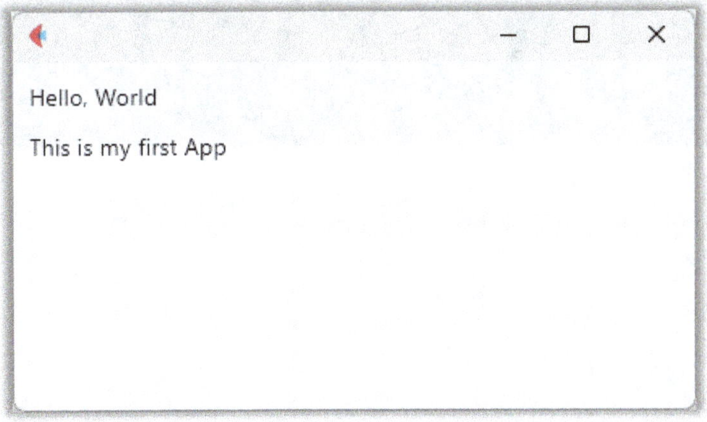

Insight

The use of the **Text** control in the examples above is intentional; its functionality will be explored more thoroughly in the next chapter.

insert(index, control)

Python

```python
import flet as ft

def main(page: ft.Page):

    def insert_function(e):
        page.insert(0, text2)
        page.update()

    text1 = ft.Text("Hello, World")
    text2 = ft.Text("This is my first App")
    button = ft.Button(content="Click me", on_click= insert_function )

    page.add(text1,button)

ft.run(main)
```

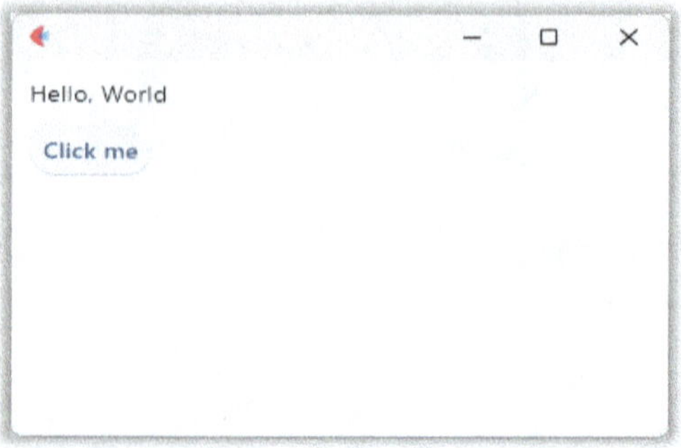

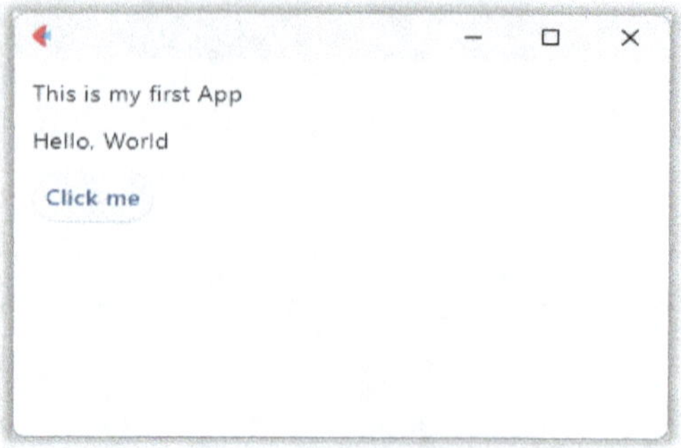

Program Explanation

The following program demonstrates how to register a function to a button in Flet and dynamically insert a control at a specific position within the page.

- A function (insert_function) is registered to a button, so when the button is clicked, the function executes.
- When the button is clicked, it inserts a Text control (*text2*) at index *0* of the page's control list, meaning it appears at the top of the page.
- The **page.update()** refreshes the page whenever a control is added, removed or modified.

remove(control)

```python
import flet as ft

def main(page: ft.Page):

    def delete(e):
        page.remove(text1)
        page.update()

    text1 = ft.Text("text1")
    text2 = ft.Text("text2")
    button = ft.Button(content="Click me", on_click = delete )

    page.add(text1, text2, button)

ft.run(main)
```

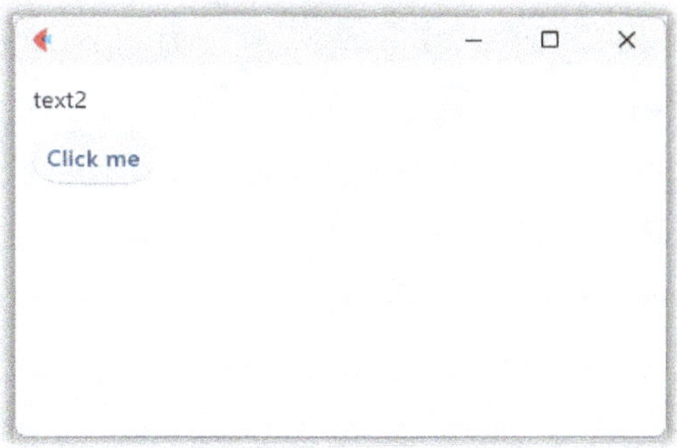

Program Explanation

This program demonstrates how to remove a control from a Flet page using the **remove()** method. A function is registered to a button and when the button is clicked, it deletes a specific control from the page.

1. A function (delete) is registered to the button using the **on_click** parameter.
2. When the button is clicked, the function executes and removes the *text1* control from the page.
3. After removing the control, **page.update()** is called to refresh the user interface and reflect the change immediately.

remove_at(index)

```python
import flet as ft

def main(page: ft.Page):

    def delete_item(e):
        page.remove_at(2)
        page.update()

    text1 = ft.Text("text1")
    text2 = ft.Text("text2")
    text3 = ft.Text("text3")
    delete = ft.Button(content="Delete", on_click = delete_item )

    page.add(text1, text2, text3, delete)

ft.run(main)
```

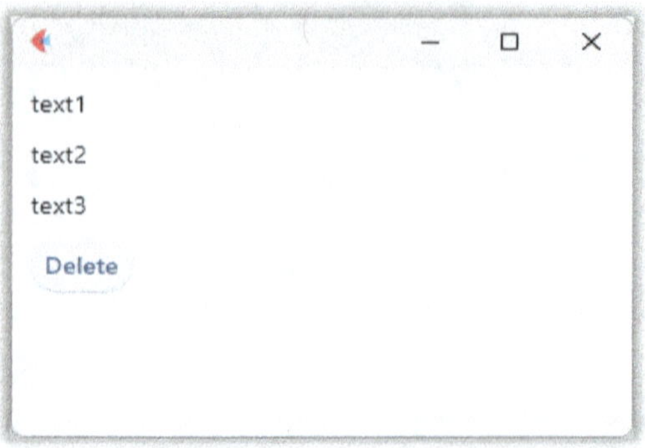

Program Explanation

This program demonstrates how to remove a control from a Flet page using the **remove_at(index)** method. A function is registered to a button and when the button is clicked, a control is deleted based on its positional index in the page's children list.

1. A function (delete) is registered to the button through the **on_click** event.
2. When the button is clicked the function executes and removes the control at index 2 (or any chosen index) using **page.remove_at(2).**

Page Appearance and Layout Properties

Table 3.2

Method/Property	Definition
bgcolor	Sets the background color of the page. Can use a color name ("red") or a hex value ("#FF5733").
padding	Defines the space between the page content and the window edges.
spacing	Sets the spacing between child controls when using a Column layout.
width/height	Returns the page's width and height.
horizontal_alignment/ vertical_alignment	Sets alignment of child controls inside the page.
expand/ expand_loose	Controls whether the page fills available space.

bgcolor = color

Python

```
import flet as ft

def main(page: ft.Page):
    page.bgcolor ="#0a8fdf"

    page.update()

ft.run(main)
```

width / height

```python
import flet as ft

def main(page: ft.Page):
    width = page.width
    height = page.height
    print(f"width->{width}\nheight->{height}")

ft.run(main)
```

```
Output
width->1264.0
height->681.0
```

Controls and Containers on Page

Table 3.3

Method/Property	Definition
controls	Returns the list of controls currently added to the page.
overlay	Adds invisible controls that can float over other page content.
drawer / end_drawer	Defines slide-out drawers for menus or additional content.
floating_action_button	A stationary elevated button that does not scroll with the page.
floating_action_button_location	Sets the position of the floating action button.
appbar	Defines the AppBar control for the page.
navigation_bar	Adds a bottom navigation bar to the page.

Page Behavior and Events

Table 3.4

Method/Property	Definition
on_close	Connects a function that runs when the page closes.
on_scroll / on_scroll_interval	Triggers a function when the page is scrolled.
on_route_change	Triggered when the page route changes.

on_connect / on_disconnect	Called when a client connects or disconnects.
on_keyboard_event	Handles keyboard input events.
on_media_change	Triggered when media content changes.
on_platform_brightness_change	Detects light or dark mode changes.
did_mount / will_unmount	Lifecycle events triggered after the page is added or before it is removed.
update	Refreshes the page whenever a control is added, removed or modified.

on_close = callback

```
Python

import flet as ft

def main(page: ft.Page):
    page.on_close = lambda _: print('Page closed successfully')
    page.update()

ft.run(main)
```

Utilities and Data Properties

Table 3.5

Method/Property	Definition
data	Stores custom data associated with the page.
uid	Unique identifier for the page.
client_ip / client_user_agent	Provides information about the connected client.
get_clipboard /set_clipboard	Accesses or modifies clipboard content programmatically.
session / session_id	Stores session-specific data.
theme / theme_mode / dark_theme	Manages page styling and color theme.
locale_configuration / platform / platform_	Provides device and platform-specific information.
views	Defines multiple "screens" or views that can be switched to within the page.

Navigation, URL and Web-Specific Properties

Method/Property	Definition
route / url / go() / launch_url()	Manage page navigation and opening links.
browser_context_menu / can_launch_url / can_launch_url_async	Manage browser-specific behavior.
pwa	Enables Progressive Web App behavior.
web	Indicates that the page is running as a web application.
close_in_app_web_view	Closes the web view if running inside a browser-based app.

Table 3.6

Other Important Methods

Method/Property	Definition
build() / build_update_commands()	Used internally to build or update page layout.
clean	Clears temporary states or data.
invoke_method / invoke_method_async	Calls a method on the page or its controls.
run_task / run_thread / executor	Executes background tasks or threads.
snapshot / show_semantics_debugger	Debugging tools for inspecting page content.

Table 3.7

Example : Running a background task to update the UI every two seconds

```python
import flet as ft
import asyncio

def main(page: ft.Page):
    page.vertical_alignment = ft.MainAxisAlignment.CENTER
    page.horizontal_alignment = ft.CrossAxisAlignment.CENTER


    async def sample(): #Function to run in the background
        for i in range(1, 20):
            text.value = str(i)
            page.update()
            await asyncio.sleep(2) #Pause without locking UI


    text = ft.Text("0", size=40)
```

```
    page.add(text)
    page.run_task(sample)
ft.run(main)
```

Insight

Many of the Page methods and properties introduced here will be examined more thoroughly in later chapters.

Theme

Theme is an essential part of modern application development. It provides a unified way of managing the overall look and feel of an application. A theme acts as a **template** that defines the default appearance and behavior of controls. It includes settings such as colors, fonts, sizes, shapes, button styles, card styles, dialog appearance and many other visual attributes.

In Flet, every application starts with a **default theme**, which includes predefined values for common properties such as color schemes, text styles, surface backgrounds and control shapes. Developers can customize the theme to match the branding or stylistic needs of their applications.

It is recommended that every application defines at least **two themes**, typically a *light* theme and a *dark* theme. Different users prefer different themes based on comfort, screen brightness, visual clarity and personal appeal.

The theme of a Flet application is controlled through the **Page** object.

Theme Modes

Flet provides **predefined theme modes** that allow developers or users to switch between visual styles:

- **ThemeMode.LIGHT** – Default light theme
- **ThemeMode.DARK** – Dark theme
- **ThemeMode.SYSTEM** – Follows the theme of the host device (automatic switching)

Example – Setting theme to Dark ,

Python

```python
import flet as ft

def main(page: ft.Page):
    page.vertical_alignment = ft.MainAxisAlignment.CENTER
    page.horizontal_alignment = ft.CrossAxisAlignment.CENTER
    page.theme_mode = ft.ThemeMode.DARK

    page.add(
        ft.SafeArea(content=ft.Text("Dark Theme",size= 20))
    )
```

```
ft.run(main)
```

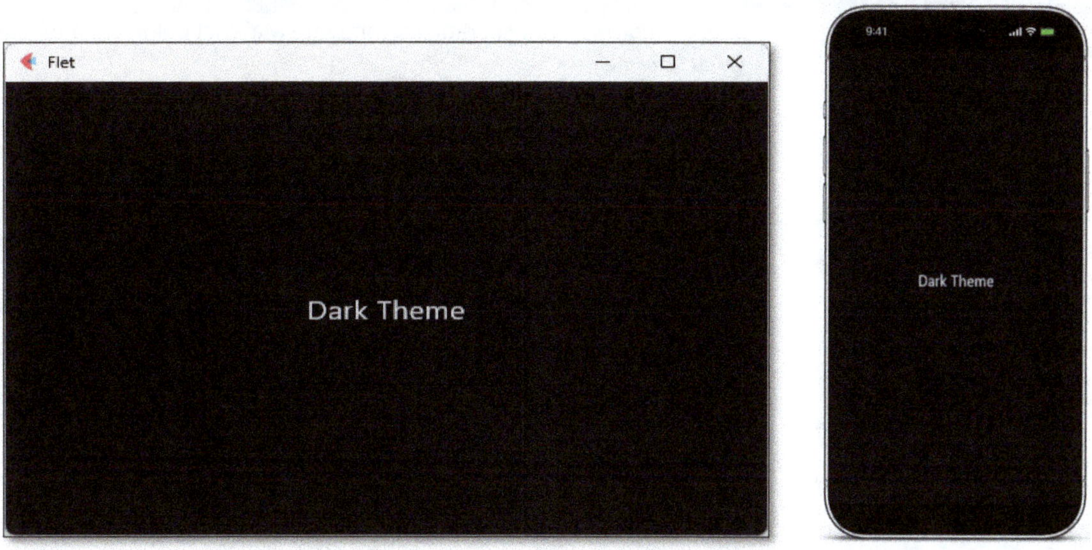

> **Note**
>
> If a property is set both in the **theme** and directly on a **control**, the property set **on the control** always overrides the value from the theme. This ensures developers can make specific adjustments without altering the global theme.

Custom Themes

Developers can customize themes by modifying the **page.theme** property. This gives access to the Theme control and all of its attributes.

Theme Properties and Settings

Below is a full description of each theme attribute. Use *dir(flet.Theme)* to return the full list of properties.

Color and Core Configuration

<table>
<tr><th>Method/Property</th><th>Definition</th><th>Table 3.8</th></tr>
<tr><td>color_scheme_seed</td><td colspan="2">Sets a seed color for generating a complete Material ColorScheme.
ColorScheme
<table>
<tr><td>secondary_container</td><td>on_tertiary_fixed_variant</td><td>on_error</td></tr>
<tr><td>error_container</td><td>surface_container</td><td>error</td></tr>
<tr><td>inverse_primary</td><td>surface_container_high</td><td>surface</td></tr>
<tr><td>inverse_surface</td><td>surface_container_highest</td><td>surface_dim</td></tr>
<tr><td>on_secondary</td><td>surface_container_low</td><td>surface_tint</td></tr>
<tr><td>on_error_container</td><td>surface_container_lowest</td><td>tertiary</td></tr>
<tr><td>primary_container</td><td>on_primary_container</td><td>on_primary</td></tr>
<tr><td>primary_fixed</td><td>on_primary_fixed</td><td>on_tertiary</td></tr>
<tr><td>primary_fixed_dim</td><td>on_primary_fixed_variant</td><td>on_surface</td></tr>
<tr><td>surface_bright</td><td>on_secondary_container</td><td>scrim</td></tr>
<tr><td>tertiary_fixed</td><td>on_secondary_fixed</td><td>secondary</td></tr>
<tr><td>on_tertiary_fixed</td><td>secondary_fixed_dim</td><td>outline</td></tr>
<tr><td>outline_variant</td><td>tertiary_container</td><td>shadow</td></tr>
<tr><td>secondary_fixed</td><td>tertiary_fixed_dim</td><td>primary</td></tr>
<tr><td>on_inverse_surface</td><td>on_secondary_fixed_variant</td><td></td></tr>
<tr><td>on_surface_variant</td><td>on_tertiary_container</td><td></td></tr>
</table></td></tr>
<tr><td>primary_swatch</td><td colspan="2">Defines a swatch of primary colors. A swatch contains variations of the main color used throughout the UI.</td></tr>
<tr><td>canvas_color</td><td colspan="2">Background color applied to the main drawing area or surfaces.</td></tr>
<tr><td>scaffold_bgcolor</td><td colspan="2">Background color for scaffold-based layouts.</td></tr>
<tr><td>card_color</td><td colspan="2">Default background color for Card controls.</td></tr>
<tr><td>divider_color</td><td colspan="2">Color for Divider controls and separator lines.</td></tr>
<tr><td>dialog_bgcolor</td><td colspan="2">Background color of dialog boxes.</td></tr>
<tr><td>indicator_color</td><td colspan="2">Color used for selection indicators, tab indicators and progress bars.</td></tr>
<tr><td>hint_color</td><td colspan="2">Color used for hint or placeholder texts.</td></tr>
<tr><td>shadow_color</td><td colspan="2">Sets the color of shadows behind controls.</td></tr>
<tr><td>secondary_header_color</td><td colspan="2">Background color for secondary headers or navigation elements.</td></tr>
<tr><td>splash_color / highlight_color / hover_color / focus_color</td><td colspan="2">Colors representing user interactions such as tap, hover and focus events.</td></tr>
<tr><td>unselected_control_color</td><td colspan="2">Color of controls in their unselected or inactive state.</td></tr>
<tr><td>disabled_color</td><td colspan="2">Default color for disabled controls.</td></tr>
</table>

Python
```python
import flet as ft
def main(page: ft.Page):
    page.theme = ft.Theme(
        card_bgcolor= "black",
        divider_color= "grey",
        color_scheme= ft.ColorScheme(
```

```
            surface = "white",
            primary= "purple",
            secondary= "cyan"
        )
    )

    page.update()

ft.run(main)
```

Typography and Fonts

Method/Property	Definition *Table 3.9*
font_family	Specifies the default font family for all Text controls.
text_theme	Defines the complete text styling including headings, labels, captions and body text.
primary_text_theme	Specifies text styles used when the primary color is applied as the background.

Python

```
import flet as ft

def main(page: ft.Page):
    page.theme = ft.Theme(
      font_family = "Georgia",
      text_theme = ft.TextTheme(
        body_small= ft.TextStyle(size= 20, color="red"),
        display_large= ft.TextStyle(size= 12, color="green"),
        headline_medium=ft.TextStyle(size=10, italic= True),
        label_medium= ft.TextStyle(size= 15, font_family="tahoma"),
        title_large= ft.TextStyle(size=25, font_family="Consolas")
        )
    )


ft.run(main)
```

Material Design Settings

Method/Property	Definition	Table 3.10
use_material3	Enables Material Design 3 styling when set to True. Controls will adopt the latest Material UI guidelines.	
visual_density	Defines how compact or spaced out controls appear.	

Control-Specific Themes

Flet provides theme sections for almost every major control. These allow developers to customize control appearance globally.

Each of these sets default properties for the corresponding control:

appbar_theme	card_theme	dialog_theme
badge_theme	checkbox_theme	divider_theme
banner_theme	chip_theme	elevated_button_theme
bottom_appbar_theme	color_scheme	outlined_button_theme
bottom_sheet_theme	data_table_theme	text_button_theme
button_theme	date_picker_theme	filled_button_theme
icon_button_theme	search_view_theme	tabs_theme
expansion_tile_theme	segmented_button_theme	time_picker_theme
floating_action_button_theme	system_overlay_style	tooltip_theme
slider_theme	radio_theme	icon_theme
snackbar_theme	scrollbar_theme	list_tile_theme
switch_theme	search_bar_theme	popup_menu_theme
navigation_bar_theme	navigation_rail_theme	progress_indicator_theme
navigation_drawer_theme	page_transitions	

Each theme object contains properties that define color, shape, padding, elevation, corner radius and typography for that control type.

Example – Configuring AppBar and Button Theme,

Python

```
import flet as ft
```

```python
def main(page: ft.Page):
    page.theme = ft.Theme(
        appbar_theme= ft.AppBarTheme(
            color= "grey",
            bgcolor = "red",
            shadow_color = ft.Colors.BROWN,
            elevation = 20,
            shape = ft.RoundedRectangleBorder(radius=10)
        ),

        button_theme= ft.ButtonTheme(
            style= ft.ButtonStyle(
                color= ft.Colors.PRIMARY,
                bgcolor= ft.Colors.SURFACE,
                icon_size = 20
            )
        )
    )


ft.run(main)
```

Window

The application window represents the main frame in which the user interface is displayed. It determines how the application appears on the user's operating system by managing properties such as size, position, background color, visibility, resizing behavior and interaction with system-level window features.

In Flet, the application window is controlled through the **page.window** property. This gives access to numerous window-level settings that help developers configure how the application behaves on the desktop platform.

It is important to note that many window properties are **platform specific** and some behave differently depending on whether the app is running on Windows, macOS or Linux.

Window Properties and Methods

Window Alignment and Positioning

Method/Property	Definition *Table 3.11*
alignment	Uses the Alignment control to position the page content inside the window. Helpful when organizing centered or responsive layouts.
left	Sets or retrieves the x-position of the window on the screen.
top	Sets or retrieves the y-position of the window on the screen.
center()	Moves the window to the center of the screen.
start_dragging()	Initiates a manual drag operation for the window. Useful when building custom title bars.

Python

```python
import flet as ft

def main(page: ft.Page):
    page.window  = ft.Window(
        alignment=ft.Alignment.CENTER_RIGHT,
        left= 100,
        top= 10
    )

ft.run(main)
```

Window Behavior

Method/Property	Definition *Table 3.12*
always_on_top	Keeps the window above all other windows when set to True.
always_on_bottom	Keeps the window below all other application windows.
prevent_close	Prevents the window from closing when the user clicks the close button, unless handled manually.
resizable	Allows or restricts the user from resizing the window.
movable	Allows or prevents the user from moving the window. Useful for fixed kiosk displays.
skip_task_bar	Hides the window from the taskbar when set to True.
full_screen	Enables full-screen mode, removing window borders and maximizing space.
frameless	Removes the standard system title bar and borders. In this mode, developers must implement custom close, minimize and maximize controls.
maximizable	Allows or prevents the window from being maximized.
minimizable	Allows or prevents the window from being minimized.
maximized	Maximizes the window programmatically when set to True.
minimized	Minimizes the window programmatically when set to True.
focused	Indicates whether the window currently has focus.

Python

```python
import flet as ft

def main(page: ft.Page):
    page.window  = ft.Window(resizable= False)

    def mini(e):
        page.window.minimized = True
        page.update()

    def maxi(e):
        page.window.maximized = True
        page.update()

    minimize = ft.Button("minimize", on_click= mini)
    maximize = ft.Button("maximize", on_click=maxi)
```

```
    ismaximize = page.window.maximizable
    isminimize = page.window.minimizable
    print(f"ismaximize->{ismaximize}\nisminimize->{isminimize}")

    page.add(minimize, maximize)
    page.update()


ft.run(main)
```

Appearance and Visual Settings

Table 3.13

Method/Property	Definition
bgcolor	Sets the window background color. Accepts color names, hex codes or predefined Flet colors.
icon	Sets the window icon displayed in the title bar and taskbar.
opacity	Controls window transparency. Value range: 0.0 (fully transparent) to 1.0 (fully opaque).
shadow	Enables or disables the window shadow effect.
badge_label	Sets a notification badge on supported operating systems.
progress_bar	Displays progress in the window's taskbar icon (mainly on Windows).
title_bar_hidden	Hides the window title bar when True.
title_bar_button_hidden	Hides the window control buttons when True.

Window Size and Constraints

Table 3.14

Method/Property	Definition
height	Gets or sets the current height of the window.
width	Gets or sets the current width of the window.
min_height / min_width	Sets minimum allowed dimensions for the window.
max_height / max_width	Sets maximum allowed dimensions for the window.

Window Interaction and Events

Method/Property	Definition *Table 3.15*
ignore_mouse_events	Allows mouse clicks to pass through the window, making it click-through. Useful for overlays.
on_event	Attaches a handler to intercept window events such as close, focus change, minimize or resize.
focused	Returns whether the window currently has focus.
page	Returns the Page object associated with the window.
visible	Hides the window when set to False. True by default.
to_front()	Brings the window to the front of all other windows.
wait_until_ready_to_show()	Ensures the window is prepared before being displayed, preventing flicker or incomplete rendering.

Closing and Destruction

Method/Property	Definition *Table 3.16*
close()	Safely closes the window and terminates the application.
destroy()	Removes and destroys the window instance. Mainly used in multi-window environments.

Note

Many **page.window** features are primarily supported on **Windows** and behavior may differ slightly on Linux or macOS. Developers should test window properties on their target platforms for consistent results.

Storage

Storage plays a vital role in application development. Applications depend on storage to save user preferences, system configurations, authentication details, application states, temporary data, and other information that supports personalization and consistent behavior.

Stored data enables applications to:

- Restore user sessions
- Apply saved themes or settings
- Remember user inputs
- Maintain continuity across app restarts

Without storage, applications would lose all user data once closed.

SharedPreferences in Flet

Flet provides a built-in storage service called **SharedPreferences**, accessible through the page object.

SharedPreferences uses a **key–value** pair model to store data. It does not require SQL queries for saving or retrieving information, making it simple and efficient for lightweight storage needs.

For most applications, SharedPreferences is sufficient. However, for complex applications requiring relational data models or large datasets, integrating an external database system may be necessary. SharedPreferences is not a visual control — it is a ***service*** that provides storage-related methods.

Core SharedPreferences Operations

SharedPreferences provides methods for:

1. Saving records
2. Retrieving records
3. Deleting records
4. Verifying key existence
5. Retrieving all keys

Saving Records

Data is saved using the **set()** method.
If a key already exists, the new value overwrites the existing value.

```
flet.SharedPreferences.set(key, value)
```

Insight

- Keys must always be strings.
- Values can be various serialized data types, such as strings, numbers, dictionaries, bytes, lists, tuples, sets and other serializable objects.
- Saved data is stored within the application's allocated storage space on the device.

Example 1 – Storing initial settings

```python
import flet as ft

def main(page: ft.Page):

    #Default settings
    async def initial():
        await database.set('appname', 'My App')
        await database.set('default_username', 'john')
        await database.set('default_password', 'pass_123')
        await database.set('default_theme', ft.ThemeMode.DARK)
        await database.set('default_bgcolor', ft.Colors.SURFACE_BRIGHT)


    database = ft.SharedPreferences()

    page.run_task(initial)
ft.run(main)
```

Example 2 – Saving user records

```python
import flet as ft
import json

async def main(page: ft.Page):

    database = ft.SharedPreferences()

    async def save(e):
        _username = username.value
        _password = password.value
        contact = [email.value, phone.value]
        serialized_contact = json.dumps(contact) #Serializing list

        #Saving Records
        await database.set('username', _username)
        await database.set('password', _password)
        await database.set('contact', serialized_contact)


    username = ft.TextField(label="Username")
    password = ft.TextField(label="Password")
    email = ft.TextField(label="Email")
    phone = ft.TextField(label="Phone")
    submit = ft.Button(content=ft.Text("Submit"), on_click = save )


    page.add(username, password, email, phone, submit, )

ft.run(main)
```

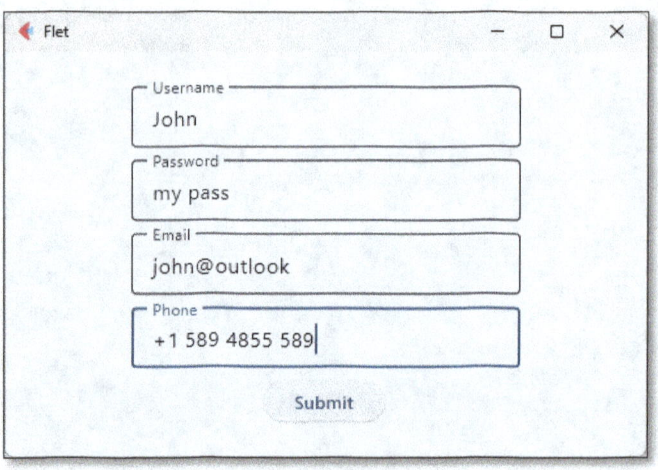

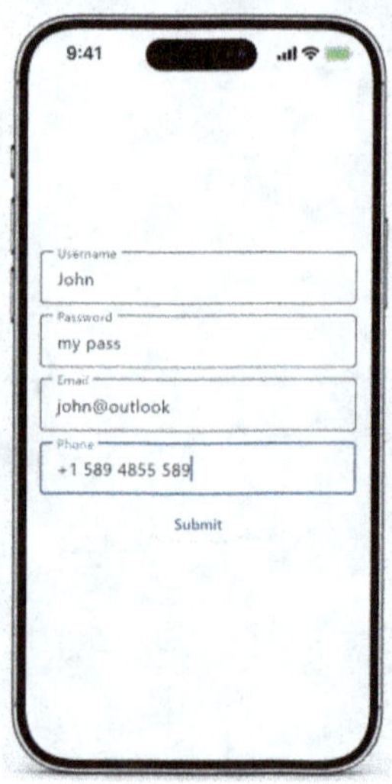

Retrieving Records

Stored values are retrieved using the **get()** method by specifying the associated key. SharedPreferences does not require SQL queries — data retrieval is direct and straightforward using the key.

```
flet.SharedPreferences.get(key)
```

```python
import flet as ft
import json

async def main(page: ft.Page):
    page.vertical_alignment = ft.MainAxisAlignment.CENTER
    page.horizontal_alignment = ft.CrossAxisAlignment.CENTER
    page.bgcolor = "white"

    database = ft.SharedPreferences()
    page.bgcolor = await database.get("bgcolor")

    async def initialize():
        info = (('appname', 'myapp'), ('version', 1.0))
        authentication = {"username":"John", "password": "mypass"}
        favorites = ['Sports', 'Fishing']

        await database.set('bgcolor', "red")
        await database.set("default_volume", str(25))
        await database.set("info", json.dumps(info))
        await database.set("auth", json.dumps(authentication))
        await database.set("favorites", json.dumps(favorites))


    async def getData(e):
        volume = await database.get("default_volume")
        info = await database.get('info')
        auth = await database.get('auth')
        print(f"AppInfo-> {info}")
        print(f"Profile-> {auth}")


    getdata = ft.Button(content=ft.Text("Get Data"), on_click = getData )
```

```
    page.add(getdata )
    page.run_task(initialize)

ft.run(main)
```

```
#Output
AppInfo-> [["appname", "myapp"], ["version", 1.0]]
Profile-> {"username": "John", "password": "mypass"}
```

Deleting Records

To remove a specific record, use the **remove()** method and provide the key. This deletes the key and its associated value.

```
flet.SharedPreferences.remove(key)
```

To delete **all stored records**, use the **clear()** method.

```
flet.SharedPreferences.clear( )
```

Note

The **clear()** method permanently removes all stored data for the application. Deleted records cannot be recovered. Use this method with caution.

Example

```python
import flet as ft

async def main(page: ft.Page):

    database = ft.SharedPreferences()

    remove_record = ft.Button(content=ft.Text("Delete"),
                on_click= await database.remove('info'))

    delete_all = ft.Button(content=ft.Text("Delete All"),
                on_click= await database.clear())

    page.add(remove_record, delete_all )

ft.run(main)
```

Verifying Key Existence

Before retrieving or overwriting data, it is good practice to verify whether a key exists. The **contains_key()** method checks for the presence of a key and returns:

- **True** – if the key exists
- **False** – if the key does not exist

This helps prevent retrieval errors and unintended overwriting.

```
flet.SharedPreferences.contains_key(key)
```

```python
import flet as ft

async def main(page: ft.Page):
```

```
    database = ft.SharedPreferences()

    async def delete(e):
        if await database.contains_key("username"):
            await database.remove("username")


    delete = ft.Button(content=ft.Text("Delete "), on_click= delete)

    page.add(delete )

ft.run(main)
```

Retrieving All Keys

To retrieve all stored keys, use the **get_keys()** method. This is useful when managing or auditing stored application data.

```
flet.SharedPreferences.get_keys( prefix )
```

Python

```python
import flet as ft

async def main(page: ft.Page):

    database = ft.SharedPreferences()

    async def getKeys(e):
        keys = await database.get_keys('')
        print(keys)


    page.add(
      ft.Button(content=ft.Text("Get Keys"), on_click = getKeys)
```

```
    )

ft.run(main)
```

🧠 **Insight**

When to Use SharedPreferences

SharedPreferences is ideal for:

- User settings
- Theme preferences
- Authentication tokens
- Small configuration data
- Lightweight caching

For large-scale, structured, or relational data storage, a dedicated database solution may be more appropriate. In Python, you can use libraries such as sqlite3 or TinyDB to handle more complex data management needs. Once created, the database file can be placed in the ***assets*** or ***storage*** directory of your Flet project.

Text

The **Text** control is used to display textual information in a Flet application. It supports extensive styling through its properties and the **TextStyle** class, allowing developers to control the appearance, formatting, layout and behavior of text.

Properties and Methods

value = string

The value defines the actual text. The value perimeter can be specified or omitted.

Python

```python
import flet as ft

def  main(page: ft.Page):
     text1 = ft.Text("Text Sample One")
     text2 = ft.Text(value = "Text Sample Two")

     page.add(text1, text2)

ft.run(main)
```

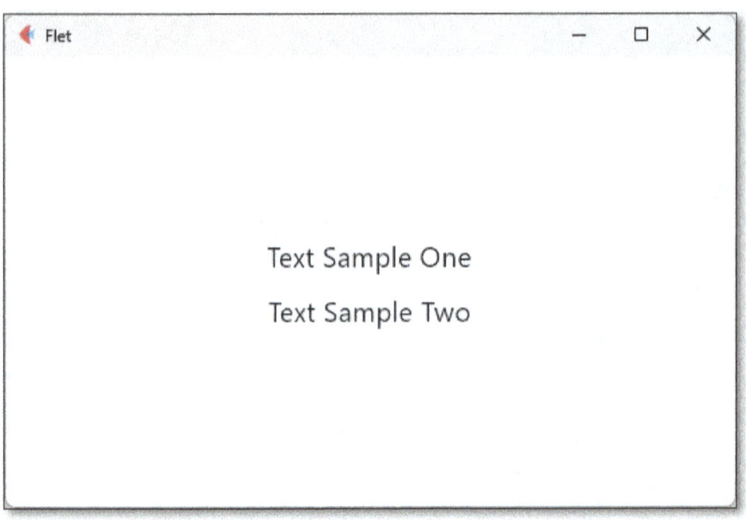

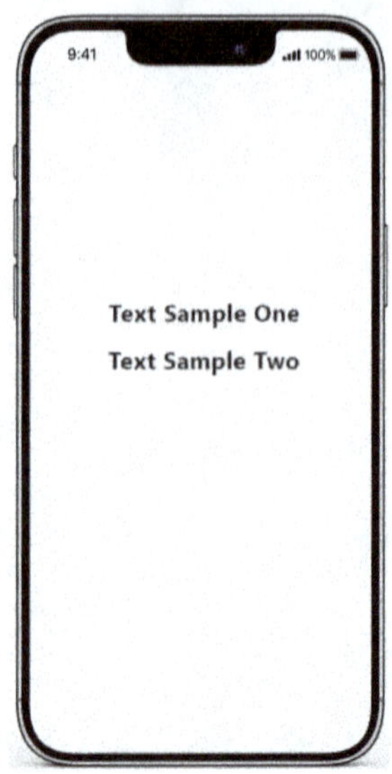

size = number

Defines the text size (font size).

weight = flet.FontWeight

Controls text boldness using **FontWeight.** FontWeight options include:
NORMAL, BOLD, W_100 ... W_900

color = color

Defines the color of the text. It accepts color names or hex values.

Python

```
import flet as ft

def main(page: ft.Page):
    page.vertical_alignment = ft.MainAxisAlignment.CENTER
    page.horizontal_alignment = ft.CrossAxisAlignment.CENTER

    text1 = ft.Text("Text Sample One", color= "orange", size=30)
    text2 = ft.Text("Text Sample Two", weight= ft.FontWeight.BOLD )

    page.add(text1, text2)

ft.run(main)
```

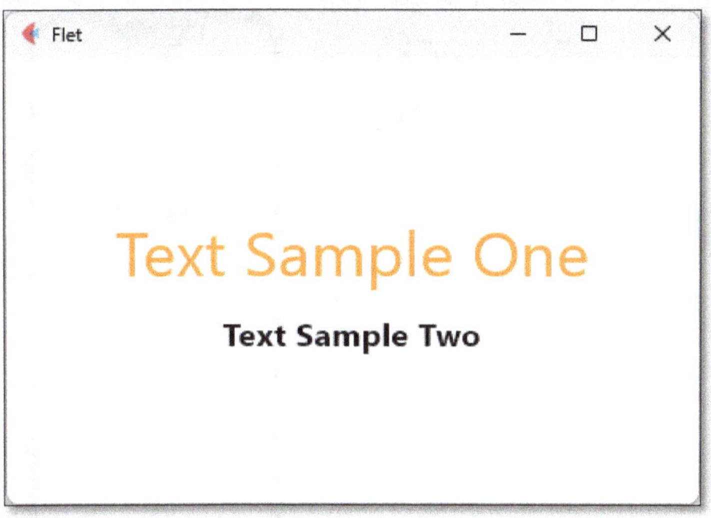

bgcolor = color

Specifies the text's background color. This highlights or marks the text area using color names (e.g., "yellow") or hexadecimal values (e.g., "#FFE7A0").

font_family = string

Specifies the name of the font. Flet includes standard families like

- "Arial"
- "Comic sans ms"
- "Georgia"
- "Helvetica"
- "Times New Roman"
- "Consolas"

Developers may also use custom fonts by specifying the path to the font file.

```python
import flet as ft

def main(page: ft.Page):
    text1 = ft.Text("Georgia", font_family="Georgia", size= 25,
                    bgcolor="green")

    text2 = ft.Text("Comic sans ms", font_family="comic sans ms",
                    size=25)

    text3 = ft.Text("Times New Roman", font_family="Times New Roman",
                     size=25)

    page.add(text1, text2, text3)

ft.run(main)
```

italic = bool

Renders the text in an italic (slanted) style when True.

scale = number

Scales the text size proportionally.

- = 1.0 → normal size
- > 1.0 → larger text
- < 1.0 → reduced text

Python

```
import flet as ft

def main(page: ft.Page):
    page.vertical_alignment = ft.MainAxisAlignment.CENTER
    page.horizontal_alignment = ft.CrossAxisAlignment.CENTER
    page.bgcolor = "white"

    text1 = ft.Text("Scaled by 1", italic=True, scale= 1)
    text2 = ft.Text("Scaled by 2.4", scale= 2.4)
    text3 = ft.Text("Scaled by 0.6", scale= 0.6)

    page.add(text1, text2, text3)

ft.run(main)
```

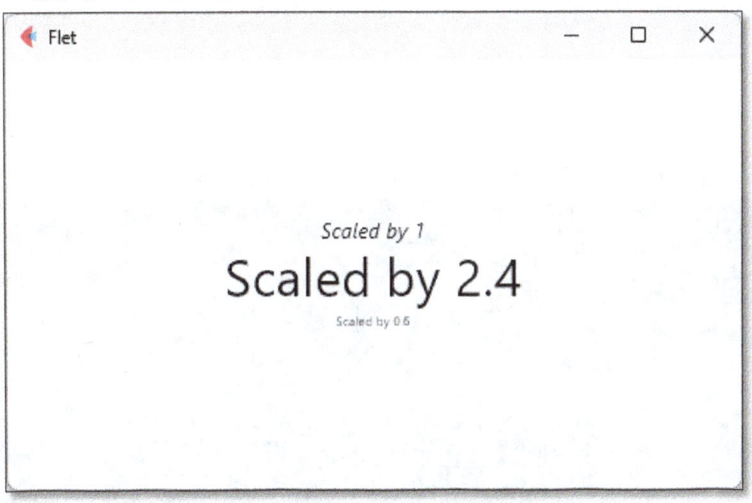

rotate = angle

Rotates the text by a given angle.

```python
import flet as ft

def main(page: ft.Page):
    text1 = ft.Text("Rotation by 60", rotate= ft.Rotate(60))
    text2 = ft.Text("Rotation by 180", rotate= 180, )

    page.add(text1, text2)

ft.run(main)
```

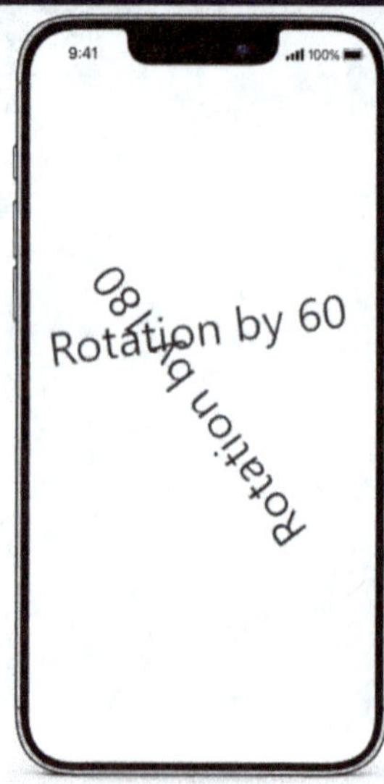

opacity = number

Sets the transparency level of the text (0.0 = invisible, 1.0 = fully visible).

```python
import flet as ft

def main(page: ft.Page):
    text1 = ft.Text("Opacity Sample One", opacity = 0.7, size= 20)
    text2 = ft.Text("Opacity Sample Two", opacity = 0.5, size=20)
    text3 = ft.Text("Opacity Sample Three", opacity = 0.2, size= 20)

    page.add(text1, text2, text3)
ft.run(main)
```

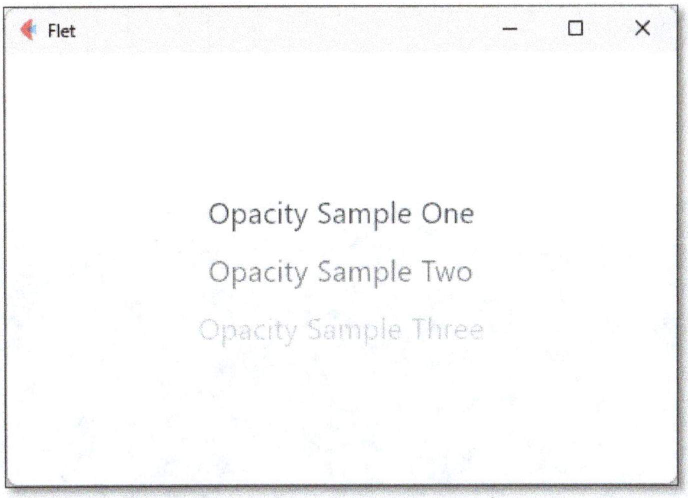

overflow = flet.TextOverflow

Determines how text behaves when it exceeds its display area using **TextOverflow**

1. **CLIP** → Excess text is simply cut off.
2. **FADE** → The endpoint fades gradually, indicating continuation.
3. **VISIBLE** → Text overflows outside the boundary freely.
4. **ELLIPSIS** → Long text is truncated with "...".

Python

```python
import flet as ft

def main(page: ft.Page):
    text = ft.Text("Text Sample", overflow=ft.TextOverflow.VISIBLE)

    page.add(text)

ft.run(main)
```

text_align = flet.TextAlign

Aligns text horizontally using **TextAlign**:

- LEFT
- START
- RIGHT
- END
- JUSTIFY
- CENTER

Python
```python
import flet as ft

def main(page: ft.Page):
    text = ft.Text("Text Sample",
        text_align=ft.TextAlign.JUSTIFY
    )

    page.add(text)

ft.run(main)
```

Lorem ipsum dolor sit amet, consectetur adipiscing elit. Integer nec odio. Praesent libero. Sed cursus ante dapibus diam.

LEFT

Lorem ipsum dolor sit amet, consectetur adipiscing elit. Integer nec odio. Praesent libero. Sed cursus ante dapibus diam.

RIGHT

Lorem ipsum dolor sit amet, consectetur adipiscing elit. Integer nec odio. Praesent libero. Sed cursus ante dapibus diam.

CENTER

Lorem ipsum dolor sit amet, consectetur adipiscing elit. Integer nec odio. Praesent libero. Sed cursus ante dapibus diam.

JUSTIFY

Lorem ipsum dolor sit amet, consectetur adipiscing elit. Integer nec odio. Praesent libero. Sed cursus ante dapibus diam.

START

Lorem ipsum dolor sit amet, consectetur adipiscing elit. Integer nec odio. Praesent libero. Sed cursus ante dapibus diam.

END

TextStyle

The TextStyle class provides advanced styling, allowing full control over text appearance.

style = flet.TextStyle()

Applies a complete text style using **TextStyle**. This allows formatting text without relying on individual Text properties.

decoration = flet.TextDecoration

Applies a decorative line using **TextDecoration**:

- UNDERLINE → A line beneath the text
- OVERLINE → A line above the text
- THROUGH → A strikethrough line
- NONE → No decoration

Python

```python
import flet as ft

def main(page: ft.Page):
```

```
    text1 = ft.Text("Overline", style= ft.TextStyle(
                      decoration= ft.TextDecoration.OVERLINE
                    )
     )
    text2 = ft.Text("Line through", style= ft.TextStyle(
                      decoration= ft.TextDecoration.LINE_THROUGH
                    )
     )
    text3 = ft.Text("Underline", style= ft.TextStyle(
                      decoration= ft.TextDecoration.UNDERLINE
                    )
     )
    page.add(text1,text2,text3)

ft.run(main)
```

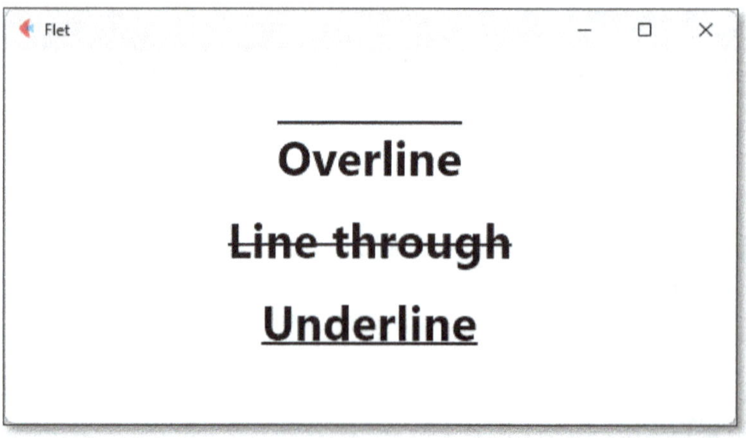

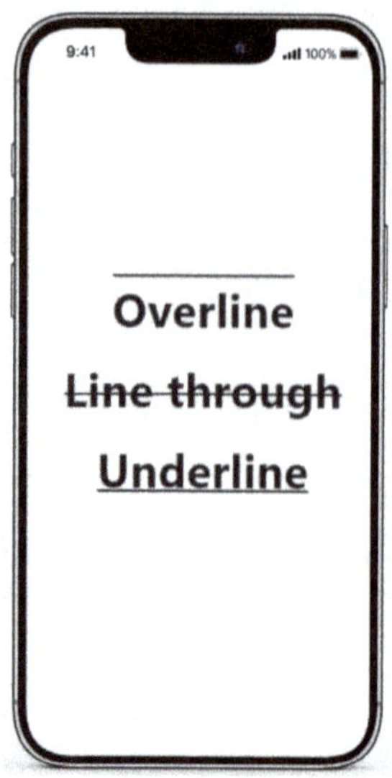

decoration_color = color

Color of the decoration line.

decoration_thickness = number

Defines the thickness (weight) of the decoration line.

decoration_style = flet.TextDecorationStyle

Specifies how the decoration appears:

- SOLID
- DOUBLE
- DOTTED
- DASHED
- WAVY

```python
import flet as ft

def main(page: ft.Page):
    text = ft.Text("Dashed Decoration", style= ft.TextStyle(
                decoration= ft.TextDecoration.UNDERLINE,
                decoration_color= "orange",
                decoration_style= ft.TextDecorationStyle.DASHED)
        )

    page.add(text)

ft.run(main)
```

Dashed

Double

Dotted

Solid

Wavy

letter_spacing = number

Controls the spacing between characters.

word_spacing = number

Specifies spacing between words.

Python

```
import flet as ft

def main(page: ft.Page):
    text1 = ft.Text("Letter Spacing Sample", style= ft.TextStyle(
                        letter_spacing = 5)
    )
    text2 = ft.Text("Word Spacing Sample", style= ft.TextStyle(
                        word_spacing = 10)
    )
    page.add(text1,text2)

ft.run(main)
```

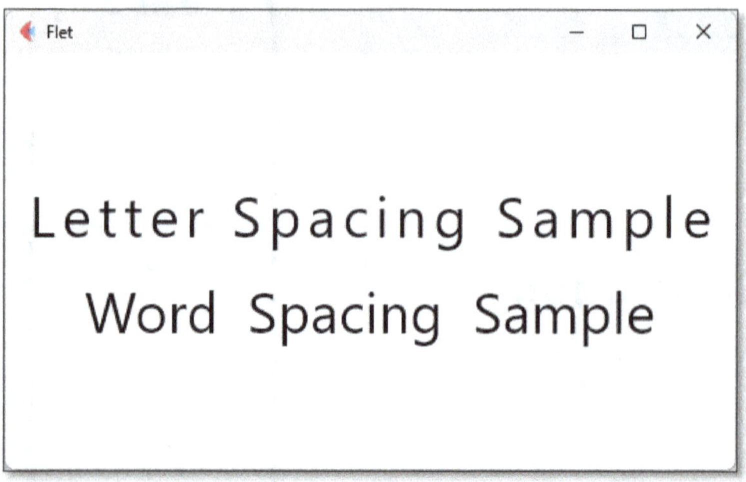

shadow = flet.BoxShadow()

Applies shadow to the text using BoxShadow.

- spread_radius → number
- blur_radius → number
- color → color
- offset → flet.Offset(x, y)

```python
import flet as ft

def main(page: ft.Page):
    text = ft.Text("Text Shadow Sample", style= ft.TextStyle(
                                shadow= ft.BoxShadow(
                                    spread_radius= 5,
                                    blur_radius= 3,
                                    color= ft.Colors.RED,
                                    offset= ft.Offset(2, 2),
                                )
                            ))

    page.add(text)

ft.run(main)
```

Other Properties and Methods of TextStyle

Table 3.17

Method/Property	Definition
baseline	Aligns the text relative to its baseline.
bgcolor	Background color applied behind the text.
color	Sets the text color.
font_family	Specifies the font name.
foreground	Defines a brush-based foreground paint for advanced text rendering.
height	Line height (line spacing multiplier).
italic	Applies italic styling.

overflow	Specifies overflow behavior (same options as TextOverflow).
size	Font size.
weight	Controls text boldness using FontWeight: • NORMAL • BOLD • W_100 ... W_900

TextSpan

The TextSpan allows rich text formatting of individual texts.

spans = flet.TextSpan()

Creates a list of TextSpan objects allowing rich text formatting. This enables individual words or characters to have different styles.

Example,

Python

```python
import flet as ft

def main(page: ft.Page):
    text=ft.Text("The", size=25, spans= [
         ft.TextSpan("\t\tbrown", style=
         ft.TextStyle(decoration=ft.TextDecoration.LINE_THROUGH)),
         ft.TextSpan("\t\tfox", style= ft.TextStyle(color="green")),
         ft.TextSpan("\t\twas too"),
         ft.TextSpan("\t\tquick", style= ft.TextStyle(italic=True)),
         ft.TextSpan("\t\tto see the", style= ft.TextStyle(
                         weight=ft.FontWeight.BOLD) ),
         ft.TextSpan("\t\tcat", style = ft.TextStyle(color="red")),
         ],
        )

    page.add(text)

ft.run(main)
```

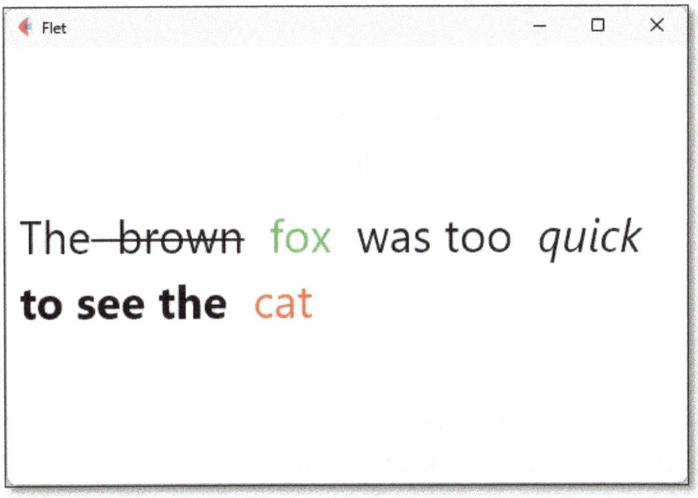

Other Methods and Properties of Text

Method/Property	Definition *Table 3.18*
enable_interractive_selection	Allows text selection even when selectable=False.
max_lines	Limits the number of visible text lines. Text beyond max_lines will be cut or handled according to the overflow property.
no_wrap	Prevents text wrapping. The text continues on a single line.
on_animation_end	Triggers when a text animation completes.
on_selection_change	Triggered when the user selects text.
on_tap	Executes a function when the text is tapped or clicked.
selectable	Enables user text selection when set to True (default is False).
selection_cursor_color	Defines the cursor color during text selection.
selection_cursor_height	Specifies the height of the selection caret.
selection_cursor_width	Specifies the width of the selection caret.
semantic_label	Provides an accessibility label for screen readers.
show_selection_cursor	Controls visibility of the cursor when selecting text.
theme_style	Applies theme-specific text styles.
update	Refreshes the UI to reflect changes.

Markdown

The **Markdown** control is a material design control that renders text formatted in Markdown syntax. Markdown allows developers to write rich text using a lightweight markup language, enabling bold, italic, headings, lists, links, code blocks, and images. The Markdown control behaves similarly to the Text control but automatically formats content according to Markdown rules.

Insight

The **Markdown** control is ideal for displaying rich, formatted content dynamically, such as articles, documentation, or any content imported from Markdown sources, while keeping a consistent and interactive user experience.

Properties and Methods

value = string
Defines the Markdown text content to be rendered.

selectable = bool
When True, allows the user to select text for copy-paste operations.

extension_set = flet.MarkdownExtensionSet
Specifies additional Markdown extensions to support advanced syntax features. Options include:

- COMMON_MARK
- GITHUB_FLAVORED
- GITHUB_WEB
- NONE

code_theme = flet.MarkdownCodeTheme
Sets the theme for syntax-highlighted code blocks within the Markdown. Options include:

DARCULA	COLOR_BREWER	ATELIER_SAVANNA_LIGHT	ATELIER_CAVE_DARK
DARK	HOPSCOTCH	ATELIER_SEASIDE_DARK	ATELIER_CAVE_LIGHT
DEFAULT	HYBRID	ATELIER_SEASIDE_LIGHT	ATELIER_DUNE_DARK
DOCCO	IDEA	ATELIER_SULPHURPOOL_DARK	ATELIER_DUNE_LIGHT

DRAGULA	IR_BLACK	TOMORROW_NIGHT	ATELIER_ESTUARY_DARK
FAR	ISBL_EDITOR_DARK	TOMORROW_NIGHT_BLUE	ATELIER_ESTUARY_LIGHT
FOUNDATION	ISBL_EDITOR_LIGHT	TOMORROW_NIGHT_BRIGHT	ATELIER_FOREST_DARK
GITHUB	KIMBIE_DARK	TOMORROW_NIGHT_EIGHTIES	ATELIER_FOREST_LIGHT
GITHUB_GIST	KIMBIE_LIGHT	ATELIER_SULPHURPOOL_LIGHT	ATELIER_HEATH_DARK
GML	LIGHTFAIR	ATOM_ONE_DARK_REASONABLE	ATELIER_HEATH_LIGHT
GOOGLE_CODE	MAGULA	RAINBOW	ATELIER_LAKESIDE_DARK
GRADIENT_DARK	MONOKAI	ROUTEROS	ATELIER_LAKESIDE_LIGHT
GRAYSCALE	MONOKAI_SUBLIME	SCHOOL_BOOK	ATELIER_PLATEAU_DARK
GRUVBOX_DARK	MONO_BLUE	SHADES_OF_PURPLE	ATELIER_PLATEAU_LIGHT
GRUVBOX_LIGHT	NIGHT_OWL	SOLARIZED_DARK	ATELIER_SAVANNA_DARK
VS	A11Y_DARK	SOLARIZED_LIGHT	ATOM_ONE_DARK
VS2015	A11Y_LIGHT	PURE_BASIC	ATOM_ONE_LIGHT
XCODE	AGATE	QT_CREATOR_DARK	BROWN_PAPER
XT256	ANDROID_STUDIO	QT_CREATOR_LIGHT	CODEPEN_EMBED
ZENBURN	AN_OLD_HOPE	RAILSCASTS	PARAISEO_DARK
ARTA	OBSIDIAN	POJOAQUE	TOMORROW
ASCETIC	OCEAN	SUNBURST	PARAISEO_LIGHT
NORD			

auto_follow_links = **bool**

When True, automatically opens links when tapped or clicked.

fit_content = **bool**

When True, the control resizes to fit the rendered content.

shrink_wrap = **bool**

When True, the Markdown control minimizes unused space and wraps tightly around its content.

soft_line_break = **bool**

Enables soft line breaks, allowing lines to wrap without requiring explicit newlines in the Markdown text.

auto_follow_links_target = **flet.UrlTarget**

Specifies the target behavior for automatically followed links (e.g. BLANK, PARENT, SELF, TOP).

img_error_content = **control**

Sets fallback content or a control to display if an image fails to load.

latex_scale_factor = number
The scale factor for LaTeX formulas rendering.

on_tap_text = callback
Registers a callback function that fires when a user taps or clicks any text element.

on_selection_change = callback
Registers a callback that triggers whenever text selection changes.

```python
import flet as ft

def main(page: ft.Page):
    page.bgcolor = "white"
    page.scroll = "auto"

    md_content = """
# 🚀 Flet Markdown Showcase

Welcome to **Flet Markdown** demo!
You can render rich formatted text easily.

---

## ✨ Text Formatting

- **Bold text**
- *Italic text*
- ~~Strikethrough~~
- `Inline code`

---

## 📋 Lists

### Ordered List
1. Install Flet
2. Write your app
3. Run `flet run`

### Unordered List
- Apple 🍎
- Banana 🍌
- Cherry 🍒
```

```
---

## 💻 Code Block

```python
def greet(name):
    return f"Hello, {name}!"

"""
    page.add(
        ft.SafeArea(
         content = ft.Markdown(
                value = md_content,
                selectable= True,
                extension_set= ft.MarkdownExtensionSet.COMMON_MARK,
                on_tap_text= lambda _:print('Text has been tapped'),
                on_selection_change= lambda _:print("text has been selected")
        ))
    )

ft.run(main)
```

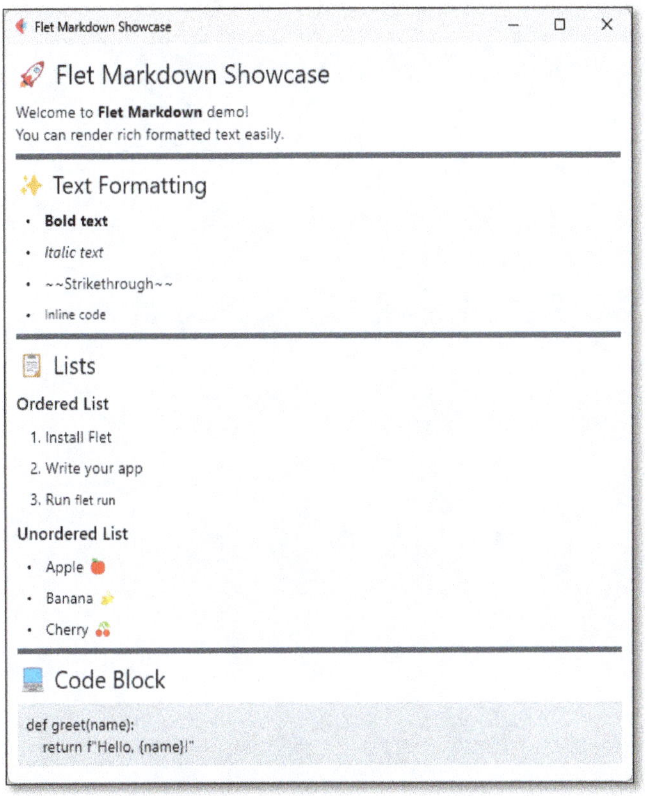

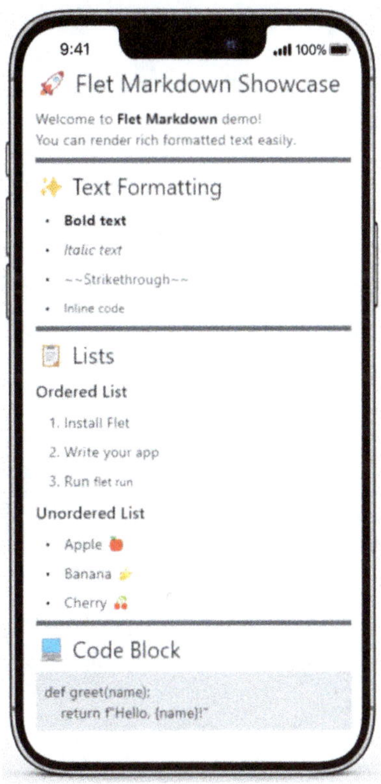
```

on_tap_link = callback

Registers a callback function that fires when a link in the Markdown content is tapped.

latex_tyle = flet.TextStyle

The text style to apply to LaTeX formulas.

code_style_sheet = flet.MarkdownStyleSheet

Defines custom styling for code blocks in the Markdown.

md_style_sheet = flet.MarkdownStyleSheet

Uses a MarkdownStyleSheet object to customize fonts, colors, and spacing for different Markdown elements.

SelectionArea

Normally, controls such as **Text**, **Markdown** and many others in Flet do not allow text selection by default. This means users cannot highlight or copy text with the mouse or keyboard.

The **SelectionArea** control solves this limitation. It acts as a selection wrapper that enables text-selection capabilities for its child content.

SelectionArea is often used for:

- Articles
- Documentation text
- Code blocks
- Markdown content
- Any region where user text selection is necessary

You wrap the control inside a SelectionArea to make it selectable.

Properties and Methods

content = control

Defines the child control whose text will be selectable.

Common controls include: Text, Markdown and any control that contains textual content.

Python

```
import flet as ft

def main(page: ft.Page):
    sa = ft.SelectionArea(
      content= ft.Text(
        """Lorem ipsum dolor sit amet, consectetur adipiscing elit. Curabitur
         quis nibh vitae purus consectetur facilisis sed vitae ipsum. Quisque
         faucibus sed nulla placerat sagittis. Phasellus condimentum risus
         vitae nulla vestibulum auctor.
       """
     )

    page.add(sa)

ft.run(main)
```

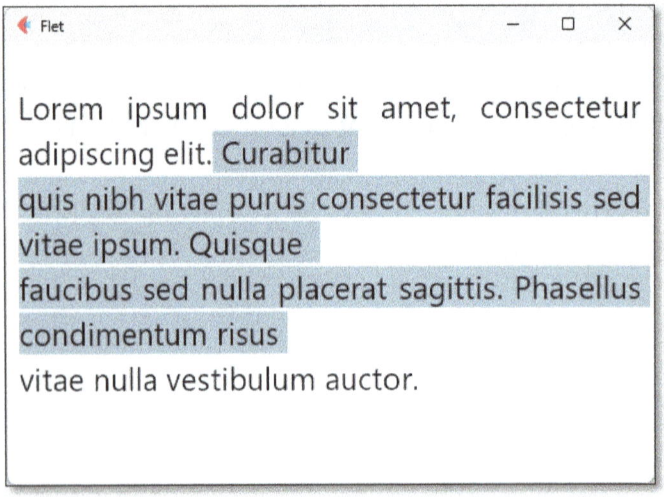

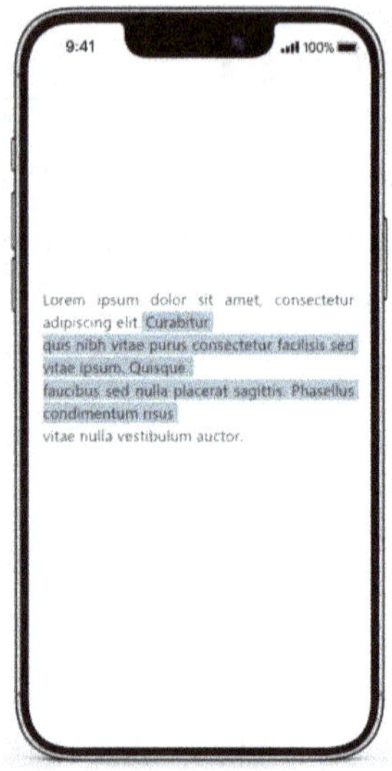

on_change = callback

Registers an event handler that fires whenever the selection changes.
For example, it triggers when the user highlights text or the selection is modified.

Python
```python
import flet as ft

def main(page: ft.Page):

    def selected(e):
        text = e.data #get selected text
        print(text)

    sa = ft.SelectionArea(
        content = ft.Markdown("Highlight to select part of me"),
        on_change = selected)

    page.add(sa)

ft.run(main)
```

Divider

In user interface design, displaying multiple sections of content on a single page can cause visual confusion. To separate or categorize content clearly, a **Divider** control is used. The **Divider** draws a horizontal or vertical line across the page, visually distinguishing different sections of the layout.

Dividers are typically used in lists, forms or content panels to improve readability and structure.

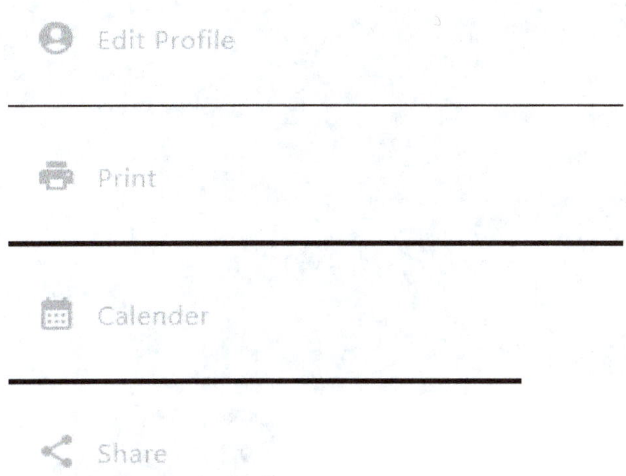

Properties and Methods

color = color

Specifies the color of the line. By default, the Divider is grey. Colors can be defined by name, hex code or predefined **ColorValue**.

thickness = number

Specifies the thickness (height) of the line.

leading_indent = number

Specifies the starting space or padding from the left (or leading side) before the line begins.

trailing_indent = number

Specifies the padding from the right(or trailing side) after the line ends.

```python
import flet as ft

async def main(page: ft.Page):
    page.vertical_alignment = ft.MainAxisAlignment.CENTER
    page.horizontal_alignment = ft.CrossAxisAlignment.START
    page.bgcolor = "#0E121A"


    page.add(
        ft.Text("Hello Flet", color="#F0F0F0"),
        ft.Divider(),
        ft.Text("Hello Flet", color="#F0F0F0"),
        ft.Divider(thickness=3, trailing_indent= 50),
        ft.Text("Hello Flet", color="#F0F0F0"),
        ft.Divider(color="cyan"),
        ft.Text("Hello Flet", color="#F0F0F0"),
        ft.Divider(thickness=3, leading_indent=50),
    )

ft.run(main)
```

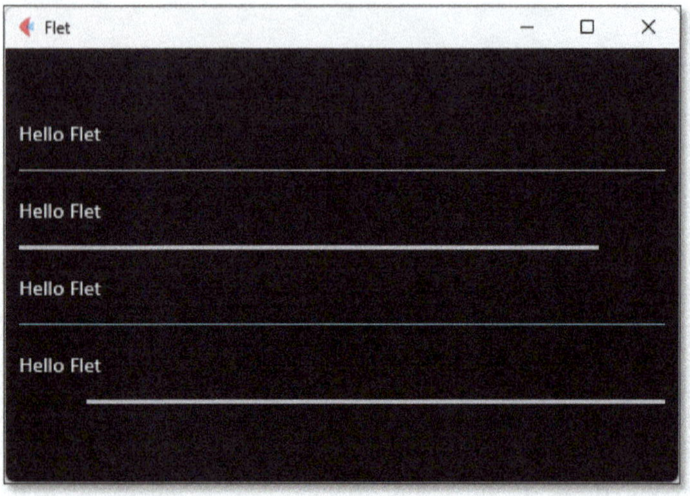

height = number

Sets the vertical size of the Divider (line thickness in the vertical dimension).

opacity = number

Sets the transparency of the Divider line. Value ranges from 0.0 (fully transparent) to 1.0 (fully opaque).

tooltip = string

Text displayed when the user hovers over or focuses on the Divider.

disabled = bool

When True, the Divider becomes inactive (non-interactive).

VerticalDivider

VerticalDivider serves the same purpose as **Divider**. While Divider renders a horizontal line, VerticalDivider renders a vertical line.

Properties and Methods

Method/Property	Definition *Table 3.19*
color	Specifies the color of the line. By default, the Divider is grey.
leading_indent	The amount of empty space to the leading edge of the divider.
trailing_indent	The amount of empty space to the trailing edge of the divider.
thickness	Specifies the thickness (height) of the line.
width	The divider's width.
radius	The border radius of the divider.

Icon

Icons are compact graphical symbols that visually communicate actions, statuses or concepts within an application's interface. Instead of using long text labels—such as *"Add account"*—a simple **plus** icon can concisely convey the same meaning. In Flet, the **Icon** control is used to display Material-style icons in your application.

Methods and Properties

icon = icon

Defines the icon name using the **Icons** enumeration.This may also be provided as the first argument without naming the parameter.

```
Python

import flet as ft

async def main(page: ft.Page):

    page.add(
        ft.Icon(ft.Icons.PRINT),
        ft.Icon(ft.CupertinoIcons.DELETE),
        ft.Icon(ft.Icons.MESSAGE_OUTLINED),
        ft.Icon(ft.CupertinoIcons.SETTINGS),
    )

ft.run(main)
```

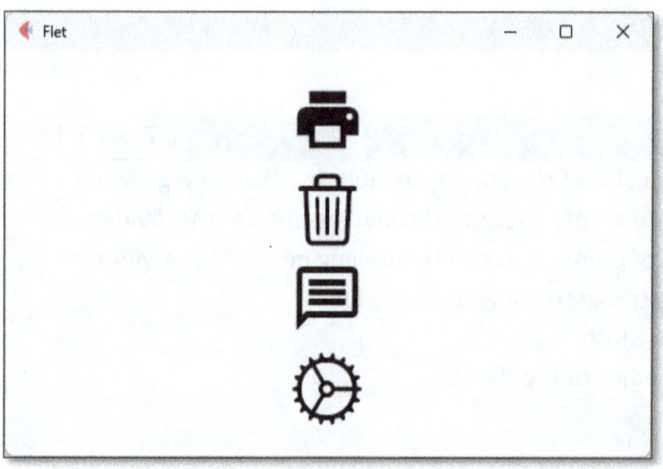

Insight

The **Icons** or **CupertinoIcons** module provides a wide range of icons suitable for use in any type of application. To view the complete list of available icons, you can call the **dir()** function on the **Icons** object.

color = color

Defines the **foreground color** of the icon. Accepts either named colors ("red", "blue") or hex codes ("#FFAA00").

size = number

Defines the icon's size (width and height). Equivalent to setting both width and height uniformly.

```python
import flet as ft

def main(page: ft.Page):

    page.bgcolor = "#24252B"

    page.add(
        ft.Icon(ft.Icons.FACEBOOK, color="orange", size=50),
        ft.Icon(ft.Icons.TIKTOK, color="green", size=50),
        ft.Icon(ft.Icons.SNAPCHAT, color="yellow", size=50),
    )

ft.run(main)
```

opacity = float

Controls the transparency level of the icon. Range: 0.0 (fully invisible) to 1.0 (fully visible).

rotate = angle / flet.Rotate(angle)

Rotates the icon by a given angle.

```python
import flet as ft

def main(page: ft.Page):

    icon1 = ft.Icon(ft.Icons.CAKE_ROUNDED, opacity= 0.5, size= 75)
    icon2 = ft.Icon(ft.Icons.CAKE_ROUNDED, rotate= 180, size=75)

    page.add(icon1, icon2)

ft.run(main)
```

weight = number

Defines the **thickness** or stroke weight of the icon (used in Material symbols). Examples: 100 (thin) , "400" (regular), 700 (bold)

scale = number

Scales the icon up or down.

- 1.0 = default size
- Values above 1 enlarge the icon
- Values below 1 shrink it

```
Python

import flet as ft

def main(page: ft.Page):

    icon = ft.Icon(ft.Icons.EMAIL_OUTLINED, scale= 2.4, weight=100)
    page.add(icon)

ft.run(main)
```

optical_size = number

Adjusts the visual sharpness and design adjustments of variable Material icons.

Other Methods and Properties of Icon

Table 3.20

Method/Property	Definition
apply_text_scaling	Determines whether the icon should scale according to the app's text scaling factor. This helps maintain accessibility and consistent visual proportions.
aspect_ratio	Sets the proportional relationship between the icon's width and height.
badge	Applies a small indicator (e.g., a number or dot) to the icon—useful for notifications or alerts.
blend_mode	Controls how the icon's colors blend with the background (e.g., multiply, overlay). Useful for special visual effects.
grade	Adjusts the weight and contrast of Material icons, depending on the icon style (Outlined, Rounded or Sharp).
shadow	Applies BoxShadow effects around the icon to create depth.

SafeArea

Modern mobile devices often feature notches, camera cutouts or rounded corners that can overlap the top or edges of an application screen. To prevent important UI elements from being obscured, the **SafeArea** control is used as a parent container. It ensures that the content starts below the notch or safe boundaries, providing proper spacing and layout for iOS and Android devices.

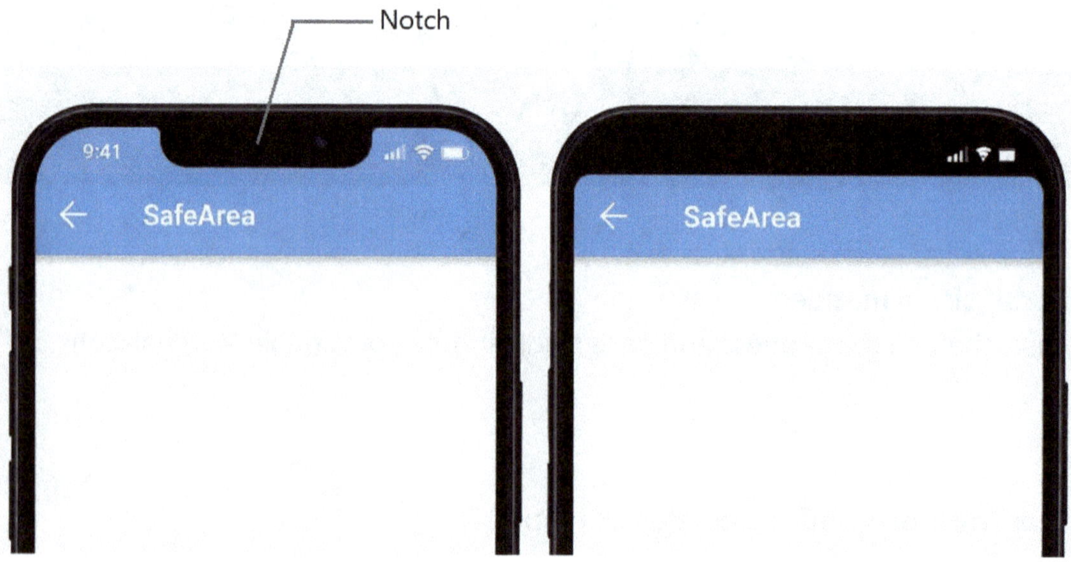

Figure 3.2: Notch in mobile devices

Key Properties and Methods

content = control
Sets the child control that will be displayed within the safe area. Additional controls can be nested inside this content.

avoid_intrusions_left = bool
When True, ensures that padding is applied to the left side of the screen to avoid unsafe areas.

avoid_intrusions_top = bool

When True, ensures that padding is applied to the top of the screen, preventing overlap with notches or status bars.

avoid_intrusions_right = bool

When True, ensures padding on the right side of the screen.

avoid_intrusions_bottom = bool

When True, ensures padding on the bottom of the screen to prevent overlap with navigation bars or gesture areas.

maintain_bottom_view_padding = bool

When True, preserves the system-defined bottom padding (e.g., for navigation gestures or keyboards).

minimum_padding = flet.Padding

Sets the minimum amount of padding to apply on all sides, even if the system safe area is smaller. This ensures consistent spacing across different devices.

Python

```
import flet as ft

def main(page: ft.Page):

    page.add(
        ft.SafeArea(
            expand=True,
            content=ft.Container(
                content= ft.Text("SafeArea", size=50),
                alignment=ft.Alignment.CENTER,
            ),
        )
    )


ft.run(main)
```

AppBar

The **AppBar** is a horizontal bar typically positioned at the top of an application page. It provides a structured area for displaying the page title, navigation controls such as a leading button or drawer icon and optional action buttons. The primary purpose of the AppBar is to offer convenient access to frequently used controls while maintaining consistent application layout.

Insight

CupertinoAppBar is the iOS-styled counterpart of AppBar, following the Cupertino design language. Most core properties are similar.

bgcolor = color

Specifies the background color of the AppBar. Colors may be defined by name such as "red" or "blue" or by hexadecimal code such as "#00334C".

leading = control

Defines a control placed at the leftmost side of the AppBar. This control is commonly a drawer icon, a back button or any other widget that performs a navigation function.

Python

```
import flet as ft

async def main(page: ft.Page):
    page.bgcolor = "white"

    page.appbar = ft.AppBar(
```

```
        leading= ft.IconButton(icon=ft.Icons.ARROW_BACK, icon_color="white"),
        bgcolor= "blue"
    )

ft.run(main)
```

leading_width = number

Specifies the horizontal space allocated to the leading control, effectively setting the distance between the leading control and the title.

title = control

Defines the main title displayed in the AppBar. The title may be the page title or the name of the application.

color = color

Specifies the foreground color applied to the title and icons in the AppBar.

```python
import flet as ft

def main(page: ft.Page):
    page.appbar = ft.AppBar(
        title=ft.Text("Home Page"),
        leading= ft.IconButton(icon= ft.Icons.MENU),
        bgcolor= "green",
        color= "white"
    )

ft.run(main)
```

title_spacing = number

Specifies the horizontal spacing between the title and the leading control.

title_text_style = flet.TextStyle()

Applies a custom text style to the AppBar title, such as font size, weight and color.

> **Note**
>
> Refer to the previously discussed **Text** control for a detailed explanation of **TextStyle**.

actions = [Control]

Defines a list of controls displayed on the right side of the **AppBar**. These controls commonly include **IconButton** widgets that trigger events when tapped or clicked.

Python

```python
import flet as ft

def main(page: ft.Page):
    page.appbar = ft.AppBar(
        actions= [
            ft.IconButton(icon= ft.Icons.ACCOUNT_CIRCLE),
            ft.IconButton(icon= ft.Icons.NOTIFICATIONS),
            ft.IconButton(icon= ft.Icons.SHOPPING_CART),
        ],
        title_spacing=2,
        title_text_style= ft.TextStyle(weight= ft.FontWeight.W_200, size=25),
        bgcolor= "#132b5c",
        #Code continues below ...
    )
```

```
ft.run(main)
```

surface_tint_color = color

Adds a tinted overlay on the AppBar surface. This is typically used for visual effects in Material design.

shadow_color = color

Specifies the color of the shadow that appears under the AppBar when elevation is applied.

elevation = number

Defines the perceived depth of the AppBar by adjusting the strength of the drop shadow beneath it.

```python
import flet as ft

def main(page: ft.Page):
    page.appbar = ft.AppBar(
        elevation= 15,
        shadow_color= "grey",
        bgcolor= "white",
        color="black",
        #Code continues below ...
    )

ft.run(main)
```

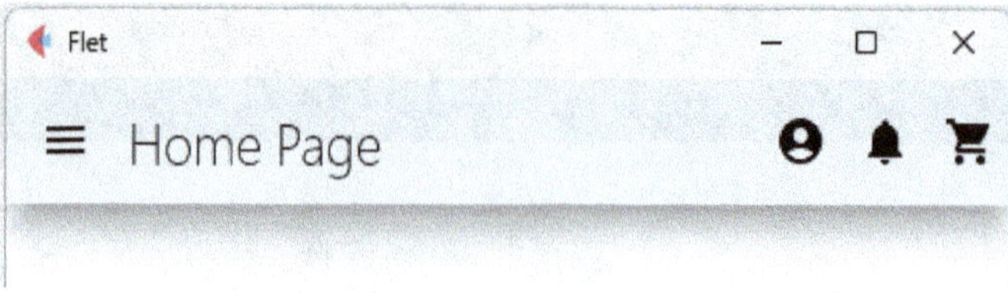

elevation_on_scroll = number

Defines the elevation when the page is scrolled.

center_title = bool

When True, the AppBar title is centered horizontally. When False, the title is aligned to the left.

automatically_imply_leading = bool

Determines whether the AppBar should automatically include a default leading control, such as a back button. When set to False, only controls explicitly supplied to the leading property will be shown.

toolbar_opacity = number

Sets the transparency level of the toolbar section specifically, separate from the overall AppBar opacity.

Python

```
import flet as ft

def main(page: ft.Page):
    page.appbar = ft.AppBar(
        toolbar_opacity=0.4,
        center_title=True,
        bgcolor= "#1C1C1C",
        color= "white",
        title= ft.Text("HomePage"),
    )


ft.run(main)
```

clip_behavior = flet.ClipBehavior

Specifies how the AppBar should clip its content when the content overflows its boundaries. Options include:

- ANTI_ALIAS
- HARD_EDGE
- NONE
- ANTI_ALIAS_WITH_SAVE_LAYER

toolbar_height = number

Defines the height of the AppBar.

toolbar_text_style = TextStyle

Applies a text style to the toolbar content when the AppBar contains text elements.

shape = Shape

Defines the shape or border outline of the AppBar. This is often used to create rounded corners or custom outlines.

```python
import flet as ft

def main(page: ft.Page):
    page.appbar = ft.AppBar(
        shape = ft.RoundedRectangleBorder(
            radius=ft.BorderRadius(
                top_left=0, top_right=0,
                bottom_left=20, bottom_right=20)
            ),

        bgcolor= "#000000",
        color="white",
        #Code continues below ...
    )


ft.run(main)
```

FloatingActionButton

The **FloatingActionButton** is a control that displays a circular or rounded elevated button positioned above the main content of the page. Unlike regular buttons that scroll with the page, the FloatingActionButton remains fixed in place. This creates a floating effect that keeps the button accessible at all times, making it ideal for primary actions such as adding items, composing messages or navigating to another view.
In Flet, the FloatingActionButton can contain text, an icon or any other control and it supports a variety of properties that customize its appearance, behavior and interaction.

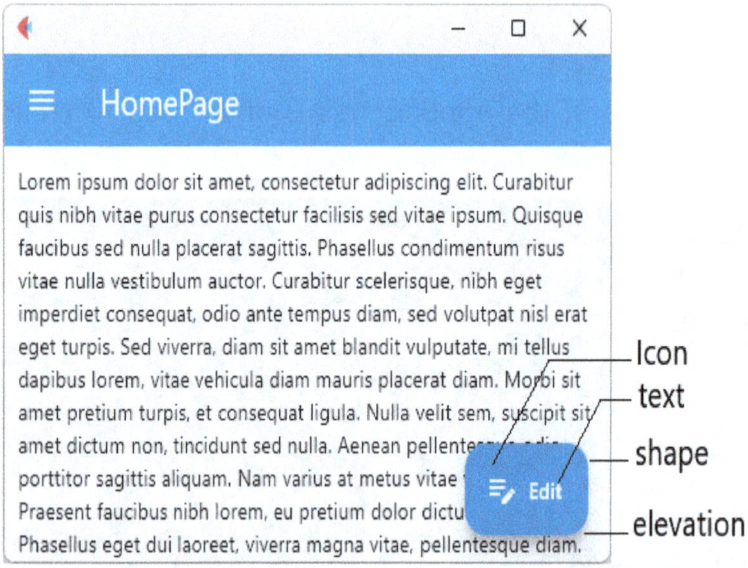

Properties and Methods

bgcolor = color

Defines the background color of the button. Colors may be provided as standard color names such as "green" or "blue" or as hexadecimal color values such as "#AAFFCC".

icon = icon

Defines the icon displayed inside the button. When icon is set, it overrides the content property.

autofocus = bool

When set to True, the button automatically receives keyboard focus when the page is loaded.

```
Python

import flet as ft

def main(page: ft.Page):
    page.floating_action_button = ft.FloatingActionButton(
        icon= ft.Icon(ft.Icons.EDIT)
    )

ft.run(main)
```

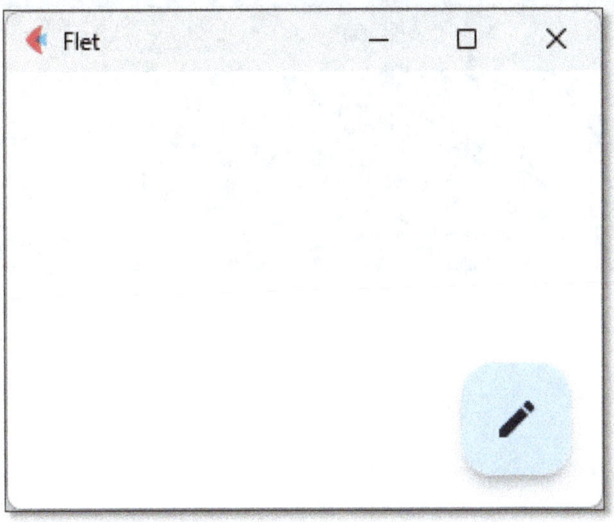

foreground_color = color

Specifies the color applied to text, icons or other foreground content within the button.

content = string/control

Defines the internal control or text displayed inside the button. This may be an icon, a text label or a more complex layout such as a Row or Column.

on_click = callback

Specifies the function that is triggered when the button is clicked or tapped.

clip_behavior = flet.ClipBehavior

Determines how content inside the button is clipped when it overflows its boundaries.

```
Python
import flet as ft

def main(page: ft.Page):

    def edit(e):
        #Actual code goes here ...
        print("Do something here")

    page.floating_action_button = ft.FloatingActionButton(
        content = "Edit",
        bgcolor="#66ccbe",
        foreground_color="white",
        on_click= edit
    )

ft.run(main)
```

elevation = number

Specifies the button's elevation when it is in its normal state. A higher value creates a stronger shadow beneath the button.

focus_elevation = number

Defines the elevation of the button when it is focused.

highlight_elevation = number

Specifies the elevation when the button is pressed.

hover_elevation = number

Specifies the elevation when the cursor hovers over the button. This is used on desktop platforms.

disabled_elevation = bool

Defines the elevation of the button when it is disabled.

focus_color = color

Sets the color used when the button receives keyboard or accessibility focus.

hover_color = color

Sets the background color used when the mover passes over the button.

Python

```python
import flet as ft

async def main(page: ft.Page):

    page.floating_action_button = ft.FloatingActionButton(
        elevation= 20,
        hover_elevation= 15,
        highlight_elevation=10,
        hover_color= "green",
        icon= ft.Icon(ft.Icons.ADD),
        content = "Add",
        bgcolor="blue",
        foreground_color="white",
    )
```

```
ft.run(main)
```

elevation = 0

elevation = 20

hover_elevation = 15

hover_color = "green"

scale = number

Controls the scale or size transformation of the button during animations.

tooltip = string

Defines the text displayed when the user hovers over the button on desktop platforms or focuses it with keyboard navigation.

shape = Shape

Specifies the shape of the button. This can be circular, rounded rectangle or any custom shape supported by Flet.

disabled = bool

When set to True, the button becomes non interactive and cannot be clicked.

opacity = number

Controls the transparency of the button. A value of 0.0 makes the button fully transparent. A value of 1.0 makes it fully visible.

mouse_cursor = fletMouseCursor

Defines the cursor style shown when the user hovers over the button.

```python
import flet as ft

async def main(page: ft.Page):

    page.floating_action_button = ft.FloatingActionButton(
        shape = ft.CircleBorder(),
        tooltip= "Submit message",
        icon= ft.Icon(ft.Icons.SEND),
        #Code continues below ...
    )


ft.run(main)
```

url = string

Defines a webpage URL that opens in the browser when the button is clicked.

url_target = flet.UrlTarget

Specifies how the URL should be opened, for example in a new tab or the same tab. UrlTarget options include:

- BLANK
- PARENT
- SELF
- TOP

mini = **bool**

When True, displays the button in a smaller variant, often used for compact UI layouts.

```python
import flet as ft

def main(page: ft.Page):

    page.floating_action_button = ft.FloatingActionButton(
        shape = ft.RoundedRectangleBorder(radius= 5),
        url= "https://google.com",
        icon= ft.Icon(ft.Icons.HOME_OUTLINED),
        #Code continues below ...
    )

ft.run(main)
```

RoundedRectangleBorder(radius = 5)

RoundedRectangleBorder(radius = 15)

enable_feedback = **bool**

When True, the button provides haptic or audible feedback during interaction. This is platform dependent.

rotate = **angle**

Defines the rotation angle of the button.

FloatingActionButtonLocation

The **FloatingActionButtonLocation** property allows you to define the position of a FloatingActionButton within a page.

By setting this property, you can control where the floating action button appears — such as at the bottom-right, bottom-center, or other predefined positions on the screen.
This helps maintain proper layout alignment and ensures the button does not overlap important content.

CENTER_DOCKED	END_FLOAT	MINI_END_DOCKED	MINI_START_TOP
CENTER_FLOAT	END_TOP	MINI_END_FLOAT	START_DOCKED
CENTER_TOP	MINI_CENTER_DOCKED	MINI_END_TOP	START_FLOAT
END_CONTAINED	MINI_CENTER_FLOAT	MINI_START_DOCKED	START_TOP
END_DOCKED	MINI_CENTER_TOP	MINI_START_FLOAT	

Python

```python
import flet as ft

def main(page: ft.Page):

    location = ft.FloatingActionButtonLocation.START_FLOAT
    page.floating_action_button_location = location

    page.floating_action_button = ft.FloatingActionButton(
        shape = ft.CircleBorder(),
        icon= ft.Icon(ft.Icons.FAVORITE),
        #Code continues below ...
    )

ft.run(main)
```

START_FLOAT

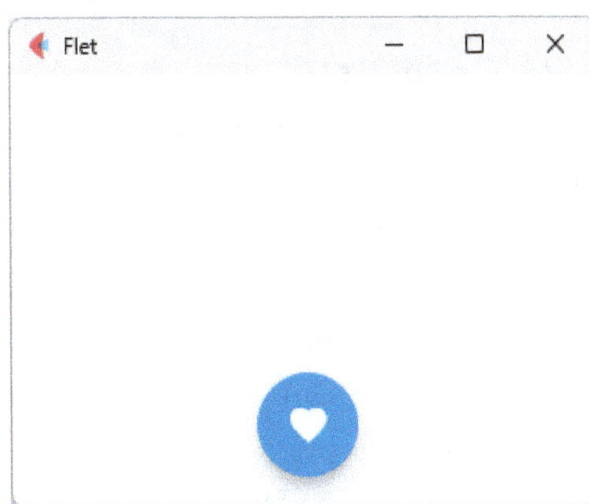

CENTER_FLOAT

BottomAppBar

The **BottomAppBar** control is similar in purpose to the standard **AppBar**, except it appears at the bottom of the application window instead of the top. It is commonly used in:

- **Web** applications to present persistent action areas at the bottom
- **Desktop and mobile apps** to display system-related details such as page status, shortcuts, navigation elements, copyright text, app version, user information, connection status (e.g., *Online / Offline*)

The BottomAppBar serves as a container that can display simple content (like text) or complex layouts (Row, Column, GridView, etc.).

Key Properties and Methods

content = control

The main child control displayed inside the bottom bar. It can be a single control—such as a Text label—or a complex layout like Row, Column or Container to organize multiple controls.

elevation = number

Controls how "raised" the BottomAppBar appears. Higher elevation creates a more pronounced shadow.
Typical values range from 0 (flat) to around 10+ (highly raised).

bgcolor = color

Sets the background color of the BottomAppBar. Color may be a built-in name (e.g., "green", "red") or a hex code ("#FFAA99").

```python
import flet as ft

def main(page: ft.Page):

    page.bottom_appbar = ft.BottomAppBar(
        bgcolor= "#075056",
        content= ft.Row(
            alignment= ft.MainAxisAlignment.SPACE_BETWEEN,
            controls=[
            ft.IconButton(icon=ft.Icons.MENU, icon_color="white"),
            ft.IconButton(icon=ft.Icons.NOTIFICATIONS, icon_color="white"),
            ft.IconButton(icon=ft.Icons.FAVORITE, icon_color="white"),
            ft.IconButton(icon=ft.Icons.SETTINGS, icon_color="white"),
        ])
    )


ft.run(main)
```

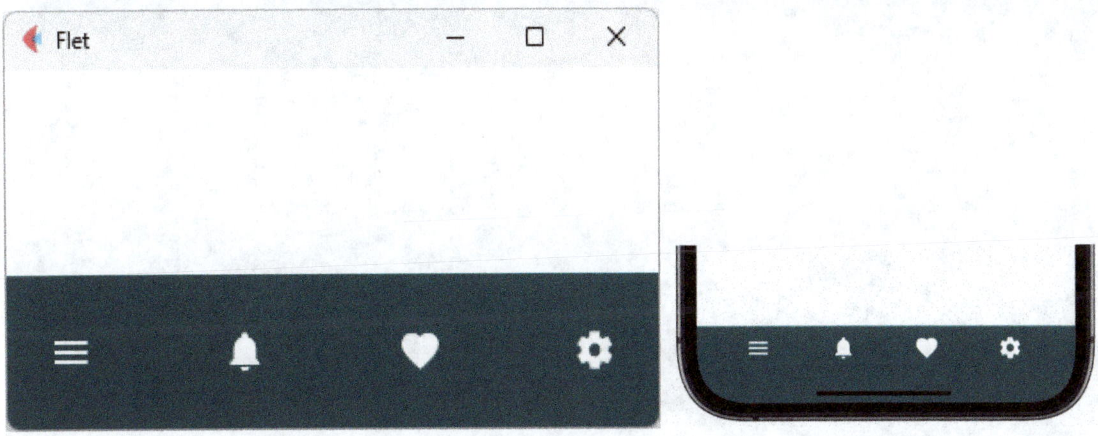

shadow_color = color

Defines the color of the shadow cast above the bar. This helps create a sense of elevation and separation from the main content.

padding = number, flet.Padding

Specifies the **inner spacing** between the bar's boundary and its content. Padding prevents elements from touching the edges.

surface_tint_color = color

Defines the subtle tint overlay applied on top of the bar's background. This creates a soft blending or elevation effect consistent with Material Design.

shape = flet.NotchSpace()

Defines the shape of the bar's top edge. Most often used when including a FloatingActionButton (FAB) with a notch cut-out.

notch_margin = number

Sets the **gap distance** between the FAB and the notch in the BottomAppBar. Used only when a notch shape is present.
Higher values = wider space around the FloatingActionButton.

```python
import flet as ft

async def main(page: ft.Page):

    location = ft.FloatingActionButtonLocation.CENTER_DOCKED
    page.floating_action_button_location = location

    page.floating_action_button = ft.FloatingActionButton(
        shape= ft.CircleBorder(),
        icon=ft.Icons.HOME_OUTLINED,
        bgcolor="green",
        foreground_color="white"
    )

    page.bottom_appbar = ft.BottomAppBar(
        shape= ft.CircularRectangleNotchShape(),
        notch_margin= 10,
        #Code continues below ...
    )


ft.run(main)
```

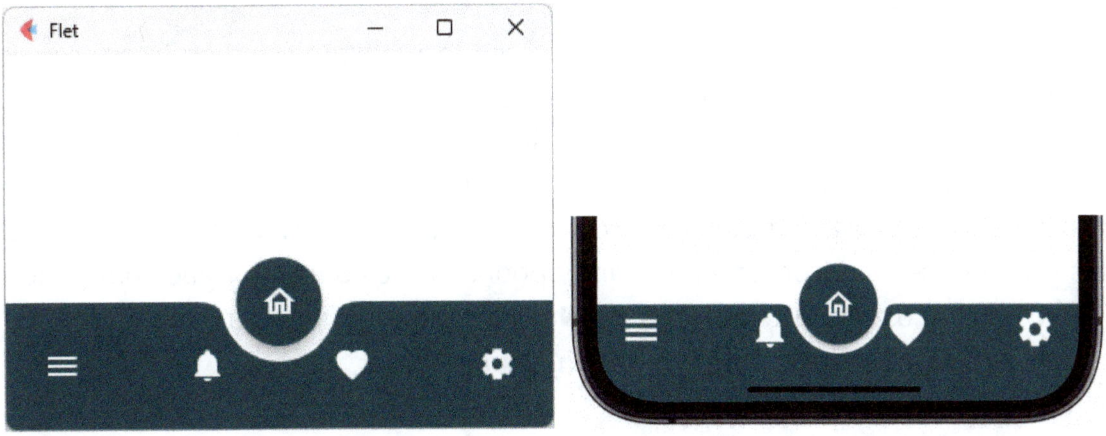

FloatingActionButtonLocation.CENTER_DOCKED

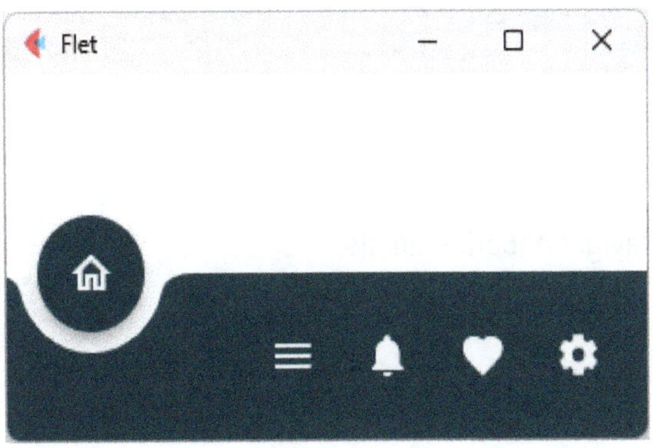

START_DOCKED

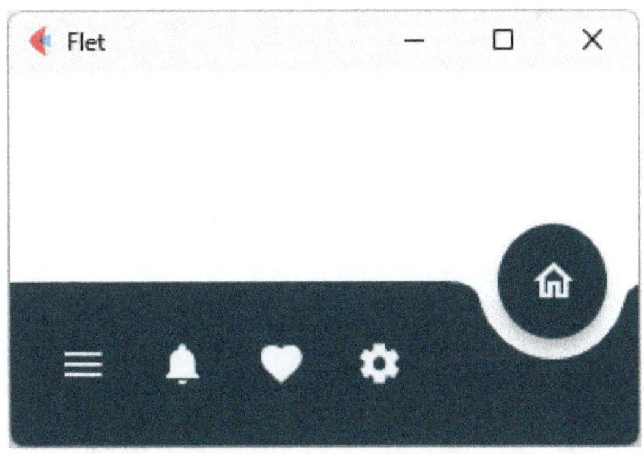

END_DOCKED

clip_behavior = flet.ClipBehavior

Determines how content is clipped when it overflows the bar's boundaries. Possible options include:

- **ClipBehavior.NONE** → Do not clip
- **ClipBehavior.HARD_EDGE** → Clip sharply
- **ClipBehavior.ANTI_ALIAS** → Smooth edge clipping

Used when content is shaped or animated to avoid overflow artifacts.

NavigationBar

The **NavigationBar** is a control commonly used in mobile and tablet interfaces. It provides a simple and convenient way for users to switch between different pages or screens of an application. The control is usually positioned at the bottom of the screen and displays a set of items that include an icon and a text label.

Each item in the **NavigationBar** is created using the **NavigationBarDestination** class. This class defines the icon, label text and optional selected icon for each navigation item. When the user selects an item, the **NavigationBar** updates its appearance and triggers a navigation action through the **on_change** event.

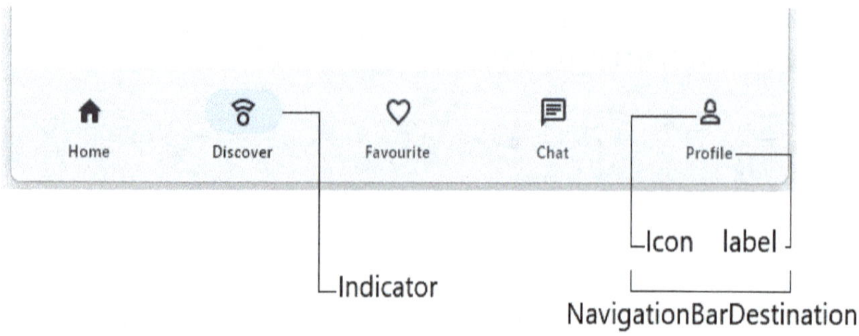

Properties and Methods

destinations = [flet.NavigationBarDestination]

A list of NavigationBarDestination objects. Each destination creates an item in the NavigationBar.

NavigationBarDestination

Method/Property	Definition *Table 3.21*
icon	The icon displayed for the item.
label	The text displayed beneath the icon.
selected_icon	An optional icon shown only when the item is selected.
bgcolor	The background color of the item when selected.

```python
import flet as ft

def main(page: ft.Page):

    page.navigation_bar = ft.NavigationBar(

        destinations=[
            ft.NavigationBarDestination(
                icon= ft.Icons.HOME_ROUNDED,
                label= "Home",
                selected_icon= ft.Icons.HOME_FILLED
            ),

            ft.NavigationBarDestination(
                icon= ft.Icons.FAVORITE,
                label= "Favorite"
            ),
            ]
    )


ft.run(main)
```

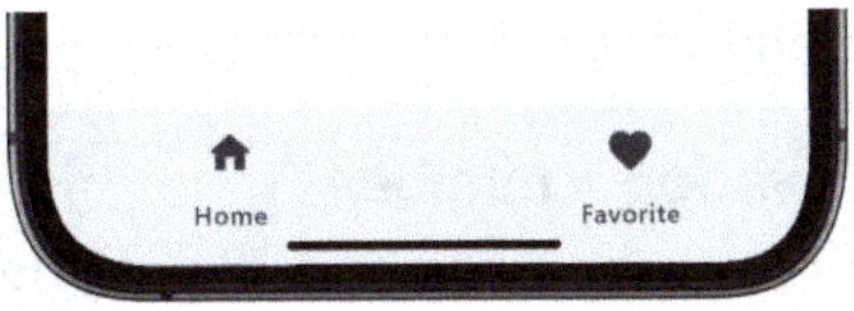

on_change = callback

Specifies a callback function that is executed when the user selects a different navigation item. This is commonly used for page switching.

Python

```python
import flet as ft

def main(page: ft.Page):

    def onChange(e):
        #Actual logic goes here ...
        index = e.data
        print(f"selected index ->{index}")

    page.navigation_bar = ft.NavigationBar(
        on_change = onChange,
        destinations=[
            ft.NavigationBarDestination(
                icon= ft.Icons.HOME_ROUNDED,
                label= "Home",
                selected_icon= ft.Icons.HOME_FILLED
            ),
            ft.NavigationBarDestination(
                icon= ft.Icons.FAVORITE,
                label= "Favorite"
            ),
        ]
    )

ft.run(main)
```

indicator_color = color

Specifies the color of the selection indicator that appears behind the selected item.

indicator_shape = Shape

Defines the shape of the selection indicator. It can be circular, rounded rectangular or any shape allowed by Flet.

elevation = number

Specifies the visual elevation of the NavigationBar by controlling the shadow beneath it.

bgcolor = color

The background color of the NavigationBar. Accepts color names such as "red" or "blue", as well as hexadecimal values such as "#DDDDDD".

Python

```
import flet as ft

async def main(page: ft.Page):
    page.theme = ft.Theme(
        navigation_bar_theme= ft.NavigationBarTheme(
            label_text_style= ft.TextStyle(color="white")
          )
    )


    page.navigation_bar = ft.NavigationBar(
        bgcolor="green",
        indicator_color= "grey",
        indicator_shape= ft.RoundedRectangleBorder(radius=5),
        elevation = 5,
        destinations=[
            ft.NavigationBarDestination(
                icon= ft.Icon(ft.Icons.HOME_ROUNDED, color="white"),
                label= "Home",
                selected_icon=ft.Icons.HOME_FILLED
            ),

            ft.NavigationBarDestination(
                icon= ft.Icon(ft.Icons.FAVORITE_OUTLINE,color="white"),
                label= "Favorite",
                selected_icon= ft.Icons.FAVORITE
            ),

            ft.NavigationBarDestination(
                icon= ft.Icon(ft.Icons.SEARCH_OUTLINED,color="white"),
                label= "Search",
            ),
            ]
     )


ft.run(main)
```

selected_index = integer

Specifies the index of the selected navigation item. The index starts at 0.

border = flet.Border

Defines the border decoration of the NavigationBar, including color, thickness and border style.

overlay_color = color

Defines a faded or tinted overlay color applied to the NavigationBar.

label_behavior = flet.NavigationBarLabelBehavior

Specifies how navigation item labels should behave. It accepts values from NavigationBarLabelBehavior. Options include:

- ALWAYS_SHOW
- ALWAYS_HIDE
- ONLY_SHOW_SELECTED

label_padding = umber, flet.Padding

Defines the padding around the text label of each item.

shadow_color = color

Defines the color of the shadow generated by the NavigationBar.

surface_tint_color = color

Specifies a tint color applied to the surface of the NavigationBar.

Python
```
import flet as ft

async def main(page: ft.Page):

    def onChange(e):
        #Actual logic goes here ...
        index = navi_bar.selected_index
        print(f"selected index ->{index}")


    navi_bar = ft.NavigationBar(
        selected_index=1,
        label_padding= ft.Padding.all(5),
        label_behavior= ft.NavigationBarLabelBehavior.ONLY_SHOW_SELECTED,
        on_change= onChange,
        #Code continues below ...
```

```
    )

    page.navigation_bar = navi_bar


ft.run(main)
```

```
#Output
selected index ->2
```

tooltip = string

Defines the tooltip text displayed when the NavigationBar gains mouse focus or hover, mostly on desktop platforms.

opacity = number

Controls the transparency of the NavigationBar. A value of 0.0 makes it fully transparent, while 1.0 makes it fully visible.

CupertinoNavigationBar

The CupertinoNavigationBar is the iOS-styled version of the **NavigationBar**. Its properties and methods include:

destinations	selected_index	bgcolor
active_color	inactive_color	border
icon_size	on_change	

NavigationDrawer

The **NavigationDrawer** is a sliding panel that appears from the left side of the application. It is commonly used when an interface contains many controls or navigation options that should remain hidden until needed. This helps maintain a clean and organized layout while giving users quick access to additional pages or features.

The drawer is typically opened by tapping the menu icon (often represented by three horizontal lines) located on the **AppBar**. It remains hidden by default and automatically closes when the user dismisses it, selects an item or clicks outside the drawer area.

The contents of the NavigationDrawer are arranged vertically. Developers can populate it with various controls such as navigation destinations, text, icons, buttons or custom layouts.

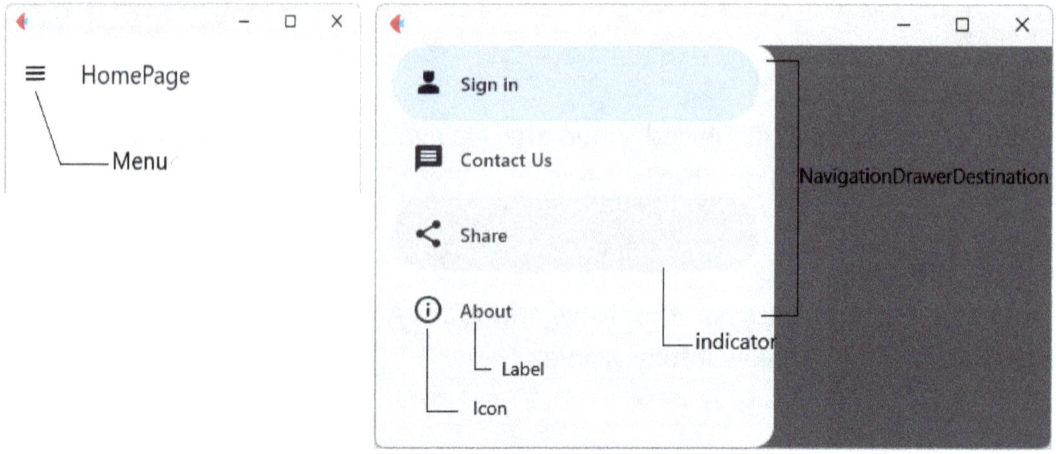

Key Properties and Methods

controls = [control]

Specifies a list of controls or **NavigationDrawerDestination** items to render inside the drawer. These controls are arranged in a vertical column by default. Items are displayed in the order they appear in the list.

NavigationDrawerDestination

Table 3.22

Method/Property	Definition
icon	The leading icon displayed for the item.
label	The text displayed beside the icon.
selected_icon	An optional icon shown only when the item is selected.
bgcolor	The background color of the item when selected.

page.show_drawer()

Programmatically opens the NavigationDrawer. Useful when developers want to trigger the drawer from a button or event.

bgcolor = color

Defines the background color of the drawer. Accepts both color names like "blue" and hexadecimal values like "#F5F5F5".

```
Python
import flet as ft

def main(page: ft.Page):

    page.drawer = ft.NavigationDrawer(
        controls=[
            ft.NavigationDrawerDestination(
                label= "Sign in",
                icon= ft.Icons.PERSON_4
            ),
            ft.NavigationDrawerDestination(
                label= "Contact Us",
                icon= ft.Icons.MESSAGE
            ),
        ]
    )
    page.appbar = ft.AppBar(
        title = ft.Text("HomePage"),
        bgcolor="blue", color="white"
    )


ft.run(main)
```

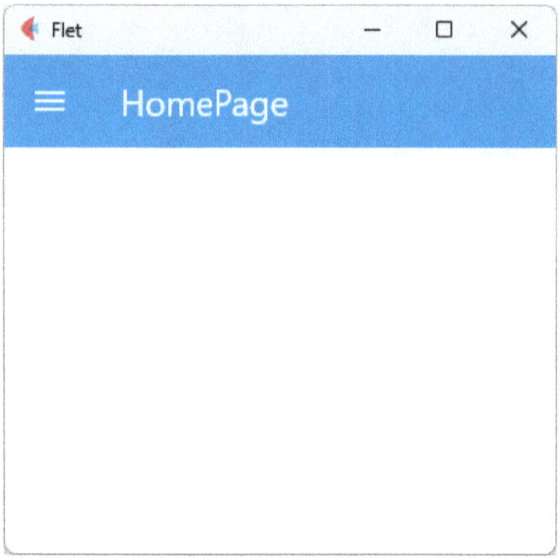

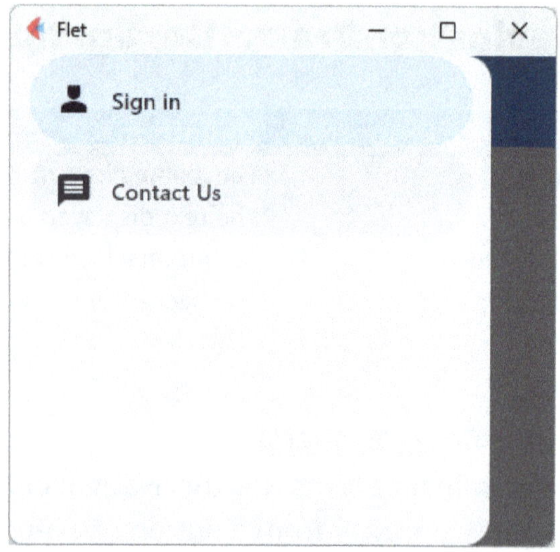

elevation = number

Defines the shadow depth of the drawer panel, giving it a raised appearance above the main content.

indicator_color = color

Defines the color applied to a drawer item when it is selected or gains focus.

Python

```
import flet as ft

def main(page: ft.Page):

    page.theme = ft.Theme(
        navigation_drawer_theme= ft.NavigationDrawerTheme(
            label_text_style= ft.TextStyle(size=20, color="black")
        )
    )

    page.drawer = ft.NavigationDrawer(
        indicator_color= ft.Colors.TEAL_100,
        #Code continues below ...
    )

ft.run(main)
```

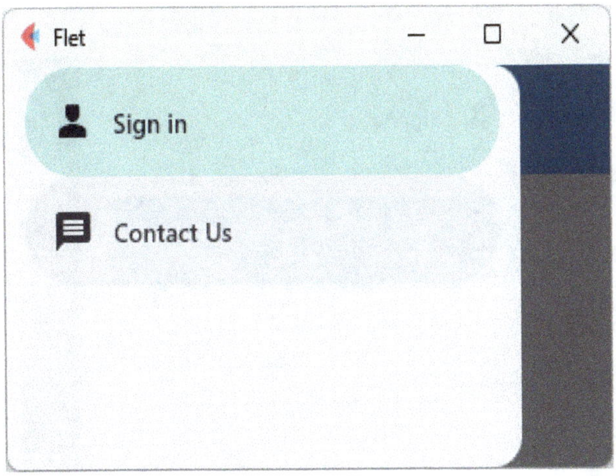

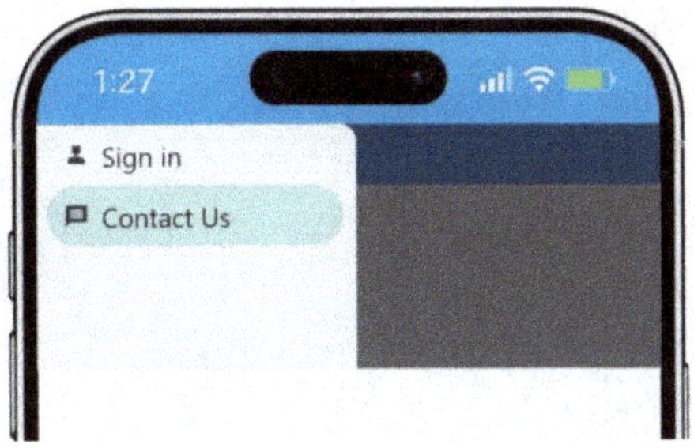

surface_tint_color = color

Applies a tint or faded overlay color to the drawer's surface.

tile_padding = flet.Padding

Defines the internal padding around drawer items. Used to adjust spacing and improve visual layout.

indicator_shape = Shape

Specifies the shape of the selection indicator for a focused or selected drawer item. This can be rounded, circular, rectangular or any shape supported by Flet.

```
Python
import flet as ft

def main(page: ft.Page):

    page.drawer = ft.NavigationDrawer(
        tile_padding= ft.Padding.symmetric(horizontal=20, vertical=10),
        indicator_shape= ft.RoundedRectangleBorder(
        radius= ft.BorderRadius(
              top_left=0, top_right=20,
              bottom_left=20, bottom_right=0
          )),
        indicator_color= "blue",
       #Code continues below ...
    )

ft.run(main)
```

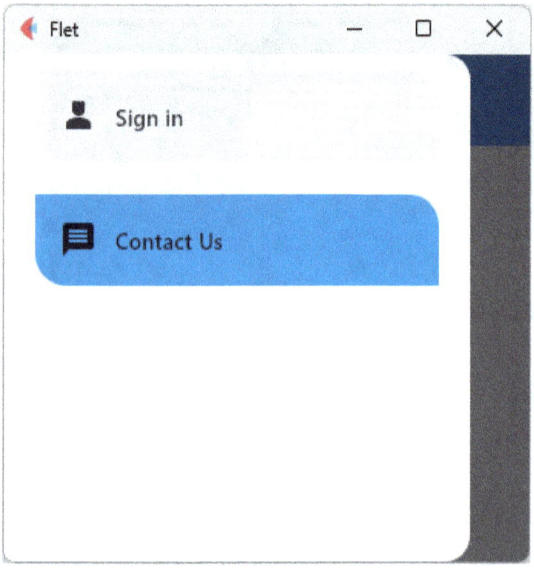

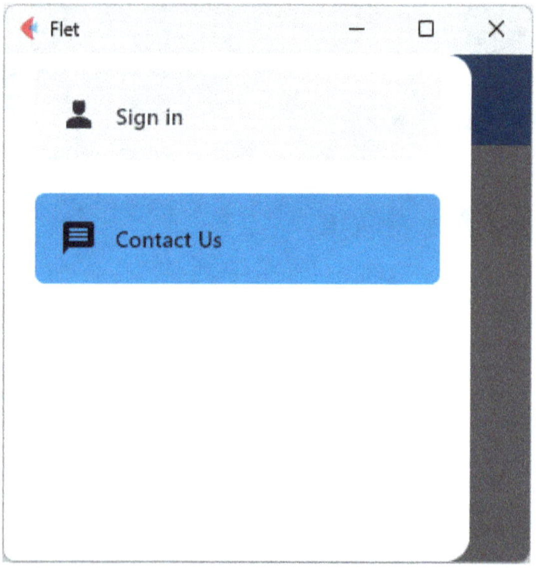

RoundedRectangularBorder(radius=10)

selected_index = integer

Returns or sets the index of the currently selected drawer item. The first item has an index of 0.

on_change = callback

Triggers a callback function when the user selects a drawer item. The function receives the index of the selected item.

on_dismiss = callback

Triggers a callback function when the drawer is closed manually by the user.

```python
import flet as ft

def main(page: ft.Page):

    def getSelectedItem(e):
        #Actual code goes here ...
        value = e.data
        print(value)

    def onClosed(e):
```

```
        #Actual code goes here ...
        print("Drawer has been closed")

    page.drawer = ft.NavigationDrawer(
        on_change = getSelectedItem,
        on_dismiss= onClosed,
        #Code continues below ...
    )

ft.run(main)
```

shadow_color = color

Specifies the color of the drawer's shadow. The default is typically a grey tone.

Page.end_drawer

By default, a **NavigationDrawer** opens from the left side (the start side) of the page. The Page.end_drawer property allows you to display a NavigationDrawer from the right side (the end side) of the page instead.

This is useful when you want the main navigation drawer on the left while placing additional options, settings, or secondary menus on the right side of the interface.

Example,

```python
import flet as ft

def main(page: ft.Page):

    page.end_drawer = ft.NavigationBar()


ft.run(main)
```

Image

The **Image** control displays image files inside a Flet application. Images can be loaded from:

- The assets directory (recommended for packaged apps)
- A file system path (desktop-only or when full path access is allowed)
- A base64-encoded string
- A URL (if supported by host environment)

For packaged applications, images should be placed in **assets/** inside the **src** folder. Example:

assets/
 logo.png
 pizza.jpg

Properties and Methods

src = string / bytes

Specifies the source of the image.

```python
import flet as ft

def main(page: ft.Page):

    image1 = ft.Image(
        src="younggirl.jpg",  #From the assets folder
        width= 100,
        height= 100
    )

    image2 = ft.Image(
        src=r"D:\Downloads\image2.jpg", #From system path
        width= 100,
        height= 100
    )

    image3 = ft.Image(
        src=r"https://example.com/image3.jpg",  #Network source
        width= 100,
        height= 100
    )

    row = ft.Row(controls=[image1, image2, image3])
    page.add(row)

ft.run(main)
```

📖 Note

The recommended method for using images in an application is to place them inside the project's **assets** directory and reference them directly in the code. This ensures that the images are bundled with the final application package.
When specifying the image source, the **assets/** prefix should be omitted. For instance, if the file **avatar.jpg** is located inside the assets folder, it should be referenced as:
src="avatar.jpg"

border_radius = number, flet.BorderRadius
Sets the curvature applied to all four image corners.

```
Python
import flet as ft

def main(page: ft.Page):

    image1 = ft.Image(
        "pizza.jpg",
        border_radius= ft.BorderRadius(
            top_left=0, top_right=30,
            bottom_left=30, bottom_right=0
            ),
    )

    image2 = ft.Image(
        "pizza.jpg",
        border_radius= 30,
    )

    row = ft.Row(controls=[image1, image2])
    page.add(row)


ft.run(main)
```

cache_height /cache_width = number

Specifies the *decoded* dimensions of the image in memory. Useful for performance optimization—especially for large images.

color = color

Applies an overlay color (tint) to the image.

color_blend_mode = flet.BlendMode

Determines how the applied color should blend with the original image.

BlendMode

CLEAR	DARKEN	DST_IN	HARD_LIGHT	MODULATE
COLOR	DIFFERENCE	DST_OUT	HUE	MULTIPLY
COLOR_BURN	DST	DST_OVER	LIGHTEN	OVERLAY
COLOR_DODGE	DST_A_TOP	EXCLUSION	LUMINOSITY	PLUS
SATURATION	SOFT_LIGHT	SRC_A_TOP	SRC_OUT	VALUES
SCREEN	SRC	SRC_IN	SRC_OVER	XOR

error_content = image

Specifies a fallback control displayed if the image fails to load.

exclude_from_semantics = bool

If True, removes the image from accessibility tools like screen readers.

filter_quality = flet.FilterQuality

Determines how smoothly the image is scaled or rendered.

Uses the **FilterQuality** enum:

1. **NONE** – No filtering, lowest quality
2. **LOW** – Basic filtering
3. **MEDIUM** – Balanced
4. **HIGH** – Best quality, more processing

fit = flet.BoxFit

Controls how the image fits inside its container using **BoxFit**. Available options include:

Method/Property	Definition *Table 3.23*
CONTAIN	Fits entire image without cropping
COVER	Fills container, cropping if needed
FILL	Stretches to fill both dimensions
FILL_WIDTH	Width fills container, height adjusts
FILL_HEIGHT	Height fills container
SCALE_DOWN	Scales down if too large
NONE	No scaling applied

Python
```
import flet as ft

def main(page: ft.Page):

    fill = ft.Image(
            src="puppy.jpg",
            fit= ft.BoxFit.FILL,
            width= 200,height= 200
        )

    contain = content= ft.Image(
            src="puppy.jpg",
            fit= ft.BoxFit.CONTAIN,
            width= 200,height= 200
```

```
    )

    cover = ft.Image(
            src="puppy.jpg",
            fit= ft.BoxFit.COVER,
            width= 200,height= 200
    )

    row = ft.Row(controls=[fill, contain, cover])
    page.add(row)


ft.run(main)
```

gapless_playback = bool

If True, the old image shows instead of the new image when the image source changes.

height / width = number

Define the displayed height and width of the image.

opacity = number

Determines the transparency of the image.

- 0.0 → completely invisible
- 1.0 → fully opaque

Python

```python
import flet as ft

def main(page: ft.Page):

    img1 = ft.Image(
            src="flower.jpeg",
            width= 200,height= 200
        )
    img2 = ft.Image(
            src="flower.jpeg",
            opacity= 0.4,
            width= 200, height= 200
        )

    row = ft.Row(controls=[img1, img2])
    page.add(row)


ft.run(main)
```

repeat = flet.ImageRepeat

Controls image repetition inside its boundary using ImageRepeat. Options include:

- no-repeat
- repeat-x
- repeat-y
- repeat

●●● Python

```python
import flet as ft

def main(page: ft.Page):

    repeaty = ft.Image(
            src="boy.jpeg",
            repeat= ft.ImageRepeat.REPEAT_Y,
            width= 100, height= 300
        )
    repeatx = ft.Image(
            src="boy.jpeg",
            repeat= ft.ImageRepeat.REPEAT_X,
            width= 300, height= 200
        )

    row = ft.Row(controls=[repeaty, repeatx])
    page.add(row)

ft.run(main)
```

semantic_label = string

It is semantic description of the image.

placeholder_src = string / bytes

This is the temporal object displayed when the image is loading. It can be a string (URL) or a local assets file path.

placeholder_fit = flet.BoxFit

Controls how the placeholder fits inside its container using **BoxFit**

fade_in_animation = flet.Animation()

The Fade-in animation of the image file, when it replaces the placeholder.

placeholder_fade_out_animation = flet.Animation

Fade-out animation for the placeholder after the image loads.

```python
import flet as ft

def main(page: ft.Page):

    image = ft.Image(
        src= r"C:\Downloads\Camera.jpg",
        placeholder_src= "image-gallery.png",
        semantics_label="my image",
        fade_in_animation= ft.Animation(
            duration= ft.Duration(seconds=10),
            curve= ft.AnimationCurve.BOUNCE_IN
        ),
        placeholder_fade_out_animation= ft.Animation(
            duration= ft.Duration(seconds=10),
            curve= ft.AnimationCurve.BOUNCE_OUT
        ),
        height= 350, width=300,
        fit= ft.BoxFit.FILL,
    )

    page.add(image)
```

```
ft.run(main)
```

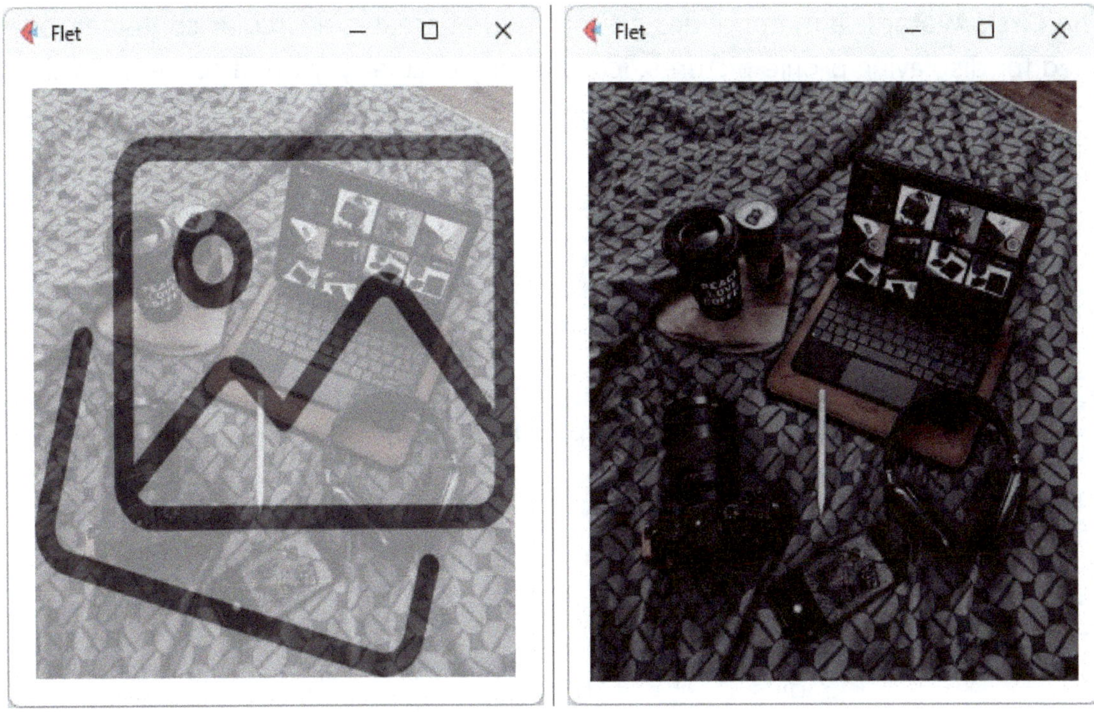

rotate = flet.Rotate, angle

Rotates the image in degrees (0–360).

CircleAvatar

The **CircleAvatar** is a material design control that creates a circular container, often used for displaying profile pictures, icons or any circularly framed content. Its size is determined by a **radius** and it can embed a child control, such as an image or text, within the circular frame.

Insight

The **CircleAvatar** provides a visually appealing **circular container** that can embed images, text or other controls, with full flexibility in styling, size and event handling.

Properties and Methods

bgcolor = color

Sets the background color of the CircleAvatar. Colors can be specified by name, hex code or **ColorValue** for predefined colors.

color = color

Specifies the foreground color (text colors) used if no image is provided.

radius = **number**

Specifies the default radius (size) of the CircleAvatar.

```python
import flet as ft

def main(page: ft.Page):

    avatar = ft.CircleAvatar(
        radius= 100,
        bgcolor= "cyan",
    )

    page.add(avatar)


ft.run(main)
```

background_image_src = **string**

Specifies an image source to decorate the background of the CircleAvatar.

foreground_image_src = **string**

Specifies an image source displayed on top of the background.

content = control

Sets the child control inside the CircleAvatar, such as a Text or Icon control.

```python
import flet as ft

def main(page: ft.Page):

    avatar = ft.CircleAvatar(
        radius= 100,
        bgcolor= "cyan",
        content= ft.CircleAvatar(
            radius= 95,
            content= ft.Image("avatar_image.png")
        )
    )

    page.add(avatar)

ft.run(main)
```

max_radius = number

Specifies the maximum radius the CircleAvatar can expand to.

min_radius = number

Specifies the minimum radius of the CircleAvatar.

on_image_error = callback

Callback triggered when an image fails to load.

```python
import flet as ft

def main(page: ft.Page):

    def avatarError(e):
        #Actual logic goes here ...
        print("Error")


    avatar = ft.CircleAvatar(
        on_image_error= avatarError,
        tooltip= "Profile picture",
        opacity= 0.4,
        rotate= 45,
        #Code continues below ...
      )

    page.add(avatar)

ft.run(main)
```

Container

The **Container** control is a versatile layout element used to group, position, style and visually isolate other controls. It can contain any single child control, including layouts such as **Column**, **Row** and **GridView**. By providing styling, spacing and alignment options, the Container plays a central role in UI composition.
A Container can apply backgrounds, borders, padding, margins, gradients, shadows, transformations and decorations. It is often used to create cards, panels, tiles, banners or interactive areas.

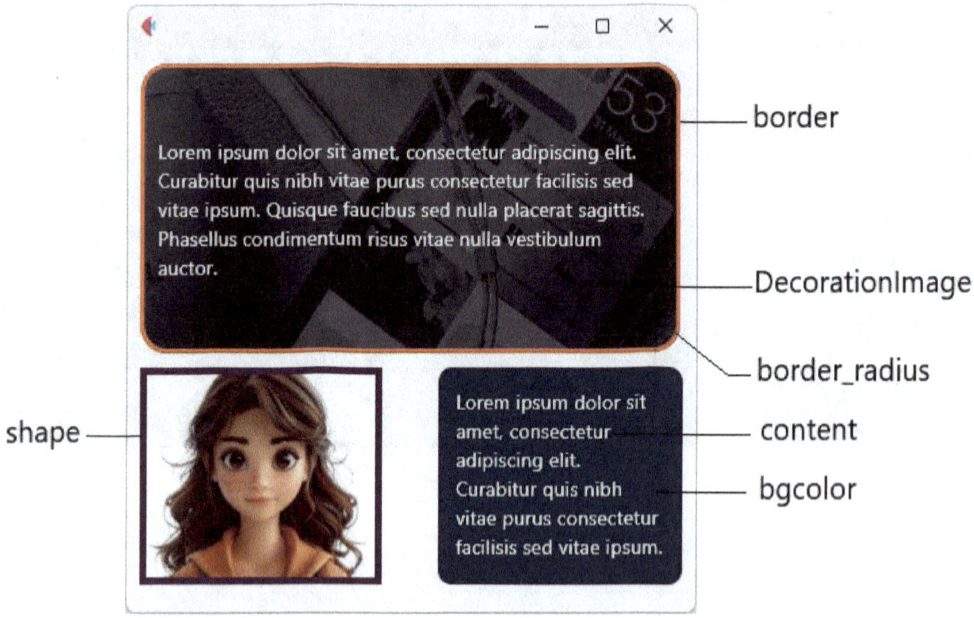

Properties and Methods

bgcolor = color

Defines the background color of the container. Colors may be specified by:

- name (e.g., "red", "blue")
- hex value
- predefined ColorValue

content = control

The child control contained inside the container.

```python
import flet as ft

def main(page: ft.Page):

    cont = ft.Container(
        content= ft.Text("Container Sample",
               style=ft.TextStyle(size=26, color="white")),
        bgcolor="#023246",
        width= 300,
        height= 100
    )

    page.add(cont)

ft.run(main)
```

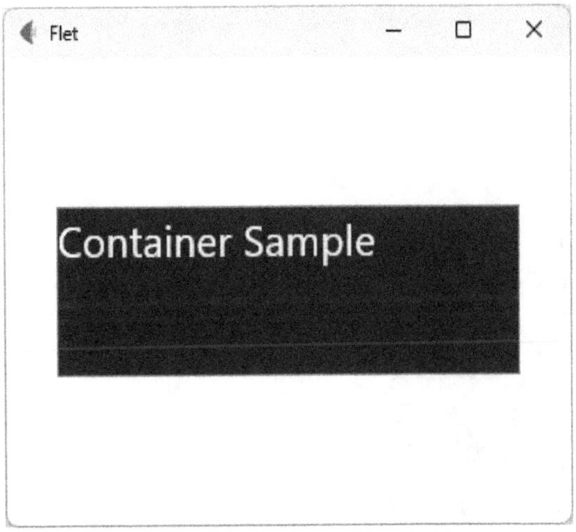

alignment = flet.Alignment

Defines how the child control is positioned inside the container. Alignment options include:

- CENTER
- TOP_LEFT
- CENTER_RIGHT
- BOTTOM_LEFT
- CENTER_LEFT
- TOP_CENTER
- TOP_RIGHT
- BOTTOM_CENTER
- BOTTOM_RIGHT

```python
import flet as ft

def main(page: ft.Page):

    cont = ft.Container(
        alignment= ft.Alignment.CENTER,
        bgcolor="orange",
        #Code continues below ...
    )

    page.add(cont)

ft.run(main)
```

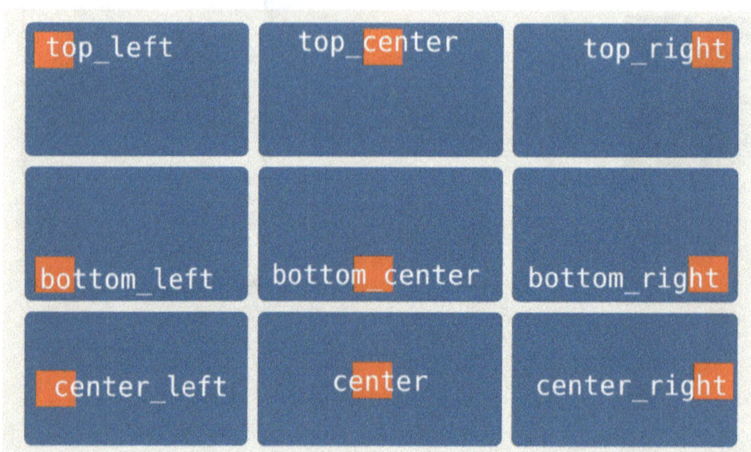

clip_behavior = **flet.ClipBehavior**

Determines how content that exceeds the container's boundaries is clipped.

ClipBehavior

Method/Property	Definition	*Table 3.24*
None	Do not clip	
HARD_EDGE	Clip sharply	
ANTI_ALIAS	Smooth edge clipping	

blur = number

Applies a blurring effect to the container, reducing visual clarity.

border = flet.Border, flet.Border.all

Defines the container's border using the Border control.

Border accepts BorderSide values for top, bottom, left and right. BorderSide includes:

- width → thickness of border
- color → border color

```
Python
import flet as ft

def main(page: ft.Page):

    cont1 = ft.Container(
        border= ft.Border.all(width=10, color="blue"),
        content= ft.Text("Container Sample  1",style=ft.TextStyle(size=26)),
        height= 200, width=400,
        bgcolor="#E9F2F9"
    )

    cont2 = ft.Container(
        border= ft.Border(
            top=ft.BorderSide(width=15, color="red"),
            left=ft.BorderSide(width=15, color="red"),
            right=ft.BorderSide(width=15, color="black"),
            bottom=ft.BorderSide(width=15, color="black"),
            ),
        content= ft.Text("Container Sample 2",style=ft.TextStyle(size=26)),
        height= 200, width=400,
        bgcolor="#9cc4e4"
    )

    page.add(cont1, cont2)

ft.run(main)
```

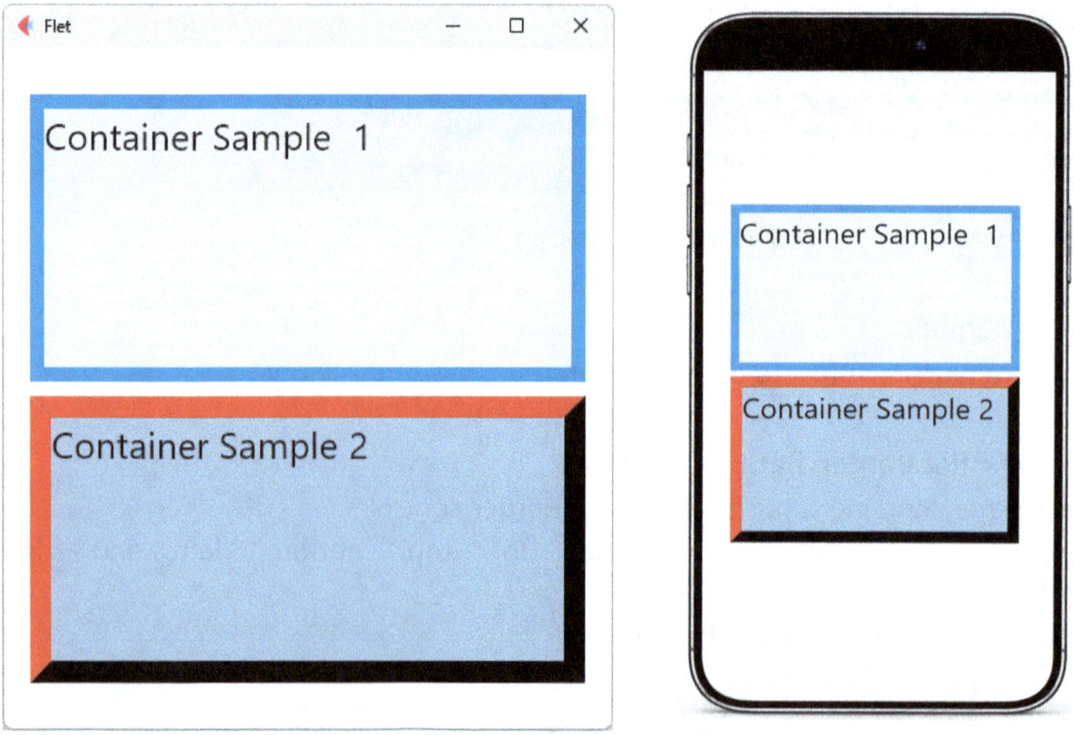

border_radius = number, flet.BorderRadius, flet.BorderRadius

Specifies the curvature of the container's corners. Supports:

- single float for all corners
- BorderRadius for individual corner values

```
Python
import flet as ft

def main(page: ft.Page):

    container1 = ft.Container(
        border_radius= 10,
        border= ft.Border.all(width=1, color="grey"),
        #Code continues below ...
    )

    container2 = ft.Container(
        border_radius= ft.BorderRadius.all(50),
        bgcolor="#E5C443",
        #Code continues below ...
    )
```

```
    container3 = ft.Container(
        border_radius= ft.BorderRadius.only(top_left=10,
                  top_right=10, bottom_left=30, bottom_right=30),
        bgcolor="#66ccbe",
        #Code continues below ...
      )

    container4 = ft.Container(
        border_radius= ft.BorderRadius(top_left=20, top_right=0,
                      bottom_left=0, bottom_right=20 ),
        bgcolor="#002c3e",
        #Code continues below ...
      )

    row1 = ft.Row(controls=[container1, container2])
    row2 = ft.Row(controls=[container3, container4])
    page.add(row1, row2)


ft.run(main)
```

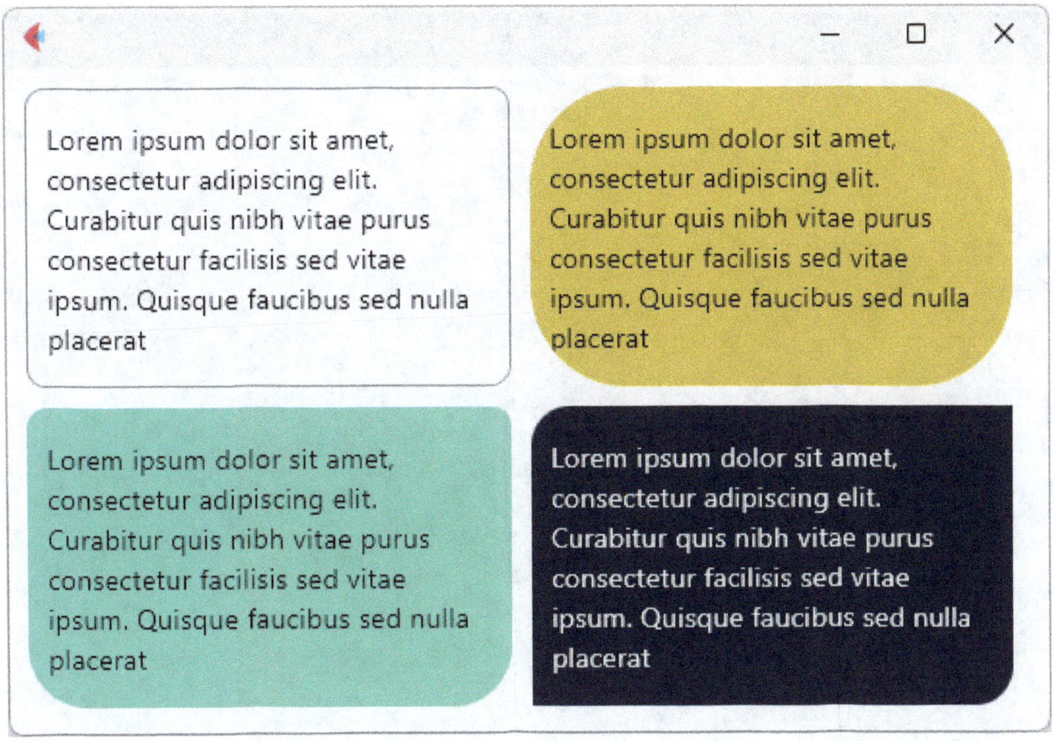

dark_theme, theme = flet.Theme

Defines theme that overrides the current theme, when the app is in dark mode.

blend_mode = flet.BlendMode

Applies blending effects when combining the container with background content.

BlendMode

CLEAR	DARKEN	DST_IN	HARD_LIGHT	MODULATE
COLOR	DIFFERENCE	DST_OUT	HUE	MULTIPLY
COLOR_BURN	DST	DST_OVER	LIGHTEN	OVERLAY
COLOR_DODGE	DST_A_TOP	EXCLUSION	LUMINOSITY	PLUS
SATURATION	SOFT_LIGHT	SRC_A_TOP	SRC_OUT	VALUES
SCREEN	SRC	SRC_IN	SRC_OVER	XOR

color_filter = flet.ColorFilter(color, blend_mode)

Applies color filtering effects using the **ColorFilter** control. Useful for foreground images.

```python
import flet as ft

def main(page: ft.Page):

    cont1 = ft.Container(
        color_filter= ft.ColorFilter("red", blend_mode=ft.BlendMode.COLOR),
        bgcolor= "green",
        #Code continues below ...
    )

    cont2 = ft.Container(
        color_filter= ft.ColorFilter("red",
            blend_mode= ft.BlendMode.SATURATION),
        bgcolor= "green",
        #Code continues below ...
    )

    cont3 = ft.Container(
        color_filter= ft.ColorFilter("red", blend_mode= ft.BlendMode.HUE),
        bgcolor= "green",
        #Code continues below ...
    )

    cont4 = ft.Container(
        color_filter= ft.ColorFilter("red",
             blend_mode= ft.BlendMode.SOFT_LIGHT),
```

```
        bgcolor= "green",
        #Code continues below ...
      )

    row1 = ft.Row(controls=[cont1, cont2])
    row2 = ft.Row(controls=[cont3, cont4])
    page.add(row1, row2)


ft.run(main)
```

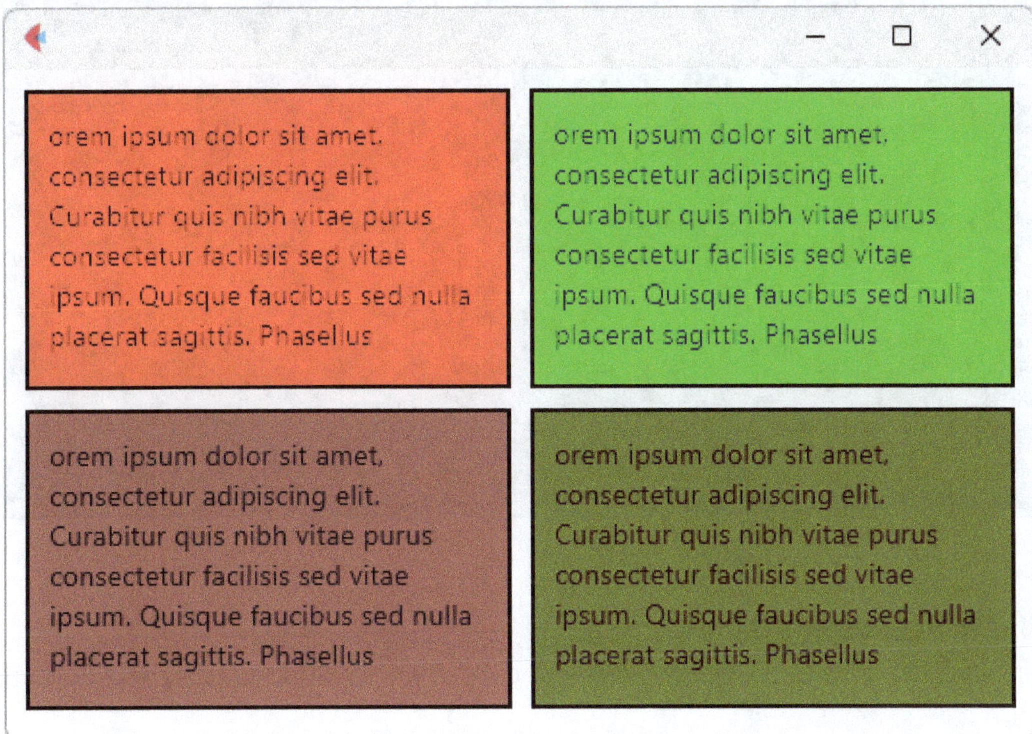

on_click = callback
Registers a function, triggered when the container is clicked.

on_hover = callback
Registers a function that fires when the pointer hovers over the container.

on_long_press = callback

Registers a function, triggered after holding the container for a long time.

on_tap_down = callback

Registers a function, triggered when the pointer presses down.

```
Python
import flet as ft

def main(page: ft.Page):

    def clicked(e):
        print("Container is clicked")

    def hovered(e):
        print("Container is hovered")

    cont = ft.Container(
        on_click = clicked,
        on_hover = hovered,
        content = ft.Text("Container Sample"),
    )

    page.add(cont)

ft.run(main)
```

padding = flet.Padding, number

Adds internal spacing between content and container boundaries using the Padding control.

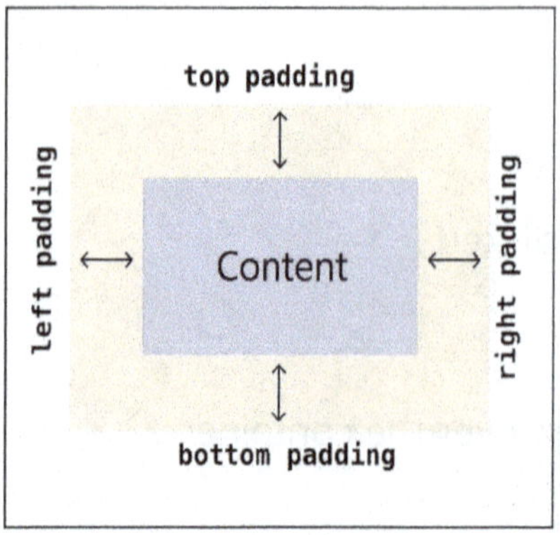

Figure 3.3 : Illustration of padding

<u>Padding Value can be</u>:

number

Padding(left, right, top, bottom)

Padding.all(value)

Padding.only(left, right, top, bottom),

Padding.symmetric(vertical, horizontal)

```python
import flet as ft

def main(page: ft.Page):

    cont1 = ft.Container(
        padding= ft.Padding.all(20),
        #Code continues below ...
        )

    cont2 = ft.Container(
        padding= ft.Padding.only(left=10, right=0, top=50, bottom=5),
        #Code continues below ...
        )

    cont3 = ft.Container(
        padding= ft.Padding.symmetric(horizontal=40, vertical=10),
        #Code continues below ...
        )

    cont4 = ft.Container(
        padding= ft.Padding(left=5, right=5, top=0, bottom=60),
        #Code continues below ...
        )

    row1 = ft.Row(controls=[cont1, cont2])
    row2 = ft.Row(controls=[cont3, cont4])
    page.add(row1, row2)


ft.run(main)
```

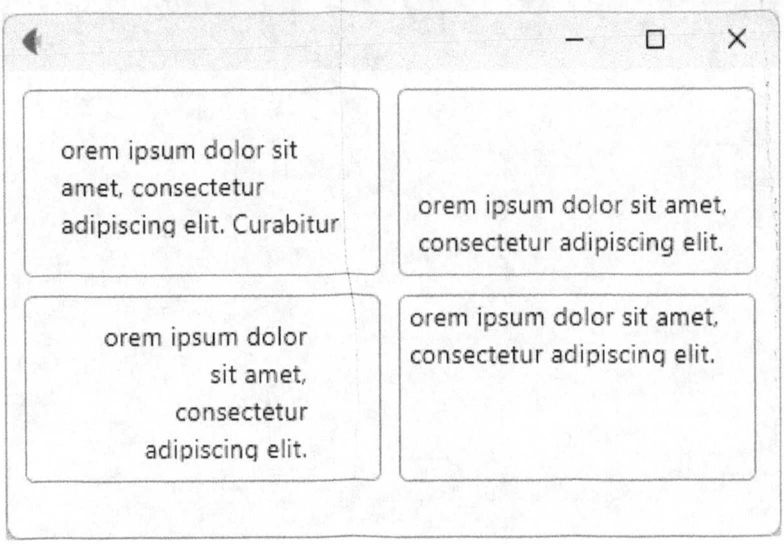

margin = number, flet.Margin

Applies spacing around the container using the Margin control.

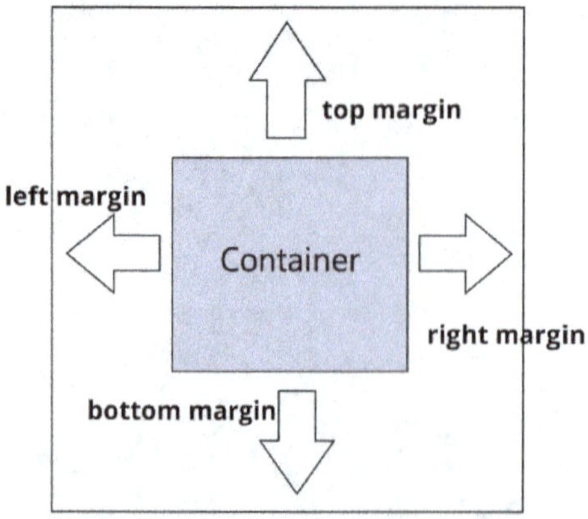

Figure 3.4 : Illustration of margin

Margin Value can :

number

Margin(left, right, top, bottom)

Margin.all(value)

Margin.only(left, right, top, bottom),

Margin.symmetric(vertical, horizontal)

```
Python
import flet as ft

def main(page: ft.Page):

    cont1 = ft.Container(
        margin= ft.Margin.all(20),
        #Code continues below ...
    )

    cont2 = ft.Container(
        margin= ft.Margin.only(left=20),
        #Code continues below ...
    )

    cont3 = ft.Container(
        margin= ft.Margin.symmetric(vertical=20),
        #Code continues below ...
    )

    cont4 = ft.Container(
        margin= ft.Margin(left=10, top= 40, right=0, bottom=0),
        #Code continues below ...
    )

    row1 = ft.Row(controls=[cont1, cont2])
    row2 = ft.Row(controls=[cont3, cont4])
    page.add(row1, row2)
```

```
ft.run(main)
```

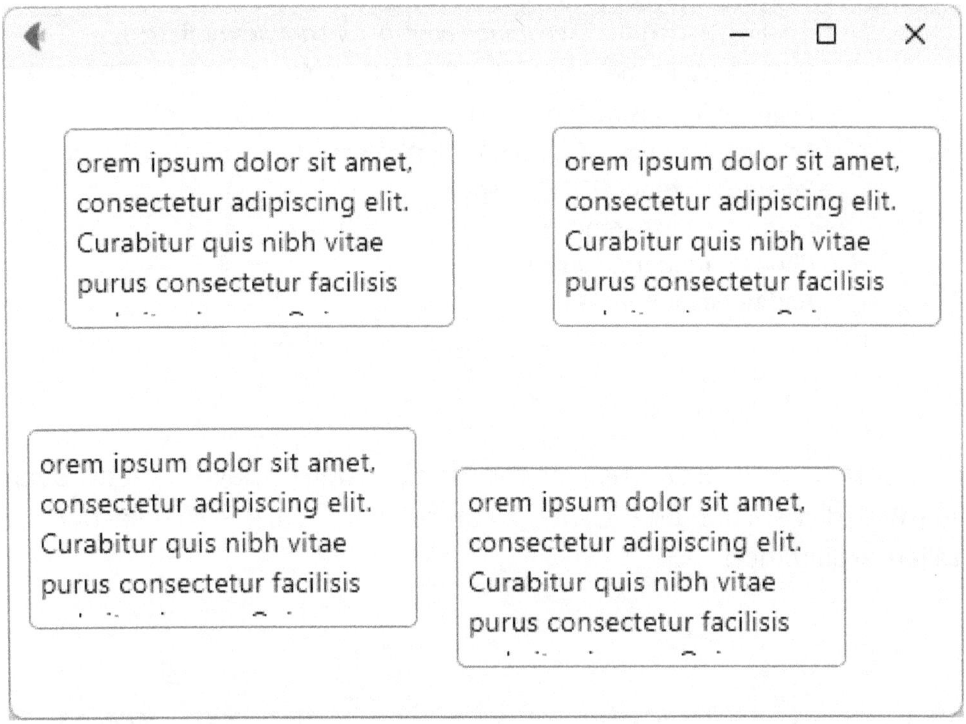

url = string
Opens a webpage when the container is clicked.

ink = bool
When True, the container shows ink ripples effect when user click or tap it .

ink_color = color
The splash color of the ink response.

image = flet.DecorationImage
A shorthand to apply a foreground DecorationImage.

DecorationImage

Method/Property	Definition	*Table 3.25*
src	Path or URL of the image	
color_filter	Applies ColorFilter. (*See Image control for samples of filters).*	
fit	Defines scaling behavior using BoxFit (contain, cover, fit_width, etc.)	
alignment	Aligns image inside the container	
repeat	Repeats the image if it cannot fill the container	
scale	Enlarges or reduces the image	
opacity	Controls transparency	
filter_quality	Chooses rendering quality	
invert_colors	Additional optional effects	

Insight

Most of the methods and properties of the **Image** control have already been discussed in the earlier section on the **Image** control. Refer back to that section for a more detailed explanation.

Python

```python
import flet as ft

def main(page: ft.Page):

    cont = ft.Container(
        image= ft.DecorationImage(
            src= "flower_bground.jpg",
            fit= ft.BoxFit.FILL,
            opacity=0.8
            ),
        content= ft.Text("Lorem ipsum dolor sit amet, consectetur ...."),
        padding= 50,
        border_radius= 10,
    )

    page.add(cont)

ft.run(main)
```

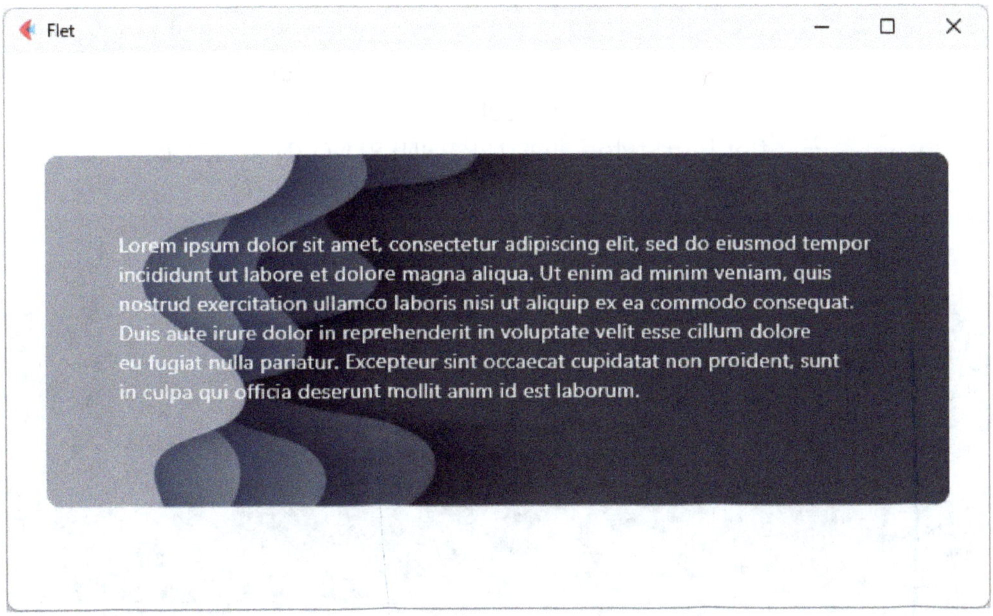

foreground_decoration = flet.BoxDecoration

Applies decorative effects on top of the container using BoxDecoration. This decoration appears above the background but below the child widget.

BoxDecoration

Table 3.26

Method/Property	Definition
border	Applies a border
border_radius	The curvature of the border
bgcolor	Background color for the decoration
image	Applies a DecorationImage
gradient	Applies a gradient
shape	Determines rectangle or circle
shadows	It applies shadow effect to the container
blend_mode	The blend mode applied to the background color

shadow = flet.BoxShadow

Adds shadow effect using BoxShadow.

BoxShadow

- spread_radius → float
- blur_radius → float
- blur_style → flet.BlurStyle →[OUTER, INNER, NORMAL,SOLID]
- offset → flet.Offset(x,y)
- color → color

```python
import flet as ft

def main(page: ft.Page):

    cont = ft.Container(
        shadow= ft.BoxShadow(
            spread_radius= 2,
            blur_radius= 3,
            color= "grey",
            offset= ft.Offset(15, 15),
            blur_style= ft.ShadowBlurStyle.NORMAL
            ),
        content= ft.Text("Lorem ipsum dolor sit amet, consecte...."),
        padding= 50,
        #Code continues below ...
    )

    page.add(cont)

ft.run(main)
```

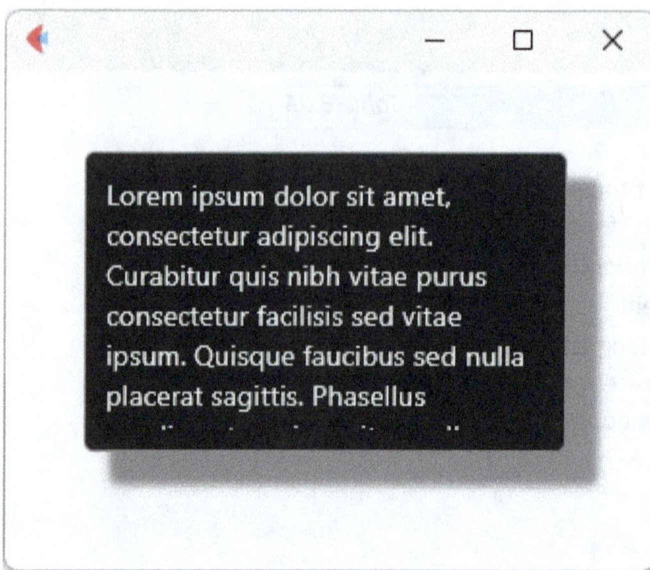

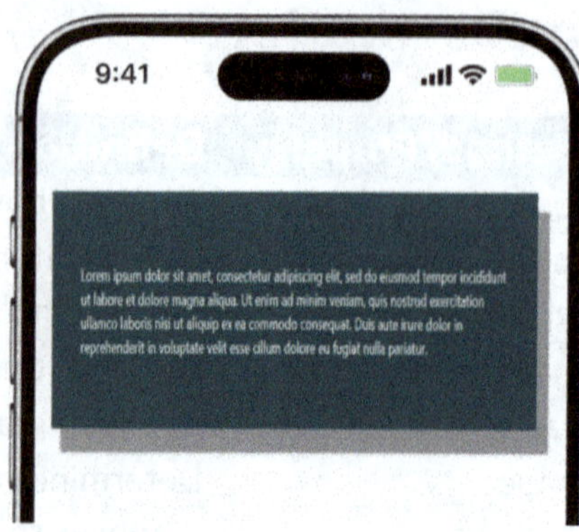

shape = flet.BoxShape

Determines whether the container is circular or rectangular using BoxShape. Options: CIRCLE, RECTANGLE

```python
import flet as ft

def main(page: ft.Page):

    circle = ft.Container(
        shape= ft.BoxShape.CIRCLE,
        #Code continues below ...
    )

    rectangle = ft.Container(
        shape= ft.BoxShape.RECTANGLE,
        #Code continues below ...
    )

    page.add(circle, rectangle)


ft.run(main)
```

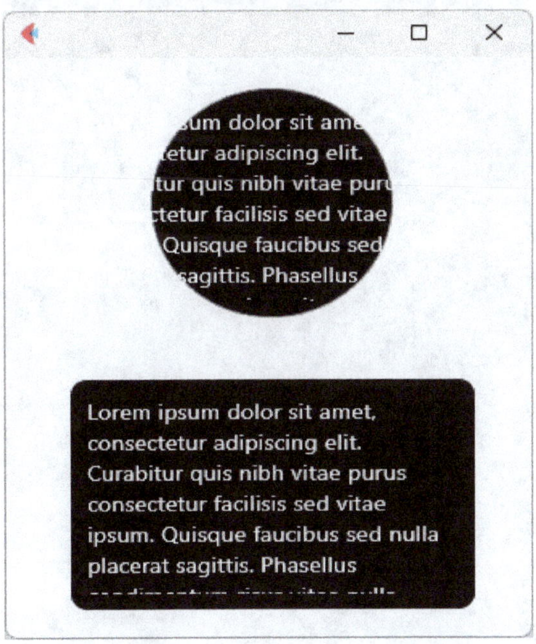

> **Note**
>
> When **BoxShape.CIRCLE** is applied, the **border_radius** property must be omitted, as it is not applicable to circular shapes.

tooltip = string
Displays text when the pointer hovers over the container.

ignore_interactions = bool
Ignores pointer interactions when set True.

theme_mode = flet.ThemeMode
Overrides theme styling within the container.

rotate = angle, flet.Rotate(angle)
Rotates the container by a given angle in radians.

Python

```
import flet as ft

def main(page: ft.Page):

    cont1 = ft.Container(
        rotate= 95,
        #Code continues below ...
    )

    cont2 = ft.Container(
        rotate= ft.Rotate(270, alignment= ft.Alignment.CENTER),
        #Code continues below ...
    )


    row = ft.Row(controls=[cont1, cont2])
    page.add(row)

ft.run(main)
```

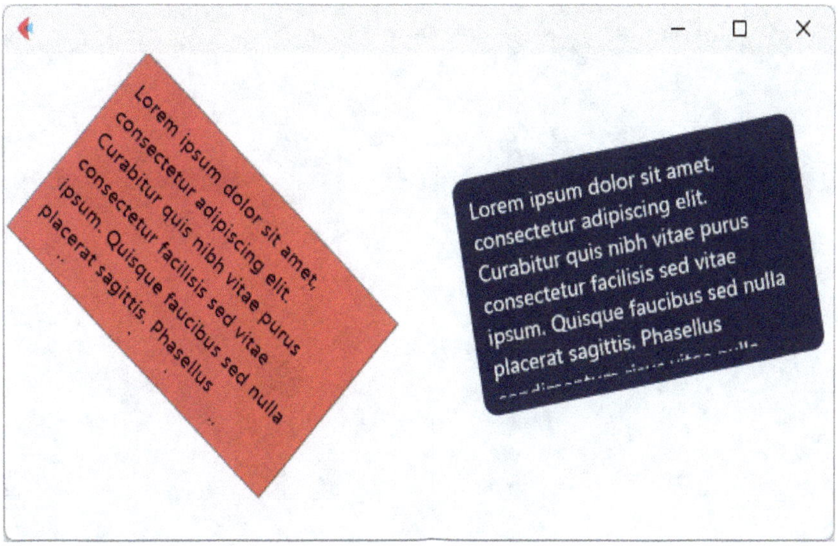

Gradient Decorations

Gradients allow smooth color transitions across the container. A Container may be decorated with gradient backgrounds using three gradient types:

- SweepGradient
- LinearGradient
- RadialGradient

SweepGradient

Creates a color sweep around a center point, rotating clockwise.

Table 3.27

Method/Property	Definition
center	Defines the center of rotation
colors	Required list of colors
start_angle	Starting angle of the sweep
end_angle	Ending angle
rotation	Rotation adjustment
stops	Numeric color positions
tile_mode	How the sweep repeats using GradientTileMode. Options include MIRROR, CLAMP, DECAL, REPEATED

```python
import flet as ft

def main(page: ft.Page):

    cont1 = ft.Container(
        gradient= ft.SweepGradient(
            colors= [ "blue","red", "yellow", "purple", "green"],
            ),
        width= 300,height=150
        #Code continues below ...
    )

    cont2 = ft.Container(
        gradient= ft.SweepGradient(
            colors= [ "#0c3b2e", "white"],
            tile_mode= ft.GradientTileMode.REPEATED,
            stops= [0.05, 0.8],
            start_angle= 0,
            end_angle= 5
            ),
        width= 300,height=150
        #Code continues below ...
    )

    row = ft.Row(controls=[cont1, cont2])
    page.add(row)


ft.run(main)
```

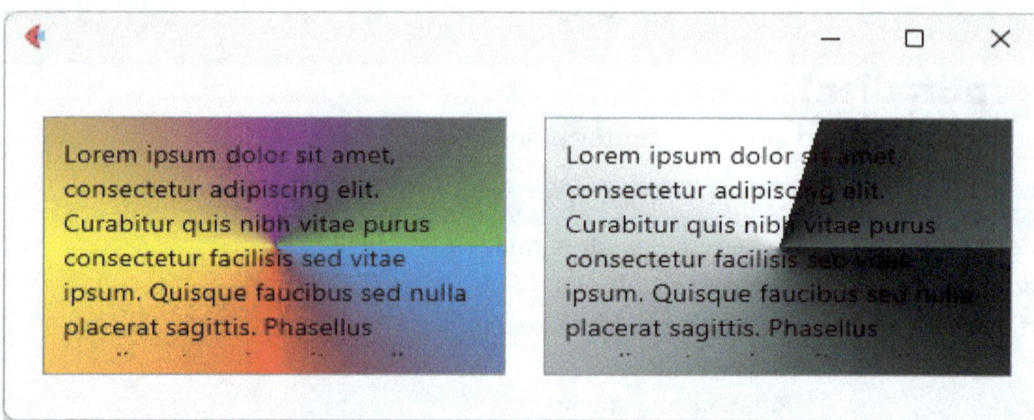

LinearGradient

Creates a straight-line gradient between two alignment points.

Method/Property	Definition
	Table 3.28
begin	starting alignment (e.g., center_left, top_center)
end	ending alignment
colors	required list of gradient colors
rotation	rotates the gradient by a given angle
stops	list of numeric positions for each color (0.0 to 1.0)
tile_mode	defines how the gradient repeats using GradientTileMode Options include MIRROR, CLAMP, DECAL, REPEATED

Python

```
import flet as ft

async def main(page: ft.Page):

    cont1 = ft.Container(
        gradient= ft.LinearGradient(
            colors= [ "red", "yellow", "purple"],
            ),
        content=ft.Text("Lorem ipsum dolor sit amet, consectetu..."),
        padding= 20, width= 300,height=150
    )

    cont2 = ft.Container(
        gradient= ft.LinearGradient(
            colors= [ "red", "yellow", "green", "blue"],
            begin= ft.Alignment.TOP_CENTER,
            end= ft.Alignment.BOTTOM_CENTER
            ),
        content=ft.Text("Lorem ipsum dolor sit amet, consectetu..."),
        padding= 20, width= 300,height=150
    )

    cont3 = ft.Container(
        gradient= ft.LinearGradient(
            colors= [ "#F1FAFE","teal", ],
            begin= ft.Alignment.BOTTOM_RIGHT,
            end= ft.Alignment.TOP_LEFT,
            stops=[0.05, 1]
            ),
        content=ft.Text("Lorem ipsum dolor sit amet, consectetu..."),
        padding= 20, width= 300,height=150
    )
```

```
    cont4 = ft.Container(
        gradient= ft.LinearGradient(
            colors= [ "white","#6d9773", "#0C3B2E"],
            tile_mode= ft.GradientTileMode.MIRROR,
            stops= [0.005, 0.09, 0.8],
            rotation= 120,
            begin= ft.Alignment.TOP_LEFT,
            end= ft.Alignment.BOTTOM_RIGHT,
           ),
        content=ft.Text("Lorem ipsum dolor sit amet, consectetu..."),
        padding= 20, width= 300,height=150
    )

    row1= ft.Row(controls=[cont1, cont2])
    row2= ft.Row(controls=[cont3, cont4])
    page.add(row1, row2)

ft.run(main)
```

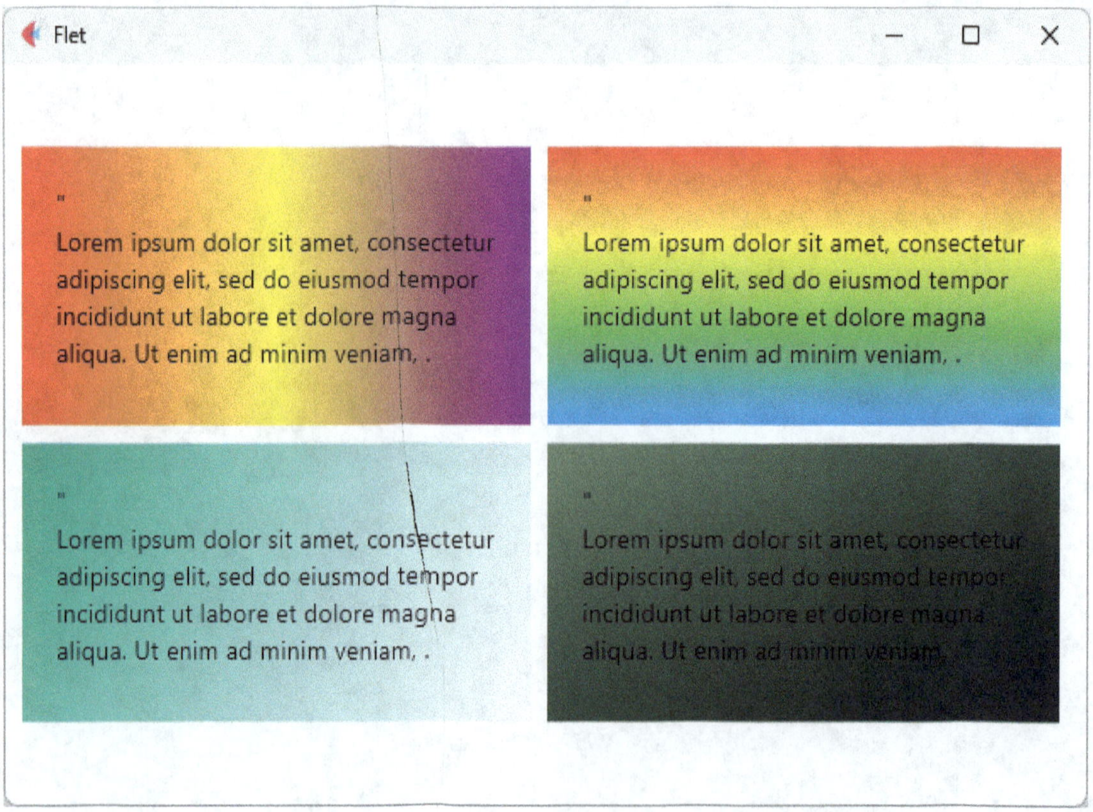

RadialGradient

Produces a circular gradient expanding from a center point.

Method/Property	Definition *Table 3.29*
center	the origin point
colors	required list of colors
radius	size of the gradient circle
focal	secondary focus point
focal_radius	size of the focal region
rotation	angle adjustment
stops	gradient transition positions
tile_mode	repeat behavior using GradientTileMode. Options include MIRROR, CLAMP, DECAL, REPEATED

Python
```
import flet as ft

def main(page: ft.Page):

    cont1 = ft.Container(
        gradient= ft.RadialGradient(
             colors= [ "blue","red", "yellow", "purple", "green"],
             radius= 4.5,
             center= ft.Alignment.TOP_LEFT
            ),
        width= 300,height=150
        #Code continues below ...
    )

    cont2 = ft.Container(
        gradient= ft.RadialGradient(
             colors= [ "#0C3B2E", "white"],
             tile_mode= ft.GradientTileMode.MIRROR,
             stops= [0.5, 0.8],
             radius=0.8,
             center= ft.Alignment.TOP_CENTER,
             focal_radius=0.1
            ),
        width= 300,height=150
        #Code continues below ...
    )

    row = ft.Row(controls=[cont1, cont2])
    page.add(row)


ft.run(main)
```

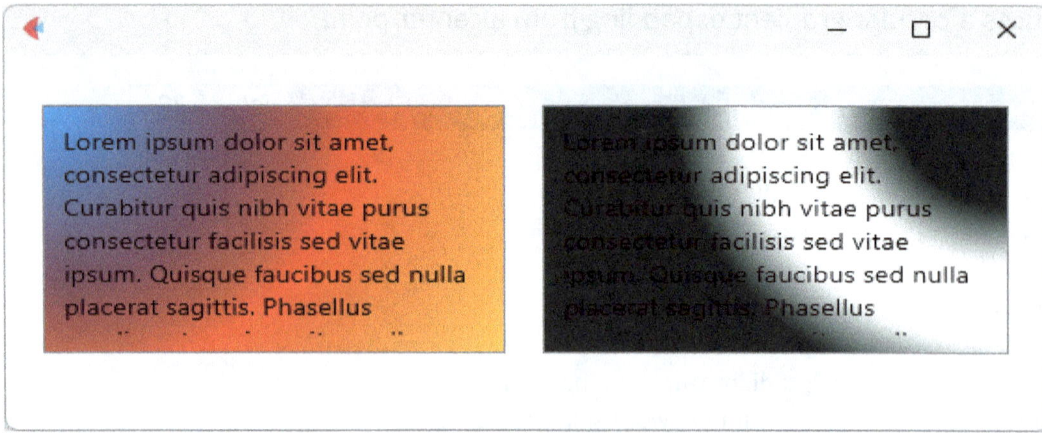
Lorem ipsum dolor sit amet, consectetur adipiscing elit. Curabitur quis nibh vitae purus consectetur facilisis sed vitae ipsum. Quisque faucibus sed nulla placerat sagittis. Phasellus
Lorem ipsum dolor sit amet, consectetur adipiscing elit. Curabitur quis nibh vitae purus consectetur facilisis sed vitae ipsum. Quisque faucibus sed nulla placerat sagittis. Phasellus

ShaderMask

The **ShaderMask** is a material design control used to decorate or mask the surface of another control with a gradient or color effect. It essentially applies a shader to the control, altering its appearance by partially or fully distorting its visibility, producing visual effects like fade, gradient overlay, or color blending.

Properties and Methods

shader = Gradient
Defines the gradient or shader effect applied to the child control. This can be any **Gradient** type (Linear, Radial, Sweep). The shader determines how the control is masked and how colors are applied across its surface.

content = control
The child control to which the shader mask is applied. This can be any UI control (Text, Image, Container, etc.).

blend_mode = flet.BlendMode
Specifies how the shader colors blend with the child control's colors. Controlled by the **BlendMode** enumeration.

Insight

See the blend_mode property of the **Container** control in the previous chapter for a detailed explanation of the available **BlendMode** options and how to use them.

border_radius = number, flet.BorderRadius
Applies rounded corners to the ShaderMask, clipping the masked content to a rounded rectangle shape.

Example 1,

Python

```python
import flet as ft

async def main(page: ft.Page):

    shader = ft.ShaderMask(
        expand= True,
        content= ft.Image(r"strawberry.jpg", fit= ft.BoxFit.COVER ),
        shader= ft.LinearGradient(
            colors=[ "black","white"],
            begin= ft.Alignment.TOP_RIGHT,
            end= ft.Alignment.BOTTOM_LEFT,
        )
    )

    page.add(shader)

ft.run(main)
```

Original Image

Image with Shader

Example 2,

```python
import flet as ft

async def main(page: ft.Page):
```

```
    original_image = ft.Image("image.jpg", fit= ft.BoxFit.COVER, expand=True )

    shader1 = ft.ShaderMask(
        expand= True,
        content= ft.Image(r"mage.jpg", fit= ft.BoxFit.COVER ),
        shader= ft.LinearGradient(
            colors=[ "blue","red", "yellow","green"],
        ),
    )
    shader2 = ft.ShaderMask(
        expand= True,
        content= ft.Image("image.jpg", fit= ft.BoxFit.COVER ),
        shader= ft.LinearGradient(
            colors=[ "blue","red", "yellow","green"],
            begin= ft.Alignment.TOP_CENTER,
            end= ft.Alignment.BOTTOM_CENTER,
        ),
        border_radius= 10,
        blend_mode= ft.BlendMode.DIFFERENCE
    )
    shader3 = ft.ShaderMask(
        expand= True,
        content= ft.Image("image.jpg", fit= ft.BoxFit.COVER ),
        shader= ft.RadialGradient(
            colors=[ "red", "orange", "yellow"],
            radius= 0.8
        ),
    )

    row = ft.Row(controls= [original_image, shader1, shader2, shader3])
    page.add(row)
ft.run(main)
```

Layout

Layout management is a core feature in application development because it determines how controls are arranged, resized, aligned and adapted to different screen sizes. In Flet, programmers do not manually adjust dimensions or spacing each time the window is resized. Instead, Flet layout controls automatically handle arrangement, spacing, scaling and overflow behavior.

Flet provides five primary layout managers:

- **Column**
- **Row**
- **Stack**
- **GridView**
- **ListView**

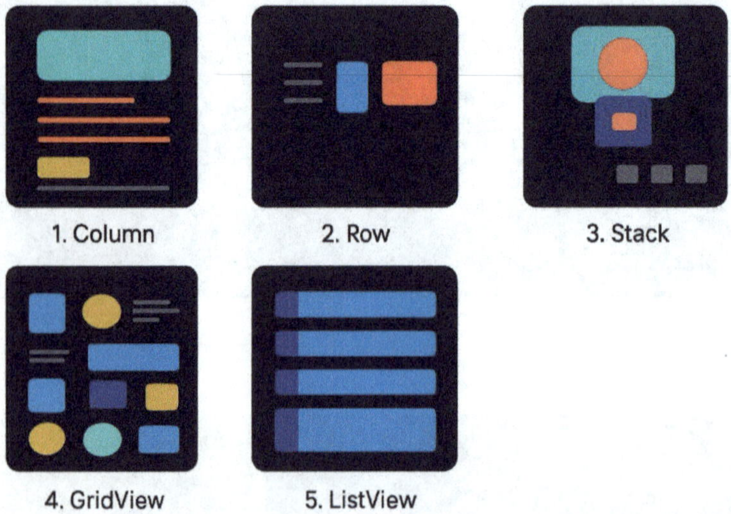

Figure 3.5: Samples of layout

Each layout solves a different structural need and helps organize the application's interface cleanly and responsively.

Column

The **Column** layout arranges its child controls in a top-down, vertical sequence. Controls appear in the order in which they are listed in the controls parameter. If the combined height of the controls exceeds the available space, the Column automatically becomes scrollable when scrolling is enabled.

The Column is ideal for forms, lists, vertical menus, stacked sections and adaptive mobile-style layouts.

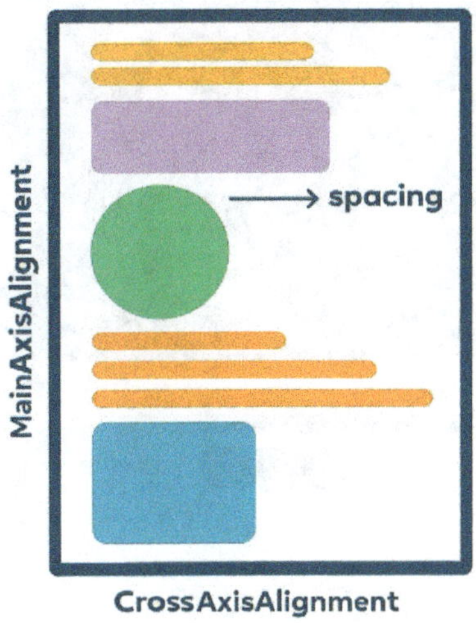

Properties and Methods

controls = [control]

A list of controls contained inside the Column. Controls are arranged vertically in the given order.

Example 1

Python

```python
import flet as ft

def main(page: ft.Page):
```

```
    column = ft.Column(

        controls=[
          ft.Container(
            content=ft.Text("Column Sample", color="white", size=25),
            bgcolor="#29282c",
            alignment= ft.Alignment.CENTER,
            height= 150
            #Code continues below ...
           ),

           ft.Image(src="burger.jpg", width=300,height=150),
           ft.Image(src="berry.jpg",width=300,height=150)
        ],
        width= page.width,
        height= page.height
    )

    page.add(column)

ft.run(main)
```

Example 2

Python

```
import flet as ft

def main(page: ft.Page):

    col = ft.Column(

      controls=[
       ft.Image(src="burg.jpg",width=200,height=150),
       ft.Text("Burger", color="orange",size=25),
       ft.Text("Lorem ipsum dolor sit amet,consecteturadipiscing elit."),
       ft.Container(content=ft.Text("$32.00"),
                    border=ft.border.all(color="red"))
        ],
    )

    cont = ft.Container(
             content=col, padding=ft.Padding.all(20),
             border= ft.border.all(width=2, color= "black"),
             border_radius=10
     )

    page.add(cont)

ft.run(main)
```

alignment = flet.MainAxisAlignment

Aligns controls along the **main axis** (vertical axis for Column). It uses MainAxisAlignment with the following options:

- START
- END
- CENTER
- SPACE_BETWEEN
- SPACE_EVENLY
- SPACE_AROUND

```python
import flet as ft

def main(page: ft.Page):

    column = ft.Column(
        alignment = ft.MainAxisAlignment.END,
        controls=[
          ft.Container(ft.Text("Box 1"), bgcolor="#023246"),
          ft.Container(ft.Text("Box 2"), bgcolor="#FF5926"),
          ft.Container(ft.Text("Box 3"), bgcolor="#F9DC5C"),
        ],
        width= 600,
        height= 400
    )

    page.add(column)


ft.run(main)
```

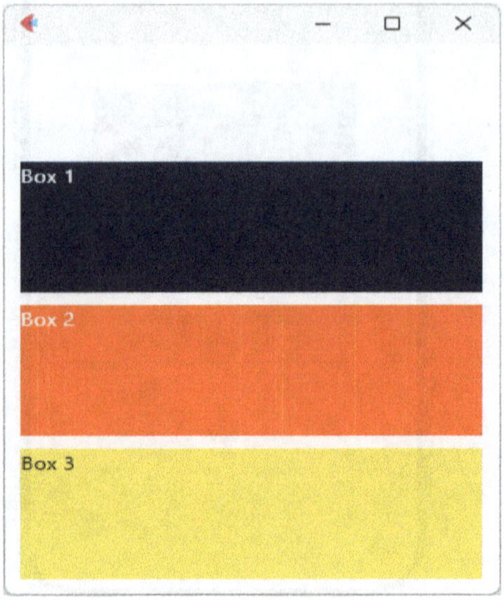

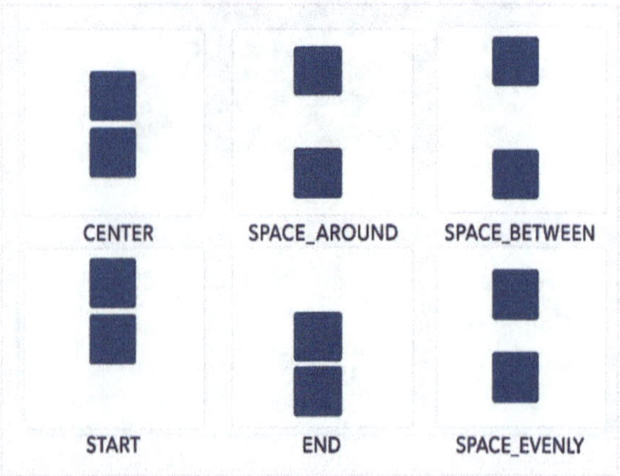

horizontal_alignment = flet.CrossAxisAlignment

Aligns controls along the **cross axis** (horizontal axis for Column) using CrossAxisAlignment. Options include:

- START
- END
- CENTER
- BASELINE
- STRETCH

```python
import flet as ft

def main(page: ft.Page):

    column = ft.Column(
        horizontal_alignment= ft.CrossAxisAlignment.END,
        controls=[
          ft.Container(ft.Text("Box 1"), bgcolor="#023246"),
          ft.Container(ft.Text("Box 2"), bgcolor="#FF5926"),
          ft.Container(ft.Text("Box 3"), bgcolor="#F9DC5C"),
        ],
        width= 600,
        height= 400
    )

    page.add(column)


ft.run(main)
```

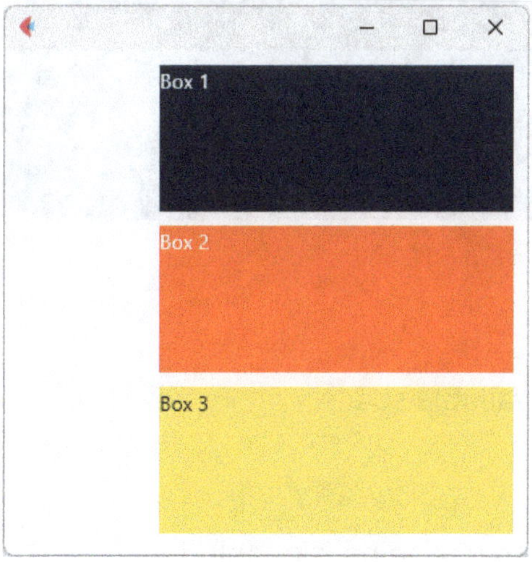

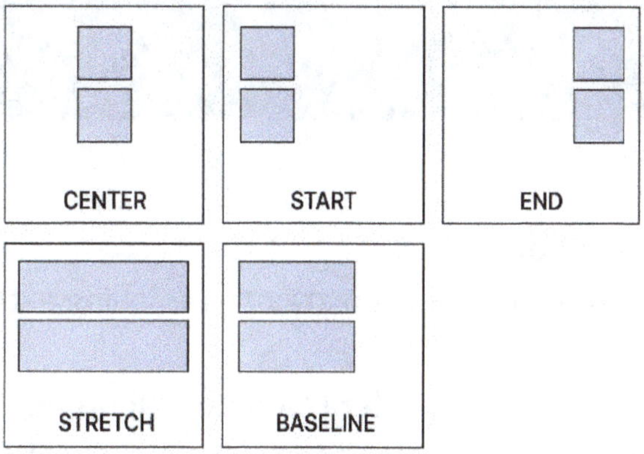

auto_scroll = bool
When set to True, the column automatically scrolls when content exceeds the visible area.

on_scroll = callback
Registers a function that triggers during scrolling.

scroll_interval = number
Defines intervals when scrolling.

spacing = number
Defines vertical spacing between child controls.

```
Python
import flet as ft

def main(page: ft.Page):

    column = ft.Column(
        spacing= 10
        controls=[
          ft.Container(bgcolor="#023246"),
          ft.Container(bgcolor="#FF5926"),
          ft.Container(bgcolor="#F9DC5C"),
        ],
    )

    page.add(column)


ft.run(main)
```

tight = bool
Forces tight layout constraints, removing extra available space.

run_alignment = flet.MainAxisAlignment
Determines how runs of controls are aligned when wrapping is enabled.

run_spacing = number

Defines spacing between lines or runs when wrap is used.

scroll = flet.ScrollMode
Enables or disables scrolling and selects the scroll mode or behavior. The ScrollMode options include:

- ADAPTIVE
- ALWAYS
- AUTO
- HIDDEN

scroll_to = number
Scrolls to a specific pixel offset or index inside the Column.

wrap = bool
Allows the Column to wrap its children into multiple runs when space is restricted. (Columns typically do not wrap, but this exists for completeness.)

Expansion in Column

Items (controls) within a **Column** can be configured to share available space unevenly. By default, a Column distributes space equally among its children. However, a control can be expanded to take up more space than others by using the common control properties **expand** and **expand_loose**.

expand = bool
When set to True, the control occupies all the remaining available vertical space within the Column. This forces the control to stretch and fill the extra space.

expand_loose = bool
When set to True, the control is allowed to expand and take up available space, but it is not forced to fill all of it. The control can occupy only the space it needs, up to the available limit.

Example,

Python

```
import flet as ft

def main(page: ft.Page):

 col = ft.Column(
      auto_scroll= True,
      controls=[
          ft.Container(
              content=ft.Text("Lorem ipsum dolor sit amet,......"),
              padding= 10, bgcolor="green",
              expand=True
          ),
          ft.Container(
              content=ft.Text("Lorem ipsum dolor sit amet,......"),
              padding= 10, bgcolor="cyan",
          )
      ],
      width=400,height=300
    )

    page.add(col)

ft.run(main)
```

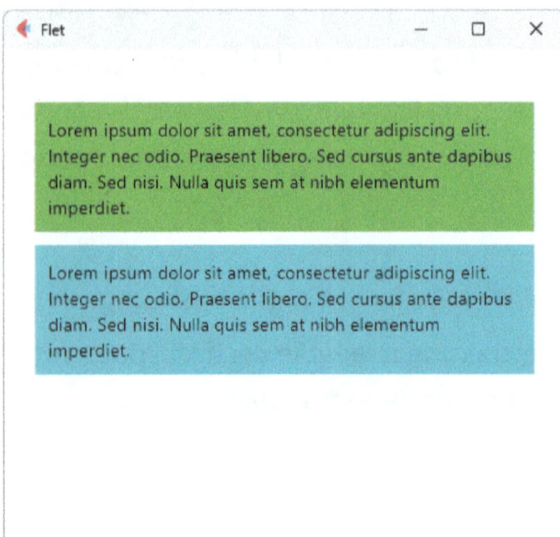

Without expansion

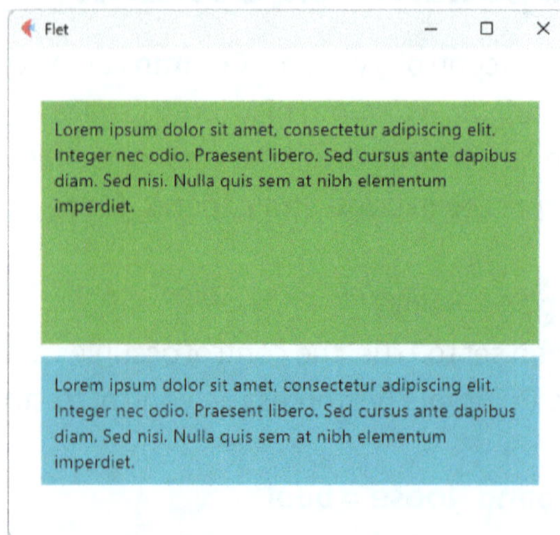

With expansion

Row

The **Row** layout arranges its child controls horizontally from left to right. Controls appear in the order they are listed in the controls parameter. Rows are typically used to position controls side by side such as buttons, icons, cards, input fields or mixed content.

If the combined width of the controls exceeds the available space, scrolling can be enabled so that the user can view overflowed content.

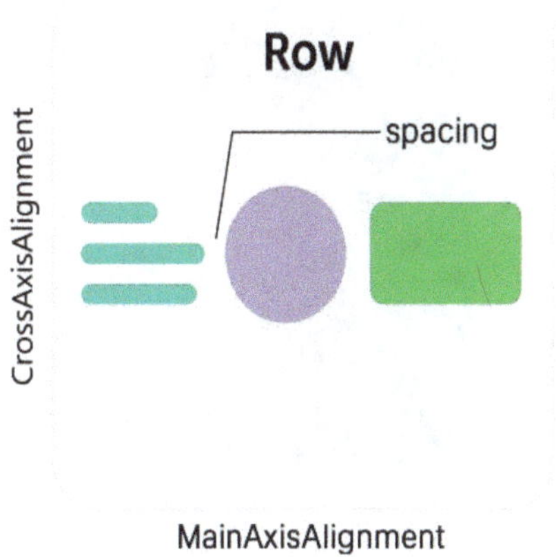

Properties and Methods

controls = [control]

A list of controls arranged horizontally in the Row.

Example 1,

```python
import flet as ft

def main(page: ft.Page):

    row = ft.Row(
       controls=[
        ft.Container(content=ft.Text("Row Sample", size=25)),
        ft.Image(src="pizza.jpg", fit=ft.BoxFit.CONTAIN),
        ft.Image(src="boy.jpg", fit=ft.BoxFit.CONTAIN),
```

```
        ],
    )

    page.add(row)

ft.run(main)
```

Example 2,

```
Python
import flet as ft

def main(page: ft.Page):

    def mycontainer(image, text):
        col = ft.Column(
          horizontal_alignment=ft.CrossAxisAlignment.CENTER,
          controls=[
            ft.Image(src=image, fit = ft.BoxFit.CONTAIN),
            ft.Text(text)],
        )

        cont = ft.Container(content=col, alignment=ft.Alignment.CENTER,
                      border = ft.Border.all(width=2, color="black"),
                      padding= ft.Padding.all(20), border_radius=10)
        return cont


    row1 = ft.Row(
```

```
        controls=[
            mycontainer("profile.jpg", "Profile"),
            mycontainer("create.jpg", "Create"),
            ],
        )
    row2 = ft.Row(
        controls=[
            mycontainer("tutor.jpg", "Tutorial"),
            mycontainer("music.jpg", "Music"),
            ],
        )

    page.add(row1, row2)

ft.run(main)
```

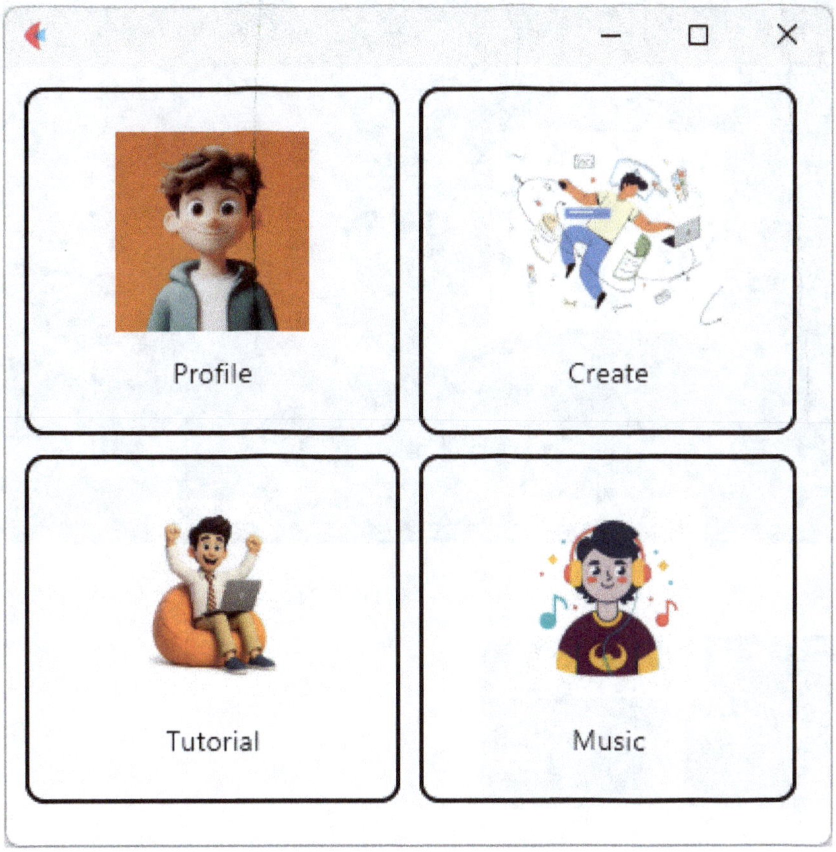

alignment = flet.MainAxisAlignment

Aligns controls along the **main axis** (horizontal axis for Row). It uses MainAxisAlignment with the following options:

- START
- END
- CENTER
- SPACE_BETWEEN
- SPACE_EVENLY
- SPACE_AROUND

Python
```
import flet as ft

def main(page: ft.Page):

    def mycontainer(text):
        return ft.Container(content=ft.Text(text, color="orange"),
                alignment=ft.Alignment.CENTER,bgcolor="#29282c",
                padding= ft.Padding.all(50), border_radius=10)


    row = ft.Row(
        alignment= ft.MainAxisAlignment.START,
        controls=[
            mycontainer("Box1"),
            mycontainer("Box2"),
            mycontainer("Box3"),
            ],
        width=page.width
        )

    page.add(row)


ft.run(main)
```

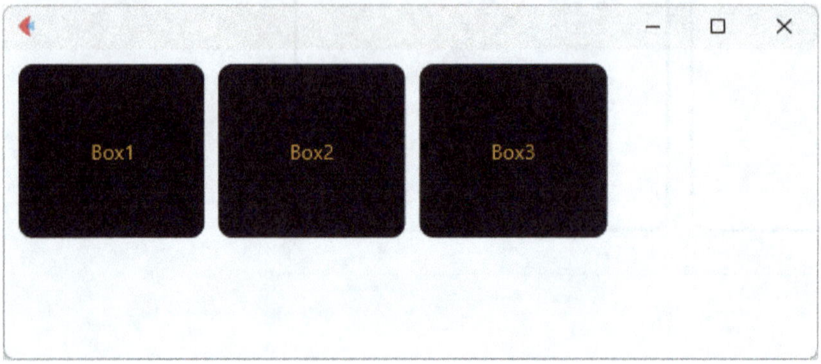

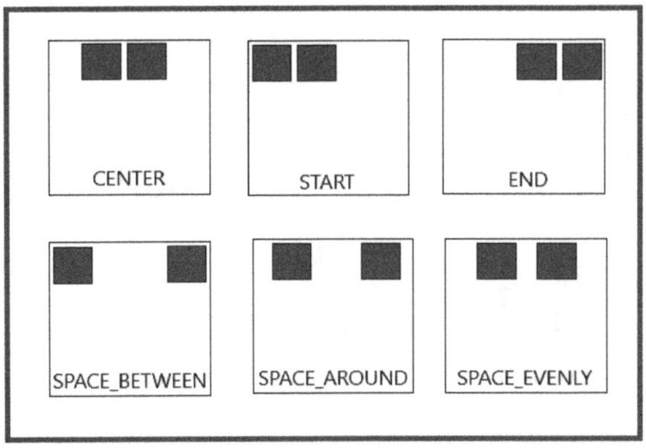

vertical_alignment = flet.CrossAxisAlignment

Aligns controls along the **cross axis** (vertical axis for a Row) using CrossAxisAlignment. Options include:

- START
- END
- CENTER
- BASELINE
- STRETCH

```
••• Python
import flet as ft

def main(page: ft.Page):

    def mycontainer(text):
        return ft.Container(content=ft.Text(text, color="orange"),
                alignment=ft.Alignment.CENTER,bgcolor="#29282c",
                padding= ft.Padding.all(50), border_radius=10)


    row = ft.Row(
        vertical_alignment = ft.CrossAxisAlignment.END,
        controls=[
            mycontainer("Box1"),
            mycontainer("Box2"),
            mycontainer("Box3"),
            ],)

    page.add(row)


ft.run(main)
```

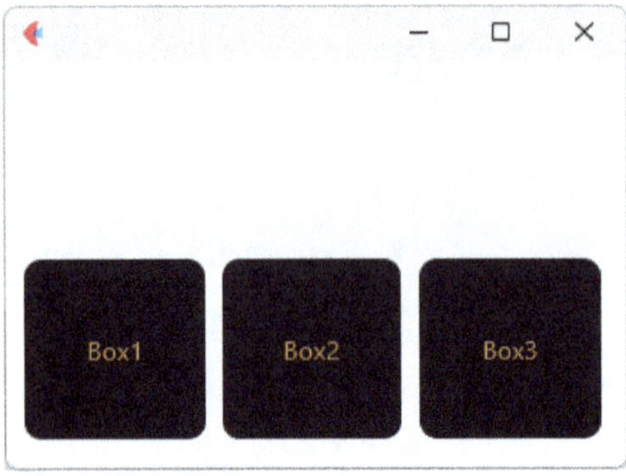

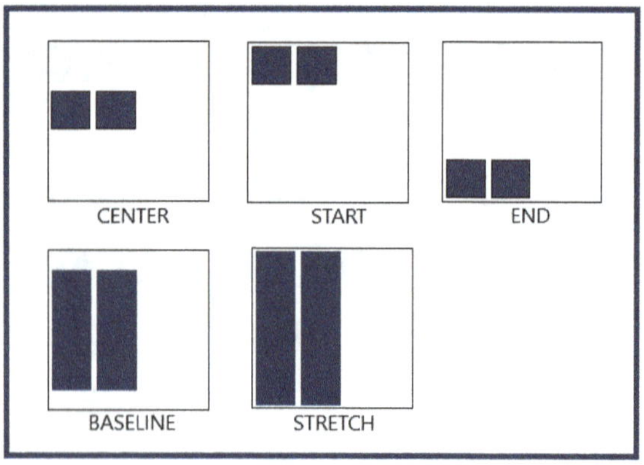

auto_scroll = bool

When set to True, the row automatically scrolls when its content exceeds available width.

on_scroll = callback

Fires when the Row's scroll position changes.

spacing = number

Defines the horizontal spacing between child controls.

```
Python
import flet as ft

def main(page: ft.Page):

    row = ft.Row(
        spacing= 5,
        vertical_alignment = ft.CrossAxisAlignment.CENTER,
        alignment= ft.MainAxisAlignment.CENTER,
        controls=[
            ft.Image(src="cake.jpg",width=200, height=200),
            ft.Image(src="cripsy.jpg",width=200,height=200),
            ft.Image(src="berry.jpg",width=200,height=200),
            ],
        )

    page.add(row)


ft.run(main)
```

scroll = flet.ScrollMode

Enables or disables scrolling and selects the scroll mode or behavior. The ScrollMode options include:

- ADAPTIVE
- ALWAYS
- AUTO
- HIDDEN

scroll_to = number

Scrolls to a specified pixel offset or index in the Row.

run_alignment = flet.MainAxisAlignment

Determines how wrapped items are aligned when wrap is True.

run_spacing = number

Defines spacing between wrapped rows of controls when wrap is enabled.

tight = bool

Forces tight layout constraints, causing the Row to occupy only the exact space required.

wrap = bool

When set to True, controls that overflow horizontally wrap into additional lines, similar to text wrapping.

Expansion in Row

Items (controls) within a **Row** can also be configured to share available space unevenly. By default, a Row distributes horizontal space among its children based on their content size. However, you can make a control take up more space than others by using the common control properties **expand** and **expand_loose**.

expand = bool

When set to True, the control occupies all the remaining available horizontal space within the Row. This forces the control to stretch and fill the extra width.

expand_loose = bool

When set to True, the control is allowed to expand horizontally and use the available space, but it is not required to fill all of it. The control can take only the space it needs, up to the available limit.

Example,

```
Python
import flet as ft

async def main(page: ft.Page):
    page.vertical_alignment = ft.MainAxisAlignment.CENTER
    page.horizontal_alignment = ft.CrossAxisAlignment.START
    page.bgcolor = "white"


    col = ft.Row(

      controls=[
          ft.Image("image_1.jpg",fit= ft.BoxFit.FILL,),

          ft.Image("image_2.jpg", expand=True, fit= ft.BoxFit.FILL),
```

```
            ft.Image("image_3.jpg", fit= ft.BoxFit.FILL)
        ],
        auto_scroll= True,
        on_scroll= lambda _:print("helloo"),
        width=650,
        height=300
    )

    page.add(col)


ft.run(main)
```

Without expansion

With expansion

Stack

The **Stack** control arranges its child controls by placing them on top of each other. Each child occupies the same base area of the Stack and the last child in the controls list appears on the topmost layer. This makes Stack useful for overlaying controls, creating floating panels, badges, banners, watermarks, image overlays or layered UI elements.

Stack also supports positioning of individual children using the **top**, **bottom**, **left** and **right** properties. These properties allow precise placement of a control relative to the container's boundaries.

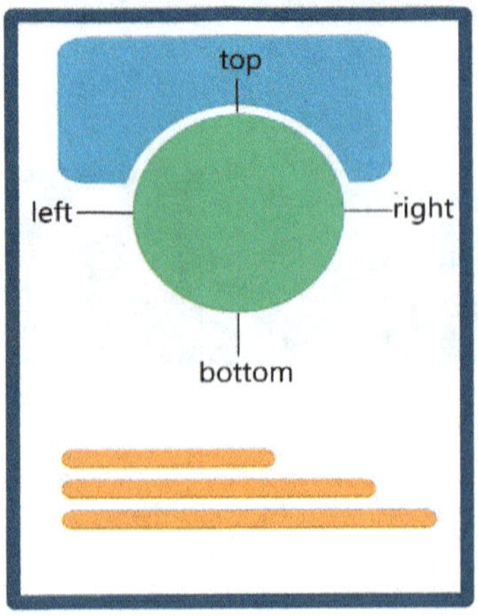

Properties and Methods

adaptive = bool

Enables adaptive layout behavior based on device or display constraints.

bottom, top, left, right = number

These values are not properties of the Stack itself but are used by children inside the Stack to define their position relative to the Stack's boundaries.

controls = [control]

A list of child controls layered on top of one another. The last control in the list appears on top.

Example 1,

```python
import flet as ft

def main(page: ft.Page):

    stack = ft.Stack(
        expand= True,
        controls=[
            ft.Container(top= 10, left= 10,
                content= ft.Text("My WebPage",size=25, color="white"),
                padding=ft.Padding.all(10),alignment=ft.Alignment.TOP_CENTER,
                bgcolor="#37324B", width= 400, height=150,
                ),

            ft.Container(top= 100, left= 40,
                content= ft.Text("Panel A", size=25, color="white"),
                padding=ft.Padding.all(10),alignment=ft.Alignment.CENTER,
                bgcolor="#075056", width= 150, height=150,
                 ),

            ft.Container(top= 100, right=40,
                content= ft.Text("Panel B", size=25, color="white"),
                padding=ft.Padding.all(10),alignment=ft.Alignment.CENTER,
                bgcolor="#FF5B04", width= 150, height=150,
                 ),

            ft.Image("support.png",height=100,width=100, top=60, left=70),
            ft.Image("24-hours.png", height=100,width=100,top=60, left=250),
        ]
    )

    page.add(stack)

ft.run(main)
```

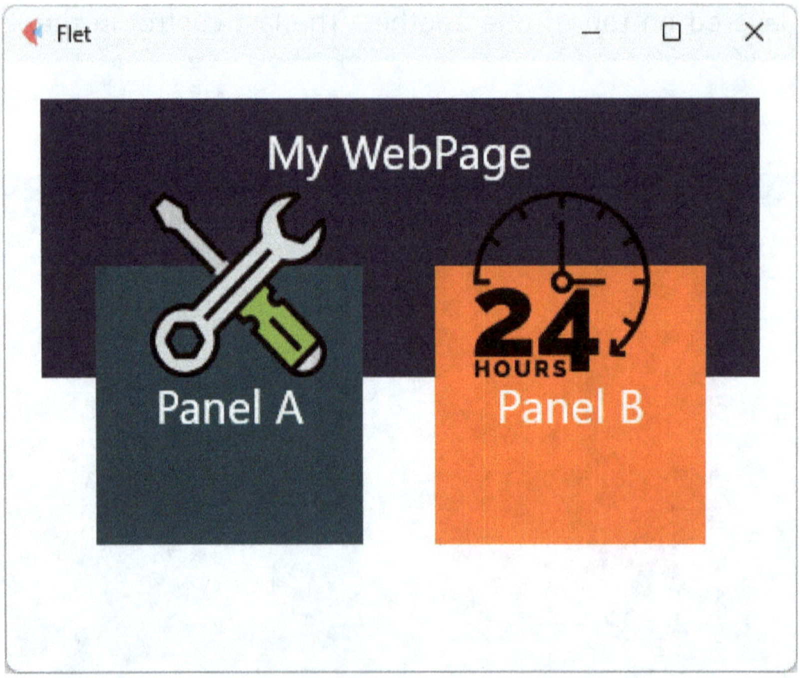

Example 2,

```python
import flet as ft

def main(page: ft.Page):

    def mycontainer(text):
        return ft.Container(content=ft.Text(text, color="white", size=35),
                alignment=ft.Alignment.CENTER,
                padding=ft.Padding.all(20),width=300, height=350,
                bgcolor="#1f1b1e", border_radius=10
              )

    stack =  ft.Stack(
        controls=[
          mycontainer("The FoodBar"),
          ft.Container(left=70,top=50,image= ft.DecorationImage("food1.jpg"),
                       shape= ft.BoxShape.CIRCLE, width=150, height=150),
          ft.Container(right=70,top=50,image= ft.DecorationImage("food2.jpg"),
                       shape= ft.BoxShape.CIRCLE, width=150, height=150),
          ft.Container(left=70,bottom=50,image= ft.DecorationImage("food3.jpg"),
                       shape= ft.BoxShape.CIRCLE, width=150, height=150),
          ft.Container(right=70,bottom=50,image= ft.DecorationImage("food4.jpg"),
                       shape= ft.BoxShape.CIRCLE, width=150, height=150),
        ],
        width=500,
```

```
        height=500,
        alignment= ft.Alignment.CENTER
    )

    page.add(stack)


ft.run(main)
```

alignment = **flet.Alignment**

Aligns controls within the Stack when they are not individually positioned. Uses Alignment values such as:

- CENTER
- TOP_LEFT
- TOP_CENTER
- TOP_RIGHT
- BOTTOM_LEFT
- BOTTOM_CENTER
- BOTTOM_RIGHT

If a child uses positional parameters (top, left, etc.), alignment does not affect that child.

clip_behavior = **flet.ClipBehavior**

Controls how content that overflows outside the Stack boundaries is handled. Options typically include:

- NONE • HARD_EDGE • ANTI_ALIAS • ANTI_ALIAS_WITH_SAVE_LAYER

fit = flet.StackFit

Controls how non-positioned children should fill the Stack. Uses StackFit with options:

- **EXPAND** → child expands to fill Stack.
- **LOOSE** → child takes minimum required space.
- **PASS_THROUGH** → child keeps its own size.

GridView

The **GridView** control arranges child controls in a grid layout consisting of rows and columns. Items are automatically positioned based on available space, scroll direction and grid configuration. It is useful for displaying collections such as images, cards or uniformly sized widgets.
Below are the primary properties and methods available in GridView.

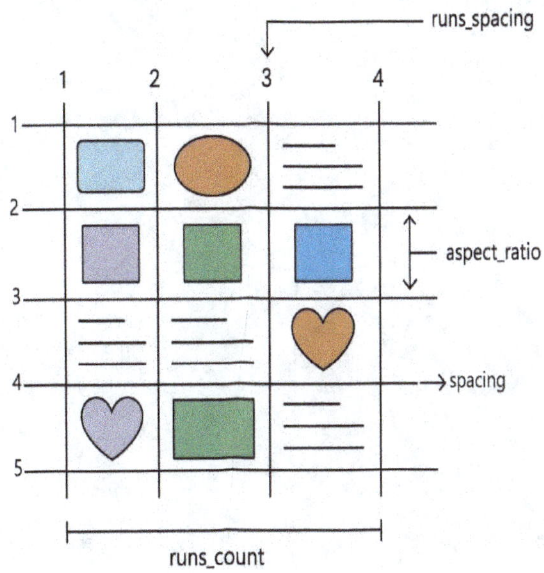

Properties and Methods

adaptive = bool

Enables adaptive layout behavior depending on screen size or platform conditions.

controls = [control]

Defines the list of child controls that populate the GridView.

max_extent = number

Specifies the maximum extent (width or height depending on orientation) for each grid tile. This determines how many tiles fit into one row. A smaller value results in more items per row.

```python
import flet as ft

def main(page: ft.Page):

    def mycontainer(text):
        return ft.Container(content=ft.Text(text,
                          color="#F7BB0E", size=20),
                alignment=ft.Alignment.CENTER,
                padding=ft.Padding.all(20),width=100, height=100,
                bgcolor="#1f1b1e", border_radius=10)

    grid =  ft.GridView(
        controls=[
          mycontainer("1"),mycontainer("2"),mycontainer("3"),
          mycontainer("4"),mycontainer("5"),mycontainer("6"),
          mycontainer("7"),mycontainer("8"),
        ],
        max_extent= 100
    )

    page.add(grid)

ft.run(main)
```

runs_count = int

Indicates the number of rows or columns, depending on scroll orientation.

```python
import flet as ft

def main(page: ft.Page):

    def cont(text, icon, color):
        return ft.Container(alignment=ft.Alignment.CENTER,
                padding=ft.Padding.all(20),width=100, height=100,
                bgcolor=color, border_radius=10,
                content= ft.Column(controls=[ft.Icon(icon,color="white"),
                                   ft.Text(text),]))

    grid =  ft.GridView(
        controls=[
          cont("Project", ft.Icons.ROCKET_LAUNCH, "#5C8BD6"),
          cont("Edit", ft.Icons.EDIT, "#66CCBE"),
          cont("Calendar", ft.Icons.CALENDAR_MONTH, "#E5C443"),
          cont("Settings", ft.Icons.SETTINGS, "#C086EA"),
          cont("Delete", ft.Icons.DELETE, "#FF8E2B"),
          cont("Share", ft.Icons.SHARE, "#075056"),
          cont("Open", ft.Icons.FOLDER_OPEN_OUTLINED, "#BE3745"),

        ],
        runs_count=3,
    )

    page.add(grid)

ft.run(main)
```

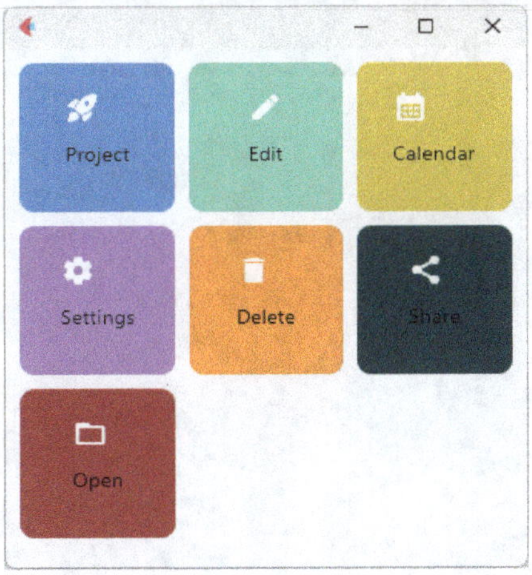

runs_count = 3

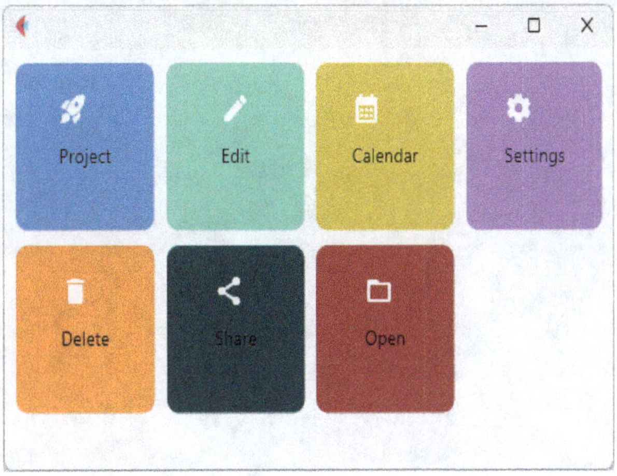

runs_count = 4

run_spacing = number

Defines the vertical spacing between rows of the grid.

spacing = number

Defines both the horizontal and vertical spacing between grid items.

child_aspect_ratio = number

Specifies the width-to-height ratio for each grid item. This ensures consistent item proportions.

Python

```python
import flet as ft

def main(page: ft.Page):

    def cont(text, image):
        return ft.Container(alignment=ft.Alignment.CENTER,
           padding=ft.Padding.all(10),width=100, height=100,
           border= ft.Border.all(1),BorderRadius=10,
           content= ft.Column(controls=[ft.Image(image), ft.Text(text),])
          )



    grid =  ft.GridView(
        controls=[
            cont("Black Chair\n$100","chair1.jpg"),
            cont("Black Brown Chair\n$280","chair2.jpg"),
            cont("Brown Chair\n$150","chair3.jpg"),
            cont("Grey Chair\n$50","chair4.jpg"),
            cont("Blue Chair\n$170","chair5.jpg"),
        ],

        run_spacing= 20,
        spacing=25,
        aspect_ratio=0.5,
        runs_count=3,
    )

    page.add(grid)

ft.run(main)
```

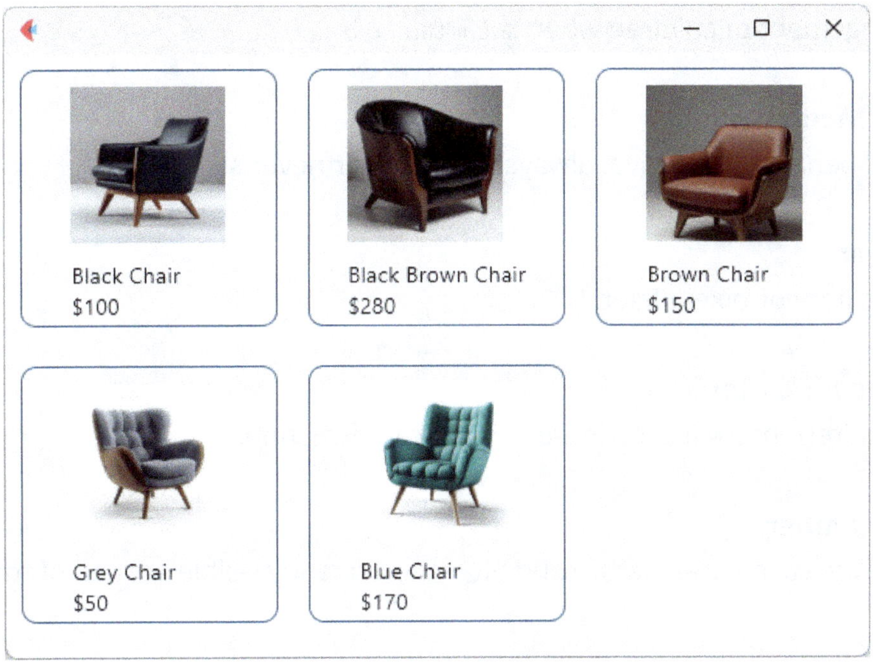

auto_scroll = bool
Automatically scrolls to the end of the GridView when new items are added.

clip_behavior = flet.ClipBehavior
Determines how overflow content should be clipped within the control's boundaries.

horizontal = bool
Changes the scroll direction. By default, GridView scrolls vertically. When set True, it scrolls horizontally.

on_scroll = callback
Calls the assigned function while the GridView is being scrolled.

padding = flet.Padding
Defines the padding inside the GridView boundary.

reverse = bool

Reverses the arrangement of children when set True.

scroll = **flet.ScrollMode**
Specifies the scroll behavior (adaptive, always scrollable or never scrollable).

scroll_to = **number**
Scrolls to a specific item or pixel offset.

semantic_child_count = **int**
The number of children that will contribute semantic information.

cache_extent = **number**
Defines the size of the cache area before and after the currently visible portion of the GridView.

build_controls_on_demand = **bool**
When set to True, controls are created only when they are needed (that is, when they are about to appear on the screen). When set to False, all controls are built at once, which may increase initial load time and memory consumption.

ListView

The **ListView** control arranges its child controls in a linear list. By default, items are laid out vertically, but the orientation can be changed. ListView is commonly used to display long, scrollable content.
Below are the important properties and methods of the ListView control.

Properties and Methods

auto_scroll = bool
Automatically scrolls to the bottom when new children are added. Useful for chat interfaces or logs.

first_item_prototype = bool
Provides a prototype control used for sizing the first item, improving scroll calculations.

prototype_item = control
Specifies a control whose size will be used as a template for all other items in the ListView.

controls = [control]
Defines the list of child controls contained in the ListView.

spacing = number
Sets the space between child controls.

```
Python
import flet as ft

def main(page: ft.Page):

    activities = ft.ListView(
      spacing=10,
       controls=[
           ft.Row(controls=[ft.Image(src="sports.png"),ft.Text("Sports")]),
           ft.Row(controls=[ft.Image(src="robot.png"),ft.Text("Robotics")],
           ft.Row(controls=[ft.Image(src="cooking.png"),ft.Text("Cooking")]),
```

```
            ft.Row(controls=[ft.Image(src="airplane.png"), ft.Text("Travel")]),
        ],
        width=400,
        height=300
    )
    page.add(activities)

ft.run(main)
```

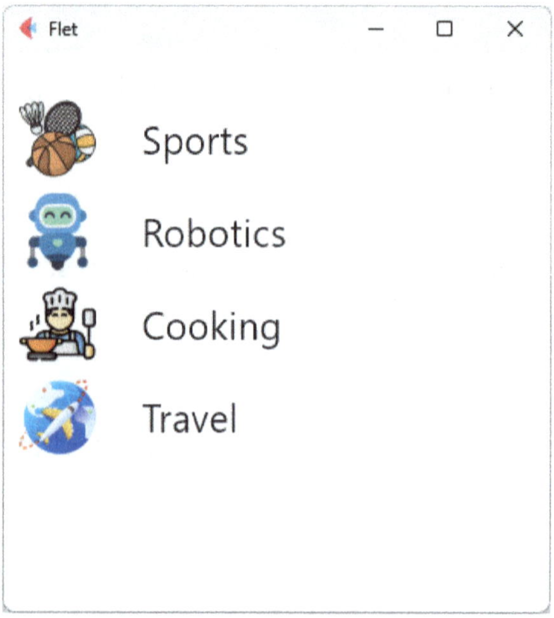

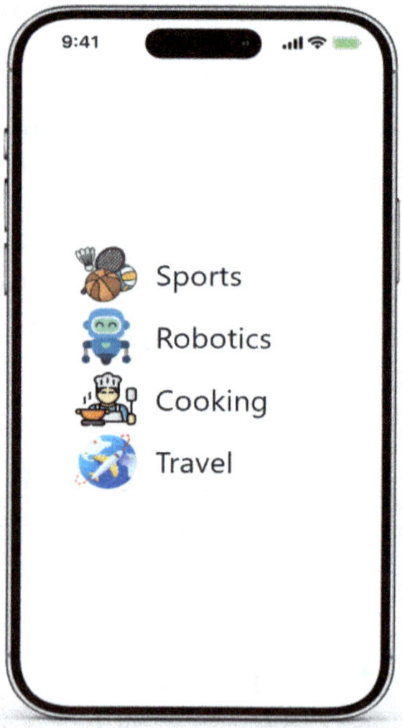

reverse = bool

Reverses the order of items when set True, so the last item appears first.

horizontal = bool

Arranges children horizontally when set True. The default is False, meaning vertical arrangement.

●●● Python

```python
import flet as ft

def main(page: ft.Page):

    listview =  ft.ListView(
      horizontal= True,
      width= page.width,
      height= 100,
      controls=[
        ft.Image("Jorge.jpg",width=150, height=150, fit=ft.BoxFit.COVER),
        ft.Image("chair.jpg",width=150, height=150, fit=ft.BoxFit.COVER),
        ft.Image("Therapy.jpg",width=150, height=150,fit=ft.BoxFit.COVER),
        ft.Image("Design.jpg",width=150, height=150, fit=ft.BoxFit.COVER),
        ],
    )

    page.add(listview)

ft.run(main)
```

clip_behavior = flet.ClipBehavior

Defines how content that overflows the control's bounds should be clipped.

item_extent = number

Defines the fixed extent (height or width) for each item, improving scroll performance.

on_scroll = callback

Assigns a function that triggers when the ListView is scrolled.

Python

```python
import flet as ft

def main(page: ft.Page):

    listview =  ft.ListView(
        spacing=20,
        expand= True,
        controls=[
            ft.Container(content = ft.Text("1", size=50), bgcolor="green"),
            ft.Container(content = ft.Text("2", size=50), bgcolor="teal"),
            ft.Container(content = ft.Text("3", size=50), bgcolor="orange"),
        ],
    )

    page.add(listview)

ft.run( main)
```

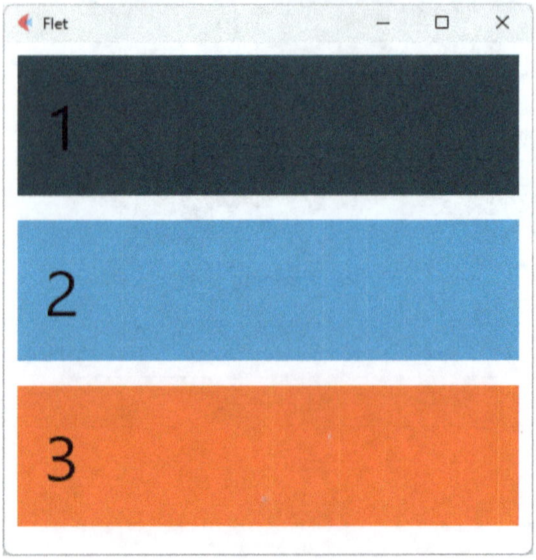

padding = flet.Padding

Defines the padding inside the ListView boundary.

divider_thickness = number

Specifies the thickness of the dividing line between list items.

```python
import flet as ft

def main(page: ft.Page):

    text = "Lorem ipsum dolor sit amet, consectetur adipiscing elit ..."
    listview =  ft.ListView(
        divider_thickness=3,
        spacing= 30,
        width=page.width,
        controls=[
            ft.Text(f"1...{text}"),
            ft.Text(f"2...{text}"),
            ft.Text(f"3...{text}"),
        ],
    )

    page.add(listview)

ft.run(main)
```

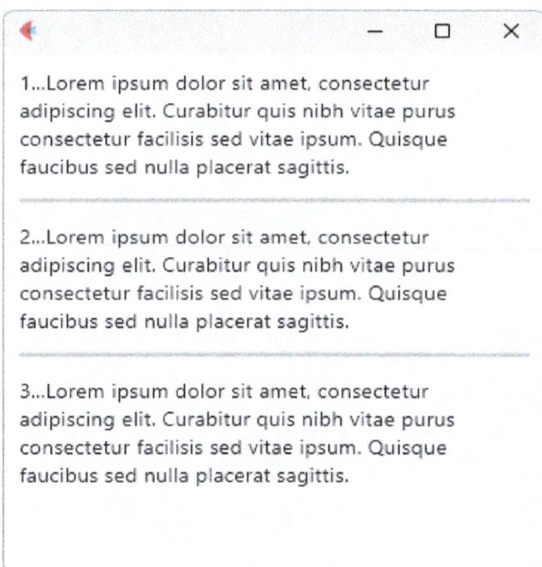

scroll_to = number

Scrolls to a specific item or offset within the list.

semantic_child_count = int

Provides a semantic count of children for accessibility tools.

cache_extent = number

Defines the size of the cache area before and after the currently visible portion of the ListView.

build_controls_on_demand = bool

When set to True, controls are created only when they are needed.

ListTile

The **ListTile** control is used to display structured information in a row format, commonly combining icons, title and subtitle. It is ideal for listing items where each item may have a **leading icon**, **title**, **subtitle** and **trailing icon**. The ListTile can also be assigned callback functions that trigger when the user interacts with it, such as taps, long presses or focus changes.

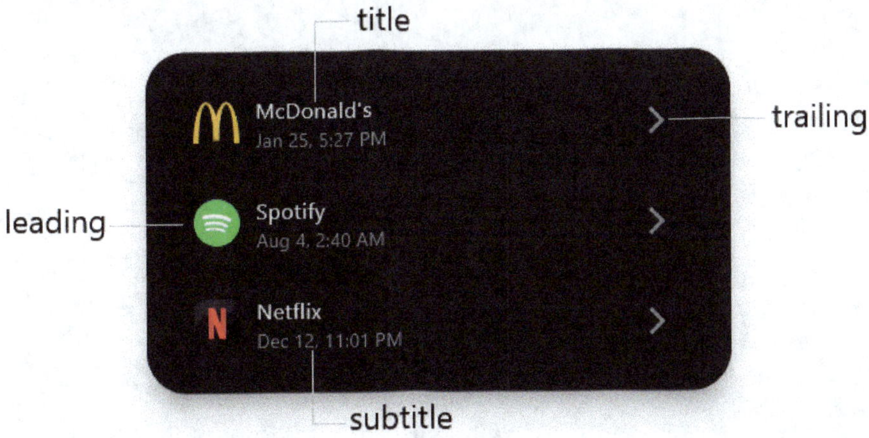

Properties and Methods

adaptive = bool
When set True, ListTile adapts its appearance to match the platform style (e.g., Material or Cupertino).

autofocus = bool
Automatically gives focus to the ListTile when set True.

bgcolor = color
Sets the background color of the ListTile. Accepts color names, hex codes or predefined ColorValue.

leading = icon/control

The leftmost control of the ListTile, commonly an icon.

```python
import flet as ft

def main(page: ft.Page):

    listile1  = ft.ListTile(
        leading= ft.Icon(ft.Icons.PERSON, size=40, color="blue"),
        bgcolor="#E4EEF0"
    )

    listile2  = ft.ListTile(
        leading= ft.Icon(ft.Icons.LOCK, size=40, color="green"),
        bgcolor="#E4EEF0"
    )

    listile3  = ft.ListTile(
        leading= ft.Image("activity.png", height=40, width=40),
        bgcolor="#E4EEF0"
    )

    page.add(listile1, listile2, listile3)

ft.run(main)
```

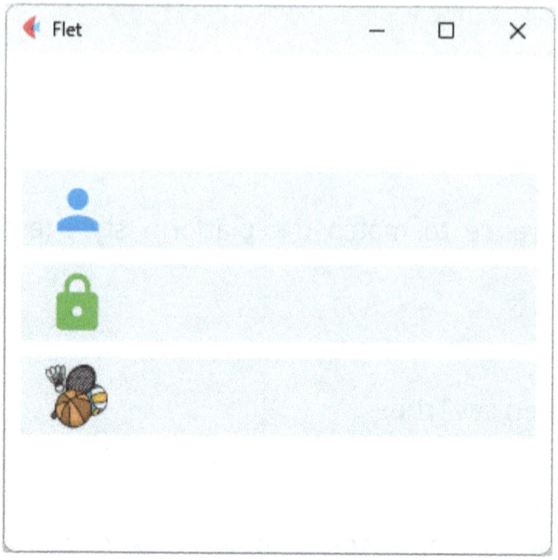

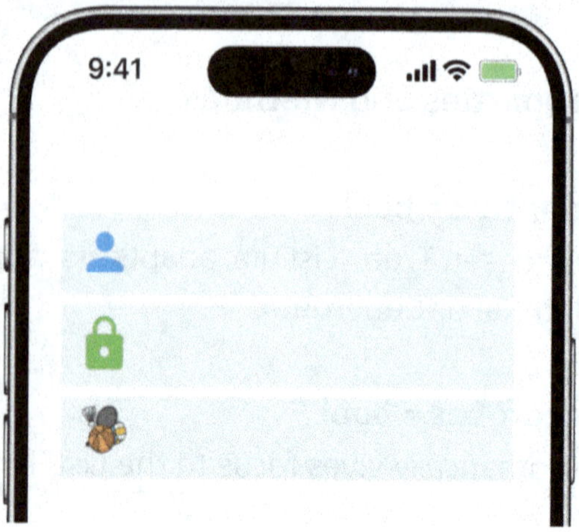

dense = bool

Reduces the vertical height of the ListTile for a compact appearance.

title = string/control

The primary text or control representing the main content.

min_height / min_leading_width / min_vertical_padding = number

Defines minimum size constraints for height, leading width and vertical padding.

title_text_style = flet.TextStyle

Applies text styling to the title using TextStyle.

Python

```
import flet as ft

def main(page: ft.Page):

    listile1  = ft.ListTile(
        title= "Account",
        title_text_style= ft.TextStyle(size=18 , color="black"),
        leading= ft.Icon(ft.Icons.PERSON, size=25,  color="blue"),
        bgcolor="#E4EEF0"
    )

    listile2  = ft.ListTile(
        title=ft.Text("Security", size=18),
        leading= ft.Icon(ft.Icons.LOCK, size=25, color="green"),
        bgcolor="#E4EEF0"
    )

    listile3  = ft.ListTile(
        title=ft.Text("Activities", size=18),
        leading= ft.Image("activity.png", height=25, width=25),
        bgcolor="#E4EEF0"
    )

    page.add(listile1, listile2, listile3)

ft.run(main)
```

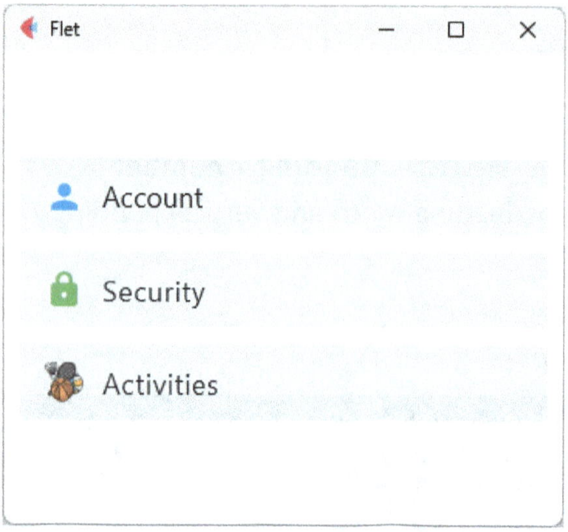

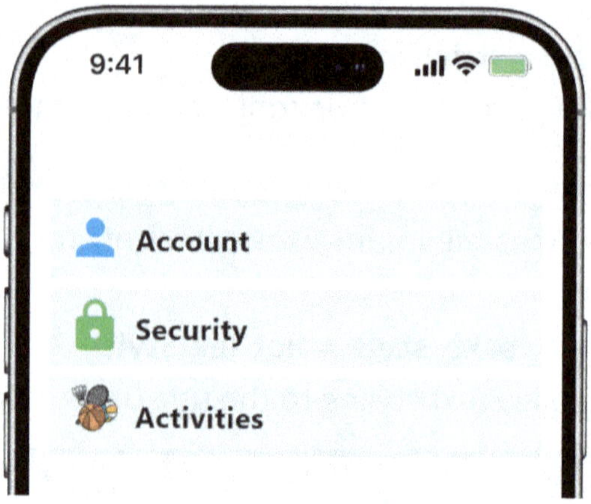

subtitle = string / control

The secondary text or control displayed below the title.

subtitle_text_style = flet.TextStyle

Applies text styling to the subtitle.

text_color = color

Applies color to the text content (title or subtitle).

```python
import flet as ft

def main(page: ft.Page):

    listile1  = ft.ListTile(
        subtitle = "Login, set username, edit profile",
        title= "Account",
        leading= ft.Icon(ft.Icons.PERSON, size=25,  color="blue"),
        #Code continues below ...
    )

    listile2  = ft.ListTile(
        subtitle = "Set passwords, encrypt message",
        title=ft.Text("Security", size=18),
        leading= ft.Icon(ft.Icons.LOCK, size=25, color="green"),
        #Code continues below ...
    )
```

```
    listile3  = ft.ListTile(
        subtitle = "See recent physical activiites",
        title=ft.Text("Activities", size=18),
        leading= ft.Image("activity.png", height=25, width=25),
        #Code continues below ...
    )

    page.add(listile1, listile2, listile3)

ft.run(main)
```

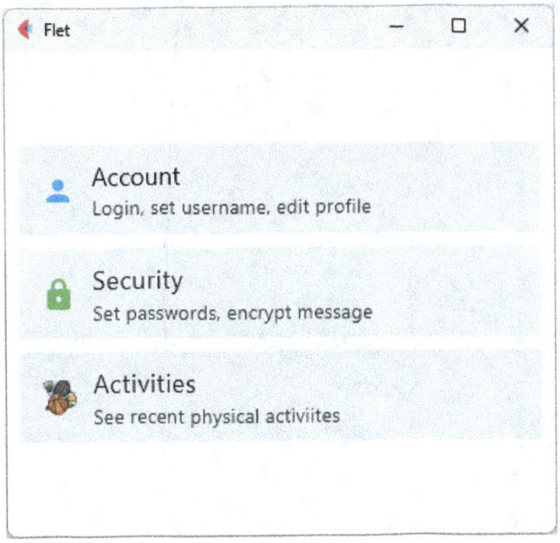

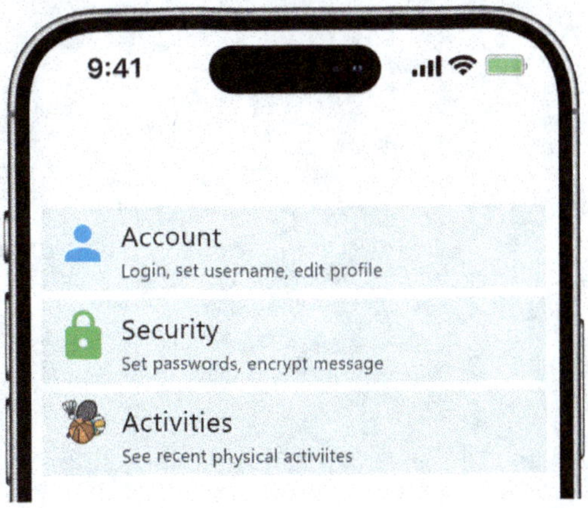

trailing = icon/control

The rightmost control, commonly an icon or button.

icon_color = color

Sets the color of leading and trailing icons, if they are icons.

is_three_line = bool

If True, allows the tile to display up to three lines of text (title + subtitle + extra).

leading_and_trailing_text_style = flet.TextStyle

Applies text styling to any leading or trailing text.

> 📖 **Note**
>
> Refer to the earlier section on the **Text** control for a detailed explanation of how **TextStyle** is used.

Python

```python
import flet as ft

def main(page: ft.Page):

    listile1  = ft.ListTile(
        trailing= ft.Icons.ARROW_FORWARD_IOS_OUTLINED,
        subtitle = "Login, set username, edit profile",
        title= "Account",
        leading= ft.Icon(ft.Icons.PERSON, size=25,  color="blue"),
        #Code continues below ...
    )

    listile2  = ft.ListTile(
        trailing= ft.IconButton(icon=ft.CupertinoIcons.LOCK_SHIELD),
        subtitle = "Set passwords, encrypt message",
        title=ft.Text("Security", size=18),
        leading= ft.Icon(ft.Icons.LOCK, size=25, color="green"),
        #Code continues below ...
    )

    listile3  = ft.ListTile(
        trailing= ft.Switch(),
        subtitle = "Enable to see recent physical activites",
        title=ft.Text("Activities", size=18),
        leading= ft.Image("activity.png", height=25, width=25),
        #Code continues below ...
    )

    page.add(listile1, listile2, listile3)

ft.run(main)
```

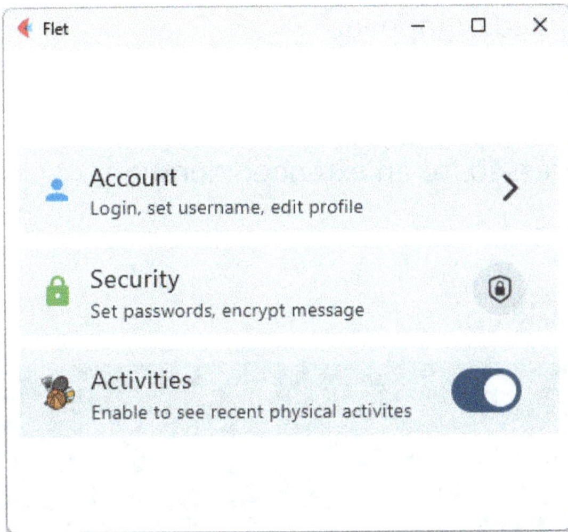

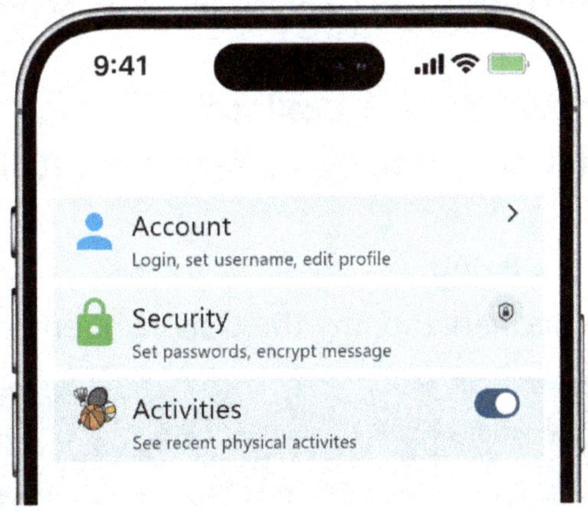

content_padding = flet.Padding

Defines padding between the ListTile content and its edges using a Padding control.

horizontal_spacing = number

Defines the space between the leading/trailing icons and text content.

hover_color = color

Background color displayed when the mouse hovers over the ListTile.

mouse_cursor = flet.MouseCursor

Specifies the mouse cursor when hovering over the ListTile. The available mouse cursors include:

ALIAS	GRABBING	RESIZE_DOWN	RESIZE_UP_DOWN
ALL_SCROLL	HELP	RESIZE_DOWN_LEFT	RESIZE_UP_LEFT
BASIC	MOVE	RESIZE_DOWN_RIGHT	RESIZE_UP_LEFT_DOWN_RIGHT
CELL	NO_DROP	RESIZE_LEFT	RESIZE_UP_RIGHT
CLICK	NONE	RESIZE_LEFT_RIGHT	RESIZE_UP_RIGHT_DOWN_LEFT
CONTEXT_MENU	PRECISE	RESIZE_RIGHT	TEXT
COPY	PROGRESS	RESIZE_ROW	VERTICAL_TEXT
DISAPPEARING	RESIZE_COLUMN	RESIZE_UP	WAIT
FORBIDDEN	GRAB	ZOOM_IN	ZOOM_OUT

on_click = callback

A function to be called when the ListTile is clicked or tapped.

on_long_press = callback

A function to be callled when the ListTile is pressed for an extended duration.

url = string

If specified, tapping the ListTile opens a web URL.

```
Python
import flet as ft

def main(page: ft.Page):

    def myfunction(e):
        #Actual code goes here ...
        print("ListTile has been clicked")

    listile  = ft.ListTile(
        on_click = myfunction,
        url = "https://google.com",
        #Code continues below ...
    )

    page.add(listile)

ft.run(main)
```

selected = bool

Boolean indicating whether the ListTile is selected.

selected_color = color

Color applied to the text when selected.

selected_tile_color = color

Background color applied when the tile is selected.

style = flet.ListTileStyle

Specifies the style type using ListTileStyle (options: LIST or DRAWER).

shape = Shape

Defines the shape of the ListTile. Shapes include

- flet.OutlinedBorder()
- flet.CircularBorder()
- flet.StadiumBorder()
- flet.RoundedRectangularBorder(radius)
- flet.ContinousRectangularBorder(radius)
- flet.BeveledRectangularBorder(radius)

Python
```python
import flet as ft

def main(page: ft.Page):

    project  = ft.ListTile(
        shape=ft.ContinuousRectangleBorder(radius=10),
        leading= ft.Image("rocket.png"),
        subtitle = ft.Text("Create,edit and save project",color="grey"),
        trailing=ft.Icon(ft.Icons.ARROW_FORWARD_IOS, color="white"),
        title= ft.Text("Project", weight= ft.FontWeight.BOLD,
                color="#E4EEF0"
            ),
        bgcolor="#023246"
    )

    calendar  = ft.ListTile(
        shape=ft.RoundedRectangleBorder(radius=ft.BorderRadius(
                            top_left=15, top_right=0,
                            bottom_left=0, bottom_right=15
                        )),
        leading= ft.Image("calendar.png"),
        subtitle = ft.Text("Open, select and edit date",color="grey"),
        trailing=ft.Icon(ft.Icons.ARROW_FORWARD_IOS, color="white"),
        title= ft.Text("Calendar", weight= ft.FontWeight.BOLD,
            color="#E4EEF0"
            ),
        bgcolor="#023246"
    )


    page.add(project, calendar)

ft.run(main)
```

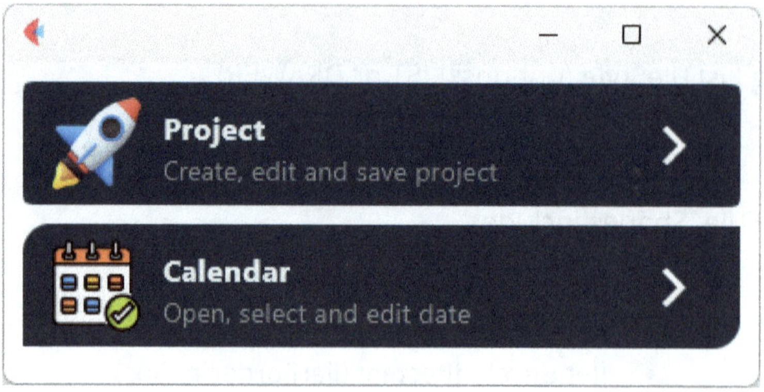

title_alignment = flet.Alignment

Aligns the title horizontally within the ListTile.

toggle_inputs = bool

Specifies if trailing toggle controls are active.

visual_density = flet.VisualDensity

Adjusts the spacing and compactness of the ListTile. Options include

- COMPACT
- STANDARD
- COMFORTABLE
- ADAPTIVE_PLATFORM_DENSITY

Example,

Python

```
import flet as ft

def main(page: ft.Page):

    Listtile  = ft.ListTile(
        visible= ft.VisualDensity.COMFORTABLE,
        #Code continues below ...
    )

    page.add(Listtile)

ft.run(main)
```

Card

The **Card** control is a container used to present related information in a visually distinct, self-contained block. It often resembles a physical card, featuring rounded corners, background color and optional elevation or shadows to create depth. Cards help organize user interface elements into structured, readable sections and can contain any Flet control, such as text, images, buttons or layouts.
Cards are commonly used to display profiles, product summaries, statistics, short forms or grouped content, offering a clean and intuitive user experience.

Properties and Methods

clip_behavior = flet.ClipBehavior
Specifies how content overflowing the Card's boundaries should be clipped.

bgcolor = color
Sets the background color of the Card.

content = control

Specifies the main control or layout contained inside the Card. This is typically a Column, Row or any single widget.

```python
import flet as ft

def main(page: ft.Page):

    card  = ft.Card(
        content= ft.Column(
            alignment= ft.MainAxisAlignment.CENTER,
            horizontal_alignment= ft.CrossAxisAlignment.CENTER,
            controls=[
                ft.Text("Current balance USD", size=25, color="#F2F4F7"),
                ft.Text("$354,935.00", size=30, color="orange"),
                ft.Row(
                    alignment= ft.MainAxisAlignment.CENTER,
                    controls=[
                        ft.OutlinedButton(text="Daily report"),
                        ft.OutlinedButton(text="Statement"),
                    ]
                ),
                ft.Container(expand=True)
            ]
        ),
        color="#141517",
    )

    page.add(card)

ft.run(main)
```

margin = number, flet.Margin

Defines the external spacing around the Card using the Margin control.

elevation = number

Defines the visual elevation of the Card. A higher value increases the depth effect, making the Card appear raised.

shadow_color = color

Specifies the color of the Card's shadow. It is typically grey by default.

```
Python
import flet as ft

def main(page: ft.Page):

    card  = ft.Card(
        elevation= 30,
        shadow_color="red",
        content= ft.Container(
            padding= ft.Padding.all(10),
            content = ft.Row(
            controls=[
                ft.Container(width=5),
                ft.Column(
                    expand=True,
                    controls=[
                        ft.Text("Premium Plan", size=25, color="#E4EEF0"),
                        ft.Text("""Upgrade to premium plan to enjoy full
                                tutorial""",size=18, color="white"),
                        ft.OutlinedButton(text="Upgrade", ),
                    ]
                ),
                ft.Image("education.png")
            ]
        )),
        color="#075056",
        height=180
    )

    page.add(card)

ft.run(main)
```

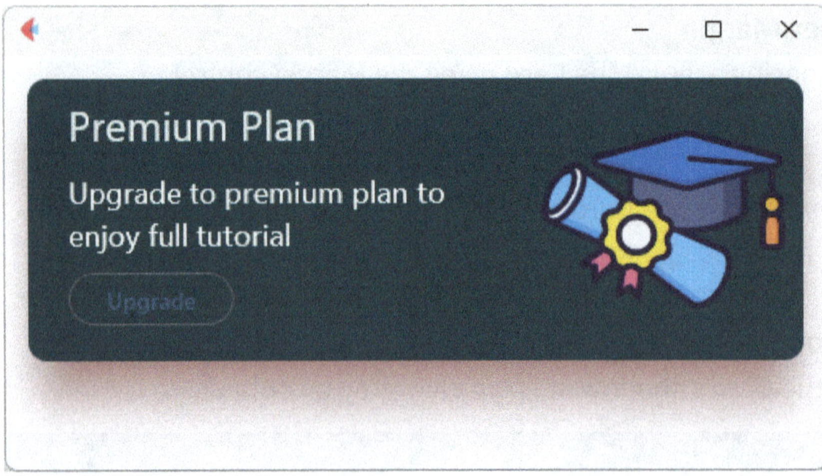

shape = **Shape**

Defines the shape of the Card. The various shapes include

- flet.OutlinedBorder()
- flet.CircularBorder()
- flet.StadiumBorder()
- flet.RoundedRectangularBorder(radius)
- flet.ContinousRectangularBorder(radius)
- flet.BeveledRectangularBorder(radius)

Example,

```
Python
import flet as ft

def main(page: ft.Page):

    card  = ft.Card(
                shape= ft.RoundedRectangleBorder(
                  radius= ft.BorderRadius(
                   top_left=0, top_right=30,
                   bottom_left=30, bottom_right=0
                )
            ),
            #Code continues below ...
    )

    page.add(card)

ft.run(main)
```

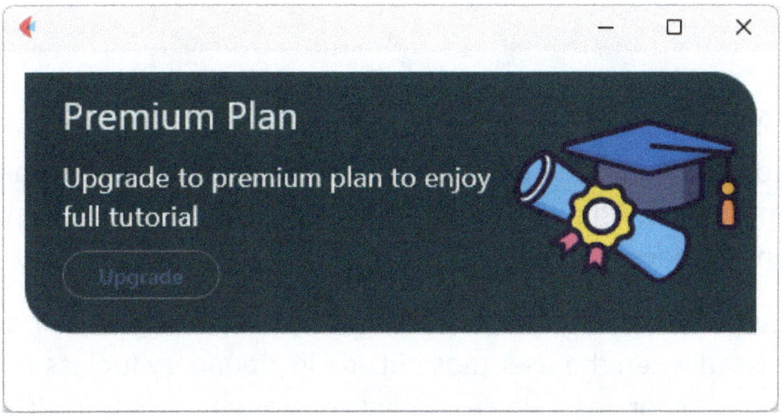

show_border_on_foreground = bool

Determines whether the Card border is painted above its content.

variant = flet.CardVariant

Specifies preset styling variations for the Card. Card variants include:

- OUTLINED
- FILLED
- ELEVATED

BottomSheet

The **BottomSheet** control is a panel that slides upward from the bottom of the application window. It is commonly used to display additional content or actions that should only appear when needed. This makes BottomSheet especially popular in mobile-style interfaces, where space is limited.

A BottomSheet is typically hidden by default. It can be opened or closed programmatically or dismissed when the user taps outside its boundary (unless this behavior is disabled). The sheet contains a single content control, which may itself be a layout holding many other controls.

Properties and Methods

animation_style = flet.AnimationStyle

Defines animation behavior for opening and closing the BottomSheet. AnimationStyle options include:

- curve
- duration
- reverse_curve
- reverse_duration

bgcolor = color

Sets the background color of the BottomSheet. You can use named colors, hex codes or predefined ColorValue options.

open = bool

Controls whether the BottomSheet is open. Setting this property to True opens the sheet programmatically.

content = control

Specifies the main control contained within the BottomSheet. This is often a layout (Column, Row, ListView, etc.) that holds multiple child controls.

Python

```
import flet as ft

def main(page: ft.Page):

    def openSheet(e):
        bottomsheet.open = True
        page.update()


    bottomsheet = ft.BottomSheet(
       bgcolor="#F0F0F0",
       content= ft.Container(
           padding=20,
           content= ft.Column(
               controls=[
                   ft.ListTile(
                       leading= ft.Icon(ft.Icons.SAVE, size= 25),
                       title= ft.Text("Save", size=18),
                       on_click= lambda _:print("Save")
                   ),
                   ft.ListTile(
                      leading= ft.Icon(ft.CupertinoIcons.DELETE,size= 25),
                      title= ft.Text("Delete", size=18),
                      on_click= lambda _:print("Delete")
                   ),

                   ft.ListTile(
                      leading= ft.Icon(ft.CupertinoIcons.PRINTER,size= 25),
                      title= ft.Text("Print", size=18),
                      on_click= lambda _:print("Print")
                   ),
               ]
```

```
            )
        )
    )

    openSheet = ft.TextButton(content="Open sheet", on_click= openSheet)
    page.add(openSheet, bottomsheet)

ft.run(main)
```

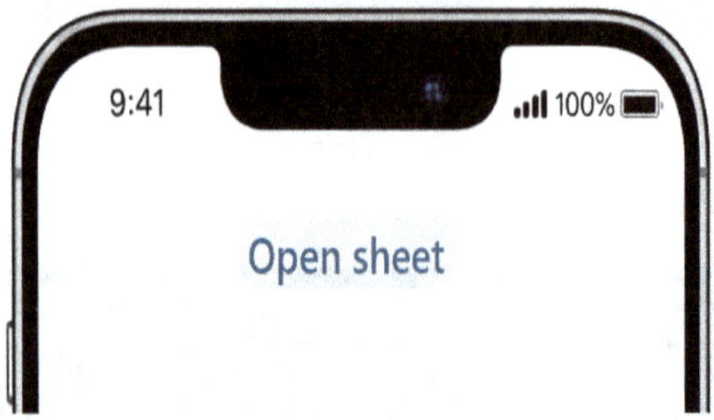

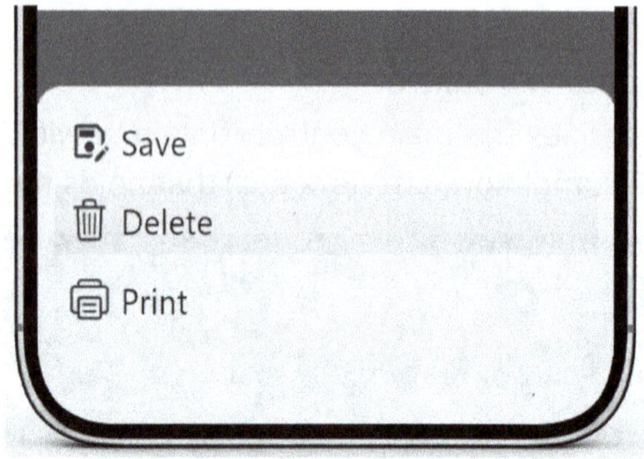

dismissible = **bool**

Controls whether the BottomSheet closes when the user taps outside its region. When set False, the sheet cannot be dismissed by tapping outside.

elevation = **number**

Applies a raised visual effect to the BottomSheet, giving the appearance of depth.

draggable = **bool**

Enables a draggable handle at the top of the BottomSheet, allowing the user to drag the sheet. When set True, a small drag bar appears.

show_drag_handle = **bool**

Displays a visible drag handle at the top of the sheet.

Python

```
import flet as ft

def main(page: ft.Page):

    sheet  =  ft.BottomSheet(
        elevation= 10,
        show_drag_handle=True,
        animation_style= ft.AnimationStyle(
           duration=ft.Duration(seconds=2),
           reverse_duration=ft.Duration(seconds=3),
           curve=ft.AnimationCurve.BOUNCE_IN_OUT,
           reverse_curve=ft.AnimationCurve.EASE_IN_OUT
        ),

        #Code continues below ...
    )

    page.add(sheet)

ft.run(main)
```

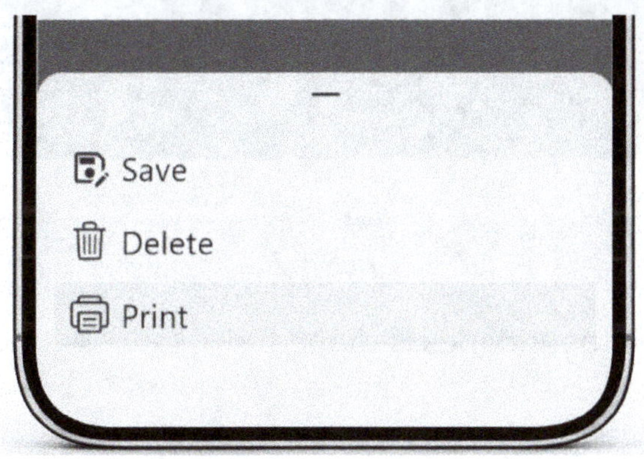

size_constraints = flet.BoxConstraints

Applies minimum and maximum size constraints to the sheet. Options of the BoxConstraints are

- max_width
- max_height
- min_width
- min_height

maintain_bottom_view_insets_padding = bool

Maintains padding when system UI elements (such as virtual keyboards) appear.

on_dismiss = callback

Registers a callback that executes when the BottomSheet closes.

```python
import flet as ft

def main(page: ft.Page):

    def onClose(e):
        #Actual logic goes here ...
        print("BottomSheet is closed!")


    sheet  =  ft.BottomSheet(
        on_dismiss= onClose,
        size_constraints= ft.BoxConstraints.max_height,
        #Code continues below ...
    )

    page.add(sheet)


ft.run(main)
```

clip_behavior = flet.ClipBehavior

Specifies how content that exceeds the sheet boundaries is clipped.

use_safe_area = bool

Ensures the BottomSheet respects the device's safe area (e.g., avoiding camera notches or system bars).

shape = Shape

Defines the shape of the BottomSheet, such as rounded or rectangular borders.

```python
import flet as ft
```

```
def main(page: ft.Page):

    sheet  =  ft.BottomSheet(
        shape= ft.RoundedRectangleBorder(radius=0),
        #Code continues below ...

    )

    page.add(sheet)

ft.run(main)
```

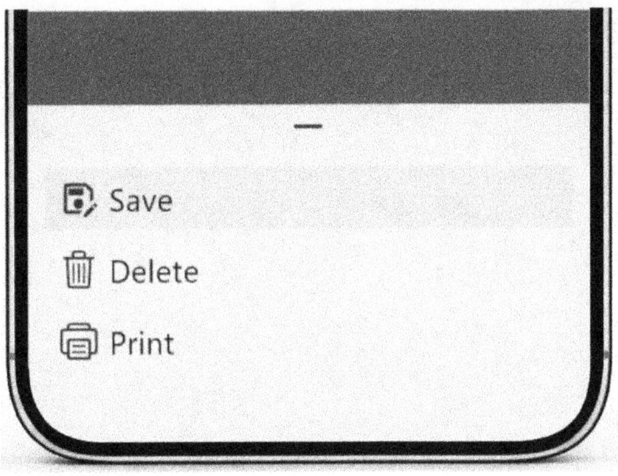

scrollable = bool
When True, the BottomSheet can scroll to display hidden controls.

fullscreen = bool
When True, the BottomSheet covers the entire screen.

barrier_color = color
Defines the background color of the screen when the BottomSheet opens.

```
Python

import flet as ft

def main(page: ft.Page):
```

```
    sheet  =  ft.BottomSheet(
        barrier_color= ft.Colors.GREEN_100,
        #Code continues below ...

    )

    page.add(sheet)

ft.run(main)
```

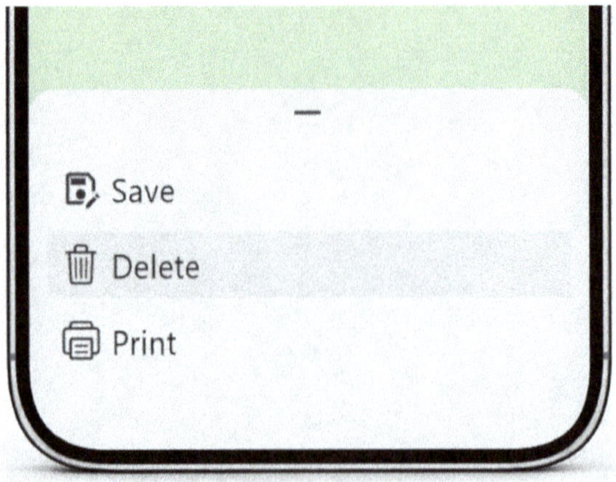

Buttons

Buttons are fundamental interactive components in user interfaces. They allow users to perform actions by tapping or clicking. A button may display **text**, **an icon** or both and each button is typically associated with a **callback function** that executes when the button is activated. Buttons therefore serve as the primary mechanism for issuing commands, triggering processes and navigating an application.

Flet provides a rich collection of built-in button controls, including:

TextButton	**Chip**	**CupertinoFilledButton**
IconButton	**FilledIconButton**	**CupertinoTintedButton**
OutlinedButton	**FilledTonalButton**	**CupertinoSegmentedButton**
FilledButton	**FilledTonalIconButton**	**CupertinoSlidingSegmentedButton**
ElevatedButton	**OutlinedIconButton**	
SegmentedButton	**CupertinoButton**	

Although these are the predefined button widgets available in Flet, the framework is intentionally flexible. Developers can build **fully customized buttons** using the base **Button** control, which allows precise control over appearance, interaction behavior and content arrangement.

Beyond the standard set, Flet also allows **any control** to function as a clickable element. This is achieved using the **GestureDetector**, which can detect gestures such as **tap**, **double tap**, **long press**, **hover** and others. When a gesture is detected, the assigned callback is triggered, effectively transforming ordinary controls—such as images, containers, text, cards or any other control—into interactive button-like components.

This flexibility enables a wide range of custom UI designs while maintaining consistent interaction behavior.

TextButton

The **TextButton** is a Material Design button control that displays text as its primary content and triggers actions when clicked, tapped or pressed. Unlike elevated buttons, it is flat and does not cast a shadow by default. Although its primary content is text, it can also host complex controls, including icons, images or layouts.

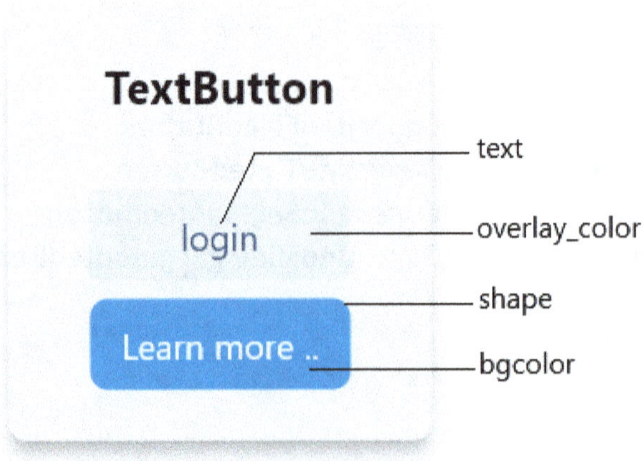

Properties and Methods

adaptive = bool
When set True, the button adopts the platform-specific Material Design style.

autofocus = bool
Gives automatic focus to the button when True.

content = string / control
Specifies the text content or any control of the button.

```
Python
```

```
import flet as ft

def main(page: ft.Page):

    button = ft.TextButton(
        content ="Send",
        width=200,
        height=50
    )

    page.add(button)

ft.run(main)
```

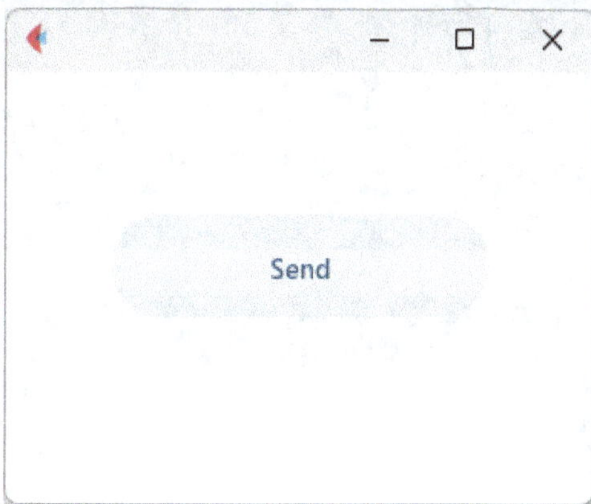

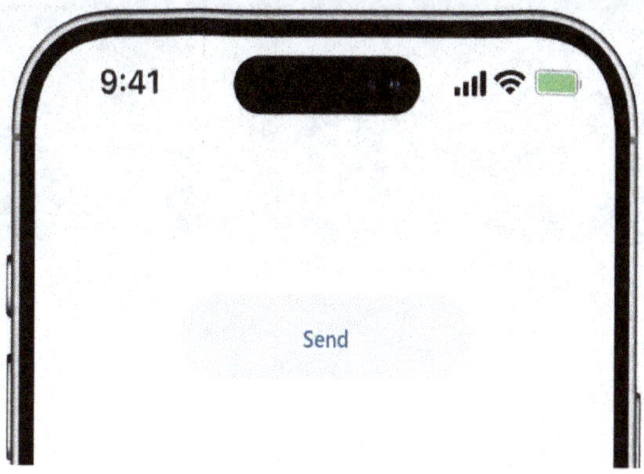

icon= icon / control

Specifies the icon content of the button. It can be used together with text

icon_color = color

Defines the color of the icon if icon is specified.

clip_behavior = flet.ClipBehavior

Defines how content is clipped inside the button (e.g., NONE, ANTI_ALIASING).

data = Any(string, number, list, tuple, set, dictionary, bytes)

Stores user-defined custom data.

disabled = bool

When True, the button is inactive and ignores user interactions.

```python
import flet as ft

def main(page: ft.Page):

    button = ft.TextButton(
        content = "Set Password",
        icon= ft.Icons.LOCK,
        icon_color="orange",
        data = "password",
        width=200, height=50
    )

    page.add(button)

ft.run(main)
```

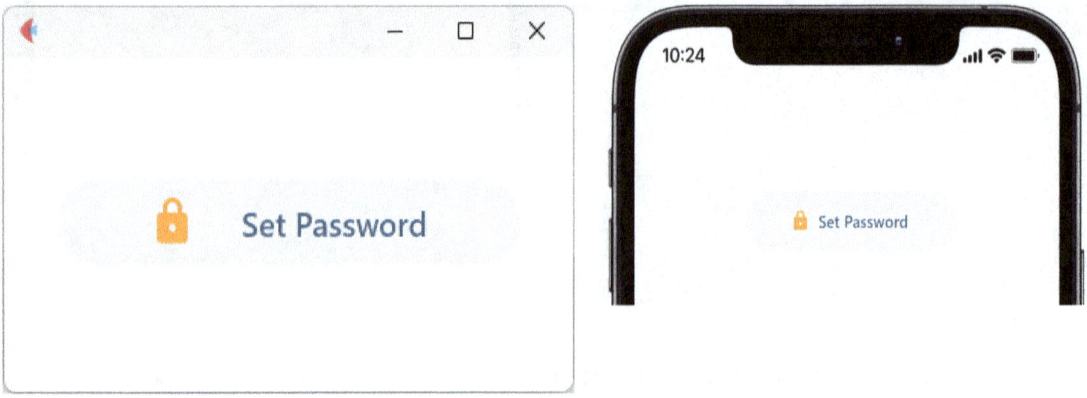

height = number

Returns or sets the button's height.

width = number

Returns or sets the button width.

opacity = callback

Controls the transparency of the button (0.0 = fully invisible, 1.0 = fully visible).

on_hover = callback
Executes a function when the mouse hovers over the button.

on_click = callback
Executes a function when the button is clicked or tapped.

```python
import flet as ft

def main(page: ft.Page):

    def isClicked(e):
        #Actual logic or code here
        print("button has been clicked")

    def isHovered(e):
        #Actual logic or code here
        print("mouse has moved over button")


    button = ft.TextButton(
        on_click= isClicked,
        on_hover = isHovered,
        #Code continues below ...
      )

    page.add(button)

ft.run(main)
```

on_focus = callback
Executes a function when the button gains focus.

on_long_press = callback
Executes a function when the button is pressed and held.

on_blur = callback
Triggered when the button loses focus.

style = flet.ButtonStyle

Customizes the button appearance using the ButtonStyle control:

ButtonStyle

Table 3.30

Method/Property	Definition
color	Sets the content (text or icon) color.
bgcolor	Sets the button's background color.
overlay_color	Temporary color displayed when clicked or pressed.
shadow_color	Shadow color if the button is elevated.
surface_tint_color	Faded background color.
elevation	Adds a raised effect and shadow.
animation_duration	Time in seconds for the click/tap splash effect.
padding	Space between content and button edges.
shape	Defines button shape: OutlinedBorder(), CircularBorder(), StadiumBorder(), RoundedRectangularBorder(radius), BeveledRectangularBorder(radius), ContinousRectangularBorder(radius),
alignment	Aligns content within the button.
text_style	Uses TextStyle to format text content. *(turn to page 65)*
icon_color	Style the icon with color
icon_size	Style the icon with size
visual_density	Adjusts compactness.
mouse_cursor	Type of mouse cursor when hovering (options: COPY, ALIAS, etc.).
enable_feedback	Enables haptic or visual feedback.
side	Uses BorderSide to define edge width and color.

Python
```
import flet as ft

def main(page: ft.Page):

    button = ft.TextButton(
        style=ft.ButtonStyle(
            color="#E4EEF0",
            text_style=ft.TextStyle( size=20, weight= ft.FontWeight.BOLD),
            overlay_color="#075056",
            padding= ft.Padding.symmetric(horizontal=10)
        ),

        content ="Let's Start",
```

```
        width=300, height=50
    )

    page.add(button)

ft.run(main)
```

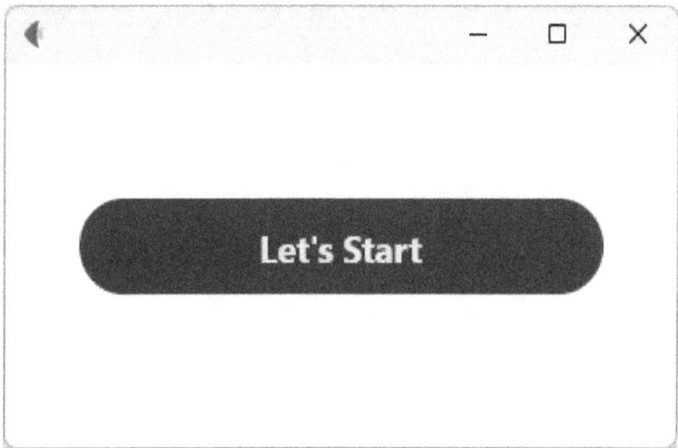

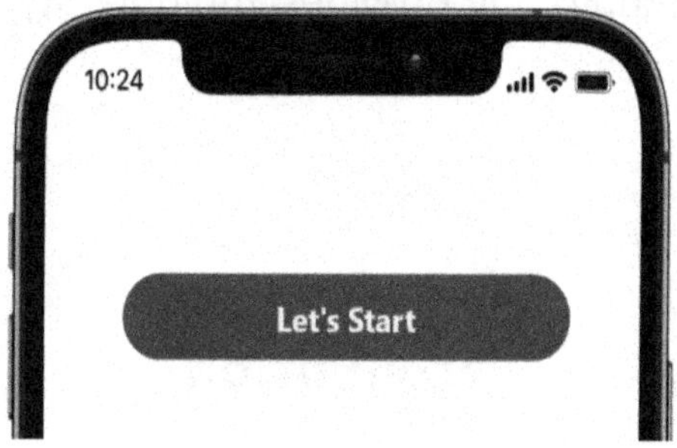

tooltip = string

Text displayed when the button gains focus or is hovered.

url = string

Opens a web URL when the button is clicked.

```python
import flet as ft

def main(page: ft.Page):

    button = ft.TextButton(
        url="https://www.google.com/data",
        #Code continues below ...
    )

    page.add(button)

ft.run(main)
```

IconButton

The **IconButton** is a Material Design button represented by an icon. When the icon is clicked, tapped or pressed, it triggers an event. The IconButton is typically used for actions that can be conveyed purely through an icon, such as "search," "delete," or "settings." It provides multiple styling and behavioral properties to customize its appearance and interaction.

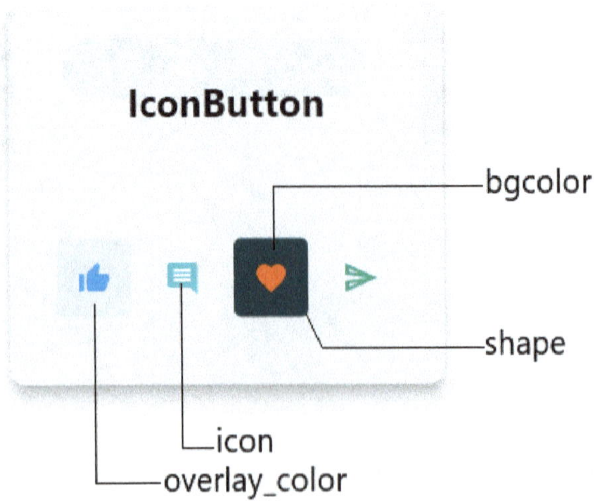

Properties and Methods

adaptive = bool
When True, the button adopts platform-specific Material Design styling.

alignment = flet.Alignment
Aligns the icon or content within the button using the alignment control. Alignment options include:

- CENTER
- TOP_LEFT
- CENTER_RIGHT
- BOTTOM_LEFT
- CENTER_LEFT
- TOP_CENTER
- TOP_RIGHT
- BOTTOM_CENTER
- BOTTOM_RIGHT

autofocus = bool

Automatically focuses the button when True.

icon = icon / control

Specifies the icon for the button or any other control.

icon_color = color

It defines the color of the icon.

icon_size = number

It defines the size of the icon.

Python

```python
import flet as ft

def main(page: ft.Page):

    button = ft.IconButton(
        icon=ft.Icons.ROCKET_LAUNCH,
        icon_color="red",
        height= 50, width=50
    )

    page.add(button)

ft.run(main)
```

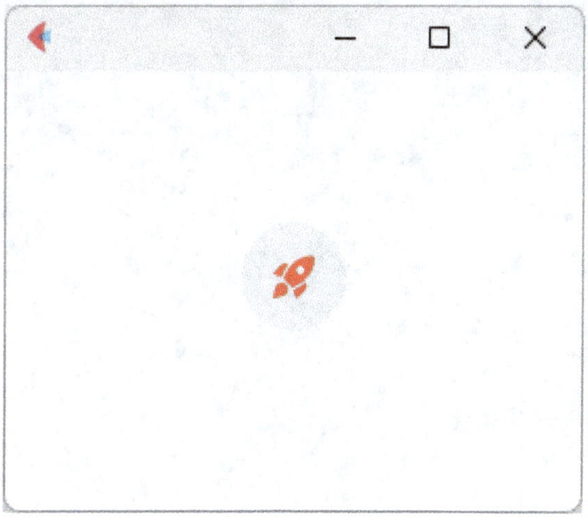

bgcolor = color
Defines the background color of the button. Colors can be specified as color names, hex codes or ColorValue.

data = Any(string, number, list, tuple, set, dictionary, bytes)
Stores custom user-defined data.

disabled / disabled_color = bool / color
When True, disables the button. disabled_color defines the icon color while disabled.

height / width / size_constraints = number/number/flet.BoxConstraints
Defines the size of the button and constrains its dimensions with BoxConstraints. Methods of the BoxConstraints are

- min_width
- min_height
- max_width
- max_height

Python

```python
import flet as ft

def main(page: ft.Page):

    button = ft.IconButton(
        size_constraints=ft.BoxConstraints(min_width= 10, min_height=5),
        icon=ft.Column(
            controls=[
               ft.Icon(ft.Icons.PRINT_OUTLINED, size=35),
               ft.Text("Print", weight=ft.FontWeight.BOLD, size=18)
            ],
        alignment=ft.MainAxisAlignment.CENTER,
        horizontal_alignment=ft.CrossAxisAlignment.CENTER,
        ),
        height= 100, width=100
    )

    page.add(button)


ft.run(main)
```

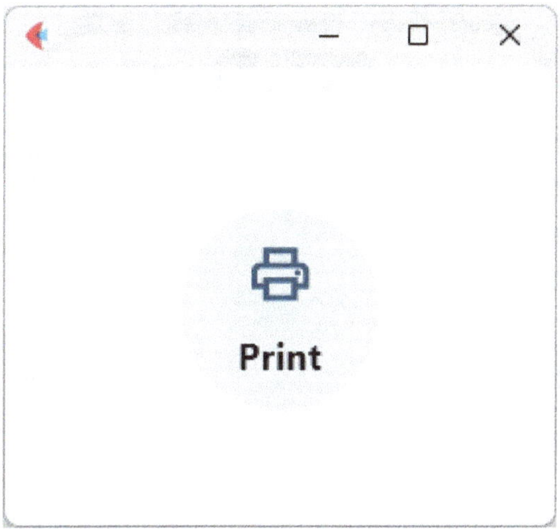

enable_feedback = **bool**

Enables visual or haptic feedback on interaction.

focus / focus_color / highlight_color / hover_color = **color**

Controls focus state and the colors applied when the button is focused, highlighted or hovered.

```
Python

import flet as ft

def main(page: ft.Page):

    button = ft.IconButton(
        highlight_color="green",
        icon= ft.Icons.CALL,
        icon_size= 15,
        #Code continues below ...
    )

    page.add(button)

ft.run(main)
```

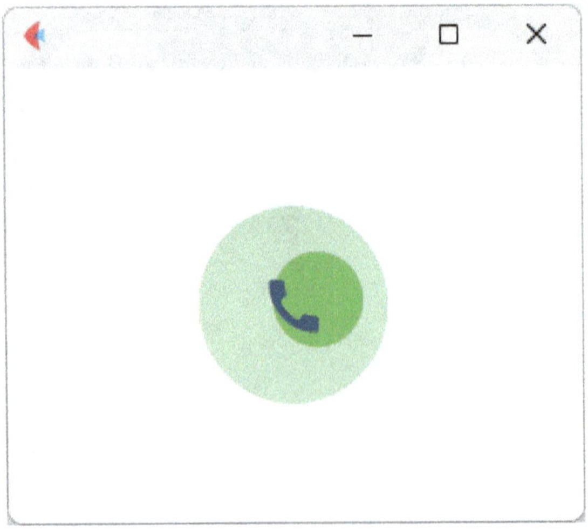

mouse_cursor = flet.MouseCursor

Sets the type of mouse cursor when interacting with the button. The available mouse cursors include:

ALIAS	GRABBING	RESIZE_DOWN	RESIZE_UP_DOWN
ALL_SCROLL	HELP	RESIZE_DOWN_LEFT	RESIZE_UP_LEFT
BASIC	MOVE	RESIZE_DOWN_RIGHT	RESIZE_UP_LEFT_DOWN_RIGHT
CELL	NO_DROP	RESIZE_LEFT	RESIZE_UP_RIGHT
CLICK	NONE	RESIZE_LEFT_RIGHT	RESIZE_UP_RIGHT_DOWN_LEFT
CONTEXT_MENU	PRECISE	RESIZE_RIGHT	TEXT
COPY	PROGRESS	RESIZE_ROW	VERTICAL_TEXT
DISAPPEARING	RESIZE_COLUMN	RESIZE_UP	WAIT
FORBIDDEN	GRAB	ZOOM_IN	ZOOM_OUT

on_blur = callback

Triggered when the button loses focus.

on_long_press = callback

Executes a function when the button is pressed and held.

on_click = callback

Executes a function when the button is clicked or tapped.

```python
import flet as ft

def main(page: ft.Page):

    def myfunction(e):
        #Actual code goes here ...
        print("Button has been pressed")


    button = ft.IconButton(
        on_click= lambda _:print("Button has been clicked"),
        on_long_press= myfunction,
        #Code continues below ...
    )

    page.add(button)

ft.run(main)
```

on_focus = callback
Executes a function when the button gains focus.

on_hover = callback
Executes a function when the mouse hovers over the button.

padding = number, flet.Padding
Space between the icon and button edges. *(Turn to page 140 or figure 3.3)*

selected = bool
Programmatically selects the button

selected_icon = icons
The selected_icon defines the icon to display when button is selected.

selected_icon_color = color
This sets the color of the selected icon.

splash_color = color, splash_radius = number

Temporary overlay color and coverage area when the button is clicked or pressed.

tooltip = string

Text displayed when the button gains focus or is hovered.

visible = bool

When False, hides the button from the UI.

style = flet.ButtonStyle

Uses ButtonStyle to format the button's appearance.

> **Insight**
>
> The properties of ButtonStyle were fully explained earlier under **TextButton** (*Table 3.30*). Please refer to that section for a detailed description of its properties and usage.

Python

```python
import flet as ft

def main(page: ft.Page):

    button = ft.IconButton(
        icon=ft.Icons.SHOPIFY_OUTLINED,
        style = ft.ButtonStyle(
          shape= ft.ContinuousRectangleBorder(radius=10),
          overlay_color="blue",
          icon_color="white",
          icon_size=50,
        ),
        width=100, height=100,
    )

    page.add(button)

ft.run(main)
```

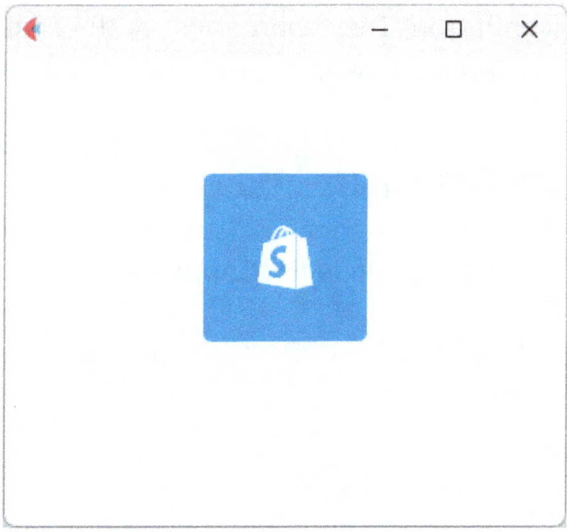

url = string
Opens a web URL when the button is clicked.

```python
import flet as ft

def main(page: ft.Page):

    button = ft.IconButton(
        url="https://www.google.com/data",
        tooltip = "Connect to Google",
        #Code continues below ...
    )

    page.add(button)

ft.run(main)
```

IconButton Variants

In addition to the standard **IconButton**, Flet provides styled variants that differ primarily in appearance while maintaining similar functionality.

These variants are pre-styled versions of IconButton. They share most of the same properties and methods, with only minor differences related to styling and visual behavior. The available variants include:

FilledIconButton

Displays the icon inside a filled container with a solid background color.

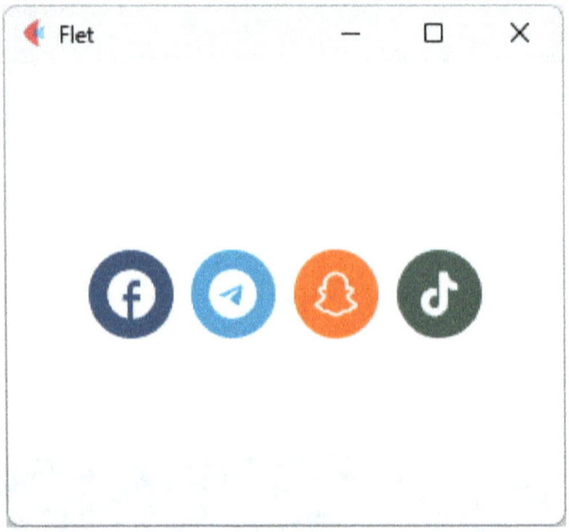

FilledTonalIconButton

Uses a softer, tonal background color for a more subtle filled appearance.

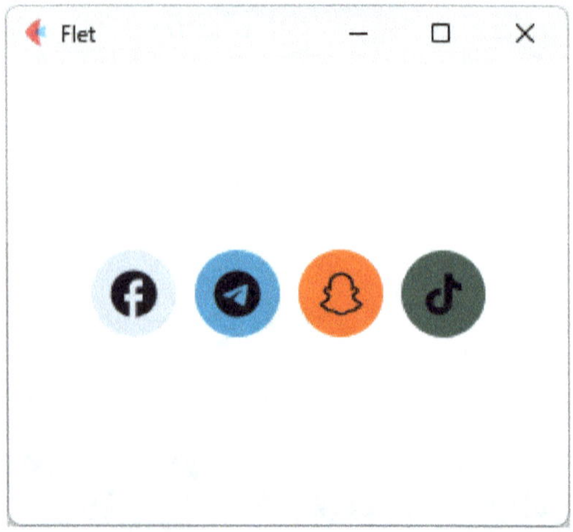

OutlinedIconButton

Displays the icon with an outlined border and no filled background.

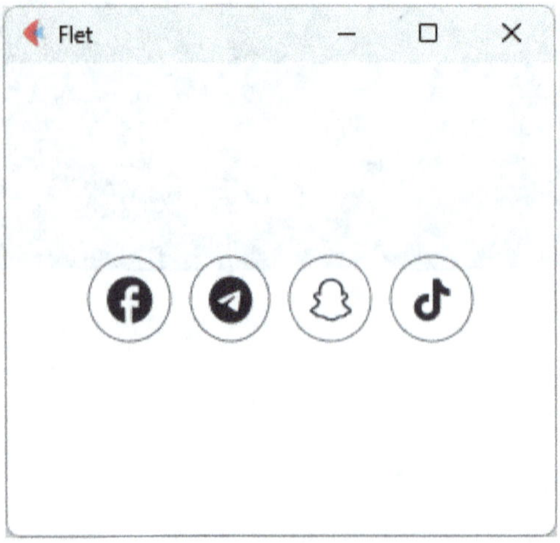

OutlinedButton

The **OutlinedButton** is a Material Design button bounded by an outline border. It can contain a child control such as an icon, text or a more complex layout. This button type emphasizes its boundary rather than a filled background, making it suitable for secondary or less prominent actions. Like other Material buttons, it supports a wide range of properties for styling and behavior.

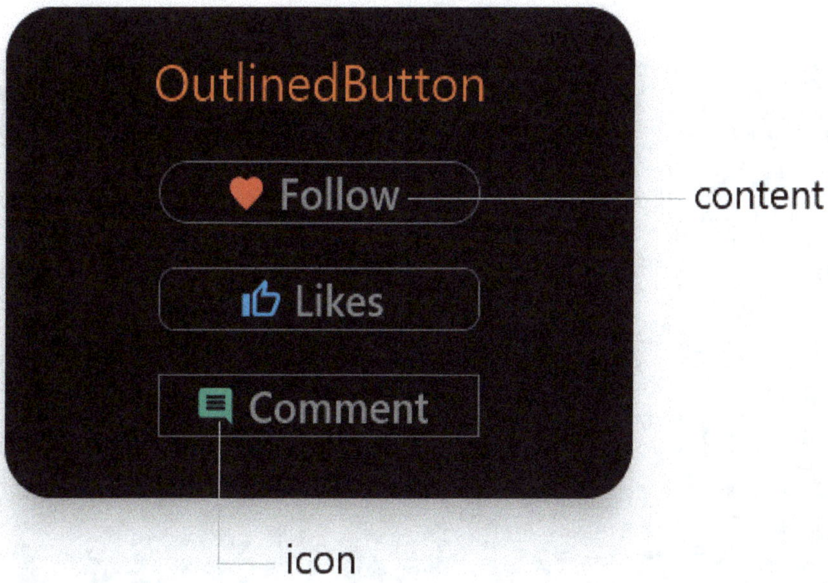

Properties and Methods

adaptive = bool
When True, the button applies platform-specific Material Design styles automatically.

autofocus = bool
Automatically focuses the button when True.

clip_behavior = flet.ClipBehavior

Defines how the button's content is clipped if it overflows the bounds.

content = string/control

Specifies the textual content or any other control of the button.

icon = flet.Icons , icon_color = color

Defines the icon to display on the button and its color. Applicable when the child control is an icon.

```python
import flet as ft

def main(page: ft.Page):

    button = ft.OutlinedButton(
        content = "Send",
        icon=ft.Icons.SEND,
        icon_color="blue",
        width=100, height=40,
    )

    page.add(button)

ft.run(main)
```

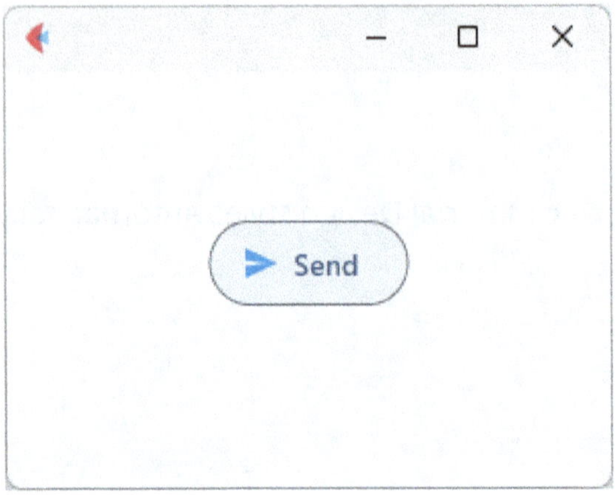

disabled = **bool**

When True, disables the button, preventing user interaction.

data = **Any(string, number, list, tuple, set, dictionary, bytes)**

Stores custom user-defined data.

Python

```python
import flet as ft

def main(page: ft.Page):

    button = ft.OutlinedButton(
        data= "shop",
        content=ft.Column(
            controls=[
                ft.Icon(ft.Icons.SHOPPING_CART_SHARP, size=50),
                ft.Text("Shop Now", size=18, weight=ft.FontWeight.BOLD)
            ],
            alignment=ft.MainAxisAlignment.CENTER,
            horizontal_alignment=ft.CrossAxisAlignment.CENTER,
        ),
        width=200, height=100,
    )

    page.add(button)

ft.run(main)
```

on_blur = **callback**

Triggered when the button loses focus.

on_long_press = callback
Executes a function when the button is pressed and held.

on_click = callback
Executes a function when the button is clicked or tapped.

on_focus = callback
Executes a function when the button gains focus.

on_hover = callback
Executes a function when the mouse hovers over the button.

Python

```
import flet as ft

def main(page: ft.Page):

    def clickFunction(e):
        #Actual code goes here ...
        print("Button has been pressed")

    button = ft.OutlinedButton(
        on_click = clickFunction,
        on_focus= lambda _: print("Button has gained focused"),
        on_blur= lambda _: print("Button has losed focused"),
        on_long_press= lambda _: print("Button has been pressed"),
        #Code continues below ...
    )

    page.add(button)

ft.run(main)
```

height / width = number
Specifies the dimensions of the button.

opacity = number
Sets the transparency of the button, ranging from 0.0 (fully invisible) to 1.0 (fully opaque).

style = flet.ButtonStyle
Uses the ButtonStyle control to format the appearance of the button, including:

Insight

The properties of ButtonStyle were fully explained earlier under **TextButton**. Please refer to that section for a detailed description of its properties and usage.

Python

```
import flet as ft

def main(page: ft.Page):

    button = ft.OutlinedButton(

        style = ft.ButtonStyle(
        icon_size=50,
        color="orange",
        text_style=ft.TextStyle(size=20, weight= ft.FontWeight.BOLD),
        shape= ft.RoundedRectangleBorder(radius=10),
        side = ft.BorderSide(width=3, color="green")
        ),

        content=ft.Column(
            controls=[
                ft.Icon(ft.Icons.SHOPPING_CART_SHARP),
                ft.Text("Shop Now")
            ],
            alignment=ft.MainAxisAlignment.CENTER,
            horizontal_alignment=ft.CrossAxisAlignment.CENTER,
        ),
        width=200, height=200,
    )
```

```
    page.add(button)

ft.run(main)
```

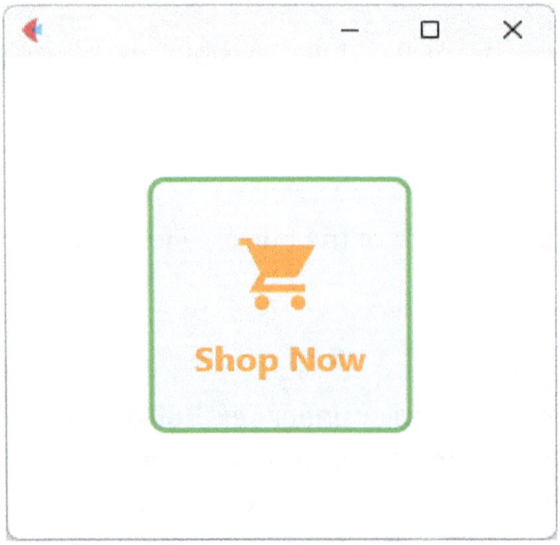

tooltip = string

Text displayed when the button gains focus or is hovered.

url = string

Opens a web URL when the button is clicked.

```python
import flet as ft

def main(page: ft.Page):

    button = ft.OutlinedButton(
        url="https://www.google.com/",
        #Code continues below ...
    )

    page.add(button)

ft.run(main)
```

FilledButton

The **FilledButton** is a Material Design button control that has a filled background color. Its child content can be text, icon or any other control. FilledButtons provide a prominent call-to-action in the interface, as the filled background makes them visually distinct compared to flat buttons.

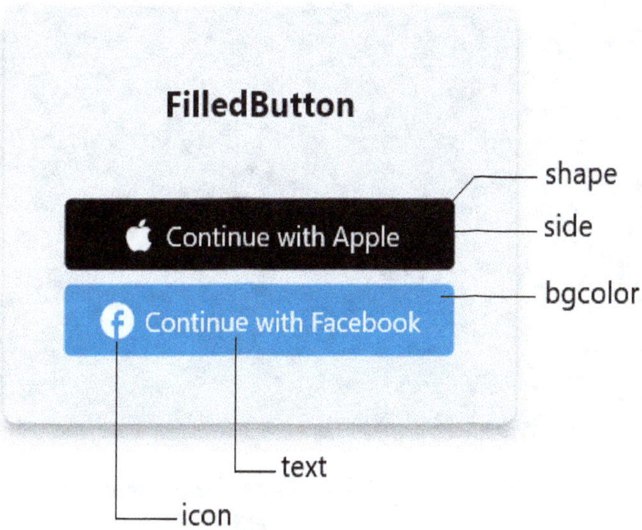

Properties and Methods

adaptive = bool

When set to True, the FilledButton adopts the platform-specific Material Design style.

autofocus = bool

Allows the button to gain focus automatically when set True.

content = string/ control

Sets the main child control of the button. Can be a Text, Icon or complex control.

icon = icon/control

Defines the icon of the button's child.

icon_color = color

Sets the color of the icon when used as the button content.

```python
import flet as ft

def main(page: ft.Page):

    button = ft.FilledButton(
        icon=ft.Icons.ACCOUNT_CIRCLE,
        content="Create Account",
        icon_color="cyan",
        width=200, height=50,
    )

    page.add(button)

ft.run(main)
```

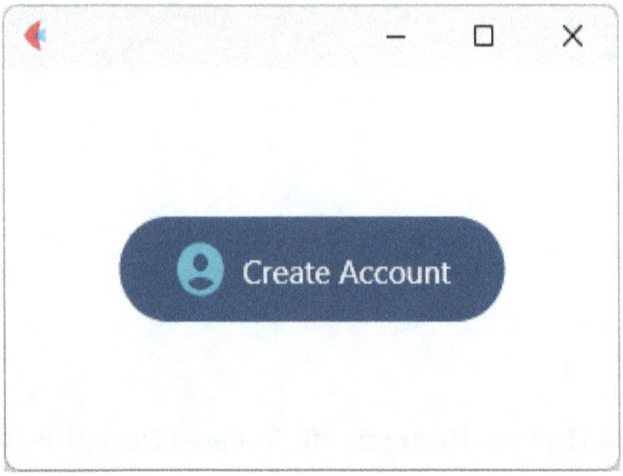

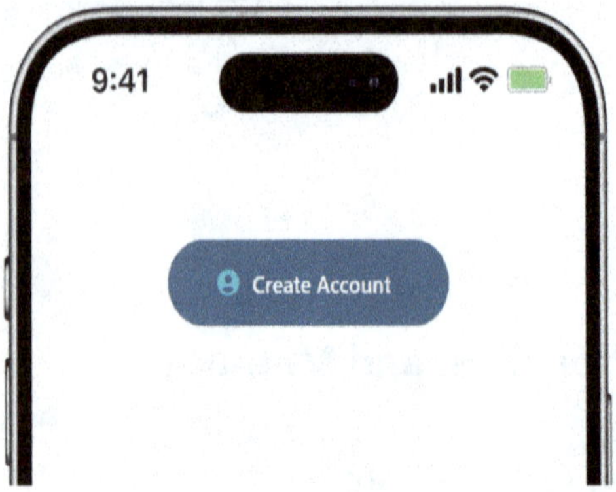

bgcolor = color

Sets the background color of the button. Accepts color names, hex codes or ColorValue.

color = color

Specifies the foreground color of the button, applied to text, icon or other content.

```
Python

import flet as ft

def main(page: ft.Page):

    button = ft.FilledButton(
        content ="Sign Up",
        color="#f7bb0e",
        bgcolor="#29282c",
    )

    page.add(button)

ft.run(main)
```

disabled = bool

Disables the button when True, preventing user interaction.

data = Any(string, number, list, tuple, dictionary, set, bytes)

User-defined custom data storage.

Python

```python
import flet as ft

def main(page: ft.Page):

    button = ft.FilledButton(
        data="order",
        bgcolor="#114155",
        content=ft.Column(
            controls=[
                ft.Image("dinner.png", width=70, height=70),
                ft.Text("Order Now", size=20,
                        weight = ft.FontWeight.BOLD, color="orange"),
            ],
            alignment=ft.MainAxisAlignment.CENTER,
            horizontal_alignment=ft.CrossAxisAlignment.CENTER,
        ),
        width=300, height=130,
    )


    page.add(button)

ft.run(main)
```

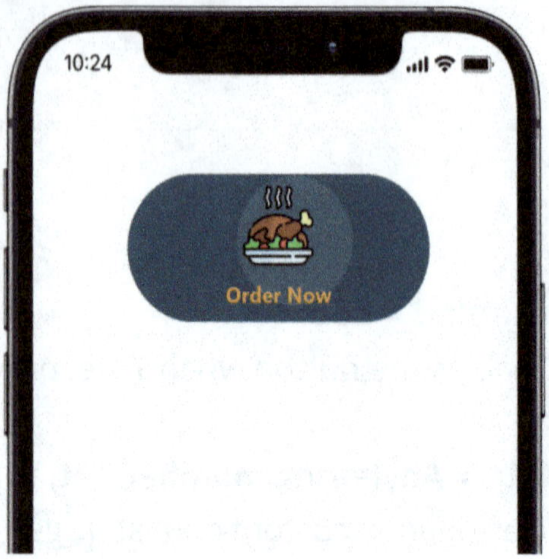

elevation = number

Raises the button to a specific level, creating a shadow effect.

```python
import flet as ft

def main(page: ft.Page):

    button = ft.FilledButton(
        elevation= 10,
        content="Shop like a Boss",
        icon=ft.Icons.SHOPIFY_OUTLINED,
        bgcolor="#1DA1F2",
        color="white",
        width=250, height=50,
    )


    page.add(button)

ft.run(main)
```

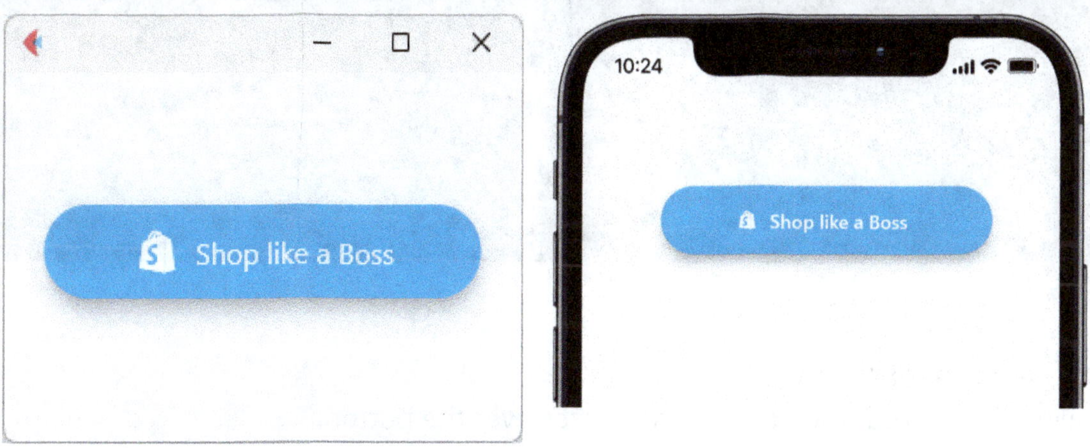

on_focus = callback

Callback triggered when the button gains focus.

on_blur = callback

Callback triggered when the button loses focus.

on_click = callback

Callback triggered when the button is clicked, pressed or tapped.

```python
import flet as ft

def main(page: ft.Page):

    def isClick(e):
        #Actual Code goes here ..
        print("Button is clicked")

    def isFocus(e):
        #Actual Code goes here ..
        print("Button has gained focus")

    def isBlur(e):
        #Actual Code goes here ..
        print("Button is has lost focus")

    button = ft.FilledButton(
        on_click= isClick,
        on_focus= isFocus,
        on_blur= isBlur,
        #Code continues below ...
    )

    page.add(button)

ft.run(main)
```

on_hover = callback

Callback triggered when the mouse passes over the button.

on_long_press = callback

Callback triggered when the button is pressed for a long duration.

style = flet.ButtonStyle

Uses the ButtonStyle control to define the appearance, including colors, padding, shape, elevation and alignment.

Insight

The properties of ButtonStyle were fully explained earlier under **TextButton**. (*Table 3.30*). Please refer to that section for a detailed description of its properties and usage.

```python
import flet as ft

def main(page: ft.Page):

    button = ft.FilledButton(
        content="Upload",
        icon=ft.Icons.CLOUD_UPLOAD,

        style = ft.ButtonStyle(
           icon_size=30,
           color="white",
           elevation=10,
           padding= ft.Padding.symmetric(horizontal=25, vertical=15),
           alignment=ft.Alignment.CENTER,
           bgcolor="#075056",
           text_style=ft.TextStyle(size=16,),
           shape= ft.RoundedRectangleBorder(radius=5),
        ),
    )

    page.add(button)

ft.run(=main)
```

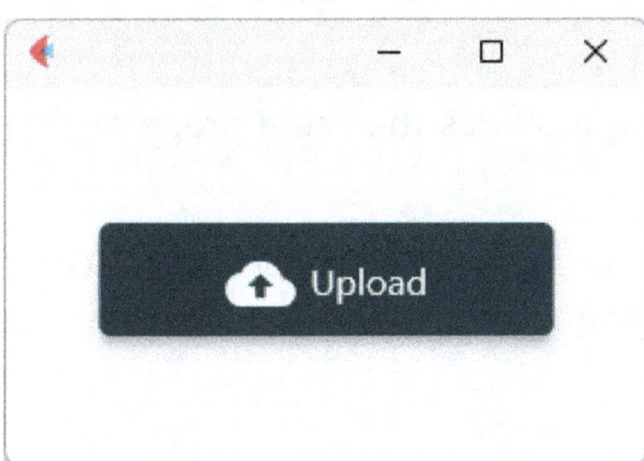

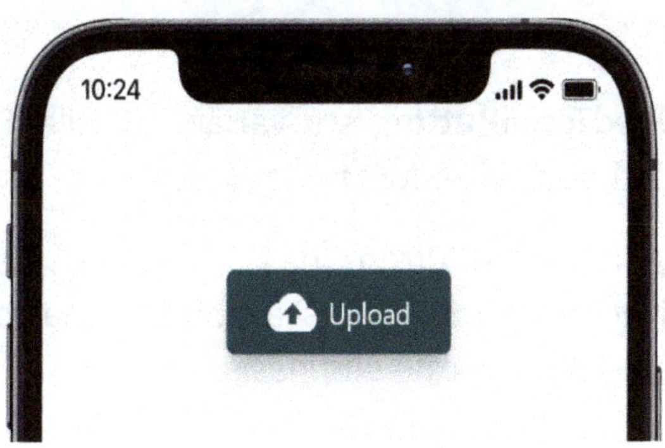

url = string

Opens a web URL in the browser when the button is clicked.

```python
import flet as ft

def main(page: ft.Page):

    button = ft.FilledButton(
        url="https://www.google.com/",
        opacity= 0.3,
        #Code continues below ...
    )

    page.add(button)


ft.run(main)
```

visible = bool

Controls the button's visibility; set False to hide it.

FilledButton Variants

FilledTonalButton is a variant of FilledButton. It shares the same properties and methods but differs in visual style.

While FilledButton has a strong, solid background for primary actions, FilledTonalButton uses a softer, tonal background and is suited for actions that require moderate emphasis.

ElevatedButton

The **ElevatedButton** is a Material Design button that appears raised above the surface due to its shadow effect. This shadow, grey by default, gives the button a sense of depth and makes it visually prominent. The button can contain any child control such as text, icon or complex layouts. It is commonly used for primary actions in an application interface.

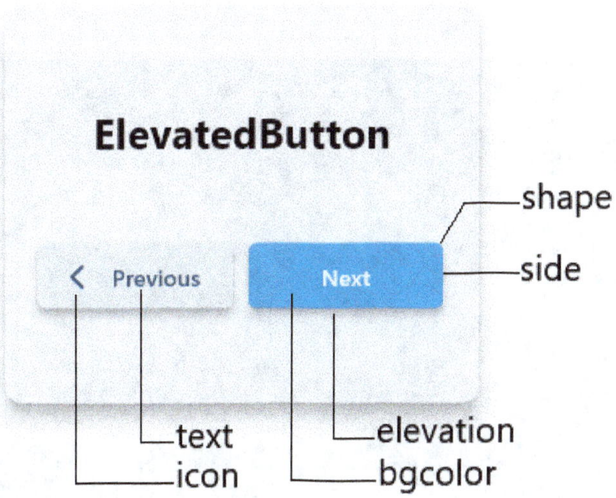

Properties and Methods

adaptive = bool
When True, applies platform-specific Material Design automatically.

autofocus = bool
Automatically focuses the button when set to True.

color = color
Specifies the color of text and icon in the button.

bgcolor = color

Specifies the background color of the button. Accepts color names, hex codes or predefined ColorValues.

content = string/control

Defines textual content of the button. It can also be an icon or any other Flet control.

icon = icons / control, icon_color = color

Sets an icon for the button and its color.

```python
import flet as ft

def main(page: ft.Page):

    button = ft.ElevatedButton(
         content="Subscribe",
         icon= ft.Icons.NOTIFICATIONS_ACTIVE_OUTLINED,
         bgcolor="orange",
         color="white",
    )

    page.add(button)


ft.run(main)
```

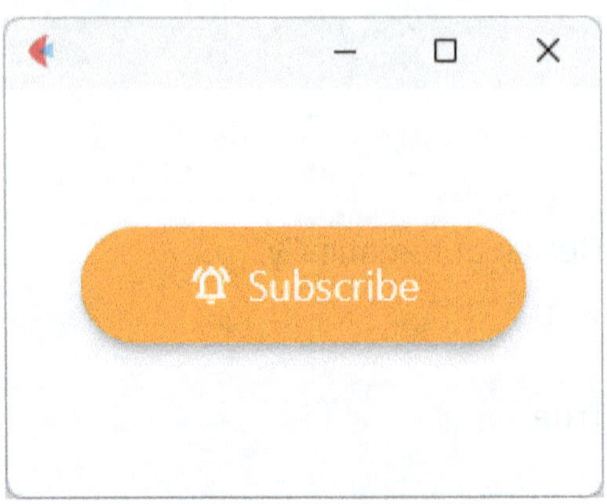

opacity = number

Sets transparency, from 0.0 (fully invisible) to 1.0 (fully opaque).

height / width = number

Specifies the dimensions of the button.

elevation = number

Controls the level of raised effect. Higher values increase the shadow's height and depth.

Python

```
import flet as ft

def main(page: ft.Page):

    button = ft.ElevatedButton(
        content="Settings",
        icon= ft.Icons.SETTINGS,
        bgcolor="#1DA1F2",
        elevation=5,
    )

    page.add(button)

ft.run(main)
```

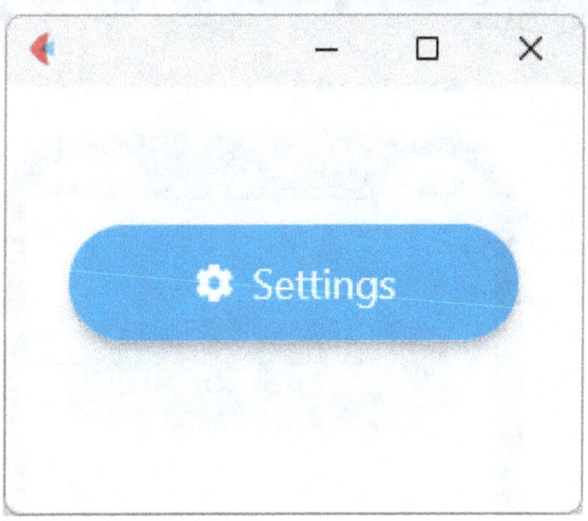

elevation = 5

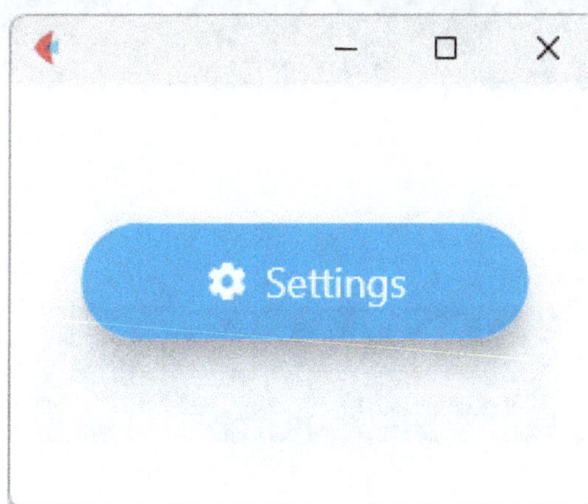

elevation = 15

clip_behavior = flet.ClipBehavior

Determines how the button's content is clipped when overflowing the bounds.

data = Any(string, number, list, tuple, dictionary, set, bytes)
Custom user-defined data storage.

Python

```python
import flet as ft

def main(page: ft.Page):

    button = ft.ElevatedButton(
        clip_behavior= ft.ClipBehavior.ANTI_ALIAS,
        data = "pizza", bgcolor="#0E121A",
        elevation=20,
        content=ft.Row(
            controls=[
                ft.Image("pizza-slice.png", width=70, height=70),
                ft.Text("Try this new taste", size=20, weight =
                        ft.FontWeight.BOLD, color="#E4EEF0"
                      ),
            ],
            alignment=ft.MainAxisAlignment.CENTER,
            vertical_alignment=ft.CrossAxisAlignment.CENTER,
        ),
        width=300, height=70,
    )

    page.add(button)

ft.run(main)
```

disabled = bool
Disables the button when True, preventing any user interaction.

on_click = callback
Callback triggered when the button is clicked, pressed or tapped.

on_hover = callback
Callback triggered when the mouse passes over the button.

```python
import flet as ft

def main(page: ft.Page):

    def myfunction(e):
        #Actual code goes here ...
        print("Button Clicked")


    button = ft.ElevatedButton(
        on_click= myfunction,
        on_long_press=lambda _:print("Button has been pressed long"),
        #Code continues below ...
    )

    page.add(button)

ft.run(main)
```

on_animation_end = callback
Callback executed when an animation ends.

on_focus = callback
Callback triggered when the button gains focus.

on_blur = callback
Callback triggered when the button loses focus.

on_long_press = callback

Callback triggered when the button is pressed for a long duration.

style = flet.ButtonStyle

Uses the ButtonStyle control to format the button's appearance and behavior, including:

Insight

The properties of ButtonStyle were fully explained earlier under **TextButton**. Please refer to that section for a detailed description of its properties and usage.

Python

```
import flet as ft

def main(page: ft.Page):

    button = ft.ElevatedButton(
        content="Create Project",
        icon= ft.Icons.ROCKET_LAUNCH_OUTLINED,
        elevation=10,

        style = ft.ButtonStyle(
          icon_size=20,
          text_style=ft.TextStyle(size=18,),
          shape = ft.RoundedRectangleBorder(
             radius= ft.BorderRadius.only(
                  top_left=10, top_right=0,
                  bottom_left=0, bottom_right=10,
             )
            ),

        ),
        width=200, height=50,
    )

    page.add(button)

ft.run(main)
```

tooltip = string

Text displayed when the button gains focus or is hovered.

update()

Dynamically updates the button's properties or content.

url = string

Specifies a web URL to open when the button is clicked.

Python

```
import flet as ft

def main(page: ft.Page):

    button = ft.ElevatedButton(
        url="https://www.google.com/",
        #Code continues below ...
    )

    page.add(button)

ft.run(main)
```

SegmentedButton

The **SegmentedButton** is a Material Design button control that appears as a **tray of multiple buttons**, segmented by vertical or horizontal borders. Each segment represents an individual button with its own **icon and label**, where the icon can change dynamically when selected. SegmentedButtons are ideal for allowing users to choose between related options in a compact, visually organized manner.

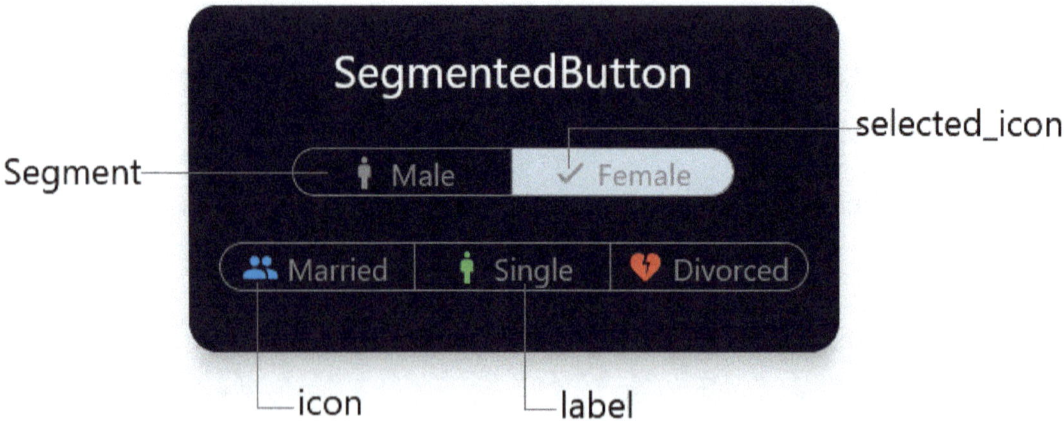

Properties and Methods

segments = **[flet.Segment]**

Defines a list of **Segment** controls. Each segment can have:

- **value** → a string representing the segment's unique value.
- **label** → a control, often Text, displaying the segment name.
- **icon** → an icon associated with the segment.

selected = **[value]**

A list of segment values that are selected by default.

Python

```python
import flet as ft

def main(page: ft.Page):

    button = ft.SegmentedButton(

        segments= [
            ft.Segment(
                value="male",
                icon=ft.Icon(ft.Icons.MAN),
                label=ft.Text("Male")
            ),
            ft.Segment(
                value="female",
                icon=ft.Icon(ft.Icons.WOMAN),
                label=ft.Text("Female")
            ),

        ],

        selected= ["female"],
    )

    page.add(button)


ft.run(main)
```

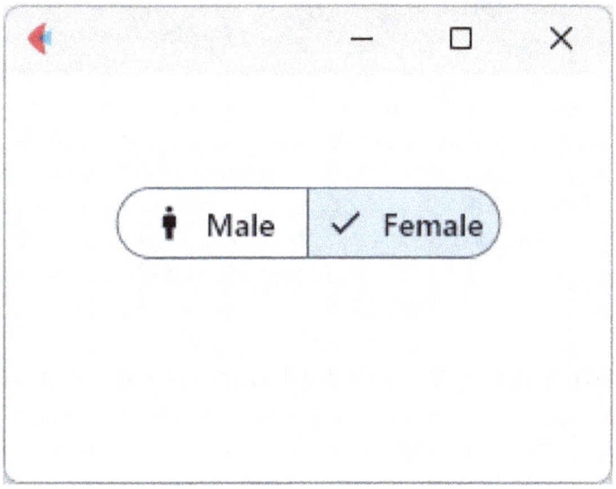

allow_empty_selection = bool

When set to True, the SegmentedButton allows all segments to remain unselected. When it is False and **selected** property is empty, an error is likely to occur.

```python
import flet as ft

def main(page: ft.Page):

    button = ft.SegmentedButton(

        allow_empty_selection= True,
        selected=['male'],
        #Code continues below ...
    )

    page.add(button)

ft.run(main)
```

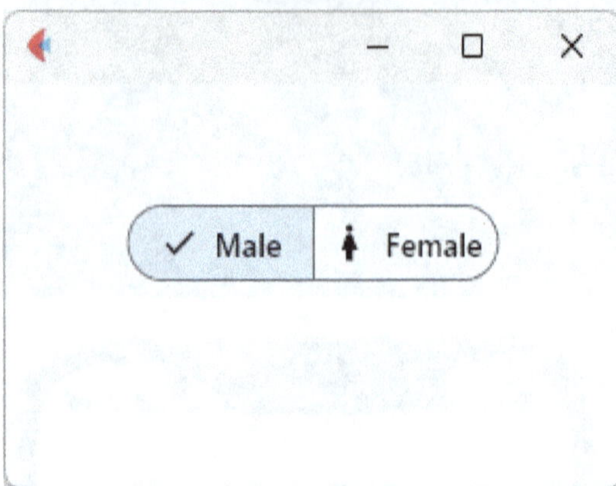

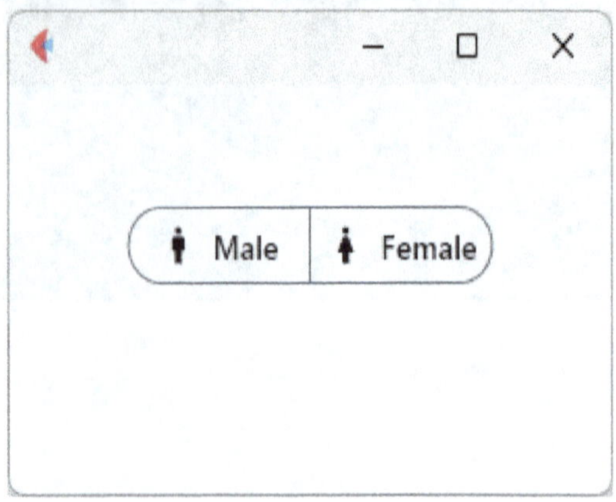

disabled = bool

Disables the entire SegmentedButton control when True, preventing user interaction.

allow_multiple_selection = bool

When True, more than one segment can be selected at the same time.

```python
import flet as ft
```

```
def main(page: ft.Page):

    button = ft.SegmentedButton(

        allow_multiple_selection= True,
        selected=['male'],
        #Code continues below ...
     )

    page.add(button)


ft.run(main)
```

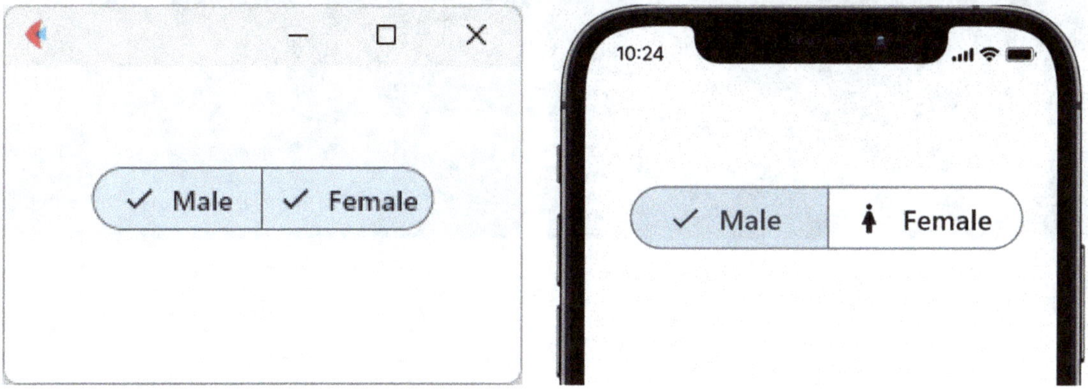

opacity = number

Applies transparency to the SegmentedButton; value ranges from 0.0 (invisible) to 1.0 (fully opaque).

tooltip = string

Text displayed when the SegmentedButton gains focus or is hovered.

show_selected_icon = bool

Determines whether the selected_icon is displayed. Defaults to True; set to False to hide the icon on selection.

selected_icon = icon

Defines an icon to display for all segments when selected.

```python
import flet as ft

def main(page: ft.Page):

    button = ft.SegmentedButton(
        selected_icon= ft.Icons.CANCEL_OUTLINED,
        segments=[
            ft.Segment(label="Gamming", value="gamming"),
            ft.Segment(label="Robotics", value="robotics"),
            ft.Segment(label="Reading", value="reading"),
            ],
        allow_empty_selection=True,
        allow_multiple_selection=True,
         #Code continues below ...
         )

    page.add(button)

ft.run(main)
```

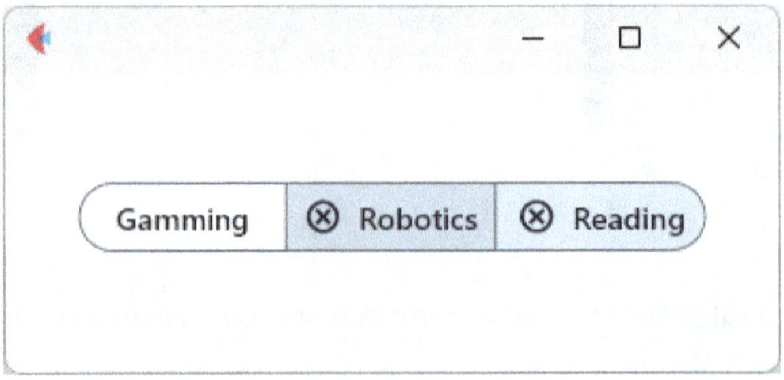

direction = **flet.Axis**

Specifies the layout direction of the segmented buttons. Default is **HORIZONTAL**. Options include HORIZONTAL and VERTICAL.

```python
import flet as ft

def main(page: ft.Page):
```

```
    button = ft.SegmentedButton(
        direction= ft.Axis.VERTICAL,
        #Code continues below ...
        )

    page.add(button)

ft.run(main)
```

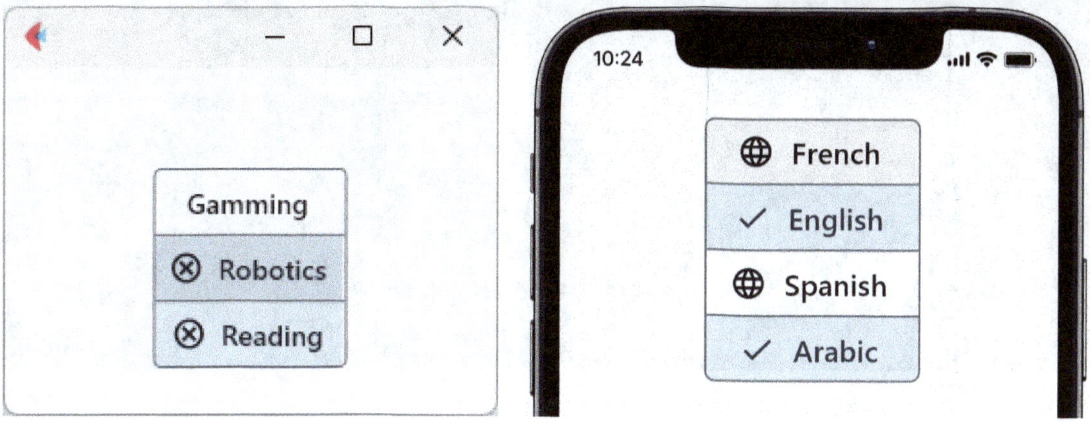

on_change = callback

Triggered whenever the user selects or deselects a segment.

```
Python

import flet as ft

def main(page: ft.Page):

    def onSelected(e):
        #Actual logic goes here ...
        print(e.data)


    button = ft.SegmentedButton(
        on_change = onSelected,

        segments= [
            ft.Segment(
                value="married",
                icon = ft.Icon(ft.Icons.GROUP),
                label=ft.Text("Married")
```

```
            ),
            ft.Segment(
                value="single",
                icon = ft.Icon(ft.Icons.MAN_3),
                label=ft.Text("Single")
            ),
            ft.Segment(
                value="divorced",
                icon = ft.Icon(ft.Icons.HEART_BROKEN),
                label=ft.Text("Divorced")
            ),

        ],
        allow_multiple_selection=True,
        selected=['single'],
        )

    page.add(button)


ft.run(main)
```

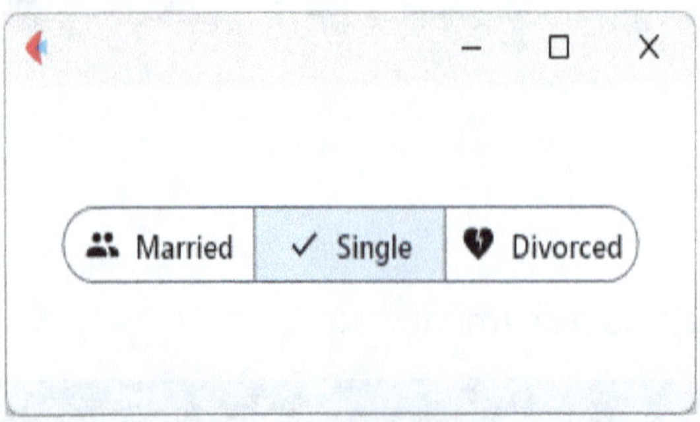

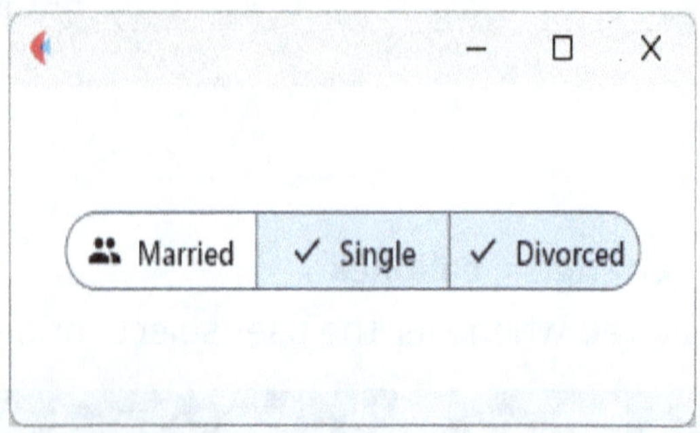


```
#Output
["single"]
["single","divorced"]
```

style = flet.ButtonStyle

Uses the ButtonStyle control to style or decorate the SegmentedButton, including colors, padding and shapes.

Insight

Refer to the sections on **TextButton** *(Table 3.30),* in the preceding chapters for a detailed discussion of **ButtonStyle**.

padding = number, flet.Padding

Space between the button content (label and icon) and button edges. The flet.Padding methods include:

- flet.Padding.all(number)
- flet.padding.only(left, right, top, bottom)
- flet.Padding.symmetry(horizontal, vertical)

Chip

The **Chip** is a Material Design **OutlinedButton**-like control used to represent compact elements such as tags, categories or actions. Chips can display text, optional icons or avatars and can often be deleted by the user. By default, Chips appear with a grey background and outlined border, but their appearance can be customized through various properties.
Chips are commonly used in applications to display clusters of options that users can interact with, select or remove from the interface.

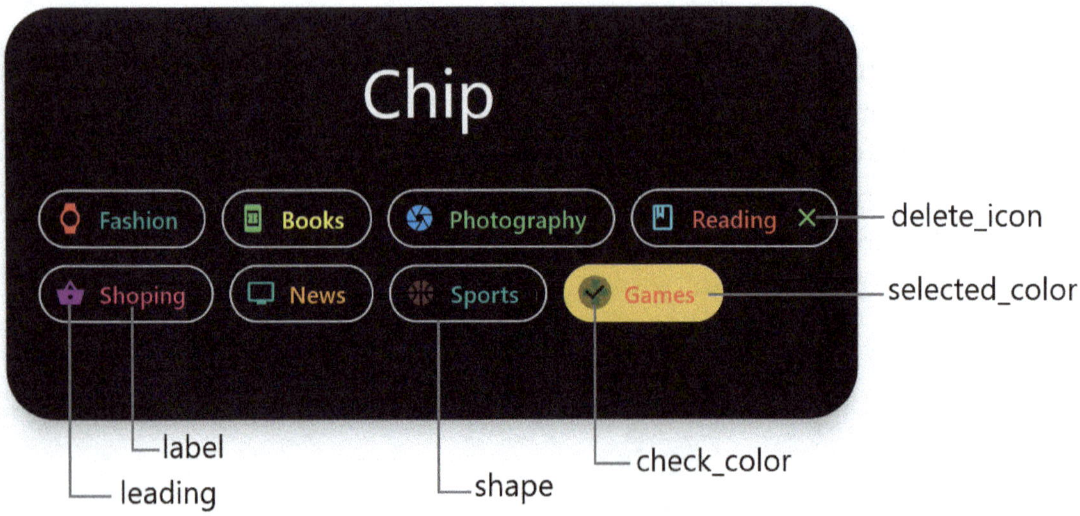

Properties and Methods

bgcolor = color
Specifies the background color of the Chip. Accepts color names, hex codes, RGB values or ColorValue.

color = color
Specifies the color of the Chip's text content.

leading = control
Properties for optional leading content (icon or avatar)
label / label_padding / label_style = control/ flet.Padding/ flet.TextStyle

Defines the Chip's main content:

- label → The text or child control displayed
- label_padding → Adds padding inside the Chip around the label
- label_style → Uses TextStyle control to format the label

on_select = callback

A callback fired when the Chip is selected.

on_delete = callback

A callback fired when the Chip is deleted.

Python

```python
import flet as ft

category = []

async def main(page: ft.Page):

    def onSelected(e):
        #Actual logic goes here ...
        if e.control.selected:
            category.append(e.control.label)
        else:
            category.remove(e.control.label)
        print(category)


    def onDeleted(e):
        page.remove(e.control)
        page.update()

    fashion = ft.Chip(
        leading= ft.Icon(ft.Icons.WATCH),
        label= "Fashion",
        color=ft.Colors.SURFACE,
        label_text_style= ft.TextStyle(color="black", size=16),
        on_select= onSelected,
        on_delete= onDeleted,
        scale= 1.5
    )

    photograohy = ft.Chip(
        leading= ft.Icon(ft.Icons.PHOTO_CAMERA),
        label= "Photography",
        color= ft.Colors.SURFACE,
```

```
        label_text_style= ft.TextStyle(color="black", size=16),
        on_select= onSelected,
        on_delete= onDeleted,
        scale= 1.5
    )

    page.add(fashion, ft.Container(height=20), photograohy)

ft.run(main)
```

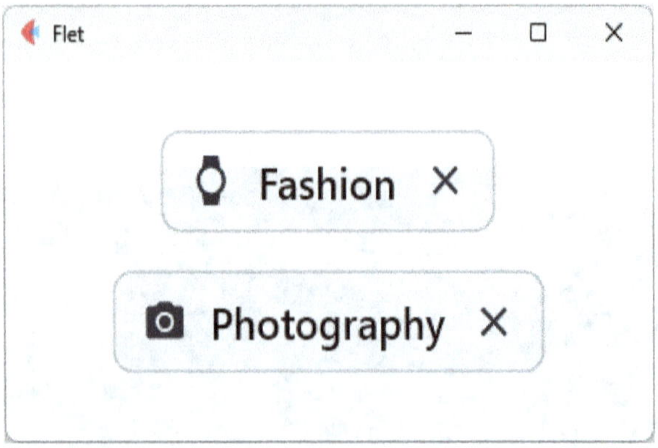

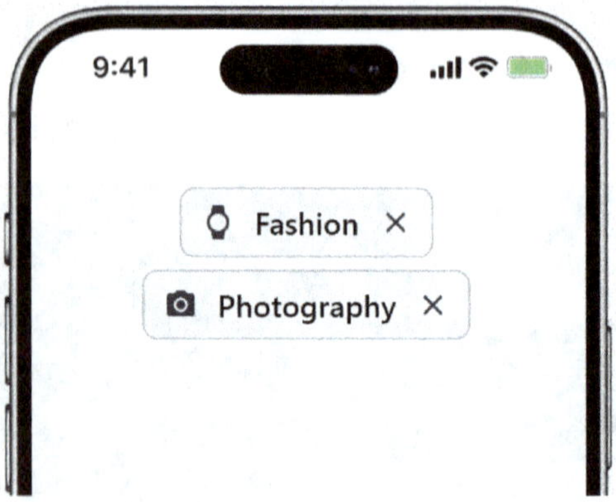

selected = bool

Programmatically selects the Chip when set True

selected_color = color

Defines the background color when the Chip is selected.

check_color = color

Specifies the color of the checkmark when show_checkmark is True.

delete_icon / delete_icon_color = icon / color

- delete_icon sets the icon to represent the delete control
- delete_icon_color sets color for the delete_icon

delete_icon_size_constraints = flet.BoxConstraints

This sets the size constraints for the delete icon using the BoxConstraints(max_height, max_widht, min_height, min_width).

delete_icon_tooltip = text

This sets the text to be displayed on hover.

disabled / disabled_color = bool / color

Disables the Chip when True, optionally setting a color for the disabled state.

enable_animation_style = flet.AnimationStyle

Enables or disables Chip animations for interactions.

delete_drawer_animation_style = flet.AnimationStyle

Defines the animation applied when the Chip is deleted.

leading_drawer_animation_style = flet.AnimationStyle

Defines the Animation style for the leading control (drawer)

padding = flet.Padding

Adds padding between the Chip's child content and its border.

Python

```python
import flet as ft


async def main(page: ft.Page):

    def onSelected(e):
        #Actual logic goes here ...
        pass

    def onDeleted(e):
        #Actual logic goes here ...
        pass


    chip = ft.Chip(
        check_color= "white",
        select_animation_style= ft.AnimationStyle(
            duration= ft.Duration(seconds=5)
         ),
        delete_drawer_animation_style= ft.AnimationStyle(
             curve=ft.AnimationCurve.BOUNCE_IN
        ),
        delete_icon= ft.Icon(ft.CupertinoIcons.DELETE),
        delete_icon_tooltip="remove category",
        delete_icon_size_constraints= ft.BoxConstraints(
```

```
            max_height=20, max_width=20
        ),
        leading= ft.Icon(ft.Icons.SPORTS_BASKETBALL, color='brown'),
        label= "Sports",
        color= ft.Colors.TEAL,
        label_text_style= ft.TextStyle(color="black", size=16),
        padding= ft.Padding.symmetric(horizontal= 20, vertical=10),
        on_select= onSelected,
        on_delete= onDeleted,
    )

    page.add(chip)

ft.run(main)
```

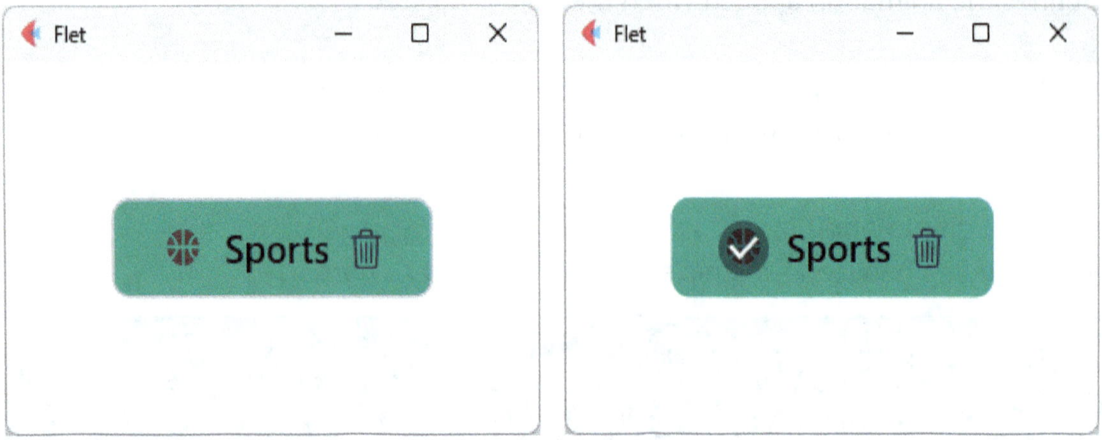

click_elevation = number

Defines the raised effect applied to the Chip when clicked, pressed or tapped.

elevation = number

Specifies the raised level of the Chip for visual depth.

clip_behavior = flet.ClipBehavior

Determines how the Chip's content is clipped when overflowing its bounds.

border_side = flet.BorderSide(color, width)

Uses BorderSide control to style the outline border. Includes:

- color – Sets the border color

- width – Sets the border thickness

shape = shape

Defines the Chip's shape, typically rectangular with rounded corners or fully circular.

shadow_color = color

Sets the shadow color of the Chip.

show_checkmark = bool

Displays a checkmark on the Chip when True.

```python
import flet as ft

async def main(page: ft.Page):

    sports = ft.Chip(
        leading= ft.Icon(ft.Icons.PHOTO_CAMERA),
        label= "Sports",
        shape= ft.RoundedRectangleBorder(radius=10),
        border_side= ft.BorderSide(width=2, color="green"),
        color=ft.Colors.SURFACE,
        #Code continues below ...
    )

    shopping = ft.Chip(
        leading= ft.Icon(ft.Icons.SHOPPING_BAG, color='brown'),
        label= "Shopping",
        shape= ft.RoundedRectangleBorder(radius=20),
        border_side= ft.BorderSide(width=2, color="read"),
        #Code continues below ...
    )

    fashion = ft.Chip(
        check_color= "white",
        leading= ft.Icon(ft.Icons.WATCH, color='brown'),
        label= "Fashion",
        color= ft.Colors.SURFACE,
        shape= ft.RoundedRectangleBorder(radius=ft.BorderRadius(
            top_left=0, top_right=10, bottom_left=10, bottom_right=0
        )),
        border_side= ft.BorderSide(width=2, color="green"),
        #Code continues below ...
        )
```

```
    row = ft.Row(controls=[sports, fashion, shopping])
    page.add(row)

ft.run(main)
```

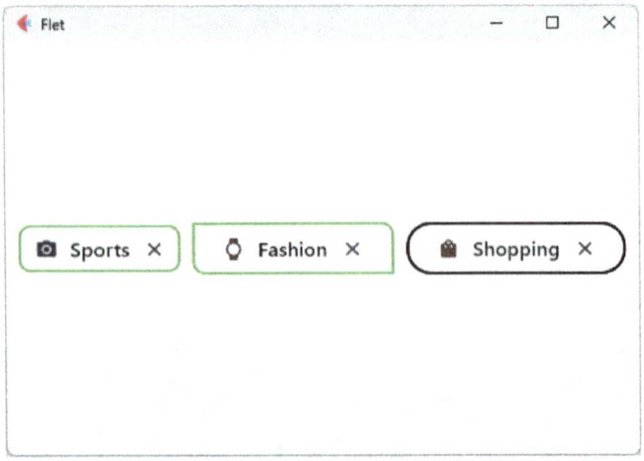

on_blur / on_click / on_focus = callback

Event callbacks for animations, focus changes, clicks/taps, deletion and selection.

selected_shadow_color = color

Defines the shadow colors of the selected Chip.

visual_density = flet.VisualDensity

Controls the spacing and sizing density of the Chip content. VisualDensity options are

- STANDARD
- COMFORTABLE
- COMPACT
- ADAPTIVE_PLATFORM_DENSITY

Button

The **Button** is a versatile Material Design control in Flet that combines the properties of all other button types (TextButton, IconButton, OutlinedButton, ElevatedButton, FilledButton, SegmentedButton, etc.). It is highly customizable and allows developers to create buttons that meet specific design and functional requirements. A Button can contain text, icons or any other control as its content.

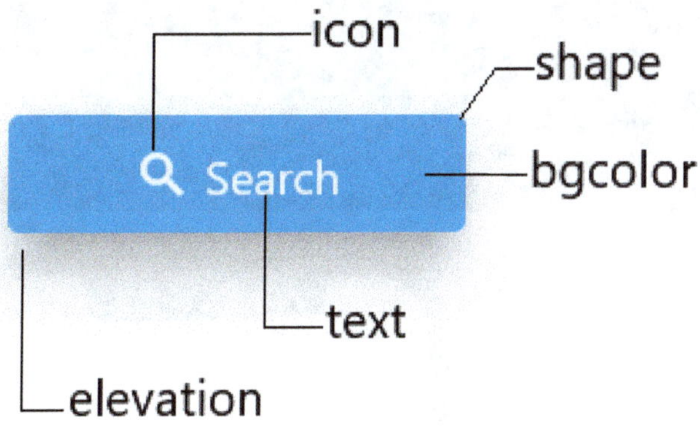

Note

This **Button** control essentially unifies all other button types into one customizable component, giving developers maximum flexibility for building interactive UIs.

Properties and Methods

content = string / control

Sets the text content of the button. The content can also be any other control.

icon = icon

Specifies an icon to be displayed on the button. Can be combined with text or other controls.

```python
import flet as ft

def main(page: ft.Page):

    button=ft.Button(
        content = "TikTok",
        icon= ft.Icons.TIKTOK,
        width= 250,
        height=  60,
    )

    page.add(button)

ft.run(main)
```

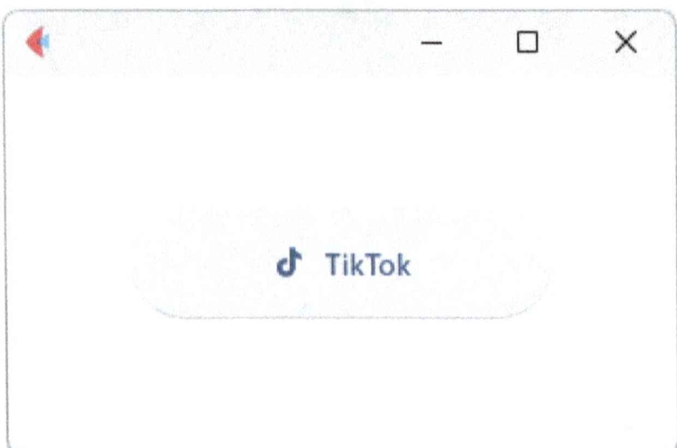

icon_color = color

Defines the color of the icon. Accepts color names, hex codes or predefined ColorValue.

color = color

Sets the foreground color of the button, including text or icon color.

bgcolor = color

Defines the background color of the button. Accepts color names, hex codes or ColorValue.

```python
import flet as ft

def main(page: ft.Page):

    button=ft.Button(
        bgcolor="#0E121A",
        color="white",
        icon_color="yellow",
        content = "TikTok",
        icon= ft.Icons.TIKTOK,
        #Code continues below ...
    )
    page.add(button)

ft.run(main)
```

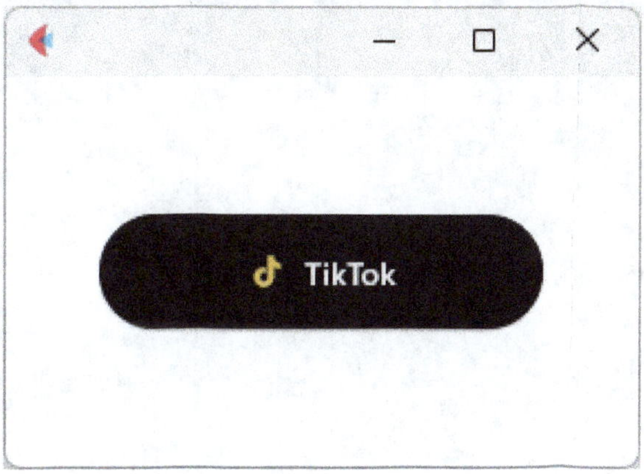

opacity = number
Applies transparency to the Button; value ranges from 0.0 (invisible) to 1.0 (fully opaque).

tooltip = string
Text displayed when the Button gains focus or is hovered.

clip_behavior = flet.ClipBehavior

Specifies how content outside the button bounds is clipped. Options include none, hard_edge, anti_alias, etc.

```python
import flet as ft

def main(page: ft.Page):

    button=ft.Button(
        clip_behavior= ft.ClipBehavior.HARD_EDGE,
        content=ft.Row(
            alignment=ft.MainAxisAlignment.CENTER,
            vertical_alignment=ft.CrossAxisAlignment.CENTER,
            controls=[
                ft.Image("dashboard.png", width=50, height=50),
                ft.Container(width=5),
                ft.Text("Data Analyzer", size=18)
            ]
        ),
        width= 250,height=  60,
        bgcolor="#0E121A",
        color="white",
    )

    page.add(button)

ft.run(main)
```

elevation = number

Applies a raised effect to the button, giving it a shadow. A higher value increases the shadow depth.

```python
import flet as ft

def main(page: ft.Page):

    button=ft.Button(
       elevation= 10,
       #Code continues below ...
    )
    page.add(button)

ft.run(main)
```

`elevation = 10` `elevation = 20`

style = flet.ButtonStyle

Uses the ButtonStyle control to format the button's appearance, including padding, shape, overlay color, text style, alignment and shadow properties.

> **Insight**
>
> Refer to the sections on **TextButton** *(Table 3.30)* in the preceding chapters for a detailed discussion of **ButtonStyle**.

Python

```python
import flet as ft

def main(page: ft.Page):

    button=ft.Button(
        style=ft.ButtonStyle(
            side=ft.BorderSide(color="#F7C846", width=3),
            shape=ft.RoundedRectangleBorder(
                    radius=ft.BorderRadius(top_left=0, top_right=0,
                        bottom_left=20, bottom_right=20)),

        ),
        #Code continues below ...
    )
    page.add(button)

ft.run(main)
```

autofocus = bool

Enables the button to gain focus automatically when the page loads or when set to True.

url = string

Assigns a web URL to the button. When clicked, the button opens the specified URL in a browser.

```
Python
import flet as ft

def main(page: ft.Page):

    button=ft.Button(
        url="https://www.google.com/",
        #Code continues below ...
    )

    page.add(button)

ft.run(main)
```

on_long_press = callback
Registers a callback function that fires when the button is pressed and held for a long duration.

on_hover = callback
Registers a callback function that executes when the mouse pointer hovers over the button.

on_focus = callback
Registers a callback function that executes when the button gains focus.

on_blur = callback
Registers a callback function that executes when the button loses focus.

on_click = callback
Registers a callback function that fires when the button is clicked or tapped.

```
Python
```

```
import flet as ft

async def main(page: ft.Page):

    def onclickFunction(e):
        #Actual logic goes here ...
        print("button is clicked")

    def onhoverFunction(e):
        #Actual logic goes here ...
        print("button is hovered")

    button=ft.Button(
        on_click = onclickFunction,
        on_hover= onhoverFunction,
        on_long_press=lambda _: print("button has been pressed")
        #Code continues below ...
    )

    page.add(button)


ft.run(main)
```

GestureDetector

The **GestureDetector** is a flexible control in Flet that allows any child control to respond to user interactions such as clicks, taps, hover, drag, long press, scale and multi-touch gestures. Essentially, it enables any control—text, image, container or complex layouts—to behave like a button or interactive element.

A GestureDetector must have a child control (content) and at least one event handler to respond to user actions. This makes it a powerful tool for creating custom interactive behaviors in your application.

Figure 3.6 : An image responding to touches

Insight

The **GestureDetector** uses events to enable any control in Flet to behave like a button, slider, canvas or interactive surface—making gesture handling a core feature of advanced Flet applications.

Properties and Methods

adaptive = bool

When set to True, the GestureDetector adapts its behavior to the platform-specific input methods.

content = control

Specifies the child control. This is the control that will respond to gestures.

Gestures

Tap Gestures

Table 3.31

on_tap	Triggered when the user performs a single tap or click and releases it successfully.
on_tap_down	Fires the moment the user touches the screen or presses a mouse button, before releasing it.
on_tap_up	Triggered when the user releases a tap or click after a successful press.
on_tap_cancel	Fired when a tap gesture is interrupted before completion.
on_tap_move	Triggered when slight movement occurs during a tap.
on_double_tap	Triggered when the user performs two quick consecutive taps or clicks.
on_double_tap_down	Fires when the second tap of a double-tap gesture touches the screen or mouse button is pressed.
on_double_tap_cancel	Triggered when a double-tap gesture is started but not completed.
on_multi_tap	Triggered when multiple fingers tap the screen simultaneously.

Python

```python
import flet as ft

def main(page: ft.Page):

    def tapFunc(e):
        #Your logic goes here ...
        print("single tapped")
```

```
    def doubleTapFunc(e):
        #Your logic goes here ...
        print("twiced tapped")

    gesture = ft.GestureDetector(
        content= ft.Text("Click to read more .."),
        on_tap= tapFunc,
        on_double_tap= doubleTapFunc,
        on_tap_up= lambda _:print("Content has been tap up")
    )


    page.add(gesture)

ft.run(main)
```

Long and Force Press Gestures

Table 3.32

on_long_press	Fired when the user presses and holds for a long period.
on_long_press_start	Triggered when the user presses and holds on a control for a defined duration.
on_long_press_end	Fires when the user releases the control after a long press.
on_long_press_move_update	Fired when the pointer moves during a long press.
on_multi_long_press	Triggered when multiple touch points perform a long press simultaneously (multi-touch).
on_long_press_down	Triggered when the pointer first touches the screen for a long press.
on_long_press_up	Triggered when the user releases after a long press.
on_long_press_cancel	Fired when a long press gesture is started but not completed.
on_force_press_start	Fired when pressure-based touch (force press) begins.
on_force_press_update	Triggered when the pressure level changes during a force press.
on_force_press_end	Triggered when the force press is released.

on_force_press_peak	Fired when maximum pressure is detected during a force press.

Hover and Pointer Entry Events

Table 3.33

on_hover	Triggered when the mouse pointer moves over a control.
on_enter	Fires when the pointer enters the bounds of a control.
on_exit	Triggered when the pointer leaves the bounds of a control.

Python

```
import flet as ft

def main(page: ft.Page):

    def whenHovered(e):
        #Actual logic goes here ...
        print("hovered")

    gesture = ft.GestureDetector(
        content= ft.Container(content=ft.Text('Hello')),
        on_hover = whenHovered,
        on_exit= lambda _:print("Mouse leaves content")
    )

    page.add(gesture)

ft.run(main)
```

Drag Gestures

Table 3.34

on_horizontal_drag_start	Triggered when a horizontal dragging gesture begins.
on_horizontal_drag_update	Fires continuously as the pointer moves horizontally during a drag.
on_horizontal_drag_end	Triggered when the horizontal drag gesture ends.
on_horizontal_drag_down	Fired when a horizontal drag gesture is detected at the moment the pointer touches down.
on_horizontal_drag_cancel	Triggered when a horizontal drag gesture is interrupted or canceled.
on_vertical_drag_start	Triggered when a vertical dragging gesture begins.
on_vertical_drag_update	Fires continuously as the pointer moves vertically during a drag.
on_vertical_drag_end	Triggered when the vertical drag gesture ends.
on_vertical_drag_down	Triggered when a vertical drag begins (pointer touches down).
on_vertical_drag_cancel	Fired when a vertical drag gesture is interrupted or canceled.

Pan (Free-Direction Drag)

Table 3.35

on_pan_start	Triggered when a free-direction drag (pan) gesture begins.
on_pan_update	Fires continuously as the pointer moves in any direction.
on_pan_end	Triggered when the pan gesture ends.
on_pan_down	Triggered when a pan gesture starts (finger touches down).
on_pan_cancel	Fired when a pan gesture is interrupted or canceled.
on_right_pan_start	Triggered when a rightward pan gesture begins.
on_right_pan_update	Fired while the pointer moves to the right during a pan.
on_right_pan_end	Triggered when the rightward pan gesture ends.

Scale and Pinch Gestures (Multi-Touch)

Table 3.36

on_scale_start	Triggered when a scaling gesture (pinch or zoom) begins.
on_scale_update	Fires continuously as the scale factor or rotation changes.
on_scale_end	Triggered when the scale gesture ends.

Scroll Gesture

Table 3.37

on_scroll	Triggered when the user scrolls using a mouse wheel, trackpad or touch-based scrolling gesture.

Python

```
import flet as ft

def main(page: ft.Page):

    def whenScrolled(e):
        #Actual logic goes here ...
        print("scrolled")

    gesture = ft.GestureDetector(
        content= ft.ListView(controls=[
            ft.Text('text1'),
            ft.Text('text2'),
            ft.Text('text3'),
        ]),
        on_scroll= whenScrolled,
        width= 300, height= 200,
    )

    page.add(gesture)
```

```
ft.run(main)
```

Secondary and Tertiary Button Gestures (Right-Click / Secondary Tap)

Table 3.38

on_secondary_tap	Triggered when the user performs a secondary click or tap (right-click).
on_secondary_tap_down	Fires when the secondary mouse button or touch is pressed.
on_secondary_tap_up	Triggered when the secondary click or tap is released.
on_secondary_tap_cancel	Triggered when a secondary (right-click) tap is started but not completed.
on_secondary_long_press	Fired when the user performs a long press using the secondary button (e.g., right mouse button).
on_secondary_long_press_start	Triggered when the user performs a long press using a secondary input.
on_secondary_long_press_end	Fires when the secondary long press is released.
on _secondary_long_press_up	Triggered when the secondary long press is released.
on_secondary_long_press_down	Triggered when the secondary button is pressed down for a long press.
on_secondary_long_press_cancel	Fired when a secondary long press is interrupted.
on_tertiary_long_press	Fired when a long press is performed using the tertiary button (e.g., middle mouse button).
on_tertiary_long_press_start	Triggered when the tertiary long press begins.
on_tertiary_long_press_end	Triggered when the tertiary long press completes.
on_tertiary_long_press_up	Fired when the tertiary button is released after a long press.
on_tertiary_long_press_cancel	Triggered when a tertiary long press is interrupted.
on_tertiary_tap_down	Fired when the tertiary button is pressed down.

Note

These gesture callbacks allow developers to:

- Detect fine-grained user interactions
- Support touch, mouse and multi-touch input
- Build highly interactive and custom UI experiences

allowed_devices = [flet.PointerDeviceType]

Specifies which input devices can interact with the GestureDetector. Methods of the PointerDeviceType are,

- MOUSE
- TOUCH
- STYLUS
- INVERTED_STYLUS
- TRACKPAD
- UNKNOWN

Python

```python
import flet as ft

def main(page: ft.Page):

    def whenTap(e):
        #Actual logic goes here ...
        print("tap")

    gesture = ft.GestureDetector(
        content= ft.Image(src="education.png"),
        on_tap= whenTap,
        allowed_devices= [
            ft.PointerDeviceType.TOUCH,
            ft.PointerDeviceType.MOUSE,
            ]
    )

    page.add(gesture)

ft.run(main)
```

disabled = bool

If True, disables all gestures and interactions on the control.

drag_interval = int

Specifies sensitivity for drag gestures.

exclude_from_semantics = bool

If True, excludes the control from accessibility tools.

height / width = number

Sets the height and width of the GestureDetector.

hover_interval = int

Sets the time interval for hover-related events.

mouse_cursor = flet.MouseCursor

Defines the type of mouse cursor for interacting with the control, using the MouseCursor control. Options include

ALIAS	GRABBING	RESIZE_DOWN	RESIZE_UP_DOWN
ALL_SCROLL	HELP	RESIZE_DOWN_LEFT	RESIZE_UP_LEFT
BASIC	MOVE	RESIZE_DOWN_RIGHT	RESIZE_UP_LEFT_DOWN_RIGHT
CELL	NO_DROP	RESIZE_LEFT	RESIZE_UP_RIGHT
CLICK	NONE	RESIZE_LEFT_RIGHT	RESIZE_UP_RIGHT_DOWN_LEFT
CONTEXT_MENU	PRECISE	RESIZE_RIGHT	TEXT
COPY	PROGRESS	RESIZE_ROW	VERTICAL_TEXT
DISAPPEARING	RESIZE_COLUMN	RESIZE_UP	WAIT
FORBIDDEN	GRAB	ZOOM_IN	ZOOM_OUT

multi_tap_touches = int

Specifies how many simultaneous taps the GestureDetector should recognize.

trackpad_scroll_causes_scale = bool

If True, trackpad scroll gestures trigger scaling events.

Forms and Input Controls

Many applications are designed to collect user input through forms, configuration panels, search interfaces, surveys and authentication screens. These inputs are commonly used for purposes such as user registration, feedback submission, comments, messaging, email composition, search queries and data entry.

In addition to data collection, user input is often required for application configuration and preference settings, such as theme selection, language choice, notification settings, accessibility options and privacy controls. Input controls also play a critical role in authentication and security, where users provide credentials such as usernames, email addresses, passwords and verification codes.

The Flet framework provides a rich set of controls for collecting and managing user input in a structured and user-friendly manner.

Common Input Controls in Flet

The following are commonly used input controls available in Flet:

TextField	**Checkbox**	**DatePicker**
Dropdown	**Switch**	**TimePicker**
Radio	**Slider**	**SegmentedButton**
Autocomplete	**DropdownM2**	

Form Enhancement and Supporting Controls

In practice, input controls are often combined with supporting controls to improve usability, validation and organization. For example:

- **RadioGroup** is used to group multiple Radio controls and manage single-choice selection.
- **Autocomplete** enhances **TextField** by suggesting values based on user input.

TextField

The **TextField** is a versatile data entry control used for accepting textual input from users. It is an essential control for forms, messages, comments, reports, search fields, login credentials and other user-generated content. Entries are processed by the application for validation, storage or interaction with other controls.

TextFields can be single-line or multi-line, support keyboard input, autofocus, password masking, helper texts, prefix/suffix controls, validation, input filtering, character counting and rich styling.
By default, a TextField provides a user-friendly interface with optional submit buttons, cursor controls and automatic focus and suggestions.

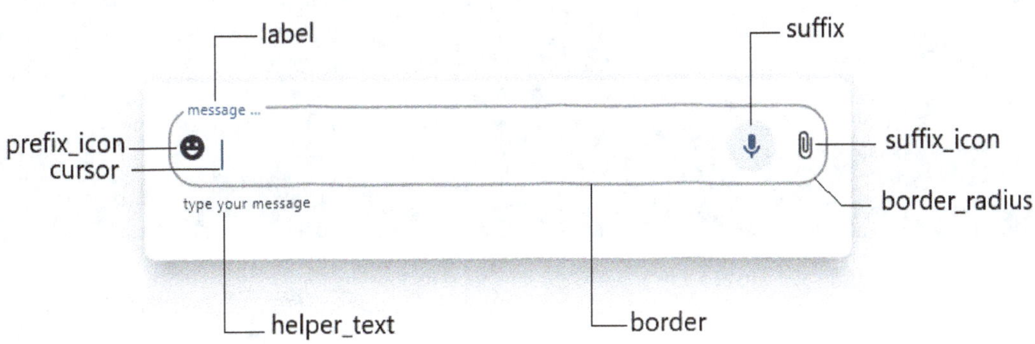

Properties and Methods

Layout, Adaptation and Positioning

adaptive = bool
The adaptive property allows the TextField to automatically adjust its appearance and behavior to match the target platform. When set to True, the control renders Material-style input fields on Android and web and Cupertino-style input fields on iOS.

width = number

Sets or returns the width of the TextField.

height = number

Sets or returns the height of the TextField.

Python

```python
import flet as ft

def main(page: ft.Page):
    page.bgcolor = "white"

    textfield = ft.TextField(
        adaptive= True,
        width= 400,
        height=80,
    )

    page.add(texfield)

ft.run(main)
```

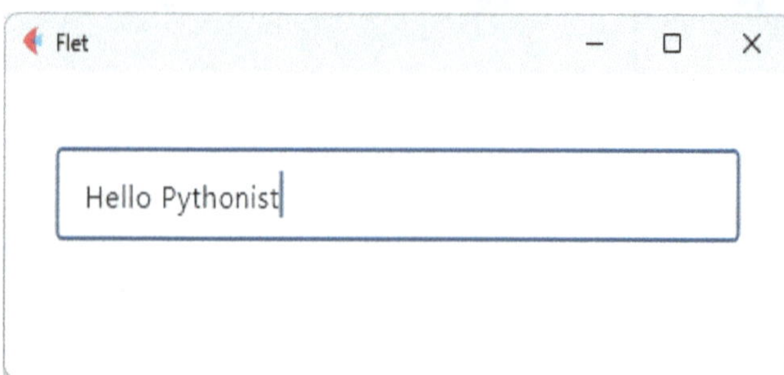

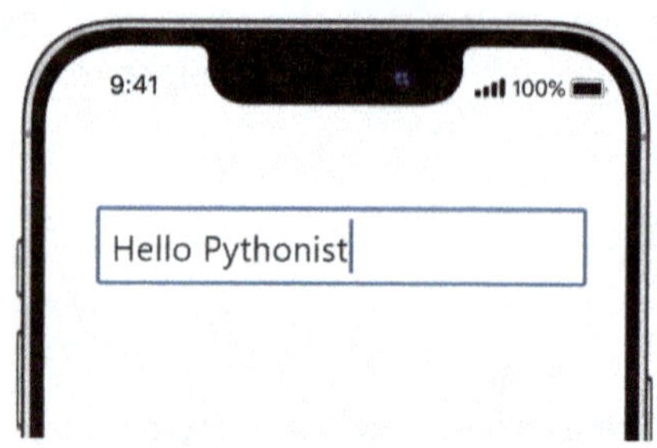

size_constraints = flet.BoxConstraints

Uses BoxConstraints to define minimum and maximum width and height limits. BoxConstraints parameters include:

- min_width
- min_height
- max_width
- max_height

dense = bool

Reduces the vertical padding, making the TextField more compact.

Background, Border and Decoration

filled = bool
When set to True, fills the background of the TextField with a color.

bgcolor = color
The bgcolor sets the background color of the TextField. Colors can be specified using color names, hexadecimal values or predefined ColorValue constants.

fill_color = color
Sets the background color of the TextField. Works similarly to bgcolor.

border = flet.InputBorder
The border implements the InputBorder control to define the boundary style of the TextField.
Available options include:

- OUTLINE (default) → a full rectangular border
- UNDERLINE → only the bottom border is visible
- NONE → no visible border

Python
```
import flet as ft

def main(page: ft.Page):
    page.bgcolor = "white"

    textfield = ft.TextField(
        border=ft.InputBorder.UNDERLINE,
        bgcolor="#eeeeee",
        width= 400,
        height=80,
    )

    page.add(texfield)

ft.run(main)
```

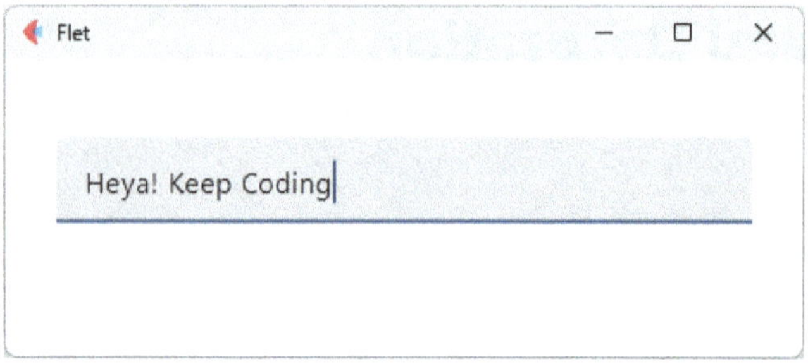

border_width = **number**

Defines the thickness of the TextField's border.

border_color = **color**

Defines the color of the outer border of the TextField.

border_radius = **number, flet.BorderRadius.all, flet.BorderRadius.only**

Defines the curvature of the TextField's border corners.

Python

```
import flet as ft

def main(page: ft.Page):
    page.bgcolor = "white"

    textfield = ft.TextField(
        border_radius= 15,
        border_color="grey",
        border_width = 2,
        #Code continues below ...
    )

    page.add(texfield)

ft.run(main)
```

```
border_radius = 15
```

```
border_radius =
flet.BorderRadius.all(25)
```

```
border_radius = flet.BorderRadius.only(
top_left=10, top_right=10, bottom_left = 0, bottom_right=0)
```

focus()

Programmatically gives focus to the TextField.

focused_bgcolor = color

Defines the background color when the TextField gains focus.

focused_border_color = color

Defines the border color when the TextField is focused.

focused_border_width = number

Defines the thickness of the border when the TextField is focused.

focused_color = **color**

Defines the text color when the TextField is focused.

hover_color = **color**

Sets a temporary background color when the mouse hovers over the TextField.

```python
import flet as ft

def main(page: ft.Page):
    page.bgcolor = "white"

    textfield = ft.TextField(
        focused_color="red",
        focused_border_color="green",
        focused_bgcolor="#eeeeee",
        focused_border_width=3,
        #Code continues below ...
    )

    page.add(texfield)

ft.run(main)
```

unfocussed

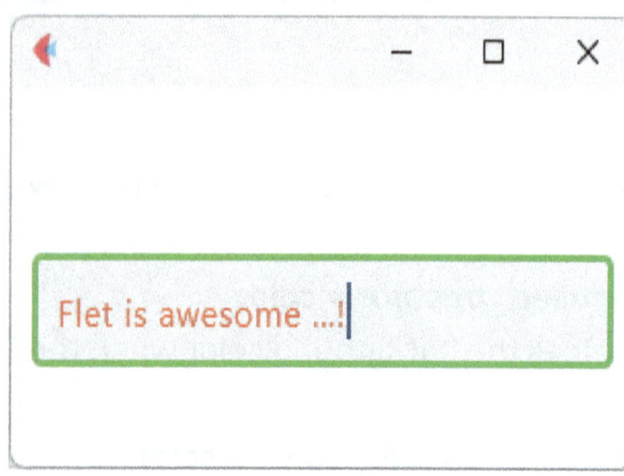

focused

autofocus = bool

The autofocus sets the TextField to gain focus automatically when set to True.

can_request_focus = bool

Determines whether the TextField is allowed to receive focus programmatically or through user interaction.

clip_behavior = flet.ClipBehavior

Defines how content is clipped when it overflows the TextField's boundaries. The ClipBehavior methods typically include:

- NONE
- HARD_EDGE
- ANTI_ALIAS
- ANTI_ALIAS_WITH_SAVE_LAYER

collapsed = bool

When set to True, removes all internal padding, causing the text to occupy the full available space.

fit_parent_size = bool

Forces the TextField to expand and fill the available size of its parent.

Cursor Configuration

show_cursor = bool

Hides the cursor when set to False.

cursor_color = color

Defines the color of the blinking text cursor.

cursor_error_color = color

Defines the cursor color when the TextField is in an error state.

cursor_height = number

Specifies the height of the text cursor.

cursor_radius = number

Defines the curvature of the cursor edges. This is more noticeable when the cursor is thick.

cursor_width = number

Defines the thickness of the text cursor.

Python

```
import flet as ft

def main(page: ft.Page):

    textfield = ft.TextField(
        cursor_color="green",
        cursor_radius=10,
        cursor_width=10,
        cursor_height=25,
        #Code continues below ...
    )

    page.add(texfield)


ft.run(main)
```

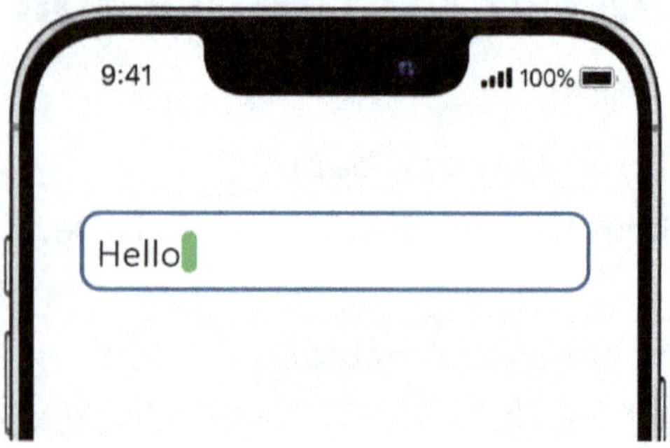

ignore_pointers = bool

Disables pointer interaction when set to True.

Text Input Behavior

disabled = bool
When set to True, the TextField becomes inactive and does not accept input.

max_length = number
Defines the maximum number of characters allowed.

max_lines = number
Specifies the maximum number of visible text lines.

min_lines = number
Specifies the minimum number of visible text lines.

mouse_cursor = flet.MouseCursor
Defines the cursor style when hovering over the TextField. MouseCursor Options include:

ALIAS	GRABBING	RESIZE_DOWN	RESIZE_UP_DOWN
ALL_SCROLL	HELP	RESIZE_DOWN_LEFT	RESIZE_UP_LEFT
BASIC	MOVE	RESIZE_DOWN_RIGHT	RESIZE_UP_LEFT_DOWN_RIGHT
CELL	NO_DROP	RESIZE_LEFT	RESIZE_UP_RIGHT
CLICK	NONE	RESIZE_LEFT_RIGHT	RESIZE_UP_RIGHT_DOWN_LEFT
CONTEXT_MENU	PRECISE	RESIZE_RIGHT	TEXT
COPY	PROGRESS	RESIZE_ROW	VERTICAL_TEXT
DISAPPEARING	RESIZE_COLUMN	RESIZE_UP	WAIT
FORBIDDEN	GRAB	ZOOM_IN	ZOOM_OUT

multiline = bool
When set to True, allows multiple lines of input.

read_only = bool
Prevents editing while still allowing text selection.

tooltip = string

Displays a message when the mouse hovers over the TextField.

value

Represents the text content of the TextField.

```python
import flet as ft

def main(page: ft.Page):

    def getText(e):
        #Actual logic goes here ...
        print(textfield.value) #Get TextField content
        textfield.value = "" #Clear all text
        page.update()

    textfield = ft.TextField(
        multiline= True,
        max_lines=5,
        min_lines=2,
        mouse_cursor= ft.MouseCursor.GRAB,
        #Code continues below ...
    )

    sender = ft.IconButton(
        icon=ft.Icons.SEND,
        bgcolor="blue",
        icon_color="white",
        on_click= getText
    )

    textpad = ft.Row(
        vertical_alignment= ft.CrossAxisAlignment.START,
        controls=[textfield, sender]
    )


    page.add(textpad)


ft.run(main)
```

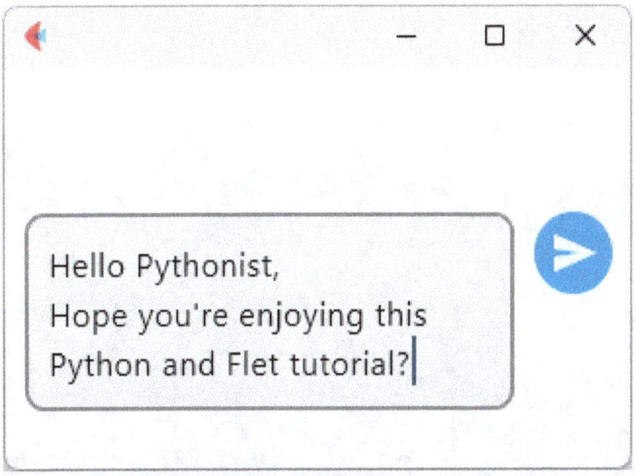

```
#Output
Hello Pythonist,
Hope you're enjoying this Python and Flet tutorial?
```

selection_color = color

Defines the highlight color when text is selected.

Text Appearance and Styling

color = color

Defines the color of the entered text.

content_padding = flet.Padding

Uses the Padding control to define spacing between the text and the TextField's border.

text_align = flet.TextAlign

Aligns text inside the TextField using the TextAlign control. Methods of TextAlign include:

- LEFT
- RIGHT
- JUSTIFY
- CENTER
- START
- END

text_size = number

Defines the size of the entered text.

```python
import flet as ft

def main(page: ft.Page):

    textfield = ft.TextField(
        color= "red",
        text_size= 25,
        text_align= ft.TextAlign.CENTER,
        content_padding= ft.Padding.all(5),
        #Code continues below ...
    )

    page.add(texfield)

ft.run(main)
```

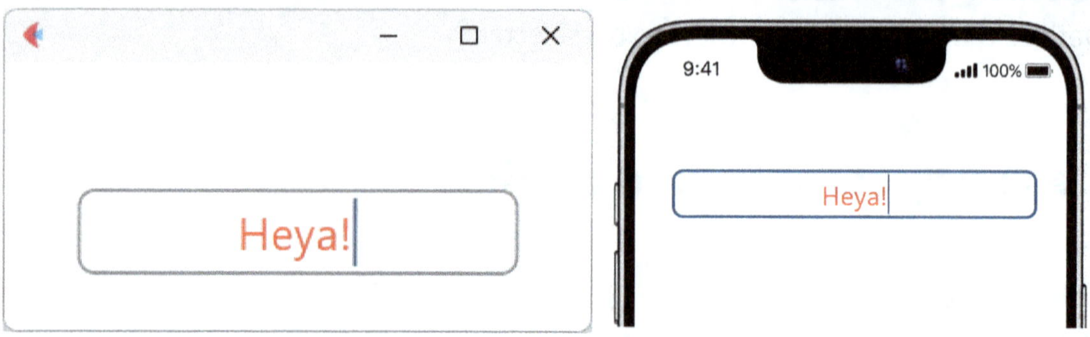

text_style = flet.TextStyle

Uses TextStyle to format the text.

Insight

For a more comprehensive discussion of text styling with **TextStyle**, see the section on the **Text** control in the preceding chapter.

Labels, Hints and Helper Text

label = string
Sets a label for the TextField. The label appears inside the field and floats above when focused.

label_style = flet.TextStyle
Uses TextStyle to format the label.

```python
import flet as ft

def main(page: ft.Page):

    textfield = ft.TextField(
        label="Username",
        label_style= ft.TextStyle(size=15),
        #Code continues below ...
    )

    page.add(texfield)

ft.run(main)
```

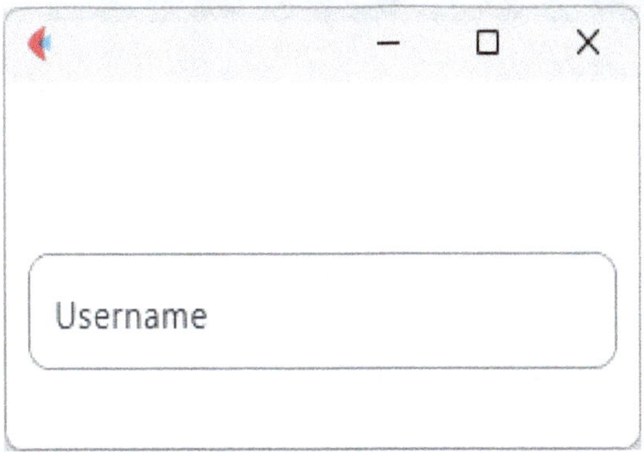

unfocussed

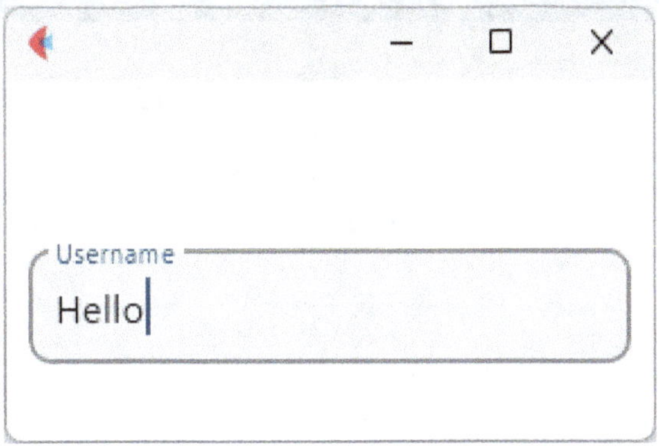

focused

hint_text = string

Displays placeholder text when the TextField is empty.

hint_style = flet.TextStyle

Uses TextStyle to format hint text.

hint_fade_duration = flet.Duration()

Controls the fade animation duration of the hint text.

hint_max_lines = number

Specifies the maximum number of lines for hint text.

```python
import flet as ft

def main(page: ft.Page):

    textfield = ft.TextField(
        hint_text="Type here ...",
        hint_max_lines= 2,
        hint_fade_duration=10,
        #Code continues below ...
    )

    page.add(texfield)

ft.run(main)
```

Before typing

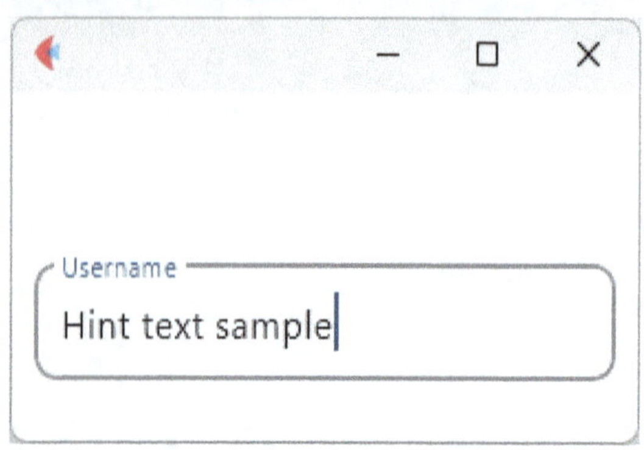

After typing

align_label_with_hint = **bool**

When set to True, this property vertically aligns the label text with the hint text. This is useful for multiline TextFields where the label should remain aligned with the hint content.

helper = **string/control**

Sets a control, usually text, displayed below the TextField to guide the user.

helper_max_lines = **number**

Specifies the maximum number of lines for helper text.

helper_style = **flet.TextStyle**

Uses TextStyle to format helper text.

```python
import flet as ft

def main(page: ft.Page):

    textfield = ft.TextField(
        helper="Username is your email",
        helper_max_lines=1,
        helper_style= ft.TextStyle(color="#00334c", size=15),
        label="Username",
        label_style= ft.TextStyle(size=15),
        #Code continues below ...
    )

    page.add(texfield)

ft.run(main)
```

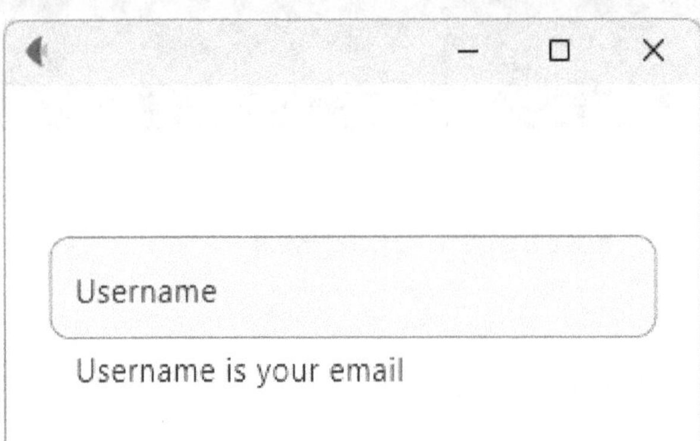

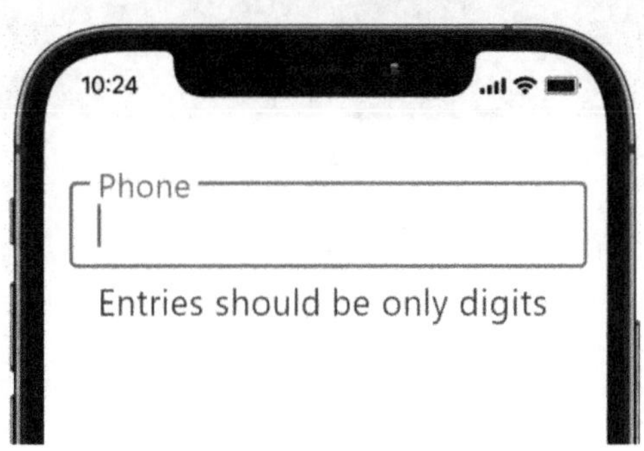

Error Handling and Validation

counter = string/control

Displays a control, usually text, below the TextField that shows the number of characters entered.

counter_style = flet.TextStyle

Uses TextStyle to format the counter text.

```python
import flet as ft

def main(page: ft.Page):

    def changed(e):
        count = len(textfield.value)
        textfield.counter = f"{count}"
        textfield.update()


    textfield = ft.TextField(
        on_change = changed,
        counter= "0",
        counter_style= ft.TextStyle(size=18, color="blue"),
        hint_text="Type anything ...",
        #Code continues below ...
    )

    page.add(texfield)

ft.run(main)
```

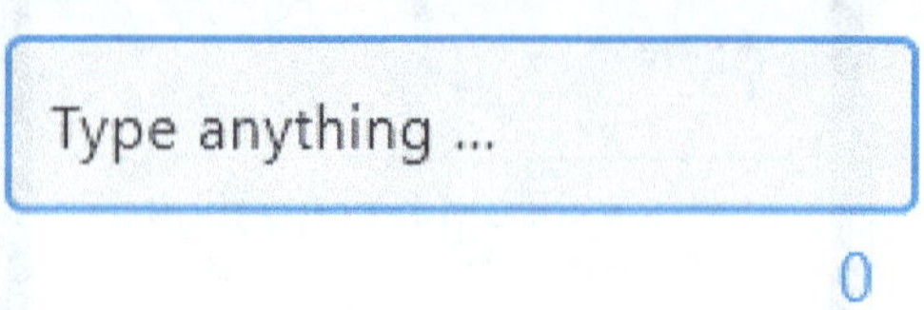

Before typing

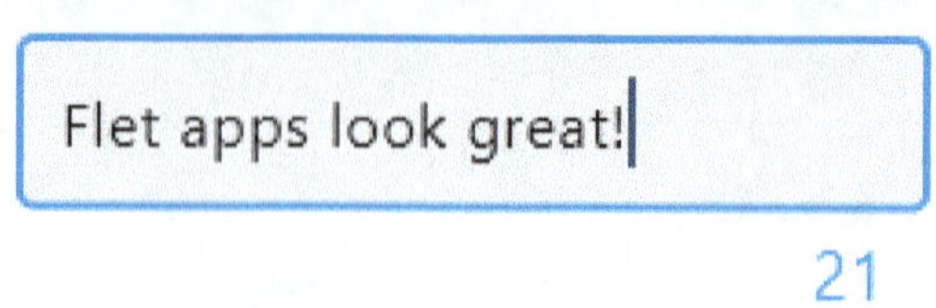

After typing

error = string/control

Sets a control—commonly a Text control—to display validation error messages.

error_max_lines = number

Specifies the maximum number of lines the error message can occupy.

error_style = flet.TextStyle

Uses TextStyle to format error text.

```
Python
import flet as ft

def main(page: ft.Page):

    def changed(e):
        text = textfield.value
        if not text.isalpha():  #If entry is not only alphabets
            textfield.error = "Entry cannot contain numbers!"
        else:
            textfield.error = None
        textfield.update()


    textfield = ft.TextField(
        on_change = changed,
        error_max_lines= 2,
        error_style= ft.TextStyle(font_family="Georgia"),
        #Code continues below ...
    )

    page.add(texfield)

ft.run(main)
```

TextField has no error

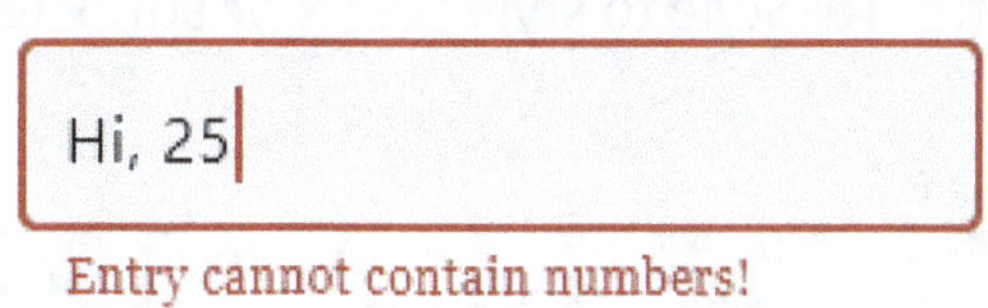

TextField has error

Prefix and Suffix Content

icon = icon

Adds a leading icon outside the TextField.

```python
import flet as ft

def main(page: ft.Page):

    textfield = ft.TextField(
        icon= ft.Icons.EMAIL,
        hint_text="Type your email ..",
        #Code continues below ...
    )

    page.add(texfield)

ft.run(main)
```

prefix / suffix = string / control

Sets a leading or a trailing control or text to the value of the TextField.

prefix_style / suffix_style = flet.TextStyle

Uses the TexStyle to style prefix or suffix text.

Example 1,

```python
import flet as ft
```

```
def main(page: ft.Page):

    textfield = ft.TextField(
      prefix = "https://",
      prefix_style= ft.TextStyle(color="green", weight=ft.FontWeight.BOLD),
      label="Website",
      #suffix = "@gmail.com"
      #Code continues below ...
    )

    page.add(texfield)

ft.run(main)
```

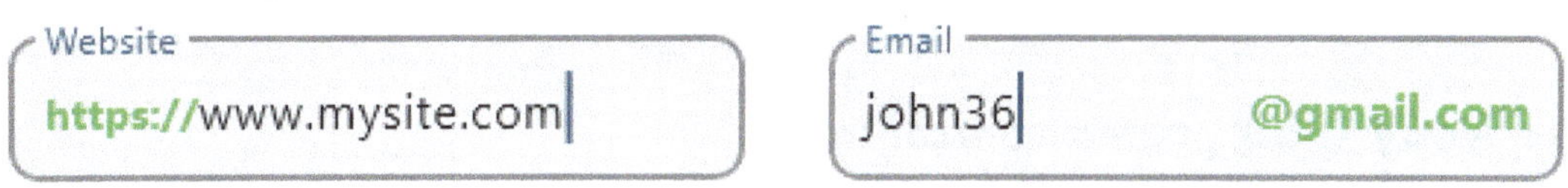

prefix = "https://"   suffix = "@gmail.com"

Example 2,

```
Python

import flet as ft

def main(page: ft.Page):

    textfield = ft.TextField(
        prefix= ft.Image("whatsapp.png",height=35, width=35),
        suffix= ft.IconButton(icon= ft.Icons.MIC),
        label="Send WhatsApp",
        #Code continues below ...
    )

    page.add(texfield)


ft.run(main)
```

> **Insight**
>
> A more comprehensive discussion of images and **IconButton** is provided in the sections covering the **Image** and Button controls.

prefix_icon / suffix_icon = icon/control

Adds icons before or after the text.

```python
import flet as ft

def main(page: ft.Page):

    textfield = ft.TextField(
        prefix_icon=ft.Icons.SEARCH,
        hint_text="Search anything ...",
        #Code continues below ...
    )

    page.add(texfield)


ft.run(main)
```

Keyboard and Input Intelligence

keyboard_brightness = flet.Brightness

Controls the keyboard theme using Brightness (LIGHT or DARK).

keyboard_type = flet.KeyboardType

Specifies the type of keyboard to display. The KeyboardType methods include:

- DATETIME
- MULTILINE
- NONE
- STREET_ADDRESS
- PHONE
- EMAIL
- NAME
- NUMBER
- VISIBLE_PASSWORD
- TEXT
- URL

autocorrect = bool

Enables or disables automatic spelling correction while the user types. When set to True, the keyboard may automatically correct misspelled words.

autofill_hints = flet.AutofillHint

Provides hints to the operating system for autofilling data such as email addresses, usernames, passwords, phone numbers and addresses. Methods of the AutofillHint include:

ADDRESS_STATE	EMAIL	FULL_STREET_ADDRESS	TELEPHONE_NUMBER_AREA_CODE
BIRTHDAY	FAMILY_NAME	STREET_ADDRESS_LINE3	TELEPHONE_NUMBER_COUNTRY_CODE
BIRTHDAY_DAY	GENDER	TELEPHONE_NUMBER	TELEPHONE_NUMBER_DEVICE
BIRTHDAY_MONTH	GIVEN_NAME	ORGANIZATION_NAME	TELEPHONE_NUMBER_EXTENSION
BIRTHDAY_YEAR	IMPP	CREDIT_CARD_NAME	TELEPHONE_NUMBER_LOCAL
COUNTRY_CODE	JOB_TITLE	CREDIT_CARD_NUMBER	TELEPHONE_NUMBER_LOCAL_PREFIX
COUNTRY_NAME	NAME	STREET_ADDRESS_LEVEL1	TELEPHONE_NUMBER_LOCAL_SUFFIX
URL	NAME_PREFIX	STREET_ADDRESS_LEVEL2	TELEPHONE_NUMBER_NATIONAL
USERNAME	NAME_SUFFIX	TRANSACTION_AMOUNT	CREDIT_CARD_FAMILY_NAME
CREDIT_CARD_TYPE	NEW_PASSWORD	CREDIT_CARD_GIVEN_NAME	CREDIT_CARD_SECURITY_CODE
LOCATION	NEW_USERNAME	STREET_ADDRESS_LEVEL3	CREDIT_CARD_EXPIRATION_YEAR
POSTAL_ADDRESS	NICKNAME	TRANSACTION_CURRENCY	CREDIT_CARD_EXPIRATION_DATE
POSTAL_CODE	ONE_TIME_CODE	STREET_ADDRESS_LINE1	CREDIT_CARD_EXPIRATION_DAY
SUB_LOCALITY	LANGUAGE	STREET_ADDRESS_LINE2	CREDIT_CARD_EXPIRATION_MONTH
MIDDLE_INITIAL	PASSWORD	POSTAL_ADDRESS_EXTENDED	CREDIT_CARD_MIDDLE_NAME
MIDDLE_NAME	PHOTO	ADDRESS_CITY_AND_STATE	POSTAL_ADDRESS_EXTENDED_POSTAL_CODE

capitalization = flet.TextCapitalization

Controls automatic text capitalization using TextCapitalization. Options include:

- CHARACTERS → capitalizes all characters.
- WORDS → capitalizes the first character of each word.
- SENTENCE → capitalizes the first character of each sentence.

Python

```
import flet as ft

def main(page: ft.Page):

    textfield = ft.TextField(
        capitalization= ft.TextCapitalization.WORDS,
        autocorrect=True,
        keyboard_type= ft.KeyboardType.NUMBER,
        autofill_hints= ft.AutofillHint.PASSWORD,
        #Code continues below ..
    )

    page.add(texfield)


ft.run(main)
```

TextCapitalization.WORDS

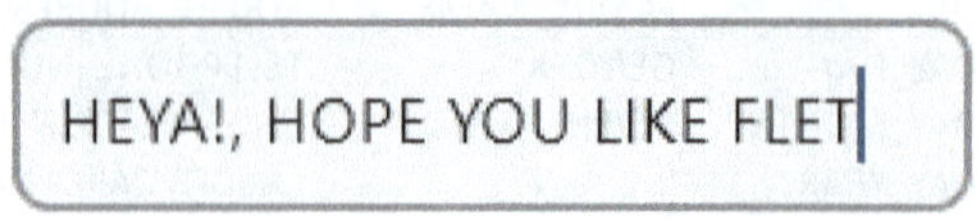

TextCapitalization.CHARACTERS

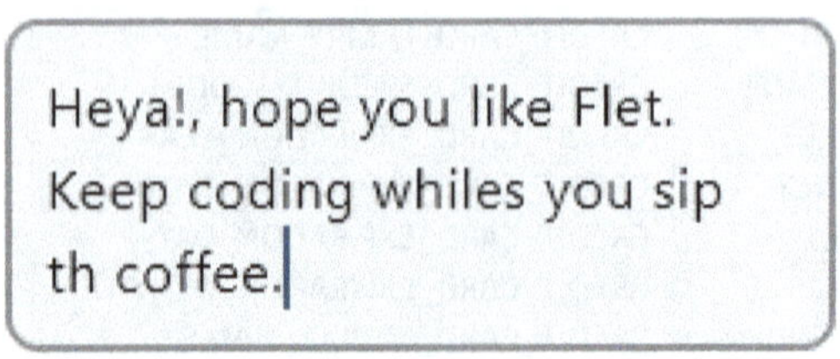

TextCapitalization.SENTENCES

enable_ime_personalized_learning = bool
Allows the system keyboard to learn from user input to improve predictions.

enable_interactive_selection = bool
Enables text selection features such as copy, cut and paste.

enable_scribble = bool
Allows handwriting input (Apple Pencil Scribble) on supported iOS devices.

enable_suggestions = bool
Allows the keyboard to suggest words and phrases while typing.

smart_dashes_type = bool
Controls smart dash conversion.

smart_quotes_type = bool
Controls smart quote conversion.

shift_enter = bool
Allows custom behavior when Shift + Enter is pressed.

input_filter = flet.InputFilter
Uses InputFilter to restrict user input using regular expressions. The InputFilter options Includes:

- regex_string
- replacement_string
- unicode
- multiline
- allow
- case_sensitive
- dot_all

Password and Security

obscuring_character = string
Defines the character used to mask sensitive input such as passwords.

password = bool

When set to True, masks the entered text.

```python
import flet as ft

def main(page: ft.Page):

    textfield = ft.TextField(
        password=True,
        obscuring_character="#",
        #Code continues below ..
    )

    page.add(texfield)

ft.run(main)
```

Default obscuring_character

obscuring_character = "#"

can_reveal_password = bool

When set to True on a password TextField, an eye icon is added as a suffix. This icon allows toggling between showing and hiding the password text.

```python
import flet as ft

def main(page: ft.Page):

    textfield = ft.TextField(
        can_reveal_password= True,
        password=True,
        obscuring_character="*",
```

```
        #Code continues below ..
    )

    page.add(texfield)

ft.run(main)
```

Masked password

Unmasked password

Events and Callbacks

update()

Forces a UI refresh for the TextField.

on_focus = callback

Fires when the TextField gains focus.

on_click = callback

Fires when the TextField is clicked.

on_change = callback

Fires whenever the TextField value changes.

Python

```python
import flet as ft

def main(page: ft.Page):

    def clicked(e):
        #Actual logic goes here ....
```

```
        print("Textfield has been clicked")


    textfield = ft.TextField(
        on_change= lambda _: print(textfield.value),
        on_focus= lambda _:print("textfield is focused"),
        on_click= clicked,
        #Code continues below ..
    )

    page.add(texfield)

ft.run(main)
```

on_selection_change = callback

Fires whenever text selection within the TextField changes.

on_blur = callback

Fires when the TextField loses focus.

on_tap_outside = callback

Fires whenever user taps outside the boundaries of the TextField.

on_submit = callback

Fires when the user submits input using the keyboard action (Enter) button.

Python

```
import flet as ft

def main(page: ft.Page):

    def submitted(e):
        #Actual logic goes here ....
        text = textfield.value
        print(text)
        textfield.value = ""    #Clear textfield
        textfield.update()
```

```
    textfield = ft.TextField(
        on_submit = submitted,
        on_blur= lambda _: print("TextField has lost focus"),
        suffix= ft.IconButton(icon=ft.Icons.SEND, on_click=submitted),
        #Code continues below ..
    )

    page.add(texfield)


ft.run(main)
```

always_call_on_tap = bool

Ensures that the on_tap callback is fired every time the TextField is tapped, even if the field is already focused.

AutoComplete

The **AutoComplete** control is a material design input field that enhances user experience by providing real-time suggestions while typing. It is based on a **TextField** but integrates a suggestion list that displays entries from a predefined dataset that matches user input. This control is particularly useful for search bars, form inputs, tagging and selection from large datasets.

AutoComplete improves accuracy, speeds up input and reduces user errors by suggesting the most relevant options.

Properties and Methods

suggestions_max_height = number

Specifies the maximum height of the suggestion dropdown. If the list exceeds this height, a scroll bar appears.

suggestions = [flet.AutoCompleteSuggestion]

A list of AutoCompleteSuggestion objects that define the possible options for the input field.

AutoCompleteSuggestion properties:

- **key** → A unique string identifier for the suggestion.

- **value** → The displayed value to match against user input.

```python
import flet as ft

def main(page: ft.Page):

    autocomplete = ft.AutoComplete(
        suggestions= [
            ft.AutoCompleteSuggestion(
                key="New York",
                value="New York",
            ),
            ft.AutoCompleteSuggestion(
                key="Arizona",
                value="Arizona",
            ),
             ft.AutoCompleteSuggestion(
                key="California",
                value="California",
            ),
              ft.AutoCompleteSuggestion(
                key="Florida",
                value="Florida",
            ),
               ft.AutoCompleteSuggestion(
                key="Georgia",
                value="Georgia",
            ),
        ]
    )

    cont = ft.Container(
        padding=ft.Padding.all(10),
        content= autocomplete,
    )


    page.add(cont)


ft.run(main)
```

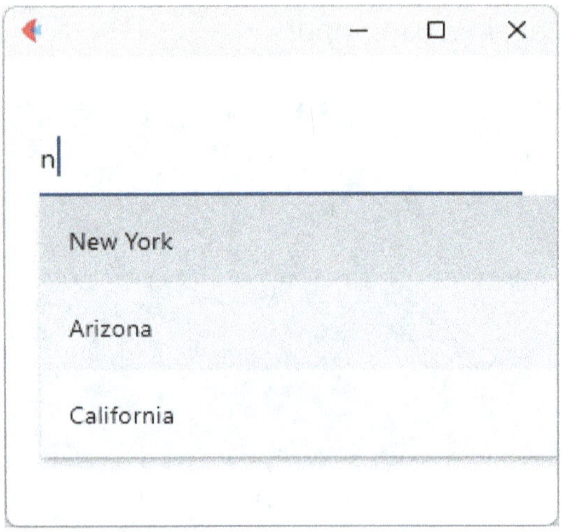 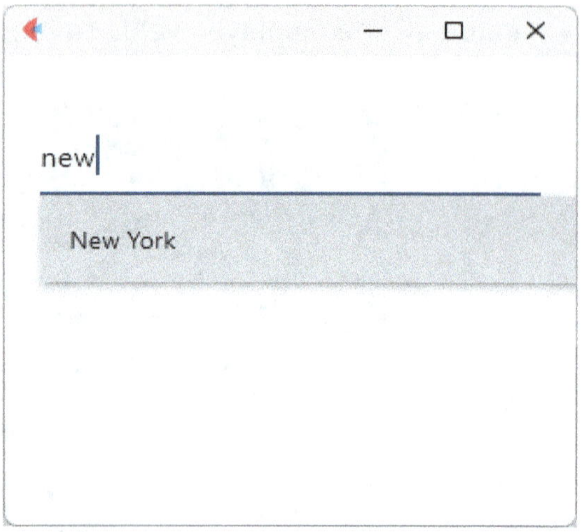

selected_index

The index of the currently selected suggestion in the list. Useful for highlighting or programmatic selection.

on_select = callback

Fires when the user selects a suggestion from the dropdown list. Receives the selected value and/or key.

```python
import flet as ft

def main(page: ft.Page):

    def selected(e):
        #Actual logic goes here
        print(autocomplete.selected_index)
        page.update()


    autocomplete = ft.AutoComplete(
        on_select= selected,
        #Code continues below ...
    )

    page.add(autocomplete)

ft.run(main)
```

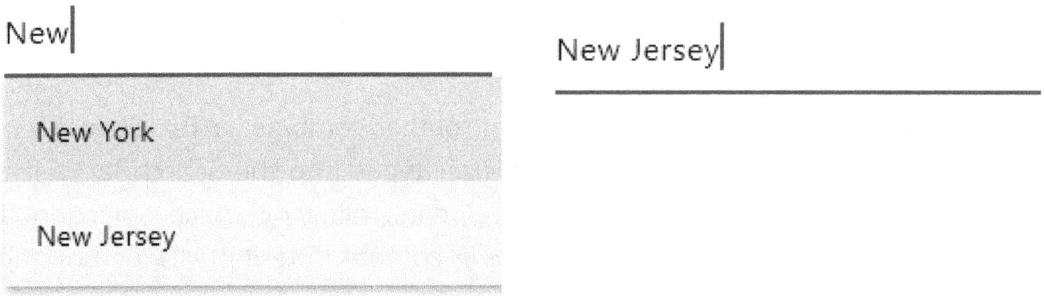


```
#Output
9
```

on_change = callback

Registers a callback that fires whenever the user selection is changed.

SearchBar

The **SearchBar** is a material design input control that combines a **TextField** for user entry with a dynamic results view. When a user types into the SearchBar, a list of controls or items that match the input appears, allowing quick selection and navigation. It is commonly used for searching content, filtering lists or navigating through large datasets.

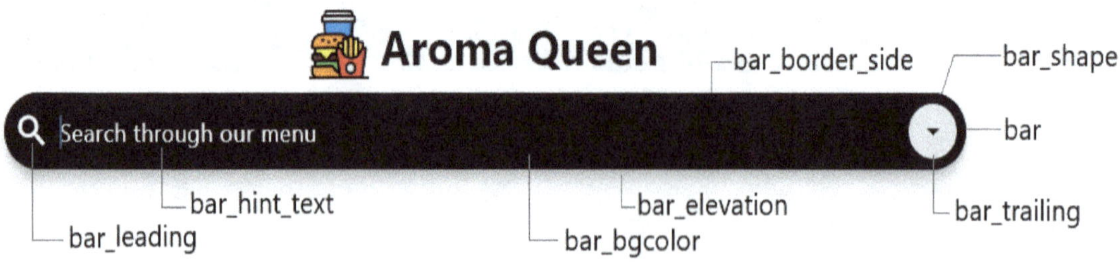

Bar

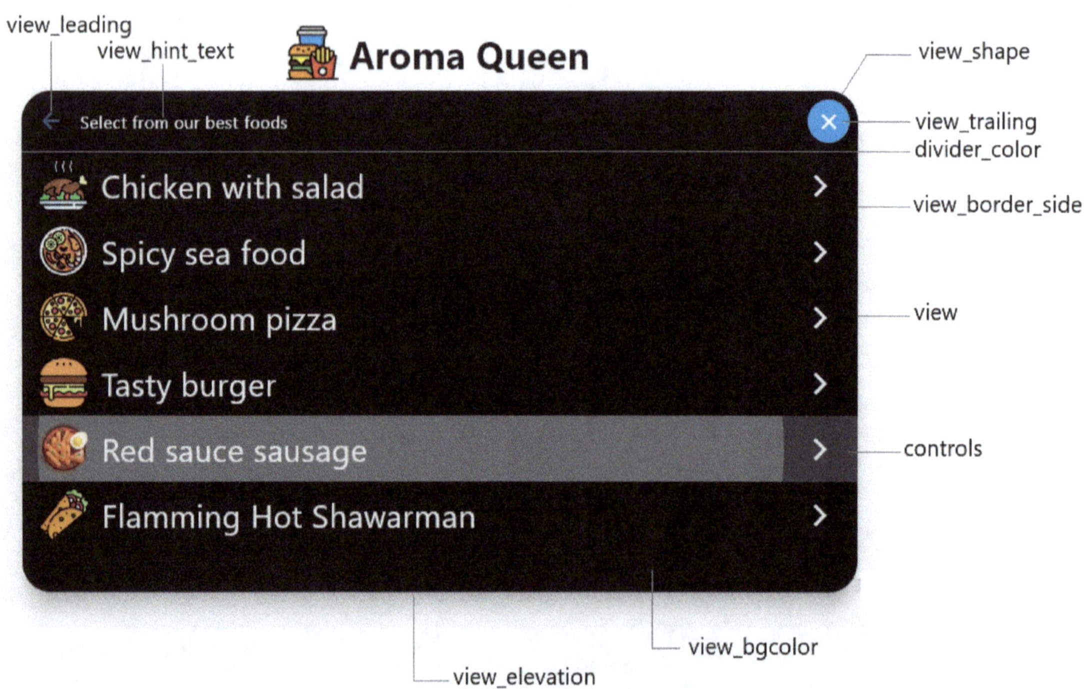

View

Properties and Methods

bar_bgcolor = color
Background color of the search input bar.

bar_border_side = flet.BorderSide, bar_shape = shape
Defines the border and shape of the search input bar.

bar_elevation = number
Controls the shadow effect of the bar.

bar_shadow_color / bar_surface_tint_color = color
Controls the shadow color and tint of the search input bar.

bar_hint_text = string, bar_hint_text_style = flet.TextStyle
Placeholder text and its styling for the input field.

bar_text_style = flet.TextStyle
Text style for the user input inside the SearchBar.

bar_padding / bar_scroll_padding = flet.Padding
Padding around the bar and within the scrollable input area.

bar_leading = control , bar_trailing = [control]
Optional leading or trailing controls, such as icons or buttons.

Python

```python
import flet as ft

def main(page: ft.Page):

    search = ft.SearchBar(
        bar_elevation= 10,
        bar_bgcolor= "#eeeeee",
        bar_shape= ft.RoundedRectangleBorder(radius= 35),
        bar_hint_text= "What will you like to eat?",
        bar_hint_text_style= ft.TextStyle(size= 20),
        bar_padding= ft.Padding.all(10),
```

```
        bar_leading= ft.Icon(ft.Icons.SEARCH),
        bar_trailing= [ft.IconButton(icon= ft.Icons.ARROW_DROP_DOWN)]

    )

    page.add(search)


ft.run(main)
```

full_screen = bool

If True, opens the search results in full-screen mode.

open_view() / close_view(string)

Boolean to programmatically open or close the search results view.

view_bgcolor = color

Background color of the results view.

view_elevation = number

Controls the shadow effect of the view.

view_surface_tint_color = color

A tint background color of the view

view_header_height = number

Height of the header

view_header_text_style = flet.TextSyle

Uses the TextStyle control to style the view_header_text

view_hint_text = string, view_hint_text_style = TextStyle

Placeholder text inside the view.

view_leading = control, view_trailing = [control]
Optional controls displayed at the start or end of the results view.

view_shape = shape, view_side = flet.BorderSide
Customizes the shape and border of the view.

view_size_constraints = flet.BoxConstraints
Controls the size limits for the results view.

```
Python
import flet as ft

def main(page: ft.Page):

    async def closeView(e):
        await search.close_view()

    async def openView(e):
        await search.open_view()

    search = ft.SearchBar(
        view_elevation= 10,
        view_header_height=60,
        view_shape= ft.RoundedRectangleBorder(radius= 35),
        view_hint_text= "Type or select food from the menu",
        view_hint_text_style= ft.TextStyle(size= 20, color="black"),
        view_leading= ft.Icon(ft.Icons.SEARCH),
        view_trailing= [
          ft.IconButton(icon= ft.Icons.CLOSE, on_click= closeView)
        ],

        bar_trailing= [
          ft.IconButton(icon=ft.Icons.ARROW_DROP_DOWN, on_click= openView)
        ]
        #Code continues below ....

    )

    page.add(search)

ft.run(main)
```

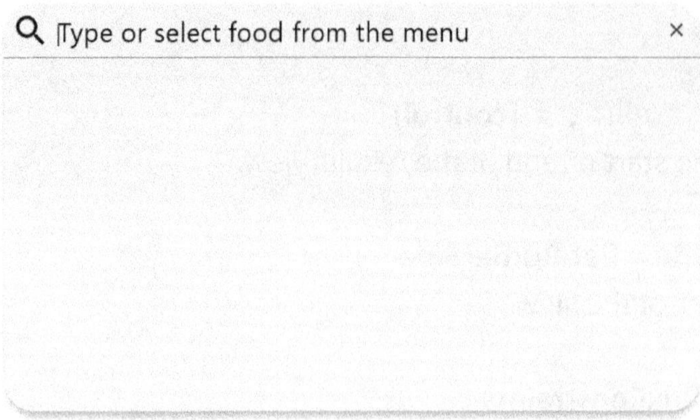

value

The current text entered in the SearchBar. Can be set programmatically or retrieved for processing.

controls = [control]

A list of child controls displayed in the results view. These can be **Text, ListTiles, Cards or any custom control**.

divider_color = color

Color of dividers between items in the results view.

autofocus = bool

Automatically focuses the SearchBar when the page loads if set to True.

on_change = callback

Fires whenever the text input changes. Useful for live filtering or updating the displayed results.

on_submit = callback

Fires when the user confirms the search input (e.g., presses Enter).

on_focus / on_blur = callback

Triggered when the SearchBar gains or loses focus.

on_tap = callback

Fires when the SearchBar is clicked or tapped.

on_tap_outside_bar = callback

Fires when the user taps outside the SearchBar input area or view.

Python

```
import flet as ft

def main(page: ft.Page):

    def submitted(e):
        print(search.value)

    def changed(e):
        print(search.value)

    async def closeView(e):
        await search.close_view(e.control.data)
        print(search.value)

    async def openView(e):
        await search.open_view()

    search = ft.SearchBar(
        view_trailing= [
         ft.IconButton(icon= ft.Icons.CLOSE, on_click= closeView)
        ],

        bar_trailing= [
         ft.IconButton(icon= ft.Icons.ARROW_DROP_DOWN, on_click= openView)
        ],

        divider_color="green",
        on_submit= submitted,
        on_change= changed,
        controls=[
            ft.ListTile(leading = ft.Image("chicken.png"),
                 trailing= ft.Icon(ft.Icons.ARROW_FORWARD_IOS) ,
                 title=ft.Text("Chicken with salad"),
                 on_click=closeView, data="Chicken with salad",),

            ft.ListTile(leading = ft.Image("sea-food.png"), trailing=
                  ft.Icon(ft.Icons.ARROW_FORWARD_IOS) ,
                  title=ft.Text("Spicy sea food"), on_click=closeView,
                  data="Spicy sea food"),
        ],
        #Code continues below ....
```

```
    )

    page.add(search)

ft.run(main)
```

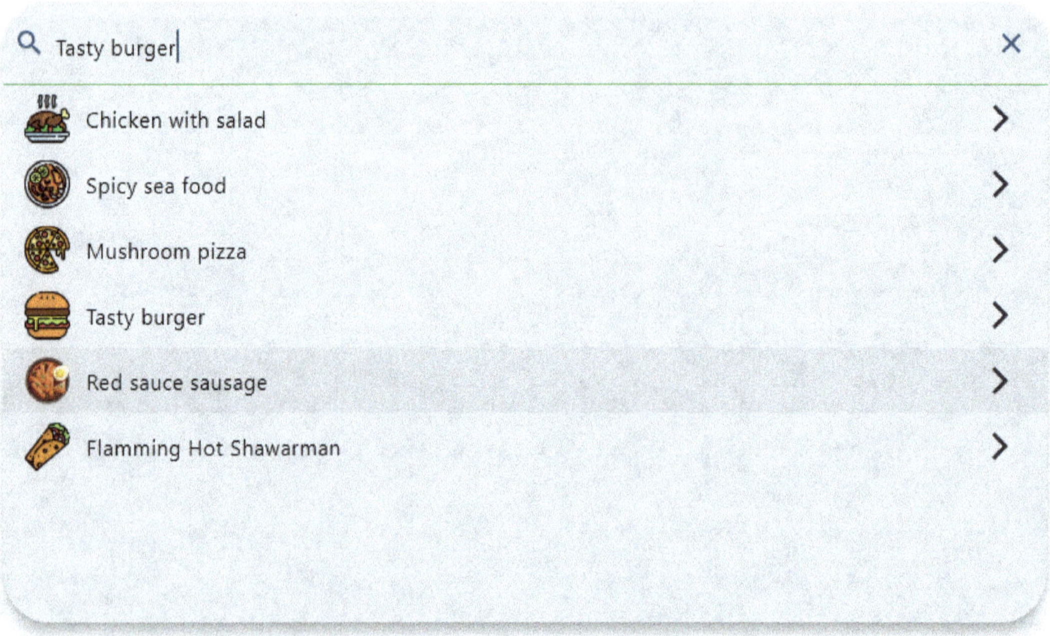

keyboard_type = flet.KeyboardType

Specifies the type of on-screen keyboard appropriate for the input, such as TEXT, NUMBER, EMAIL, URL. *See page 305 for options of the KeyboardType.*

capitalization = flet.TextCapitalization

Controls text capitalization using TextCapitalization. Options: CHARACTERS, WORDS, SENTENCE.

focus()

Programmatically sets focus on the SearchBar.

Dropdown

The **Dropdown** is a material design control used for selecting an item from a predefined list. Instead of typing values manually, the user can choose from a drop-down panel displaying available options. This improves input accuracy and enhances the user experience in forms, settings or any selection-based UI.

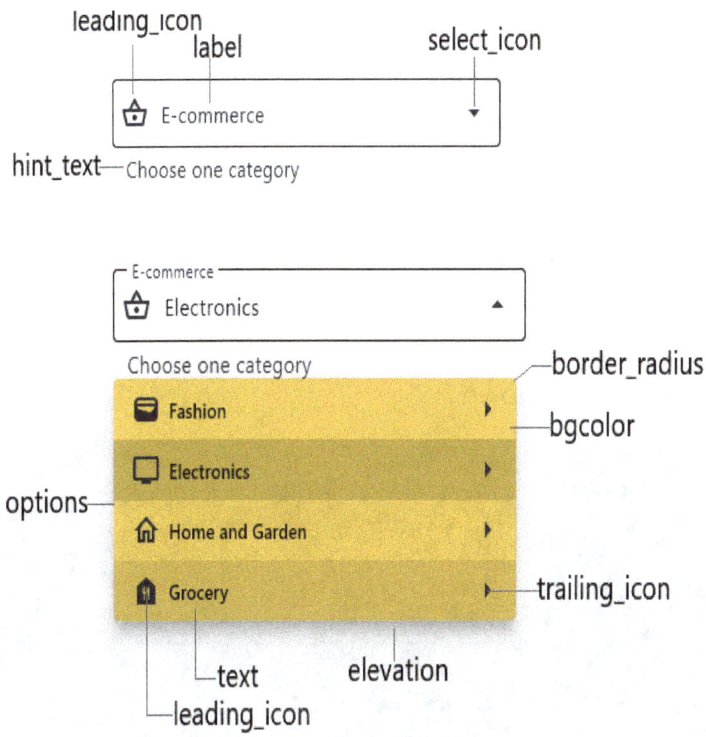

Properties and Methods

value

Returns or sets the currently selected item from the dropdown menu.

label = string, label_style = flet.TextStyle

Displays a label for the dropdown and formats it using **TextStyle**.

hint_text = string , hint_style = flet.TextStyle

Sets a placeholder when no item is selected and styling.

helper_text = string

Adds helper text below the dropdown for guidance.

helper_style = flet.TextStyle

The helper_style uses TextStyle to style the helper text.

error_text = string, error_style = flet.TextStyle

Displays validation errors below the dropdown.

leading_icon = icon / control

Sets leading or prefix icon or content inside the dropdown.

trailing_icon = icon/control

Sets trailing icon or content inside the dropdown.

Python

```
import flet as ft

def main(page: ft.Page):

    dropdown = ft.Dropdown(
        label="Country",
        helper_text="Your home of residence",
        hint_text="Select a country",
        helper_style= ft.TextStyle(size=16),
        leading_icon= ft.Icons.FLAG_OUTLINE,
        width = 350,
    )

    page.add(dropdown)

ft.run(main)
```

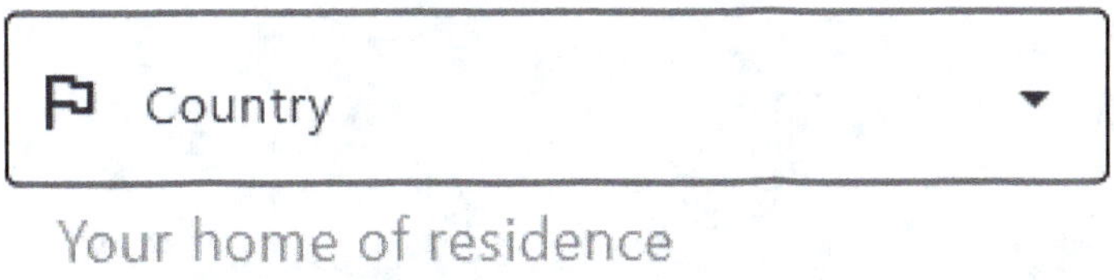

text = string

The text overrides the hint_text. It normally represents the default value.

text_align = flet.TextAlign

Aligns all text within the **Dropdown**. Methods of TextAlign include:

- LEFT
- RIGHT
- JUSTIFY
- CENTER
- START
- END

color, bgcolor, fill_color= color, filled = bool

Sets text color and background color. filled=False disables background fill.

elevation = number

Raises the dropdown menu to a specific visual depth.

options = [flet.DropdownOption]

A list of **DropdownOption** items representing the available choices.

DropdownOption

Method/Property	Definition	*Table 3.39*
key	A unique identifier for the item.	
text	A string to display as the item name.	
content	Overrides text to set a custom control.	
leading_icon	Adds a prefix icon to the item.	
trailing_icon	Adds a suffix icon to the item.	
style	Uses ButtonStyle to format or style the item button.	

```python
import flet as ft

def main(page: ft.Page):

    dropdown = ft.Dropdown(
        options=[
            ft.DropdownOption(
                text="Brazil",
                leading_icon= ft.Icons.SPORTS_FOOTBALL_OUTLINED,
                trailing_icon= ft.Icons.ARROW_RIGHT
            ),
            ft.DropdownOption(
                text="Canada",
                leading_icon=ft.Icons.FLAG_OUTLINED,
            ),
            ft.DropdownOption(
                text="United States",
            ),

        ],
        elevation = 10,
        color = 'red',
        #Code continues below ...
    )

    page.add(dropdown)


ft.run(main)
```

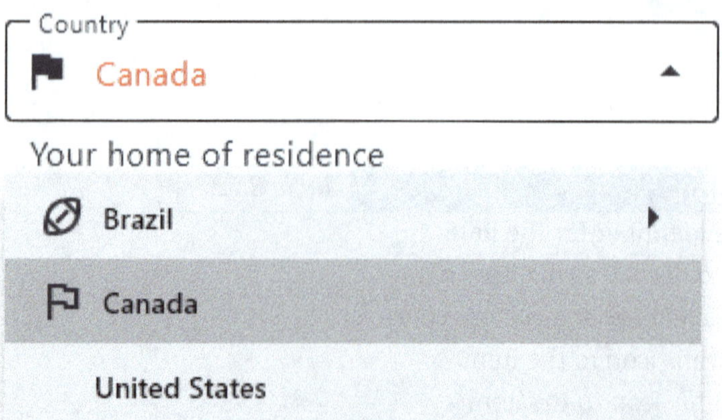

text_size = number
Sets the font size of dropdown items.

text_style = flet.TextStyle
Uses **TextStyle** to format the dropdown items.

autofocus = bool
When **True**, the dropdown gains focus automatically.

selected_suffix = control
The selected_suffix defines a control displayed at the trailing edge of the selected item in the Dropdown.

select_icon = icon
Sets the icon displayed to expand the dropdown menu.

selected_trailing_icon = icon
Sets the trailing icon displayed when Dropdown expands to show items.

on_select = callback
Callback fired when an item is selected.

on_text_change = callback
Callback fired when selected item or text changed.

on_focus / on_blur = callback
Callbacks triggered when the dropdown gains focus, loses focus or is clicked/tapped.

Python
```
import flet as ft

def main(page: ft.Page):

    def getSelected(e):
        #Actual logic goes here ...
        country = dropdown.value
        print(country)
```

```
    dropdown = ft.Dropdown(
        on_select = getSelected,
        on_text_change= getSelected,
        on_focus= lambda _:print("Dropdown is active!"),
        #Code continues below ...
    )

    page.add(dropdown)

ft.run(main)
```

editable = bool

The editable property enables the user to type text into the Dropdown field. When set to True, the Dropdown behaves like a searchable input field where the user can type to locate or filter available options. By default, editable is set to False, meaning the Dropdown is read-only and users can only select from the predefined options.

enable_search = bool

The enable_search property allows the Dropdown to actively search through the available options as the user types. enable_search is typically used together with editable=True.

enable_filter = bool

The enable_filter property refines the search behavior by filtering Dropdown options based on the typed input.

input_filter = flet.InputFilter

The input_filter implements the InputFilter control to restrict the characters that can be typed into an editable Dropdown. *See page 307 for InputFilter options*.

capitalization = flet.TextCpitalization

The capitalization property applies the TextCapitalization rule to user input. Available options include:

- CHARACTERS – capitalizes all characters
- WORDS – capitalizes the first letter of each word
- SENTENCE – capitalizes the first letter of each sentence

```python
import flet as ft

def main(page: ft.Page):

    dropdown = ft.Dropdown(
        enable_search=True,
        editable=True,
        capitalization= ft.TextCapitalization.WORDS,
        menu_height= 80,
        enable_filter=True,
        #Code continues below ...
    )

    page.add(dropdown)


ft.run(main)
```

menu_style= flet.MenuStyle

The menu_style uses MenuStyle control to apply custom styles to the Dropdown menu.

MenuStyle

Method/Property	Definition *Table 3.40*
alignment	Aligns items within the Dropdown using Alignment.
bgcolor	Background color of the menu.
elevation	The depth of shadow effect of the menu.
fixed_size	Defines the size of the menu panel.
max_size	Defines the maximum size the menu can have.
min_size	Defines the minimum size of the menu panel.
mouse_cursor	Sets the kind of mouse cursor to interact with the menu.
padding	Pads items within the Dropdown menu panel.
shadow_color	Defines the color of the shadow beneath the menu.
shape	Defines the shape (circular , rectangular etc) of the menu.
side	Applies color and thickness to the border sides of the menu.
visual_density	Adjusts the density of spacing in the Dropdown.

menu_height = number

The menu_height explicitly sets the height of the Dropdown menu panel when opened. This property overrides automatic height calculation based on the number of items.

menu_width = number

The menu_width sets the width of the expanded Dropdown menu. This allows the menu panel to be wider or narrower than the Dropdown field itself.

border = flet.InputBorder, border_color = color

Defines the dropdown's border and its color.

border_width / border_radius = number

Defines the thickness of the dropdown's border and its curvature.

focused_border_color = color, focused_border_width = number

The dropdown border_color and border_tickness when it gains focus.

```python
import flet as ft

def main(page: ft.Page):

    dropdown = ft.Dropdown(
        border= ft.OutlinedBorder(),
        border_color="blue",
        border_radius=15,
        focused_border_color="cyan",
        focused_border_width= 3,
        #Code continues below ...
    )

    page.add(dropdown)


ft.run(main)
```

unfocused

focused

content_padding = flet.Padding

Pads items inside the dropdown using **Padding** control.

expanded_insets = flet.Padding

The expanded_insets uses the Padding control to define the spacing between the Dropdown menu and the screen edges when the menu is expanded. This helps prevent clipping on smaller screens.

DropdownM2

DropdownM2 is a Material Design 2 styled dropdown control. It behaves similarly to the standard **Dropdown**, expanding to display selectable options inside a menu container.

Functionally, DropdownM2 works like Dropdown, but it follows the older Material 2 design system. Since Flet is moving toward Material 3 components, DropdownM2 may be deprecated in future versions.

Most of its properties are similar to those of Dropdown, although some are named differently while serving the same purpose.

Example:

Table 3.41

DropdownM2	Dropdown	DropdownM2	Dropdown
hint_content	hint_text	suffix/suffix_icon	trailing_icon
prefix/prefix_icon	leading_icon	helper	helper_text
focus_color	focused_border_color	item_height	menu_height
on_change	on_text_change	on_click	on_select

Key Properties of DropdownM2

Table 3.42

Method/Property	Definition
counter	Displays a counter widget, often used to show character count or selection limits.
counter_style	Uses the TextStyle to format the counter
collapse	Determines whether the DropdownM2 occupies minimal vertical space when not expanded.
fit_parent_size	Makes the DropdownM2 expand to match the size of its parent container.
prefix_icon_size_constraints	Sets size limits (min/max) for the prefix icon.
suffix_icon_size_constraints	Sets size limits (min/max) for the suffix icon.
select_icon_enabled_color	Defines the color of the DropdownM2 arrow icon when enabled.
size_constraints	Applies layout size restrictions (minimum and maximum width/height).
hint_fade_duration	Controls how long the hint text fade animation lasts.

disabled_hint_content	Specifies the hint content displayed when the DropdownM2 is disabled.
helper_max_lines	Limits the number of lines for helper text displayed below the field.
enable_feedback	Enables tactile, sound, or visual feedback when interacting with the dropdown.
align_label_with_hint	Aligns the label properly when a hint is present.
options_fill_horizontally	Forces dropdown options to stretch horizontally to fill available space.
text_vertical_align	Controls the vertical alignment of text inside the dropdown field.
error_max_lines	Sets the maximum number of lines for error text display.
alignment	Defines how the dropdown content is aligned within its container.
on_click	Fires when a menu item is selected.

Radio

The **Radio** is a material design input control that allows the user to select one option from a set of choices. It is commonly used in forms, settings or preference selections, such as choosing gender, application themes or system configurations.
The **value** of a Radio is a string, that is returned whenever the radio is selected. To group multiple radios so that only one option can be selected at a time, use the **RadioGroup** control.

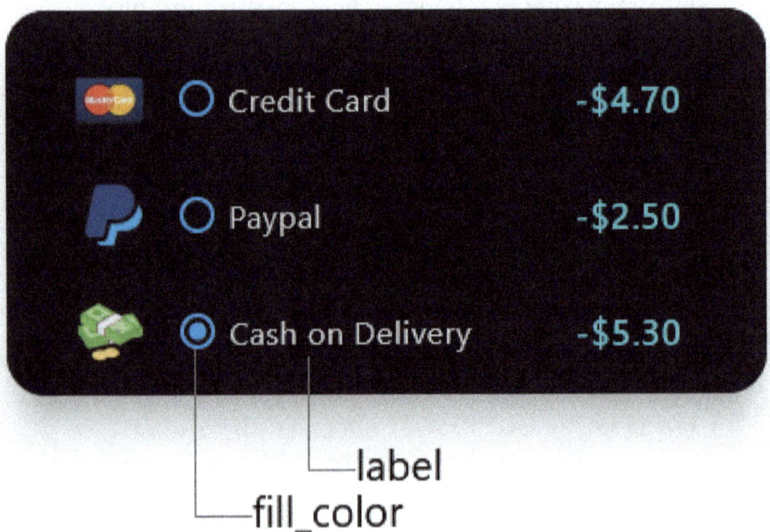

> **Insight**
>
> The **Radio** control is an essential input element in Flet for single-choice selections. Its flexibility with labels, colors and events allows it to fit seamlessly into forms and settings in both desktop and mobile applications.

RadioGroup

The **RadioGroup** is a material design control that groups related Radio controls, allowing the user to select only one option from a set of choices. By using RadioGroup, all child Radio controls are logically linked, ensuring that selecting one automatically deselects the others.

Method/Property	Definition *Table 3.43*
content	Defines the layout or container that holds the child Radio controls within the RadioGroup.
value	Represents the currently selected Radio's value in the group. This can be read or programmatically set.
on_change	Assigns a function that triggers whenever a child Radio is selected. This function can access the currently selected Radio's value.

Properties and Methods

adaptive = bool

When set to True, the Radio adopts the platform-specific material design style.

value = string

It represents the return value as a string when the radio is selected.

label = string

Defines the text for the Radio button, describing the option.

label_style = flet.TextStyle

Uses the TextStyle control to format the Radio label's appearance.

on_animation_end, on_blur, on_focus = callback

Event callbacks for animations, losing focus and gaining focus.

active_color = color

Sets the color of the Radio when it is selected. Colors can be color names, hex codes or predefined ColorValue.

```python
import flet as ft

def main(page: ft.Page):
```

```
    def getSelected(e):
        #Actual logic goes here ...
        print(radio.value)


    radio = ft.RadioGroup(
        on_change = getSelected,
        value= "female",
        content= ft.Column(
            controls=[
              ft.Radio(label= "Male", value = "male"),
              ft.Radio(label= "Female", value = "female"),
            ]
        )
    )

    page.add(radio)

ft.run(main)
```

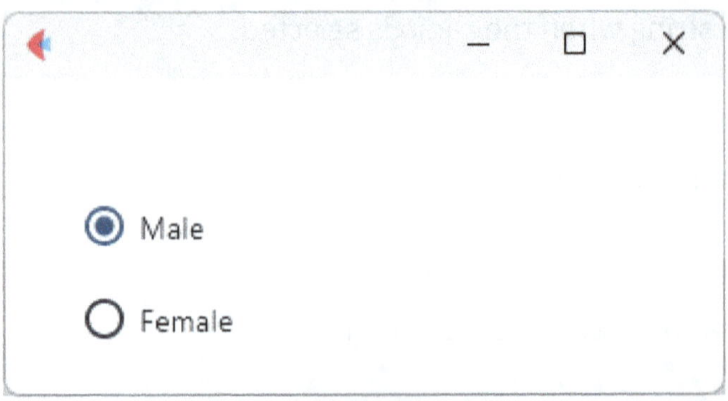

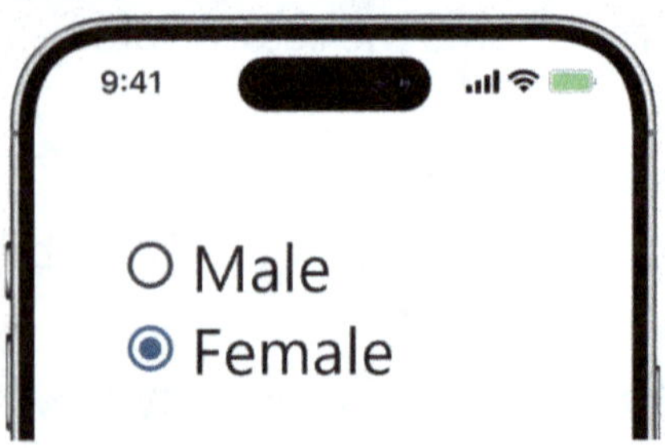


```
#Output
male
female
```

overlay_color = color

Defines the temporary background color of the Radio and its label when toggled.

splash_radius = number

Defines the radius of the splash effect when the Radio is clicked.

toggleable = bool
If False, allows the Radio to be untoggled by the user.

fill_color = color
Specifies the background color of the Radio circle when selected.

label_position = flet.LabelPosition
Sets the position of the label relative to the Radio using LabelPosition. Options: **LEFT** or **RIGHT**.

Python
```
import flet as ft

def main(page: ft.Page):

    def getTheme(e):
        #Actual logic goes here ...
        print(radio.value)


    radio = ft.RadioGroup(
        on_change= getTheme,
        value= "light",
        content= ft.Column(
            controls=[
              ft.Radio(
                  label= "Dark", value= "dark", fill_color="cyan",
                  label_position= ft.LabelPosition.LEFT,),

              ft.Radio(
                  label= "Light", value= "light",fill_color="cyan",
                  label_position= ft.LabelPosition.LEFT,),
            ]
        )
    )

    page.add(dropdown)

ft.run(main)
```

focus_color = color

Defines the color of the Radio when it gains focus.

autofocus = bool

Automatically gives focus to the Radio when the page loads if True.

hover_color = color

Specifies the color displayed when the mouse hovers over the Radio.

```
Python
import flet as ft

def main(page: ft.Page):

    def favorite(e):
        #Actual logic goes here ...
        print(radio.value)

    radio = ft.RadioGroup(
      on_change= favorite,
      value= "Python",
      content= ft.Row(
        controls=[
          ft.Radio(label= "Python", value= "python", focus_color="red",
                   overlay_color="red"),

          ft.Radio(label= "JavaScript", value= "js", focus_color="cyan",
                   overlay_color="green"),

          ft.Radio(label= "C++", value= "c++", focus_color="brown",
                  overlay_color="blue"),
            ]
        )
    )

    page.add(radio)

ft.run(main)
```

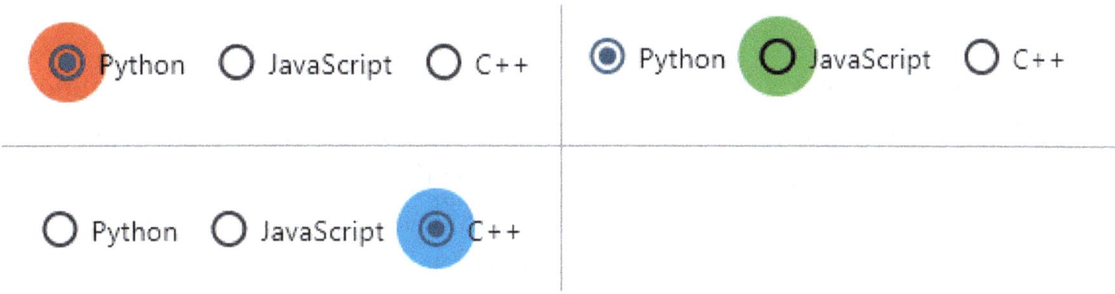

mouse_cursor = flet.MouseCursor
Specifies the mouse cursor type when hovering over the Radio, using MouseCursor options such as DEFAULT, POINTER, TEXT, etc.

visual_density = flet.VisualDensity
Adjusts the spacing and density of the Radio relative to other controls.

CupertinoRadio

CupertinoRadio is the **iOS-styled** version of the standard **Radio** control. It provides the same functionality as Radio, with the difference being its visual appearance, which follows Apple's Cupertino design language.

It shares almost all the same properties and methods as Radio, with a few notable additions:

use_checkmark_style = bool
When set to True, a checkmark icon is displayed instead of the default circular indicator.

inactive_color = color
Defines the color of the radio button when it is in the unselected state.

Checkbox

The **Checkbox** is a material design input control used for selecting multiple options. Unlike **Radio**, which allows only a single selection within a group, Checkbox allows users to choose any number of options independently.
It is visually represented as a square box that displays a checkmark when selected. The value of a Checkbox is either ***True*** or ***False***, where True indicates the box is checked and False indicates it is unchecked.

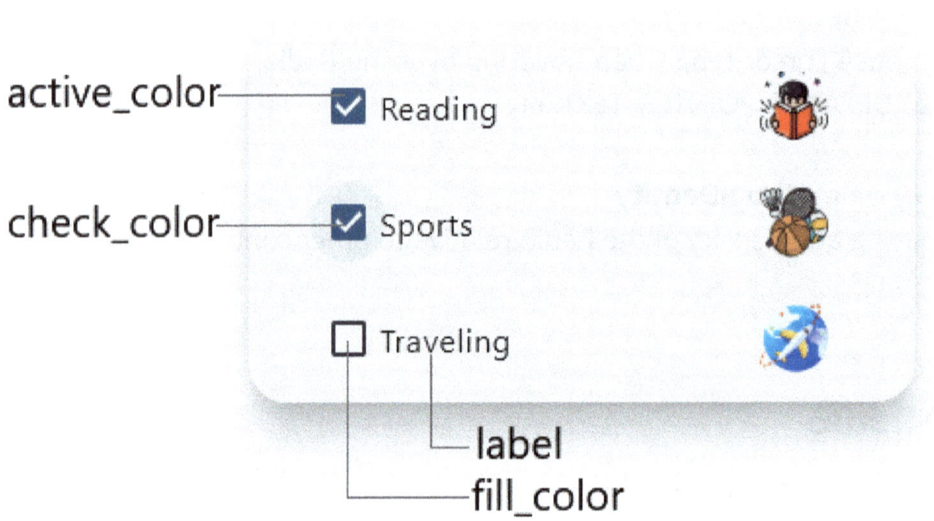

Properties and Methods

adaptive = bool
When set to True, the Checkbox applies platform-specific material design.

aspect_ratio = number
Defines the width-to-height ratio of the Checkbox.

autofocus = bool
Enables the Checkbox to automatically gain focus when the page loads.

label = string/control

Text or control that describes the Checkbox.

label_position = flet.LabelPosition

Specifies the position of the label relative to the Checkbox. Options: LEFT, RIGHT.

label_style = flet.TextStyle

Formats the label using **TextStyle** control.

value = bool

The current value of the Checkbox. True if checked, False if unchecked and None if *tristate* is enabled and unchecked.

on_change = callback

Triggers a function whenever the value of the Checkbox changes (True ↔ False).

```
Python
import flet as ft

def main(page: ft.Page):

    def isChecked(e):
        #Actual logic goes here ...
        state = check.value
        print(f"Check is {state}")


    check = ft.Checkbox(
        label= "Reading",
        label_style= ft.TextStyle(size=20),
        on_change= isChecked
    )

    page.add(check)


ft.run(main)
```

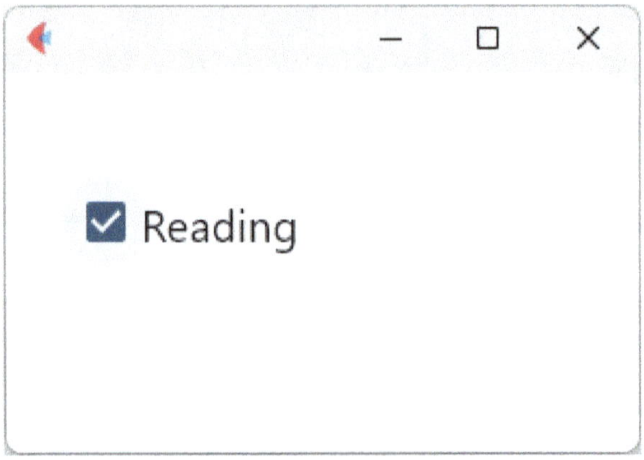

```
#Output
Check is False
Check is True
```

on_animation_end, on_blur, on_focus = callback
Event handlers for animation completion, loss of focus and gaining focus.

active_color = color
Specifies the color of the Checkbox when it is selected.

check_color = color
Specifies the color of the checkmark displayed inside the box when selected.

fill_color = color
Sets the background color of the Checkbox when selected.

focus_color = color
Specifies the color when the Checkbox gains focus.

overlay_color
Specifies the temporary splash color when interacting with the Checkbox.

hover_color = color
Defines the background color when the mouse hovers over the Checkbox.

```python
import flet as ft

def main(page: ft.Page):

    def language(e):
        #Actual logic goes here ...
        lang = e.control.label
        value = e.data
        print(f"{lang} = {value}")


    checkers = ft.Column(
       controls=[
         ft.Checkbox(label="English", check_color="blue",
                    active_color="#eeeeee",
                    on_change=language
              ),

         ft.Checkbox(label="French", check_color="blue",
                    active_color="#eeeeee",
                    on_change=language
              ),
        ]
    )

    page.add(checkers)

ft.run(main)
```

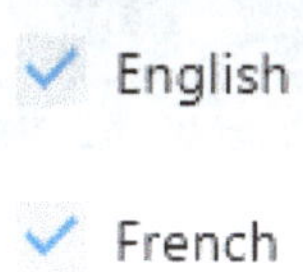

`active_color = "grey",`
`check_color = "blue"`

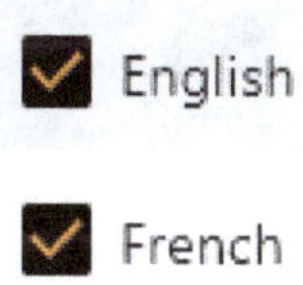

`active_color = "black",`
`check_color = "orange"`

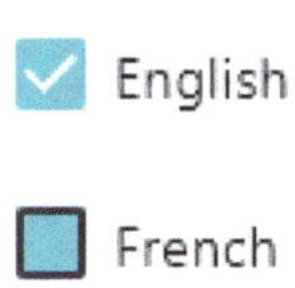

`fill_color = "cyan"`

`overlay_color = "green"`

semantics_label = string

Provides an accessibility label for screen readers.

shape = shape

Defines the visual shape of the Checkbox (e.g., square, rounded). *See pages 201 or 206 for samples of shapes.*

```python
import flet as ft

def main(page: ft.Page):


    checkers = ft.Column(
       controls=[
            ft.Checkbox(
                shape= ft.CircleBorder(),
                #Code continues below ...
            ),

            ft.Checkbox(
                shape= ft.RoundedRectangleBorder(radius=5),
                #Code continues below ...
            ),
        ]
    )

    page.add(checkers)

ft.run(main)
```

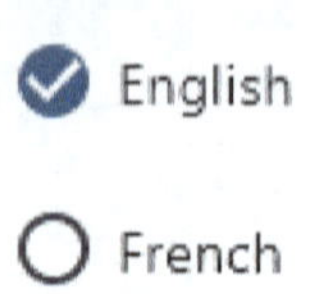

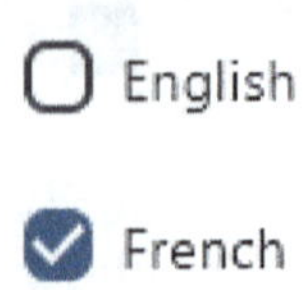

`shape= ft.CircleBorder()`

`shape= ft.RoundedRectangleBorder(radius=5)`

border_side = flet.BorderSide

Uses the **BorderSide** control to style the edges of the Checkbox. You can specify color and width for the border.

Python

```python
import flet as ft

def main(page: ft.Page):

    check = ft.Checkbox(
        label = "Accept terms and conditions",
        border_side= ft.BorderSide(width=2, color="Green"),
        #Code continues below ...
    )

    page.add(check)

ft.run(main)
```

☐ Accept terms and conditions

splash_radius = number

Specifies the radius of the splash effect when the Checkbox is clicked or tapped.

mouse_cursor = flet.MouseCursor

Specifies the type of mouse cursor when hovering over the Checkbox.

tristate = bool

If True, the Checkbox supports a third state (None) in addition to True and False.

Python
```python
import flet as ft

def main(page: ft.Page):

    def isChecked(e):
        #Actual logic goes here ...
        state = check.value
        print(f"Check is {state}")

    check = ft.Checkbox(
        label = "Subscribe to our newsletter",
        tristate= True,
```

```
        on_change= isChecked,
        #Code continues below ...
    )

    page.add(check)

ft.run(main)
```

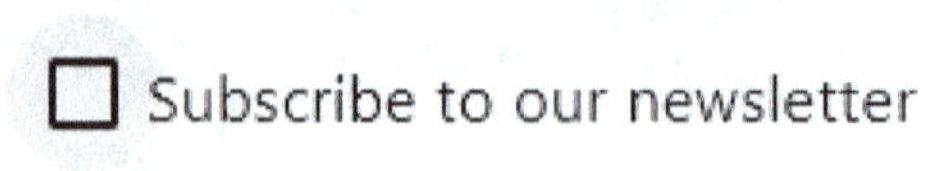


```
#Output
Check is False
```

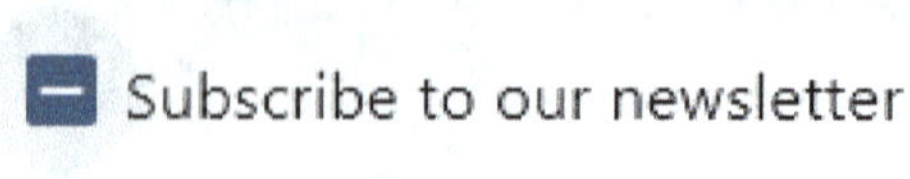


```
#Output
Check is None
```

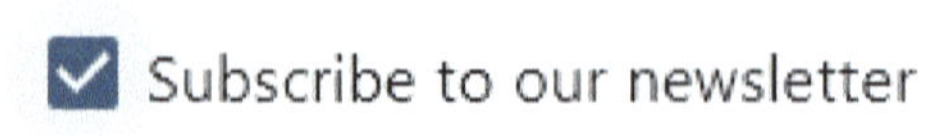


```
#Output
Check is True
```

visual_density = flet.VisualDensity
Adjusts the spacing and compactness of the Checkbox. *See page 472 for options of VisualDensity.*

CupertinoCheckbox

CupertinoCheckbox is the **iOS-styled** version of the standard **Checkbox** control. It performs the same function and supports the same properties and methods as Checkbox, differing only in design style.

spacing = number
Defines the space between the checkbox and its label.

Switch

The **Switch** is a material design toggle control used to select between two mutually exclusive states, usually ***True*** or ***False***. It visually consists of a **thumb** (**knob**) that slides along a **track** from left to right or vice versa to indicate the state. The track provides a visual guide for the thumb movement.
Switch controls are commonly used in settings, preferences and other UI elements where a binary choice is required.

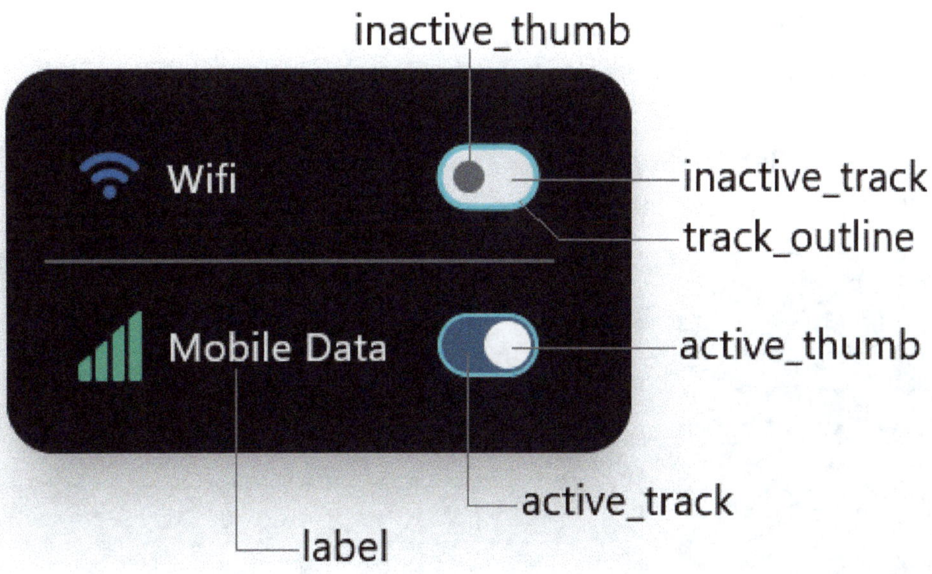

Properties and Methods

adaptive = bool
When set to True, the Switch adopts platform-specific material design styles.

autofocus = bool
Automatically sets focus to the Switch when the page loads.

on_change = callback
Triggers a function whenever the Switch state changes.

value = bool
Gets or sets the state of the Switch. True indicates on, False indicates off.

label = string /control
Text or any control that describes the purpose or function of the Switch.

label_position = flet.LabelPosition
Specifies the position of the label relative to the Switch. Options: LEFT, RIGHT.

label_text_style = flet.TextStyle
Uses **TextStyle** to format the label.

```python
import flet as ft

def main(page: ft.Page):

    def getValue(e):
        #Actual logic goes here ...
        print(switch.value)

    switch = ft.Switch(
        label="Night Mode",
        label_text_style=ft.TextStyle(size=20),
        on_change = getValue,
        label_position=ft.LabelPosition.LEFT,
    )

    page.add(switch)


ft.run(main)
```

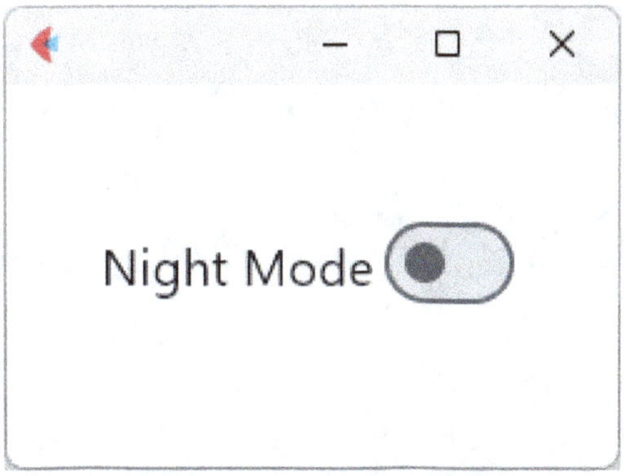


```
#Output
False
```

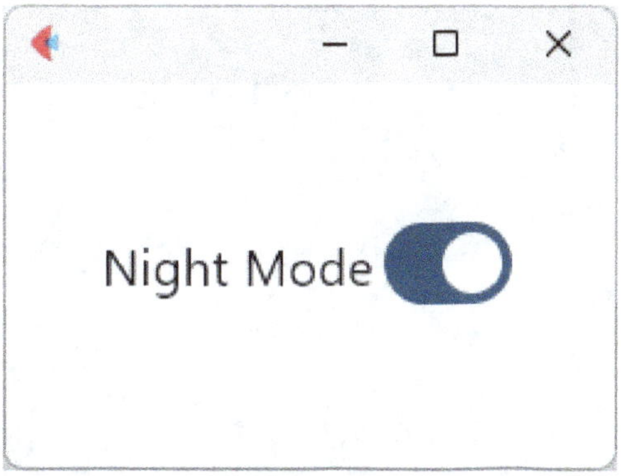


```
#Output
True
```

thumb_color = color

Specifies the color of the thumb.

inactive_thumb_color = color

Specifies the color of the thumb when the Switch is off (False).

thumb_icon = icon

Sets an icon for the thumb.

```python
import flet as ft

def main(page: ft.Page):

    def getMode(e):
        #Actual logic goes here ...
        print(f"Night mode -> {e.control.value}")

    def getNotify(e):
        #Actual logic goes here ...
        if notify.value:
            notify.thumb_color = "red"
        else:
            notify.thumb_color = None

        print(f"Notification -> {notify.value}")
        notify.update()


    nightmode = ft.Switch(
```

```
            label="Night Mode",
            thumb_icon= ft.Icons.BRIGHTNESS_2,
            on_change = getMode,
            #Code continues below ...
        )

    notify = ft.Switch(
            label="Notification",
            inactive_thumb_color="cyan",
            on_change = getNotify,
            #Code continues below ...
        )


    cont = ft.Container(
            content= ft.Column(controls=[nightmode, notify]),
    )

    page.add(cont)

ft.run(main)
```

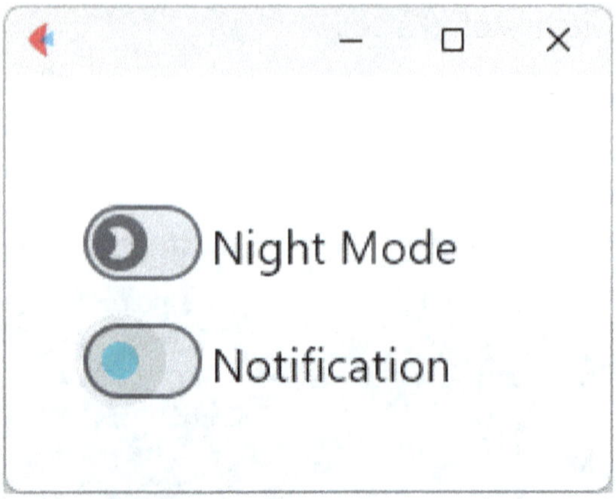


```
#Output
Night mode -> False
Notification -> False
```

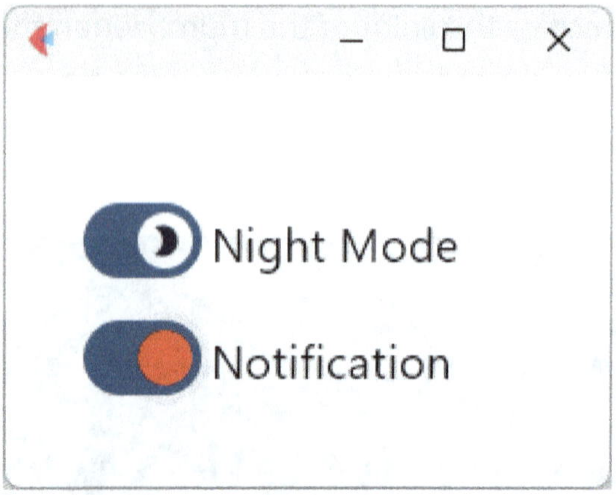


```
#Output
Night mode -> True
Notification -> True
```

active_track_color = color

Specifies the color of the track when the Switch is active.

inactive_track_color = color

Specifies the color of the track when the Switch is off (False).

```python
import flet as ft

def main(page: ft.Page):

    switch = ft.Switch(
        label="Notification",
        active_track_color="blue",
        inactive_track_color="orange",
        #Code continues below ...
      )

    page.add(switch)

ft.run(main)
```

Inactive track

Active track

active_color = color

Specifies the color of the Switch thumb when it is active (True).

track_color = color

Specifies the default color of the track.

```python
import flet as ft

def main(page: ft.Page):

    switch = ft.Switch(
        label="Notification",
        active_color="blue",
        track_color="black",
        #Code continues below ...
      )

    page.add(switch)
```

```
ft.run(main)
```

Inactive switch

Active switch

on_animation_end, on_blur, on_focus = callback
Event handlers for animation completion, losing focus and gaining focus.

focus_color = color
Specifies the color of the Switch when it gains focus.

hover_color = color
Specifies the background color when the mouse hovers over the Switch.

overlay_color = color
Specifies the color that appears temporarily when the Switch is toggled.

splash_radius = number
Defines the radius of the splash effect when the Switch is toggled.

track_outline_color = color, track_outline_width = number
Define the outline color and thickness of the track.

Python
```
import flet as ft

def main(page: ft.Page):

    switch = ft.Switch(
        label="Notification",
        track_outline_color= "blue",
        track_outline_width= 5,
        overlay_color="teal",
        splash_radius= 10,
```

```
        on_focus= lambda _:print("switched is focused"),
        #Code continues below ...
    )

    page.add(switch)

ft.run(main)
```

Inactive switch

Active switch

CupertinoSwitch

CupertinoSwitch is the **iOS-styled** version of the standard Switch control. It serves the same purpose as Switch—toggling between two states (on/off)—but follows Apple's Cupertino design style.

It supports the same core properties and methods as Switch, with a few additional styling-related properties:

Table 3.44

Method/Property	Definition
off_label_color	Defines the color of the label when the switch is inactive (False).
on_label_color	Defines the color of the label when the switch is active (True).
active_thumb_image_src	Specifies the image path(string) to be used for the thumb when the switch is in the active (on) state, replacing the default circular thumb.
inactive_thumb_image_src	Specifies the image path (string) to be used for the thumb when the switch is in the inactive (off) state.
on_image_error	Triggered when loading the thumb image fails.

Slider

The **Slider** control is a material design input control that allows users to select a numeric value from a defined range by moving a **thumb** (**knob**) along a track. Sliders are commonly used for adjusting settings such as volume, brightness, temperature or any numeric scale input.
The value of the Slider corresponds to the position of the thumb along the track, which can optionally snap to defined divisions for discrete input.

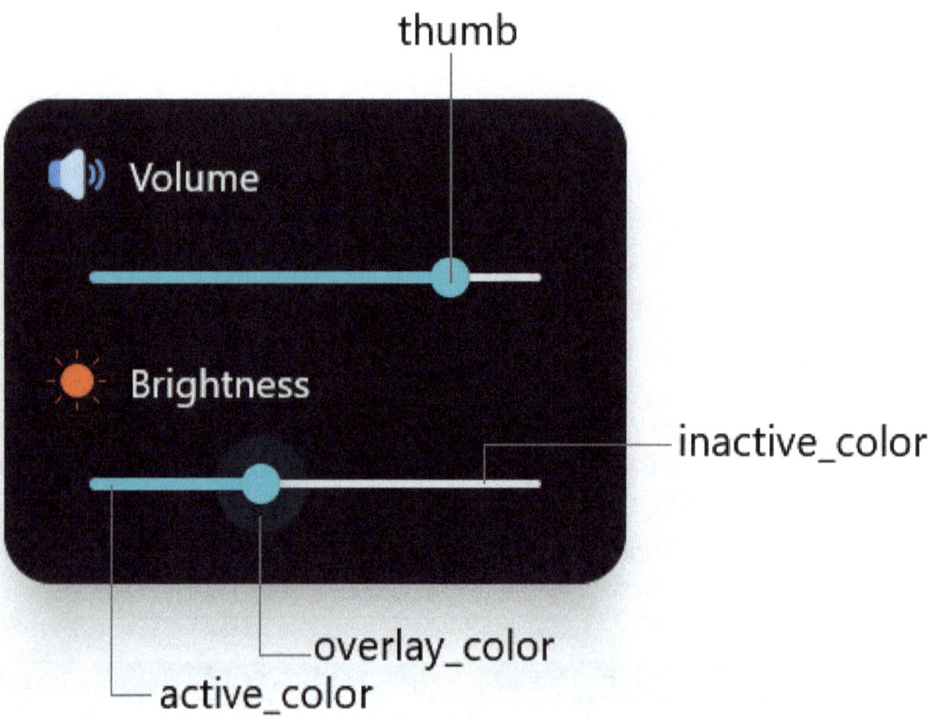

Properties and Methods

value = number
Sets or returns the current position of the thumb on the slider track. Default: (0.0 – 1.0)

label = string
A string that can be displayed near the thumb to indicate the current value.

min = number

Defines the minimum value of the slider, representing the lower end of the range.

max = number

Defines the maximum value of the slider, representing the upper end of the range.

on_change = callback

Registers a callback that triggers whenever the slider value changes (continuously while dragging).

on_change_start = callback

Registers a callback that fires once when the user starts sliding the thumb.

on_change_end = callback

Registers a callback that fires once when the user stops dragging the thumb.

```python
import flet as ft

def main(page: ft.Page):

    def adjustment(e):
        #Actual logic goes here ...
        value = int(volume.value)
        print(f"volume -> {value}")

    volume = ft.Slider(
        value = 5, #Initial value
        min=1,
        max=10,
        on_change = adjustment
    )

    cont = ft.Container(
        content= ft.Column(controls=[ft.Text("Volume"), volume]),
    )

    page.add(cont)

ft.run(main)
```

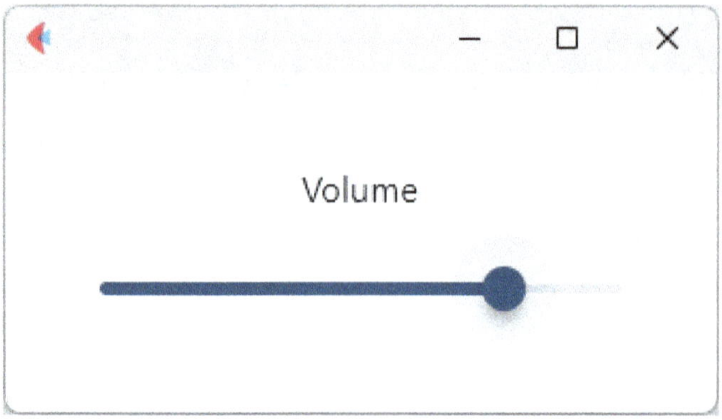

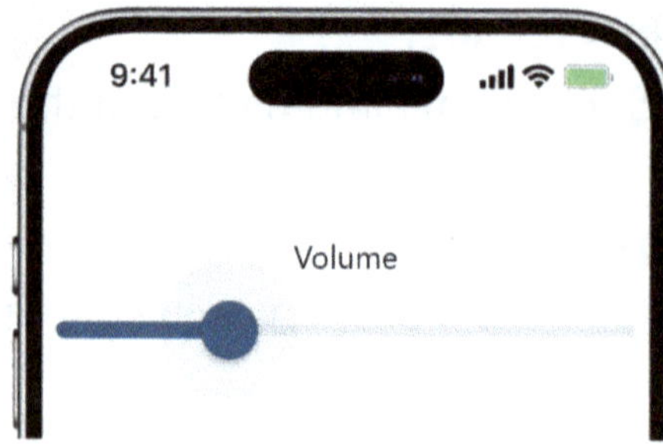


```
#Output
volume -> 5
volume -> 7
```

autofocus = bool

When **True**, the slider automatically gains focus when the page is loaded.

divisions = int

Specifies the number of discrete intervals in the slider. If set, the slider snaps to these division points.

round = int

Determines whether the thumb value should be rounded to integer or decimal precision.

interaction = flet.SliderInteration

Uses **SliderInteraction** to specify allowed user interactions. Options include:

- **TAP_ONLY** → Can only tap on the track to move the thumb.
- **SLIDE_ONLY** → Can only slide the thumb.
- **TAP_AND_SLIDE** → Allows both tapping on the track and sliding the thumb.
- **SLIDE_THUMB** → Only allows direct sliding of the thumb.

```python
import flet as ft

def main(page: ft.Page):

    def adjustment(e):
```

```
        #Actual logic goes here ...
        value = volume.value
        print(f"volume -> {value}")

    volume = ft.Slider(
        divisions= 10,
        round= 2,
        value = 20, #Initial value
        min=0,
        max=100,
        interaction= ft.SliderInteraction.TAP_AND_SLIDE,
        on_change = adjustment,
        on_change_start=lambda _:print("Volume is adjusting"),
        on_change_end=lambda _:print("Volume is adjusted")
    )


    cont = ft.Container(
        content= ft.Column(controls=[ft.Text("Volume"), volume]),)

    page.add(cont)


ft.run(main)
```

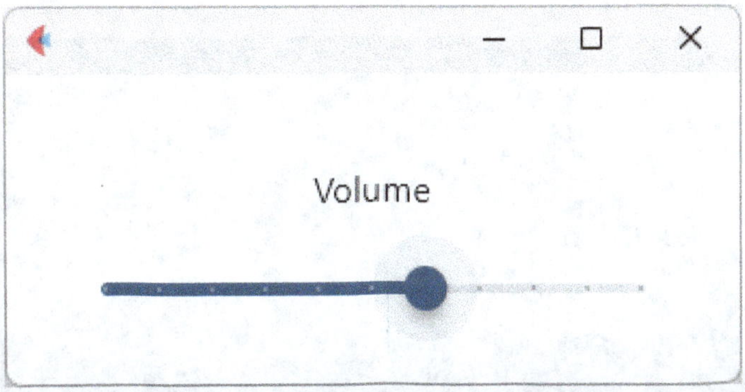

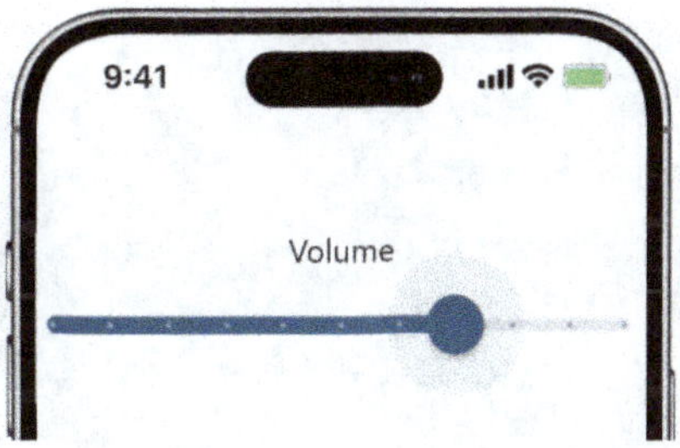


```
#Output
Volume is adjusting
volume -> 30.0
volume -> 40.0
volume -> 50.0
volume -> 60.0
Volume is adjusted
```

active_color = color

Sets the color of the portion of the track between the minimum and the thumb (filled track).

inactive_color = color

Sets the color of the portion of the track from the thumb to the maximum (unfilled track).

thumb_color = color

Sets the color of the knob or thumb that slides along the track.

secondary_active_color = color

Sets the color for a secondary active track if used.

overlay_color = color

Sets a temporary highlight color when the thumb is pressed or dragged.

secondary_track_value = number

Can set a secondary progress marker along the slider track.

```
Python
import flet as ft

def main(page: ft.Page):

    volume = ft.Slider(
        thumb_color="blue",
        active_color="cyan",
        inactive_color="orange",
        overlay_color="#F0F0F0",
        #Code continues below ...
    )


    cont = ft.Container(
        content= ft.Column(controls=[ft.Text("Volume"), volume]),)

    page.add(cont)

ft.run(main)
```

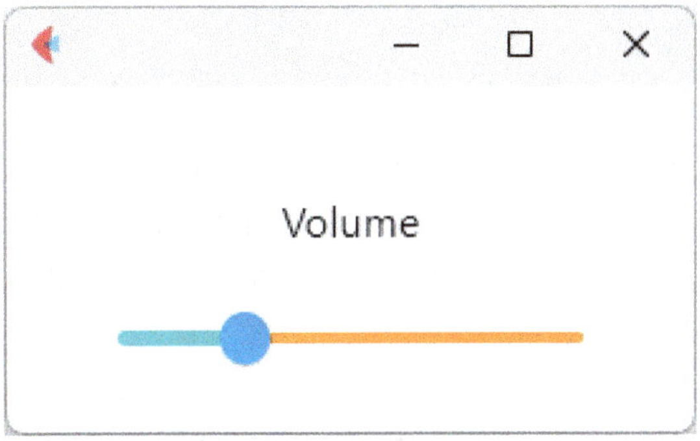

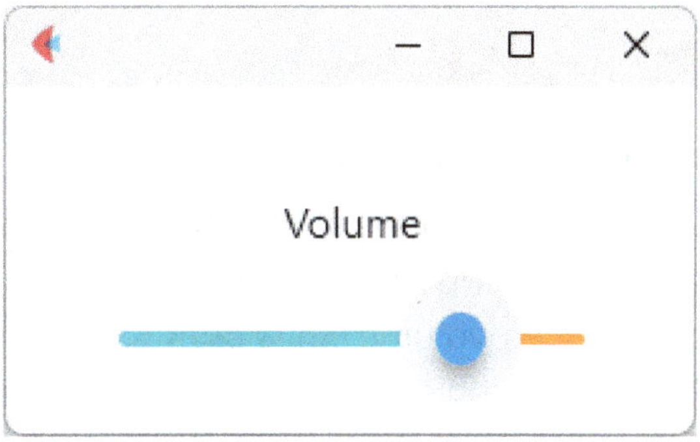

mouse_cursor = flet.MouseCursor
Sets the mouse cursor type when hovering over the slider. *See page 293 for MouseCursor options.*

padding = number, flet.Padding
Applies padding around the slider track and thumb.

on_focus = callback
Registers a callback that fires when the slider gains focus.

on_blur = callback
Registers a callback that fires when the slider loses focus.

CupertinoSlider

CupertinoSlider is the **iOS-styled** version of the standard Slider control. It is used for the same purpose as the regular Slider—allowing users to select a value within a specified range—but follows Apple's Cupertino design language.

It provides the same core properties and methods as the Material Design Slider, with the primary difference being its visual appearance.

RangeSlider

The **RangeSlider** is a material design input control that allows users to select a range of values by sliding two thumbs (knobs) along a track. It is commonly used in applications where a user needs to define a range for settings such as price filters, date ranges, volume limits or any numeric range selection.
The left thumb represents the *minimum* value and the right thumb represents the *maximum* value. The slider track visually indicates the selected range, with different colors for selected and unselected regions.

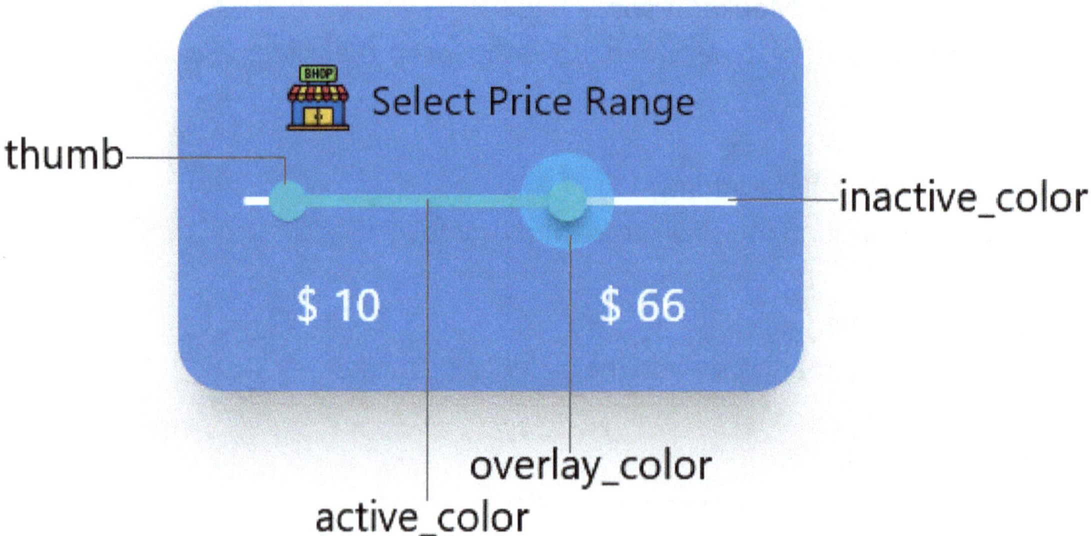

Insight

Usage Example:
A **RangeSlider** can be used in an e-commerce app to filter products by price. The user can slide the left thumb to set the minimum price and the right thumb to set the maximum price. The selected track can be highlighted in green (active_color), while the remaining track is gray (inactive_color).

Properties and Methods

start_value = number

Sets or returns the initial **minimum value** of the range.

end_value = number

Sets or returns the initial **maximum value** of the range.

label = string

Optional string or control to display the current range value near the thumbs.

min = number

Defines the **minimum value** for the range slider, setting the lower bound of the track.

max = number

Defines the **maximum value** for the range slider, setting the upper bound of the track.

on_change = callback

Registers a callback function that fires whenever either thumb moves along the track. This is useful for continuously updating displayed values.

on_change_start = callback

Registers a callback function that fires when the user starts moving the minimum thumb.

on_change_end = callback

Registers a callback function that fires when the user stops moving the maximum thumb.

```python
import flet as ft

def main(page: ft.Page):

    def adjust(e):
        lower_reading.value = "$ " + str(int(range.start_value))
```

```
        upper_reading.value = "$ " + str(int(range.end_value))
        page.update()


    range = ft.RangeSlider(
        min=1,
        max=20,
        start_value= 5,
        end_value=18,
        on_change= adjust,
    )

    lower_reading = ft.Text(str(range.start_value), size=23 )
    upper_reading = ft.Text(str(range.end_value), size=23)

    readings = ft.Row(
            alignment=ft.MainAxisAlignment.SPACE_AROUND,
            controls=[lower_reading, upper_reading]
        )

    col = ft.Column(
            alignment= ft.MainAxisAlignment.CENTER,
            controls=[range, readings],
        )


    page.add(col)

ft.run(main)
```

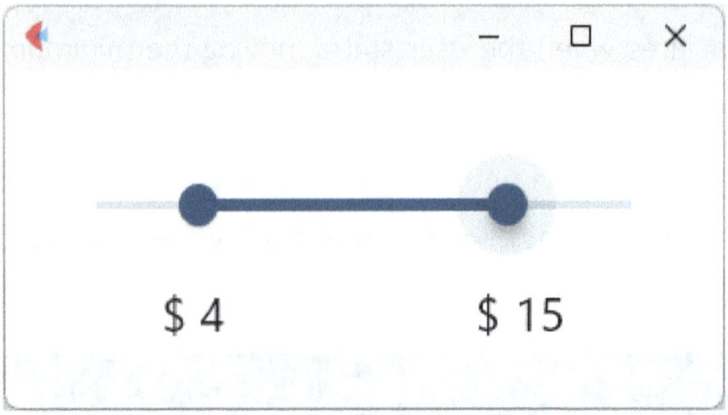

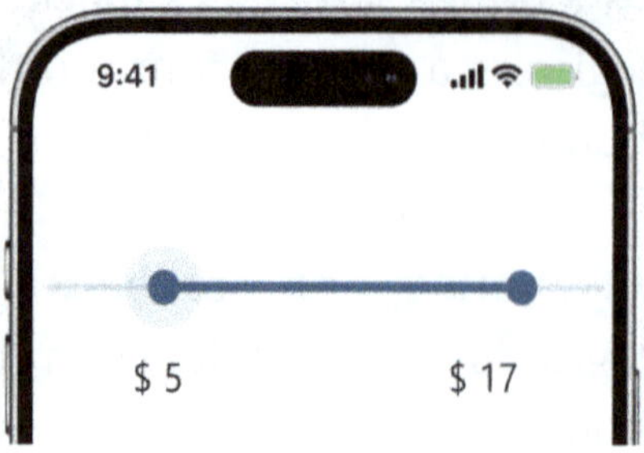

divisions = int

Specifies the number of discrete intervals along the track. If set, the thumbs snap to these interval points.

round = int

Determines whether the slider values are rounded to integer or decimal precision.

active_color = color

Sets the color of the track between the two thumbs (selected range).

inactive_color = color

Sets the color of the portions of the track outside the selected range.

overlay_color = color

Sets a temporary highlight color that appears when a thumb is pressed or dragged.

mouse_cursor = flet.MouseCursor

Uses the **MouseCursor** control to define the type of cursor when hovering over the RangeSlider.

DatePicker

The **DatePicker** is an input control that allows users to select a date easily without manually typing it. It is widely used in forms that require date input such as date of birth, program start and end dates, event schedules, deadlines, booking dates and more. The DatePicker provides two primary entry methods: a **calendar view** for visual selection and a **manual input field** for typing the date. By default, the initial date is set to the device's current date.

Input Mode

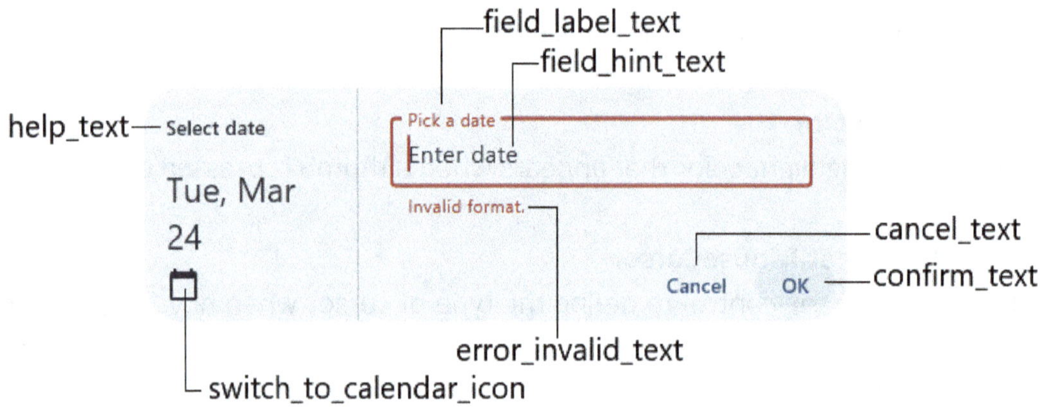

Calender Mode

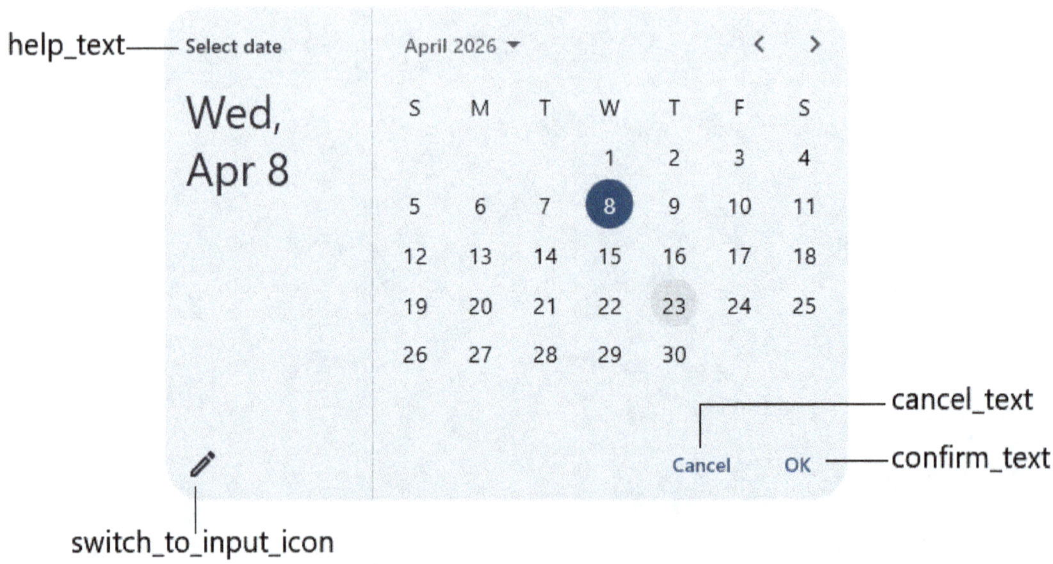

Insight

The **DatePicker** simplifies date entry, ensures consistency in formatting and enhances the user experience in forms and scheduling applications.

Properties and Methods

open = bool
Programmatically opens the DatePicker when set to True.

value = DateTime
Gets or sets the currently selected date.

cancel_text = string
Specifies the text for the cancel button in the DatePicker dialog. Default is *cancel.*

confirm_text = string
Specifies the text for the confirm button in the DatePicker dialog. Default is *Ok.*

error_format_text = string
Text displayed when the entered date does not match the required format.

error_invalid_text = string
Text displayed when the entered date is outside the allowed range.

field_hint_text = string
Hint text shown in the input field to guide the user.

field_label_text = string
Label displayed above the DatePicker input field.

help_text = string
Optional descriptive text providing guidance for selecting a date.

on_change = callback

Registers a callback that executes when the user selects or changes the date.

```python
import flet as ft

def main(page: ft.Page):

    def openCalendar(e):
        datepicker.open = True
        page.update()

    def getdate(e):
        #Actual logic goes here ...
        date = datepicker.value
        print(f"date -> {date}")
        print(f"full date -> {date.strftime("%d, %B %Y")}")
        print(f"day-> {date.day} - {date.strftime("%A")}")
        print(f"month-> {date.month} - {date.strftime("%B / %b")}")
        print(f"year-> {date.year}"
      )

    datepicker = ft.DatePicker(
        field_hint_text="Enter date",
        field_label_text="Pick a date",
        on_change= getdate
       )

    button = ft.ElevatedButton(icon= ft.Icons.CALENDAR_MONTH,
        content="Select date", on_click= openCalendar,)

    col = ft.Column(controls=[button, datepicker],)

    page.add(col)

ft.run(main)
```

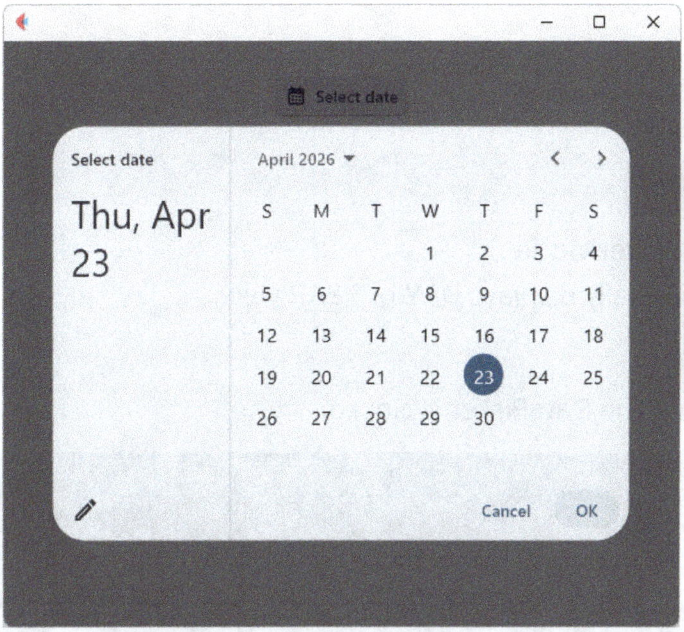

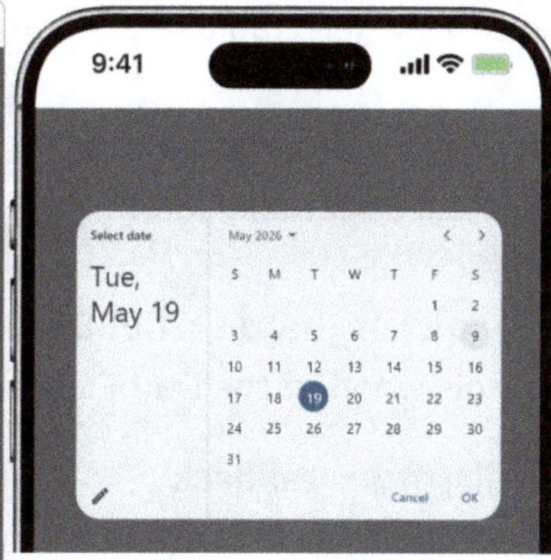


```
#Output
date -> 2026-04-23 00:00:00
full date -> 23, April 2026
day-> 23 - Thursday
month-> 4 - April / Apr
year-> 2026
```

opacity = number

Applies transparency to the DatePicker. Values range from 0.0 (transparent) to 1.0 (opaque).

current_date = DateTimeValue

Sets the initial date for the DatePicker using a DateTimeValue. Defaults to the device's current date (datetime.now()).

barrier_color = color

Sets a background overlay color for the application when the DatePicker dialog is open. Colors can be names, hex codes or predefined ColorValues.

first_date = DateTimeValue

The earliest selectable date.

last_date = DateTimeValue

The latest selectable date.

date_picker_mode = flet.DatePickerMode

Controls whether the DatePicker initially displays **DAY** or **YEAR** view.

on_dismiss = callback

Registers a callback triggered when the DatePicker is closed.

```python
import flet as ft
from datetime import datetime

def main(page: ft.Page):

    def openCalendar(e):
        datepicker.open = True
        page.update()


    datepicker = ft.DatePicker(
        current_date = datetime(year=2028,month=12,day=5),
        first_date=datetime(year=1900,month=1,day=1),
        last_date=datetime(year=2040,month=1,day=1),
        date_picker_mode= ft.DatePickerMode.YEAR,
        barrier_color= ft.Colors.with_opacity(0.5, "black"),
        on_dismiss= lambda _: print("DatePicker closed"),
        #Code continues below ...
      )

    button = ft.TextButton(icon= ft.Icons.CALENDAR_MONTH,
        content="Select date", on_click= openCalendar,)

    col = ft.Column(controls=[button, datepicker],)

    page.add(col)

ft.run(main)
```

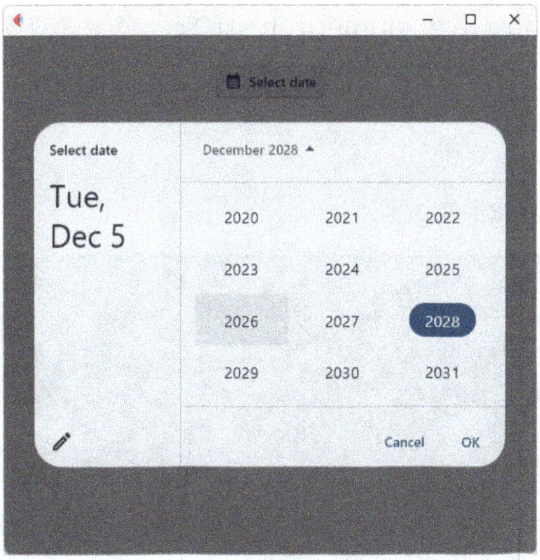

`flet.DatePickerMode.YEAR,`

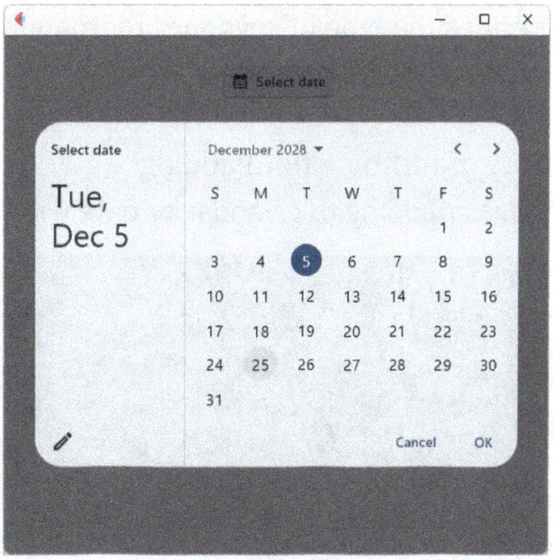

`flet.DatePickerMode.DAY,`

date_picker_entry_mode = flet.DatePickerEntryMode

Specifies the preferred entry mode for the DatePicker. Options include:

- CALENDAR → Shows a calendar or input for picking a date.
- INPUT → Allows manual typing of the date or calendar.
- CALENDAR_ONLY → Shows only calendar for picking a date
- INPUT_ONLY → Allows only manual typing of the date.

on_entry_mode_change = callback

Registers a callback that executes when the user switches between calendar and input modes.

switch_to_calendar_icon = icon

Sets the icon that switches the entry mode to calendar view.

switch_to_input_icon = icon

Sets the icon that switches the entry mode to input view.

keyboard_type = flet.KeyBoardType

Specifies the type of keyboard for manual entry (e.g., numeric, text). *See page 305 for options of the KeyboardType.*

inset_padding = flet.Padding

Applies padding to calendar or date within the dialog.

```
Python
import flet as ft
from datetime import datetime

def main(page: ft.Page):

    def openCalendar(e):
        datepicker.open = True
        page.update()


    datepicker = ft.DatePicker(
        date_picker_entry_mode= ft.DatePickerEntryMode.INPUT,
        switch_to_input_icon= ft.Icons.KEYBOARD,
        switch_to_calendar_icon=ft.Icons.CALENDAR_MONTH,
        field_hint_text="Enter date",
        field_label_text="Pick a date",
        help_text="Date of birth",
        error_format_text="Date format has errors",
        barrier_color= ft.Colors.with_opacity(0.5, "blue"),
        #Code continues below ...
    )

    button = ft.TextButton(icon= ft.Icons.CALENDAR_MONTH,
        content="Select date", on_click= openCalendar,
    )

    col = ft.Column(controls=[button, datepicker])

    page.add(col)

ft.run(main)
```

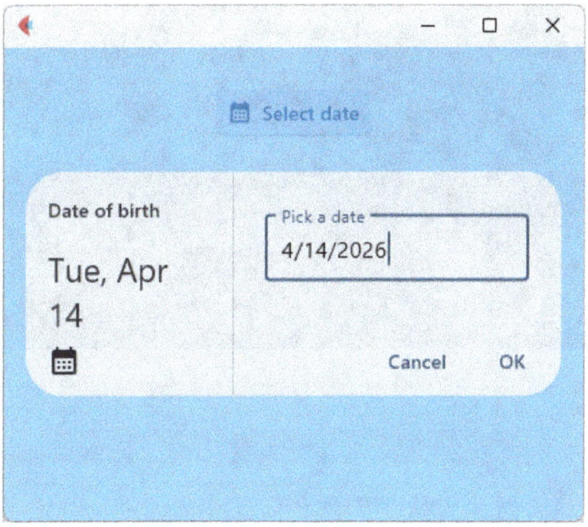

flet.DatePickerEntryMode.INPUT

flet.DatePickerEntryMode.CALENDAR

locale = flet.Locale

Sets the language and regional formatting for the date picker. Locale options include:

- country_code → The standard country code (e.g., "US", "GB").
- language_code → The language code (e.g., "en", "fr").
- script_code → Specifies the writing script, where applicable.

Python
```
import flet as ft

def main(page: ft.Page):


    datepicker = ft.DatePicker(
        #Setting langauge to French
        locale= ft.Locale(language_code="fr"),
        barrier_color= ft.Colors.with_opacity(0.4, ft.Colors.PURPLE_600)
        #Code continues below ...
      )

    button = ft.TextButton(
        icon= ft.Icons.CALENDAR_MONTH,
        content="Select date",
```

```
        on_click= openCalendar
      )

    col = ft.Column(controls=[button, datepicker])

    page.add(col)


ft.run(main)
```

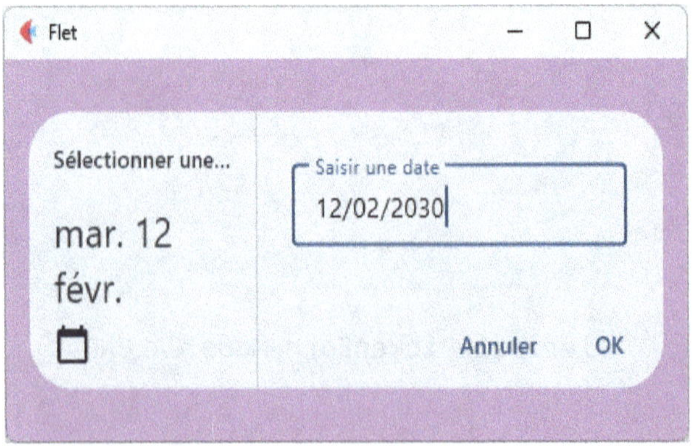

CupertinoDatePicker

CupertinoDatePicker is the **iOS-styled** version of **DatePicker**. It performs the same function—allowing users to select a date—but follows Apple's Cupertino design style. While it shares many properties with DatePicker, it includes some additional styling and behavior-related properties.

Common Properties

first_date	on_change	value
last_date	locale	

Key Properties

Table 3.44

Method/Property	Definition
bgcolor	Sets the background color of the date picker.
date_order	Defines the order in which date components (day, month, year) are displayed.(CupertinoDatePickerDateOrder). Options: DAY_MONTH_YEAR, MONTH_DAY_YEAR, YEAR_MONTH_DAY, YEAR_DAY_MONTH
date_picker_mode	Specifies the picker mode, such as date, time, or date-and-time selection.(CupertinoDatePickerMode). Options: MONTH_YEAR, DATE, TIME, DATE_AND_TIME
item_extent	Sets the height of each selectable item in the picker wheel.(number)
maximum_year	Defines the maximum selectable year.(int)
minimum_year	Defines the minimum selectable year.(int)
minute_interval	Sets the interval between selectable minutes (e.g., 1, 5, 10, 15).
show_day_of_week	Determines whether the day of the week is displayed alongside the date.(bool)
use_24h_format	Enables 24-hour time format when set to True.(bool)

Example

Python
```python
import flet as ft

def main(page: ft.Page):


    def getDate(e):
```

```
        value = datepicker.value
        print(f"Date-> {value}")

    def openDate(e):
        page.show_dialog(ft.AlertDialog(content=datepicker))


    datepicker = ft.CupertinoDatePicker(
        date_picker_mode= ft.CupertinoDatePickerMode.DATE_AND_TIME,
        date_order= ft.CupertinoDatePickerDateOrder.DAY_MONTH_YEAR,
        minimum_year=1998,maximum_year= 2030,
        item_extent= 40,
        use_24h_format= True,
        on_change= getDate,
    )

    button = ft.TextButton(
        icon= ft.Icons.CALENDAR_MONTH, content="Select date",
        on_click= openDate
    )

    col = ft.Column(controls=[button, datepicker],)
    page.add(col)

ft.run(main)
```

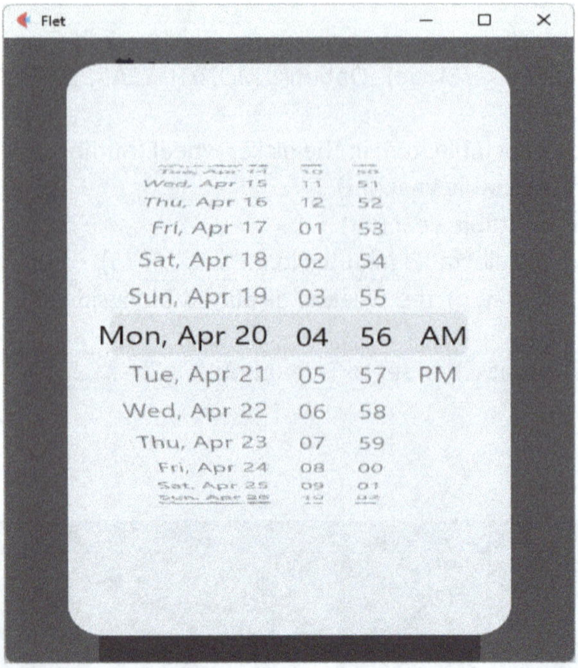

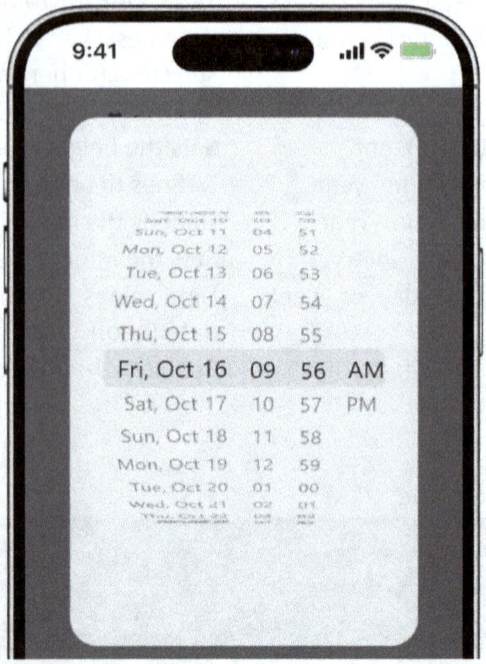

DateRangePicker

DateRangePicker allows users to select or enter a range of dates, consisting of a ***start date*** and an ***end date***. The start date marks the beginning of the range, while the end date marks the final date in the selected period.

> **Insight**
>
> **DateRangePicker** shares many properties and methods with DatePicker. Refer to the **DatePicker** section for a detailed explanation of common features.

Key Properties and Methods

Table 3.45

Method/Property	Definition
start_value	Sets the initially selected start date.
end_value	Sets the initially selected end date.
field_start_label_text	Defines the label for the start date input field.
field_end_label_text	Defines the label for the end date input field.
field_start_hint_text	Sets the placeholder text displayed inside the start date field.
field_end_hint_text	Sets the placeholder text displayed inside the end date field.
error_invalid_range_text	Defines the error message shown when the selected date range is invalid (for example, when the end date is earlier than the start date).
save_text	Defines the text for the ***save*** button which saves selected dates.
modal	If True, the panel exit when clicked outside its region.

Example,

Python

```
import flet as ft
from datetime import datetime

def main(page: ft.Page):

    def getDate(e):
```

```
        print(f"Date-> {datepicker.start_value}\n{datepicker.end_value}")

    def openDate(e):
        datepicker.open = True
        page.update()


    datepicker = ft.DateRangePicker(
        start_value= datetime(year=2026,month=1, day=1),
        end_value= datetime(year=2026,month=2, day=8),
        first_date= datetime(year=2000,month=12, day=1),
        last_date= datetime(year=2030,month=8, day=1),
        modal= True,
        on_change= getDate
    )

    button = ft.TextButton(
        icon= ft.Icons.CALENDAR_MONTH, content="Select date",
        on_click= openDate
    )

    col = ft.Column(controls=[button, datepicker])

    page.add(col)

ft.run(main)
```

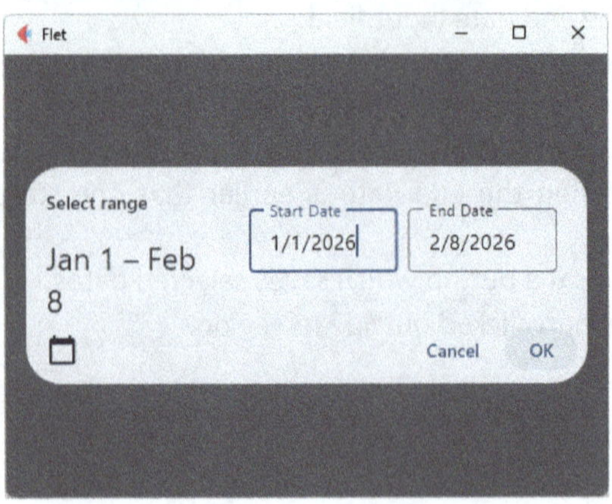

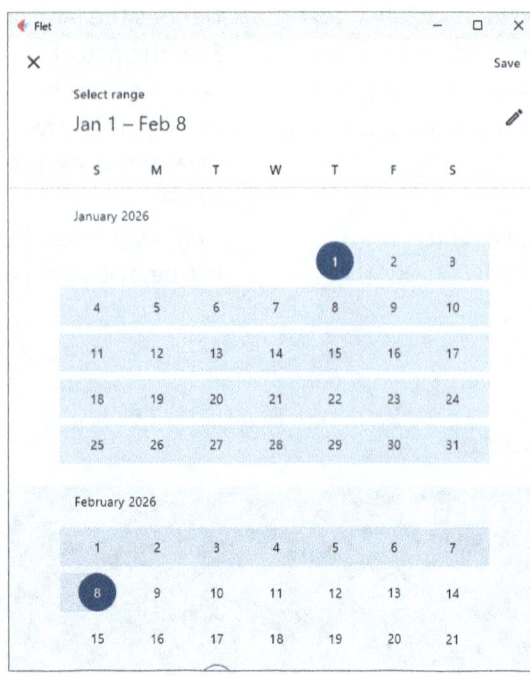

TimePicker

The **TimePicker** is an input control that allows users to select or enter a time efficiently. Similar to the DatePicker, it provides two modes for entering time: manual input and visual selection. The initial time defaults to the device's current time. TimePickers are commonly used in forms and applications that require time input, such as meeting schedules, alarm settings, event planning, reminders or shift management.

Input Mode

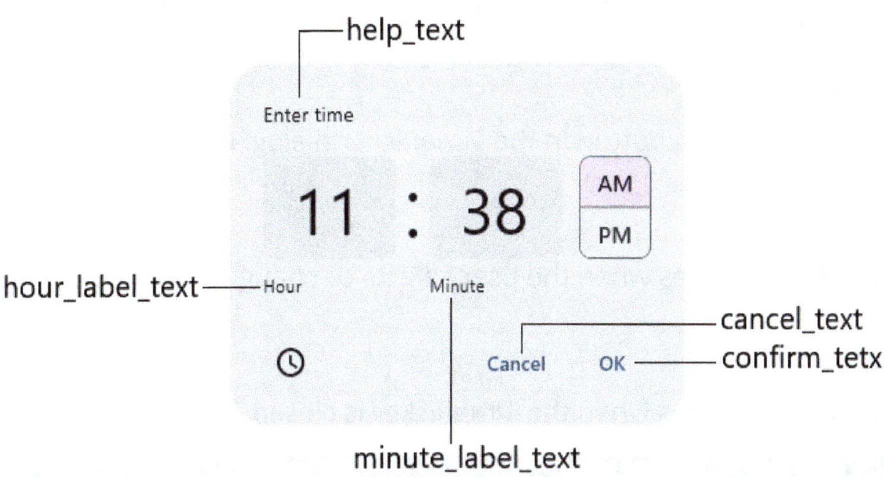

Dial Mode

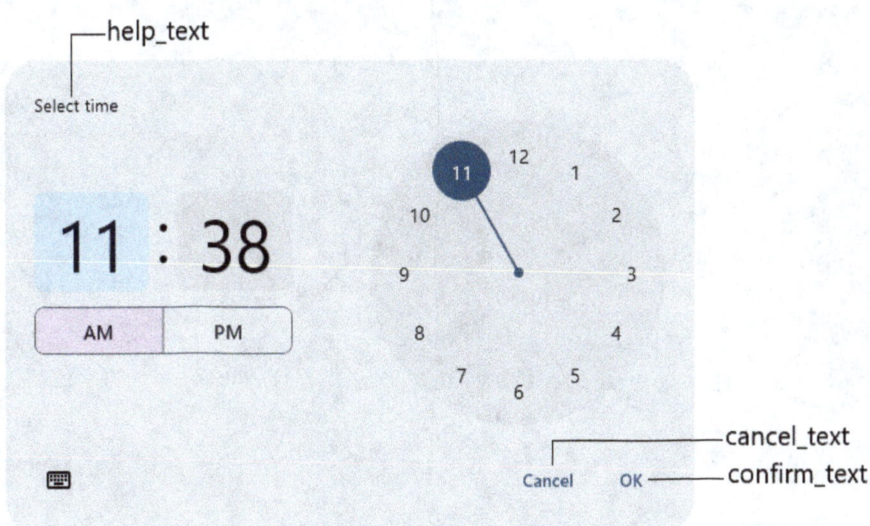

Properties and Methods

open = bool

Programmatically opens the TimePicker when set to True.

value = DateTimeValue

Gets or sets the currently selected time.

cancel_text = string

Specifies the text for the *cancel* button in the TimePicker dialog. Default is *Cancel.*

confirm_text = string

Specifies the text for the *confirm* button in the TimePicker dialog. Default is *OK.*

on_change = callback

Registers a callback that executes when the user selects or changes the time.

on_dismiss = callback

Registers a callback that executes when the TimePicker is closed.

Python

```python
import flet as ft

def main(page: ft.Page):

    def openTime(e):
        timepicker.open = True
        page.update()

    def gettime(e):
        #Actual logic goes here ...
        time = timepicker.value
        print(f"date -> {time}")
        print(f"hour -> {time.hour}")
        print(f"minute -> {time.minute}")
        print(f"second -> {time.second}")
        print(f"microsecond -> {time.microsecond}")


    timepicker = ft.TimePicker(
        on_change= gettime,
        on_dismiss= lambda _: print("Time successfully closed")
    )
```

```
    button = ft.TextButton(icon= ft.Icons.TIMER,
        content="Select Time", on_click= openTime
    )

    col = ft.Column(controls=[button, timepicker])
    page.add(col)

ft.run(main)
```

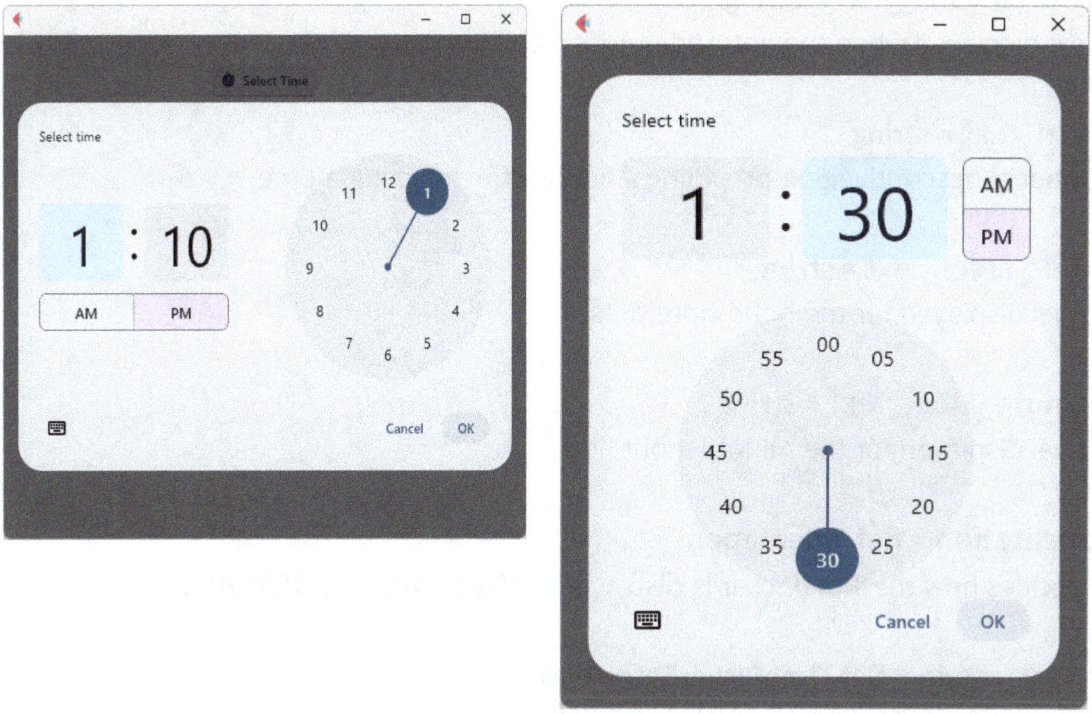

switch_to_timer_icon = icon
Sets the icon that switches the entry mode to dial mode.

switch_to_input_icon = icon
Sets the icon that switches the entry mode to input view.

locale = flet.Locale(language_code, country_code)
Sets the language and regional formatting for the time picker. Example of language codes include: "en" (English) and "fr" (French).

modal = **bool**

Determines whether the timer should be closed when outside it's region is clicked.

barrier_color = **color**

Sets a background overlay color for the application when the TimePicker dialog is open. Colors can be names, hex codes or predefined ColorValues.

error_invalid_text = **string**

Text displayed when the entered time is invalid.

help_text = **string**

Optional descriptive text providing guidance for selecting a time.

hour_label_text = **string**

Label displayed for the hour input field.

minute_label_text = **string**

Label displayed for the minute input field.

orientation = **flet.Orientation**

Specifies how the TimePicker is displayed: **LANDSCAPE** or **PORTRAIT**.

entry_mode = **flet.TimePickerEntryMode**

Sets the preferred entry mode: either **input** for manual typing or **dial** for visual selection. Options include:

- DIAL
- INPUT
- DIAL_ONLY
- INPUT_ONLY

on_entry_mode_change = **callback**

Registers a callback, triggered when switching between input and selection modes.

```
Python
import flet as ft

def main(page: ft.Page):

    def openTime(e):
        timepicker.open = True
        page.update()
```

```
    timepicker = ft.TimePicker(
        orientation= ft.Orientation.PORTRAIT,
        time_picker_entry_mode= ft.TimePickerEntryMode.INPUT,
        barrier_color= ft.Colors.with_opacity(0.7, "#023246"),
        on_entry_mode_change= lambda _: print("Time entry mode change"),
        #Code continues below ...
       )

    button = ft.ElevatedButton(icon= ft.Icons.TIMER,
        text="Select Time", on_click= openTime
     )

    col = ft.Column(controls=[button, timepicker])


    page.add(col)

ft.run(main)
```

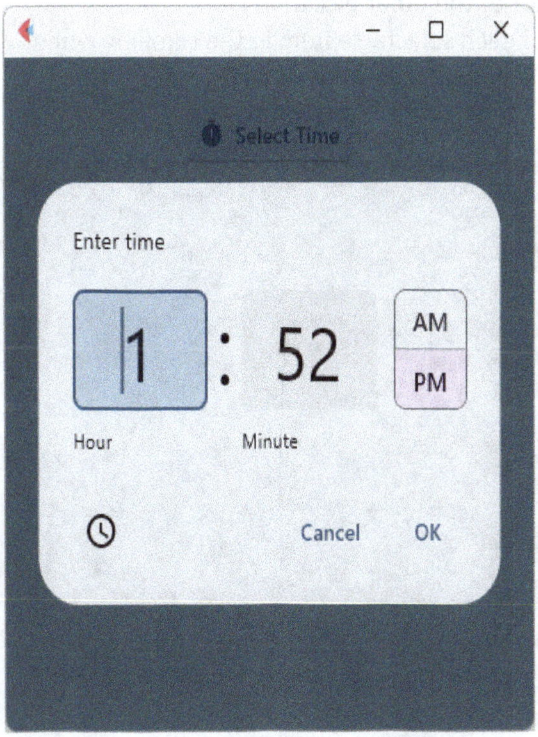

`flet.TimePickerEntryMode.INPUT`

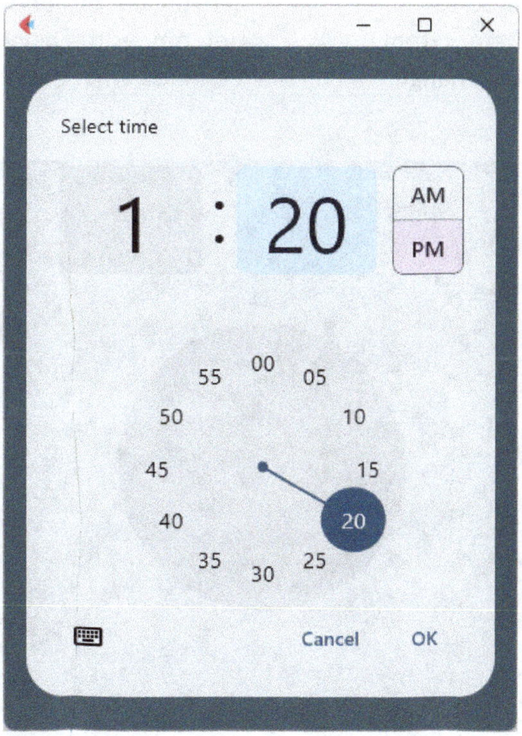

`flet.TimePickerEntryMode.DIAL`

CupertinoTimerPicker

CupertinoTimerPicker is an iOS-styled time selection control that allows users to pick a duration or time value using a scrolling wheel interface, following Apple's Cupertino design.

Key Properties

Table 3.46

Method/Property	Definition
value	Represents the selected time value in DateTime format.
alignment	Controls how the timer picker is aligned within its parent container or dialog.
second_interval	Defines the interval between selectable seconds (e.g., 1, 5, 10).
minute_interval	Defines the interval between selectable minutes.
mode	Specifies the timer display mode using CupertinoTimerPickerMode. For example: HOUR_MINUTE_SECONDS, HOUR_MINUTE, MINUTE_SECONDS
bgcolor	Sets the background color of the timer picker.
item_extent	Determines the height of each selectable item in the scrolling wheel.
on_change	Triggered whenever the selected time value changes.

```python
import flet as ft

def main(page: ft.Page):

    def getTime(e):
        value = timepicker.value
        print(f"Time-> {value}")

    def openTime(e):
        page.show_dialog(ft.AlertDialog(content=timepicker))


    timepicker = ft.CupertinoTimerPicker(on_change= getTime,
        mode= ft.CupertinoTimerPickerMode.HOUR_MINUTE_SECONDS,
    )

    button = ft.TextButton(content="Select Time", on_click=openTime)
    page.add(button)

ft.run(main)
```

System Notifications and User Feedback

Every application should maintain effective communication with the user. Beyond providing real-time feedback for interface interactions such as clicks, presses, taps, scrolling, selections and gestures, an application must also inform the user about events occurring within its internal logic or backend processes.

System notifications help users understand what the application is doing at any given moment. These notifications may communicate processing states, loading durations, updates, errors, warnings, crash reports, confirmations or the successful completion of operations. By providing such feedback, users can anticipate system behavior, avoid confusion and develop trust in the application.
User feedback can be delivered through various on-screen messages, including alerts, warnings, informational messages, success confirmations, recommendations, tips and status updates. These messages may appear temporarily or persist until the user takes an action, depending on their importance and context.

For long-running or background operations—such as downloading, uploading, file processing, data synchronization, execution of tasks or network requests—the application should visually notify the user that an operation is in progress. This is typically achieved through timed animations, indicators or progress components that reflect the current state or completion level of the task. Such indicators prevent the user from assuming the application is unresponsive and improve overall usability.
Flet provides several controls specifically designed for system notifications and user feedback, including:

AlertDialog **ProgressBar** **Shimmer** **Placeholder**
SnackBar **ProgressRing**

These notification controls enable developers to build responsive, informative and user-friendly applications by clearly communicating application states and system behavior.

AlertDialog

The **AlertDialog** is a material design control that displays a panel above the main application to inform, warn or alert the user about specific events. It is often used to acknowledge user actions, system status or critical operations. AlertDialogs can either require user interaction (e.g., confirm deletion, format a file, cancel a process) or be informational without requiring action (e.g., successful upload, completed process, notifications).

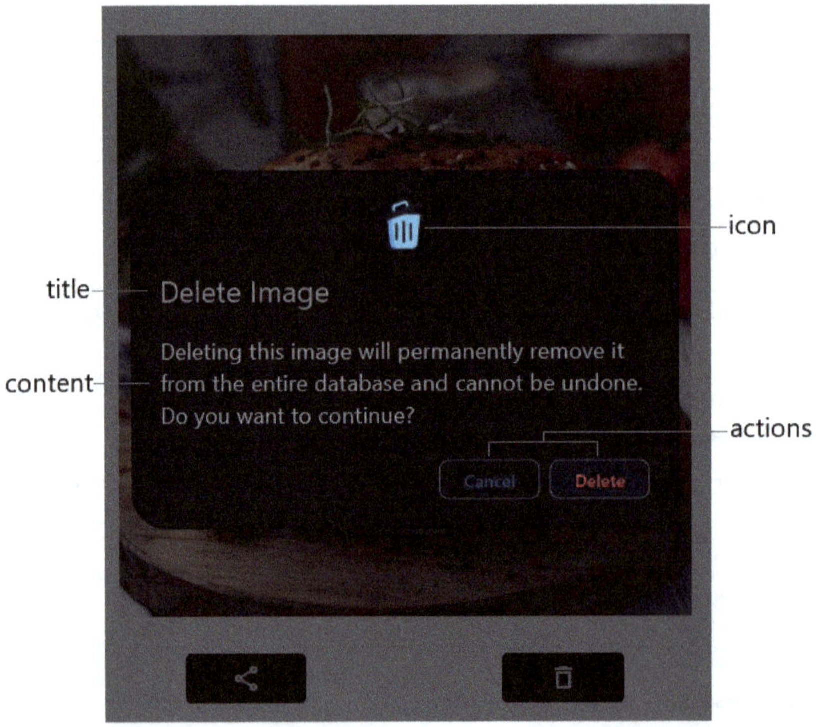

Insight

Common Use Cases

1. Battery is low.
2. Deleting or formatting a file or item.
3. File successfully uploaded or downloaded.
4. Network errors or connectivity issues.
5. Unsaved changes or form validation warnings.

6. System errors or critical notifications.

Properties and Methods

modal = bool

When **True**, the dialog blocks interaction with the underlying UI until dismissed.

open = bool

When **True**, displays the dialog programmatically. Alternatively, you can use **page.show_dialog(dialog)** to open the dialog.

title = string/control

Sets the main control (usually a **Text** control) as the dialog title.

content = control

Sets the main message or information control inside the dialog.

actions = [controls]

A list of controls, usually **Buttons**, that the user can interact with to perform actions like "OK", "Cancel", "Delete".

bgcolor = color

Sets the background color of the dialog panel.

elevation = number

Sets the visual depth or raised level of the dialog.

icon = control

Adds an icon (typically an **Icon** control) to represent the intent of the dialog (e.g., warning, info, error).

```python
import flet as ft

async def main(page: ft.Page):

    def openDialog(e):
        page.show_dialog(dialog)

    def deleteAction(e):
        #Actual code goes here ...
        print("Confirmed delete")

    dialog = ft.AlertDialog(
        title="Delete Item",
        icon= ft.CupertinoIcons.DELETE,
        content= ft.Text("Are you sure you want to delete this contact?"),
        actions=[
            ft.OutlinedButton(content="Delete", on_click= deleteAction),
            ft.OutlinedButton(content="Cancel",
                          on_click= lambda _:page.pop_dialog()
             ),
        ]
   )

    delete_item = ft.IconButton(icon=ft.Icons.DELETE, on_click=openDialog)

    page.add(delete_item)

ft.run(main)
```

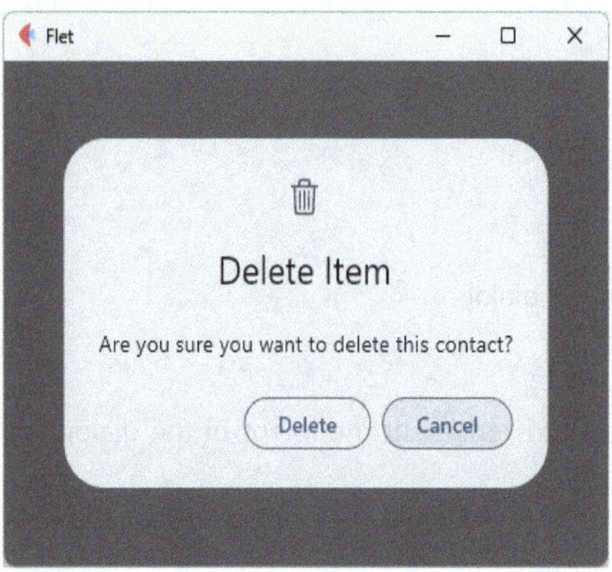

title_padding = number, flet.Padding

Uses **Padding** to add space around the title. *See page 140 for Padding options.*

content_padding = number, flet.Padding

Pads the content (message) within the dialog.

actions_padding = number, flet.Padding

Adds padding around the actions area.

actions_alignment = flet.MainAxisAlignment

Aligns the action buttons using an alignment control. *See pages 162 or 170 or MainAxisAlignment options.*

shape = shape

Sets the shape of the dialog. Defaults to OutlinedBorder. Can use RoundedRectangularBorder for customization.

content_text_style = flet.TextStyle

Uses TextStyle to format or style the dialog's message text.

title_text_style = flet.TextStyle

Uses **TextStyle** to format or style the dialog title.

Python
```
import flet as ft

def main(page: ft.Page):

    style = ft.ButtonStyle(bgcolor="blue", color="white",
        shape=ft.RoundedRectangleBorder(radius=5)
    )

    alertdialog = ft.AlertDialog(
        title= ft.Text("Tour", color="grey",text_align= ft.TextAlign.LEFT),
        modal= True,
        content= ft.Text("Take a quick tour to see how to create...",
             size=18, color="#F0F0F0"
          ),
        icon= ft.Image("lightbulb.png", width= 40, height = 40),
        shape= ft.RoundedRectangleBorder(radius=10),
        elevation= 20,
        actions_alignment= ft.MainAxisAlignment.START,
```

```
        title_padding= ft.Padding.symmetric(horizontal=20),
        bgcolor=  "#0E121A",
        actions= [
            ft.Button(content="Skip", style=style),
            ft.Button(content="Close", style=style,
                 on_click= lambda _:page.pop_dialog()
               ),
            ft.Button(content="Ok", style=style,
                 on_click= lambda _:print("Ok")
               ),
        ],)

    tour = ft.Button(content="Take a tour",
            on_click= lambda _:page.show_dialog(alertdialog)
    )

    page.add(tour)

ft.run(main)
```

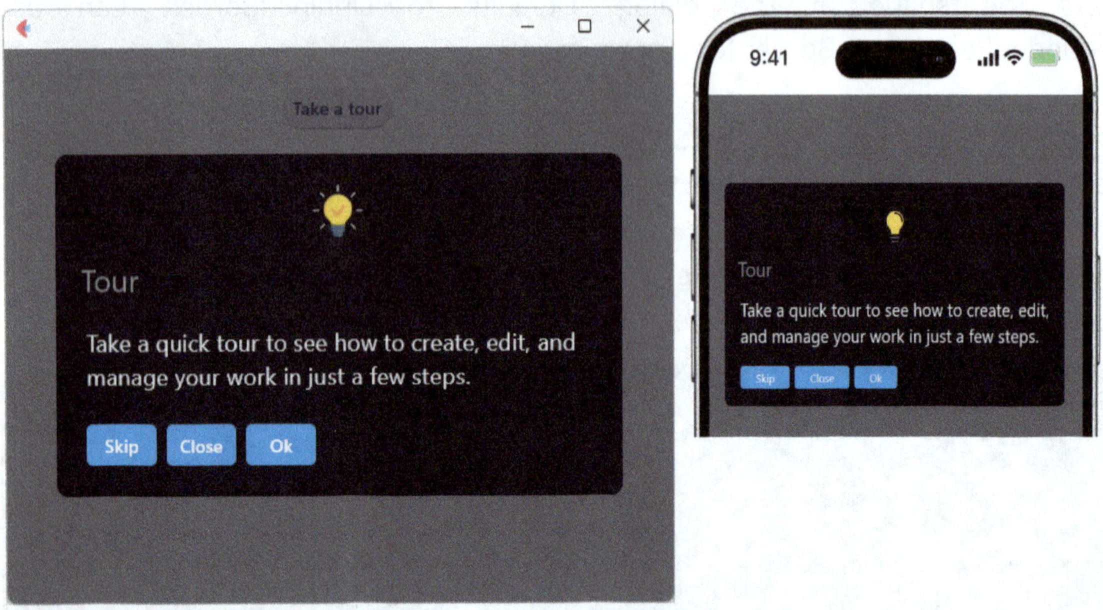

inset_padding = flet.Padding

Adds padding between the dialog edge and the screen.

icon_padding = flet.Padding

Pads the icon inside the dialog.

action_button_padding = flet.Padding
Adds padding around individual action buttons.

shadow_color = color
Sets the shadow color for the dialog. Default is gray.

icon_color = color
Sets the color of the dialog icon if the **icon** property is set as an icon.

scrollable = bool
When **True**, makes content scrollable if it overflows the dialog's bounds.

barrier_color = color
Sets the background color behind the dialog, dimming the underlying UI.

on_dismiss = callback
Registers a callback that fires when the dialog is dismissed from the screen.

alignment = flet.Alignment
Aligns the content inside the dialog. *See page 222 for Alignment options.*

Python
```
import flet as ft

def main(page: ft.Page):

    alertdialog = ft.AlertDialog(
        title= ft.Text("Terms & Conditions", color="#F7C846" ),
        content= ft.Text("By downloading, ...", size=18, color="#F0F0F0"),
        icon= ft.Icon(ft.Icons.CHECK_CIRCLE,size=25),
        icon_color= "green",
        barrier_color="white",
        on_dismiss= lambda _:print("Dialog closed"),
        scrollable= True,
        modal = True,
        actions= [
            ft.OutlinedButton(content="Cancel",
                on_click=lambda _:page.pop_dialog()
                ),
            ft.OutlinedButton(content="Accept"),
        ],
        #Code continues below ...
```

```
    )

    button = ft.Button(content="Terms and Conditions ",
            on_click= lambda _:page.show_dialog(alertdialog)
        )


    page.add(button)

ft.run(main)
```

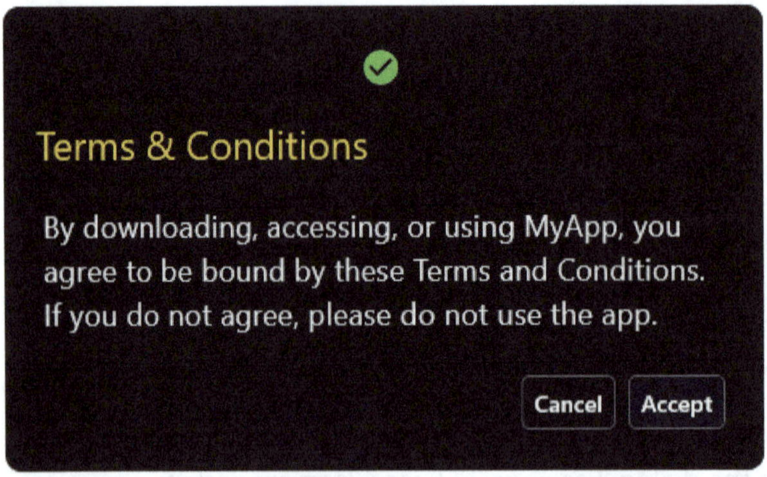

clip_behavior = flet.ClipBehavior
Uses **ClipBehavior** to control clipping. *See table 3.24 for ClipBehavior options.*

actions_overflow_button_spacing = number
Sets spacing when multiple action buttons overflow.

semantics_label = string
Sets an accessibility label for screen readers.

Snackbar

The **Snackbar** is a material design control that briefly appears on the screen to display messages generated by the system. It is commonly used to notify the user about events such as:

- Success (e.g., form submitted successfully)
- Failure (e.g., network request failed)
- Warnings or alerts (e.g., unsaved changes, low battery)
- Informational messages (e.g., new updates available)

The Snackbar can automatically disappear, be dismissed manually and even include interactive actions like buttons for the user to respond.

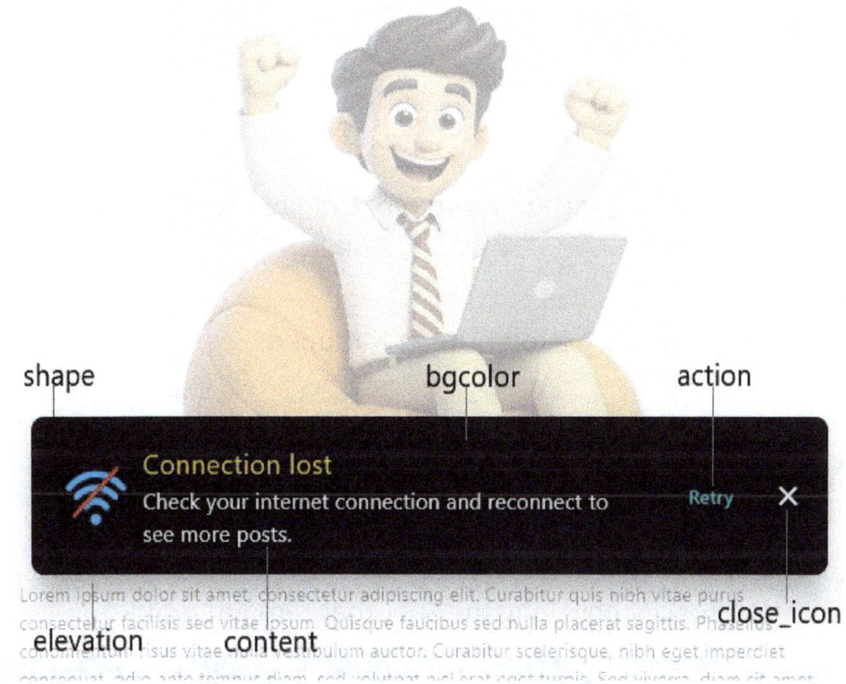

Insight

The **Snackbar** is a powerful tool for temporary messaging in applications, ensuring users are notified without interrupting the workflow.

Methods and Properties

open = bool

When set to **True**, programmatically shows the Snackbar. Another way to open the Snackbar is to use **page.show_dialog(snackbar)**.

content = string/control

Sets the child control of the Snackbar, typically a Text control showing the message.

show_close_icon = bool

When True, displays a close icon that the user can tap to dismiss the Snackbar.

close_icon_color = color

Defines the color of the close icon.

action = string

Adds an interactive button or control for the user to tap. Example 'OK', 'Cancel' etc.

on_action = callback

Registers a callback that fires when the **action button** is tapped.

bgcolor = color

Sets the background color of the Snackbar.

duration = number, flet.Duration()

Uses the **Duration** control to specify how long the Snackbar remains visible.

```
Python
import flet as ft

def main(page: ft.Page):

    snackbar =  ft.SnackBar(
        content= ft.ListTile(
            leading= ft.Image("upload.png"),
            title= ft.Text("Upload Successful", size=20, color="blue"),
            subtitle= ft.Text("Your file has been uploaded ...",size=16)
        ),
        action="Ok",
        show_close_icon= True,
```

```
        close_icon_color= "black",
        bgcolor="#F0F0F0",
        duration= 10,  #Milliseconds
    )

    upload = ft.Button(
        content="Upload File",
        on_click= lambda _:page.show_dialog(snackbar),
        #Code continues below ...
    )

    page.add(upload)

ft.run(main)
```

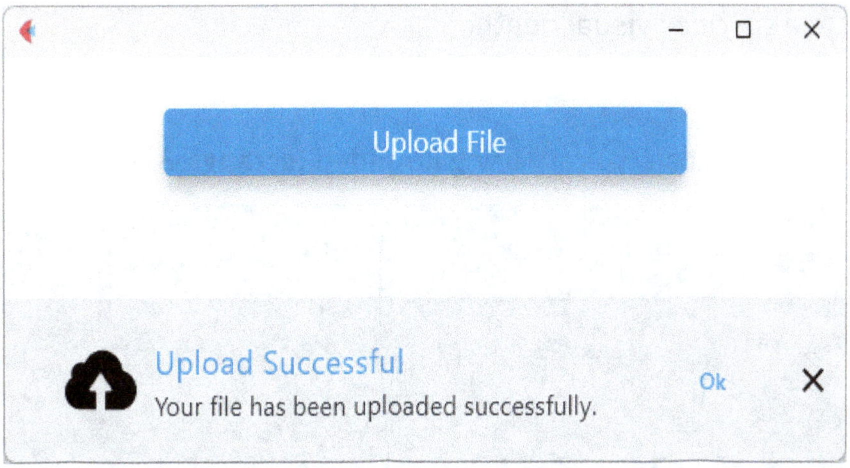

behavior = flet.SnackbarBehavior

Uses **SnackbarBehavior** to control how the Snackbar appears. Options:

- **FIXED** → Snackbar stays at the bottom with zero margin, no elevation.
- **FLOATING** → Snackbar floats above content with margin and elevation.

dismiss_direction = flet.DismissDirection

Specifies the exit direction using **DismissDirection**. Options include,

- DOWN
- UP
- HORIZONTAL
- VERTICAL
- START_TO_END
- END_TO_START
- NONE

persist = bool

When set True, the snackbar stays on the screen until the user closes it.

margin = number, flet.Marging

Sets space between the Snackbar and the edges of the screen using the **Margin** control (works if behavior is **FLOATNG**).

padding = flet.Padding

Pads the content and edges of the Snackbar using the **Padding** control.

elevation = number

Raises the Snackbar to a specified **visual depth**.

shape = shape

Defines the shape of the Snackbar, typically using **RoundedRectangleBorder**.

```
Python
import flet as ft

def main(page: ft.Page):

    def onSuccess(e):
        #Actual logic goes here ...
        return "See submitted file"

    snackbar =  ft.SnackBar(
        content= ft.Row(controls=[
            ft.Icon(ft.Icons.CHECK_CIRCLE, color="green", size=50),
            ft.Text("Your submission was sent ...",color="white", size=18),
        ]),

        shape= ft.RoundedRectangleBorder(radius= 10),
        behavior= ft.SnackBarBehavior.FLOATING,
        elevation=20,
        margin= ft.Margin.only(bottom=50, left=30, right=30),
        padding= ft.Padding.all(10),
        dismiss_direction= ft.DismissDirection.END_TO_START,
        action="view",
        on_action= onSuccess,
        bgcolor="#023246",
        duration= ft.Duration(seconds=2),
        persist= False
        #Code continues below ...
    )
```

```
    submit = ft.Button(
        content="Submit File",
        on_click= lambda _:page.show_dialog(snackbar),
        #Code continues below ...
    )

    page.add(submit)


ft.run(main)
```

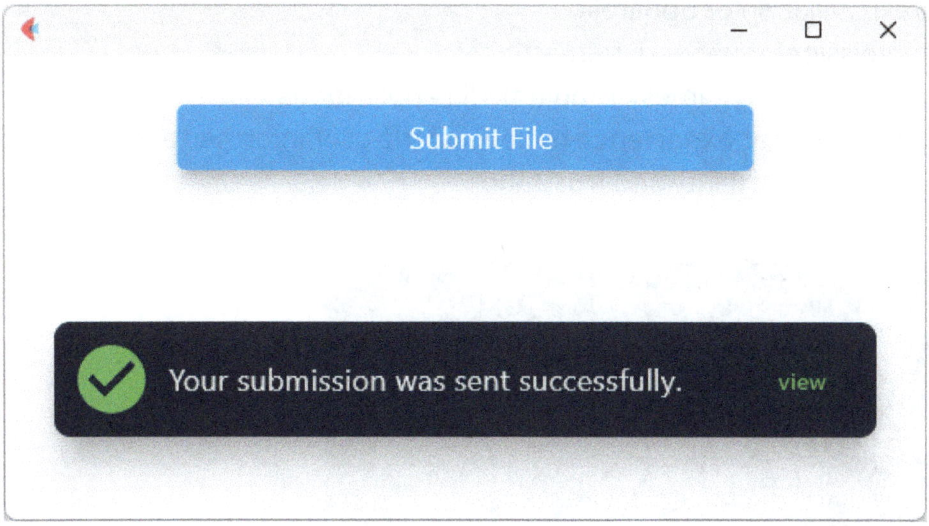

clip_behavior = flet.ClipBehavior
Controls how content inside the Snackbar is clipped. *See table 3.24 for clip options.*

action_overflow_threshold = number
Specifies a threshold for overflowing actions (e.g., if multiple actions exist).

on_visible = callback
Registers a callback that fires when the Snackbar becomes visible.

ProgressBar

The **ProgressBar** is a material design control that visually indicates the progress of a task or computation. It displays a horizontal bar that fills over time, reflecting the completion percentage of a process. ProgressBar is widely used in applications where users need real-time feedback, such as:

- File uploading and downloading
- Data processing and computation tasks
- Software installation or updates
- Form submission or network requests
- Loading resources in games or multimedia applications

This control **enhances user experience** by keeping the user informed about ongoing operations, reducing uncertainty and frustration.

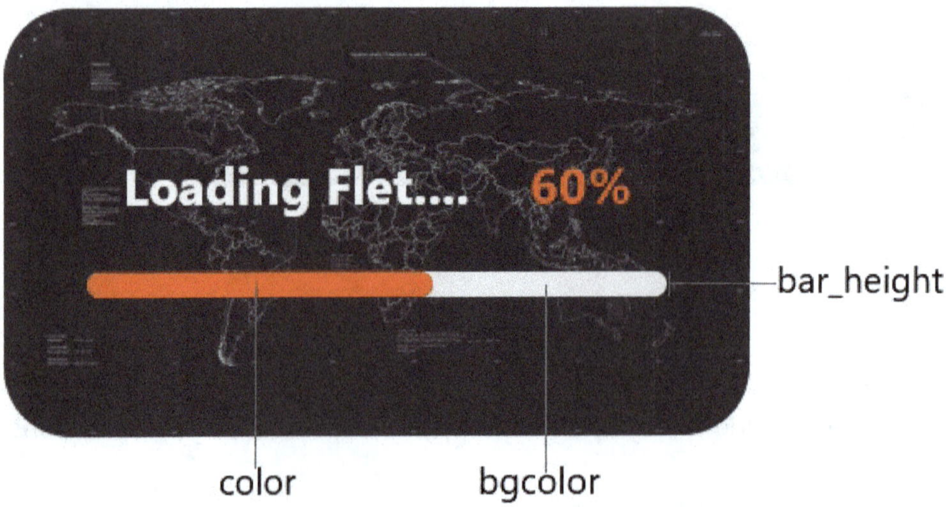

Insight

The **ProgressBar** is an essential visual feedback component, keeping users informed of long-running tasks and enhancing the interactivity and professionalism of an application.

Methods and Properties

value = number

The value sets or returns the current progress of the task. It is a float ranging from **0.0** to **1.0**, where 1.0 represents **100%** completion. If no value is set, the ProgressBar displays a repeating animated fill, indicating ongoing activity.

bar_height = number

Sets the height (thickness) of the progress bar. Increasing this value makes the bar visually thicker.

```python
import flet as ft

def main(page: ft.Page):

    progressbar = ft.ProgressBar(
        #value=0.4,
        height= 15,
        width= 350,
    )

    page.add(progressbar)

ft.run(main)
```

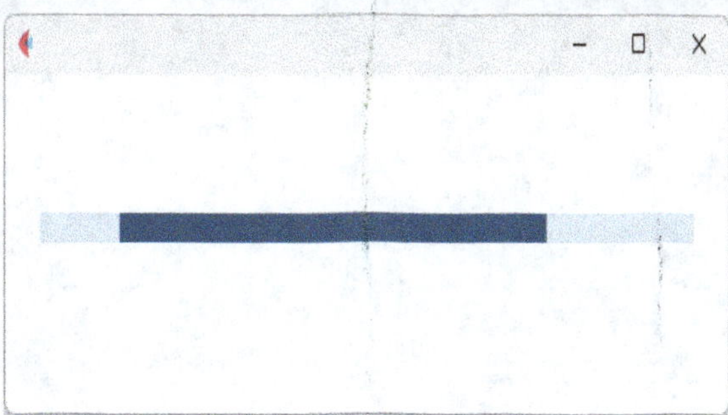

value = None,

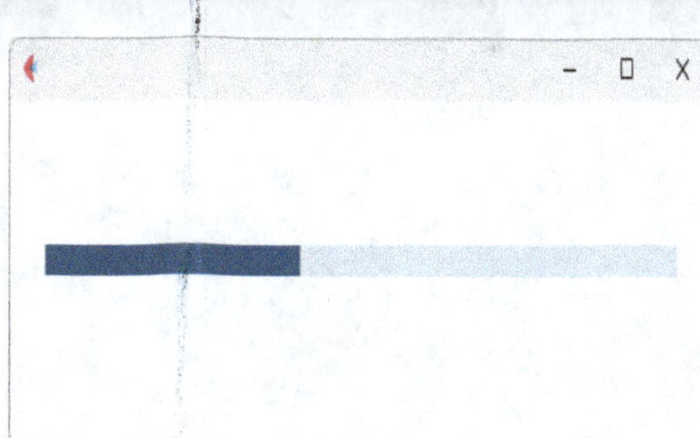

value = 0.4

color = color

Defines the **fill color** of the progress portion of the bar.

bgcolor = color

Defines the background color, representing the unprocessed portion of the task.

border_radius = number, flet.BorderRadius

Sets the curvature of the ProgressBar edges. Higher values make the bar appear rounded, which is more noticeable on thicker bars.

```python
import flet as ft
import asyncio

async def main(page: ft.Page):

    async def processData(e):
        #Actual logic goes here ....
        i = 1
        while i <= 100:
            await asyncio.sleep(0.2)
            progressbar.value = i  / 100
            i = i + 1
            reader.value = str(int(progressbar.value * 100)) + "%"
            reader.update()
            progressbar.update()


    progressbar = ft.ProgressBar(
        value= 0.0,
        color= "#0096c7",
        border_radius= 10,
        #Code continues below ...
    )

    reader = ft.Text("0%", size=20, weight= ft.FontWeight.BOLD,)

    col = ft.Column(horizontal_alignment= ft.CrossAxisAlignment.CENTER,
        controls=[ progressbar, reader,
            ft.Button(content="Execute", width= 200, height=40,
                elevation=5, on_click = processData
               ),
        ])

    page.add(col)


ft.run(main)
```

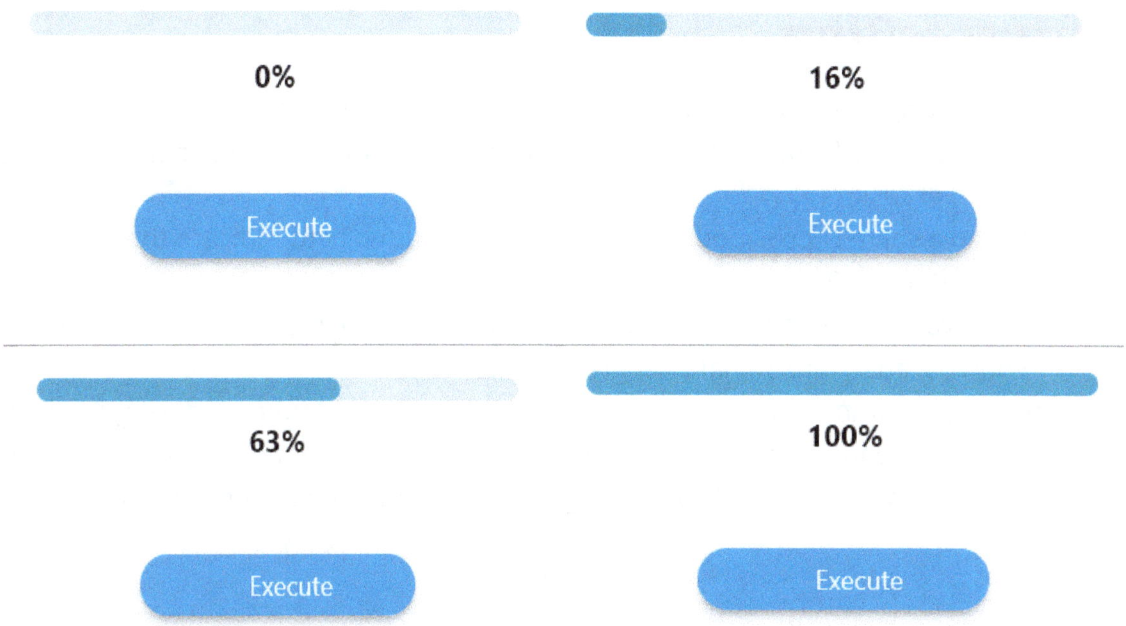

semantics_label = string

A text label that describes the purpose of the ProgressBar for accessibility tools.

semantics_value = number

A textual description of the current progress value for accessibility purposes.

stop_indicator_color = color

Defines the color of the end indicator at the current progress point (if used).

stop_indicator_radius = number

Sets the radius of the stop indicator, making it appear rounded or circular.

track_gap = number

Sets the spacing or gap between multiple tracks if using segmented or multi-track progress bars.

ProgressRing

The **ProgressRing** is a material design control similar to ProgressBar, but it displays progress in a circular form. It visually communicates the status of an ongoing process, computation or task.

- When a value is provided, the ring fills proportionally to indicate the progress (from 0.0 to 1.0).
- If no value is specified, the ring continuously animates in a circular motion, showing an indeterminate progress state.

ProgressRing is commonly used in applications to indicate progress during loading, uploading, downloading, processing tasks or network operations. Its circular design provides a compact and visually appealing alternative to a linear progress bar.

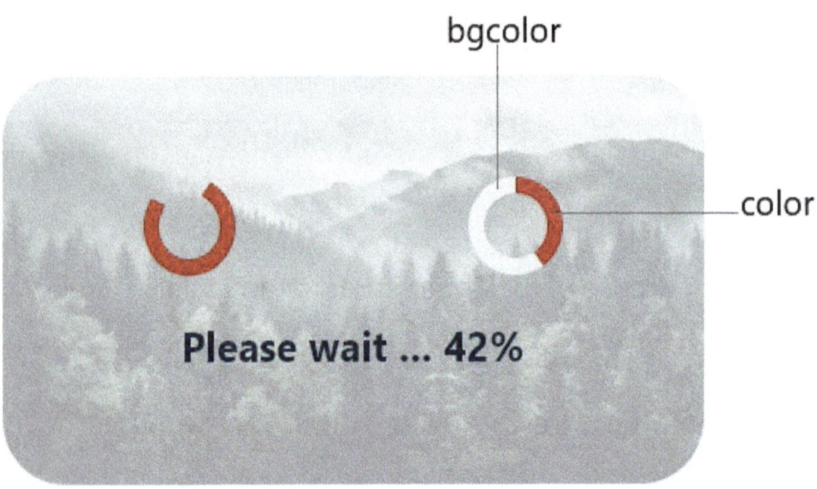

Insight

The **ProgressRing** is ideal for applications that require compact, visually appealing progress indicators, especially when space is limited or circular indicators fit better with the UI design.

Methods and Properties

value = number

Sets or returns the progress value. Accepts a float between **0.0 (0%)** and **1.0 (100%)**. If unspecified, the ring continuously rotates to indicate ongoing activity.

stroke_width = number

Sets the thickness of the ring. Increasing this value makes the progress ring more prominent.

```
Python
import flet as ft

def main(page: ft.Page):

    progressring = ft.ProgressRing(
        #value=0.6,
        stroke_width= 5,
        height= 50,
        width= 50,
    )

    page.add(progressring)

ft.run(main)
```

value = None (Spinning),

value = 0.6

color = color

Sets the color of the progress portion of the ring. Can be specified using color names, hex codes or predefined ColorValues.

bgcolor = color

Sets the color of the ring's track, representing the uncompleted portion of the process.

stroke_cap = flet.StrokeCap

Defines the shape of the stroke's ends. Options include **ROUND, SQUARE or BUTT**.

size_constraints = flet.BoxConstraints

Uses **BoxConstraints** to define the maximum and minimum dimensions of the ring:

- max_height → Maximum height of the ring
- min_height → Minimum height of the ring
- max_width → Maximum width of the ring
- min_width → Minimum width of the ring

Python
```
import flet as ft
import asyncio

async def main(page: ft.Page):

    async def processData(e):
        #Actual code goes here ....
        i = 1
        while i <= 100:
            await asyncio.sleep(0.2)
            progressring.value = i  / 100
            i = i + 1
            reader.value=f"Please wait...{str(int(progressring.value * 100))}%"
            reader.update()
            progressring.update()

    progressring = ft.ProgressRing(
        value= 0.0,
        color= "#1A1440",
        bgcolor="#7f5bfd",
        stroke_width= 10,
        stroke_align= 5,
        size_constraints= ft.BoxConstraints(max_height=50, max_width=50),
        #Code continues below ...
    )
```

```
    reader = ft.Text("0%", size=20, weight= ft.FontWeight.BOLD)

    col = ft.Column(
        controls=[ progressring, reader,
                  ft.Button(content="Execute", width= 200, height=40,
                            elevation=5, on_click = processData
                            )
                 ]
    )

    page.add(col)

ft.run(main)
```

track_gap = number

Sets the spacing or gap between the start and end of the progress stroke, allowing partial ring displays.

stroke_align = number

Specifies how the stroke is aligned relative to the ring's path. Options control whether the stroke is inside, outside or centered along the ring.

semantics_label = string

Provides an accessibility label for the ring.

semantics_value = number

Provides a textual description of the current progress for accessibility purposes.

padding = flet.Padding

Sets the padding around the ProgressRing.

Shimmer

Shimmer is a visual loading indicator that applies an animated color-highlight effect to a placeholder control. It is commonly used **temporarily** while content is loading, refreshing or being fetched asynchronously. Shimmer helps inform users that a page or control is in the process of rendering and has not yet completed loading.

Once the actual data or UI content becomes available, the shimmer effect is removed and replaced with the real control.

Shimmer is typically used in the following scenarios:

- During initial page loading
- While fetching data from an API
- During network or connectivity delays
- While refreshing content
- As a placeholder for images, lists, cards or text blocks

Properties and Methods

content = control

The control to which the shimmer effect is applied. This is usually a placeholder UI element displayed while loading.

gradient = flet.Gradient

Defines a gradient used for the shimmer animation.

> **Note**
>
> Gradients are fully explained under the **Container** control (page 149) in previous chapters. Refer to that section for gradient implementation details.

base_color = color

The primary background color of the shimmer placeholder.

highlight_color = color

The lighter color that moves across the base color to create the shimmering effect.

period = flet.Duration()

Specifies the duration of one shimmer animation cycle. It uses the **Duration** class, which allows time to be defined in various units:

microseconds	→	Time in microseconds	minutes	→	Time in minutes
milliseconds	→	Time in milliseconds	hours	→	Time in hours
seconds	→	Time in seconds	days	→	Time in days

direction = flet.ShimmerDirection

Determines the direction in which the shimmer animation moves. Options include

- LTR → Left-to-Right
- RTL → Right-to-Left
- TTB → Top-to-Bottom
- BTT → Bottom-to-Top

loop = number(int)

Specifies whether the shimmer animation should repeat continuously.

```
Python

import flet as ft

def main(page: ft.Page):
    page.bgcolor = "white"

    page.appbar = ft.AppBar(
        title= ft.Text("Shimmer", color="#F0F0F0"),
        bgcolor="#6693EB")

    cont = ft.Row(
        alignment= ft.MainAxisAlignment.CENTER,
        controls=[
            ft.CircleAvatar(radius=40, color= "grey"),
            ft.Column(controls=[
                ft.Container(width=300, height=60, bgcolor="grey"),
                ft.Container(width=300, height=20, bgcolor="grey"),
            ])
        ]
    )

    shimmer = ft.Shimmer(
        content= ft.Column(controls=[
```

```
                    cont, ft.Container(height=20),
                    cont, ft.Container(height=20),
                    cont
                         ]
            ),
        base_color= ft.Colors.GREY,
        highlight_color="white",
        period= ft.Duration(seconds=2),
    )

    page.add(shimmer)

ft.run(main)
```

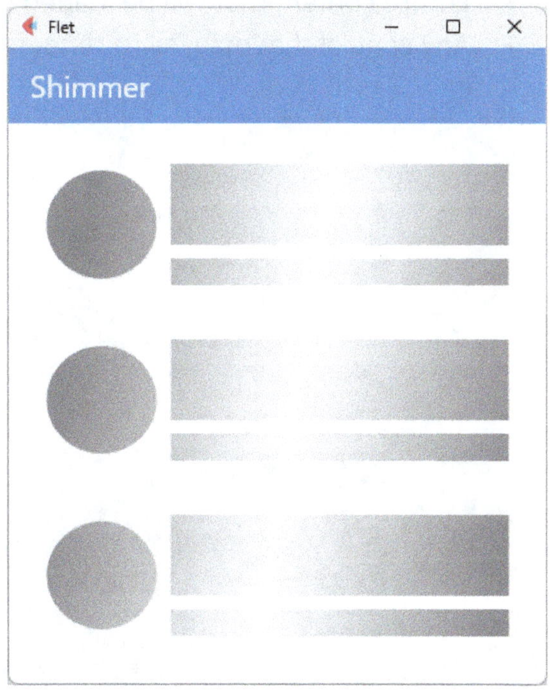

Placeholder

The **Placeholder** is a material design control used to represent a region reserved for a control that fails to load or is not yet available. It provides a visual cue for fallback content or future content, ensuring the UI layout remains consistent and the user knows that content is intended for that space.

Use cases:

- Image loading errors
- Connectivity issues (e.g., failed data fetch)
- Future content that will be loaded dynamically
- Any control that may fail to render due to errors or delays

Properties and Methods

content = control

Sets the child control that the Placeholder should represent or display when the fallback is active.

color = color

Sets the color of the placeholder. This can help indicate the placeholder's state (e.g., grey for loading, red for error). Accepts color names, hex codes or predefined ColorValues.

fallback_height = number

Specifies the height of the placeholder when the original control fails to load. Ensures layout consistency.

fallback_width = number

Specifies the width of the placeholder when the original control fails to load.

stroke_width = number

Sets the thickness of the border or outline of the placeholder, making it more visible or subtle depending on design needs.

Page Navigation and Application Routing

Applications range from simple interfaces with minimal content to complex systems containing numerous widgets, views and interactive components. One of the key factors that makes an application intuitive and user-friendly is how well its content and interface elements are organized across the available screen space.
Simple applications may present all their content within a single screen. However, as applications grow in complexity, it becomes impractical to display all content on one screen. In such cases, the application must be divided into multiple screens or pages, each responsible for displaying a specific set of content or user interface elements.

This separation improves usability, readability and overall user experience.
These multiple screens or pages are typically managed within a main application container that allows users to navigate or route from one screen to another. Navigation can occur through menus, tabs, navigation bars, buttons, drawers, links or programmatic routing logic. Proper navigation design ensures that users can easily move between different sections of the application without confusion.

Routing refers to the mechanism by which an application determines which page or view should be displayed at a given time. Routing may be static or dynamic and can respond to user interactions, application state changes or URLs (in web-based applications). Effective routing helps maintain a clear structure and logical flow throughout the application.
Flet provides several controls and concepts that support page navigation and routing, including:

Tabs	**MenuBar**	**NavigationRail**	**NavigationDrawer**
View	**NavigationBar**	**BottomSheet**	

> **Note**
>
> **NavigationBar, BottomSheet** and **NavigationDrawer** are covered in earlier chapters; refer back to those sections for additional details.

Tabs

In complex applications, content is often organized into categories, with each category displayed on a separate screen. Instead of navigating to different pages, these screens can be embedded within a single view, allowing users to switch between them easily.
In Flet, the **Tabs** control is used to create multiple views within one screen. Users can switch between these views by selecting the corresponding tab.

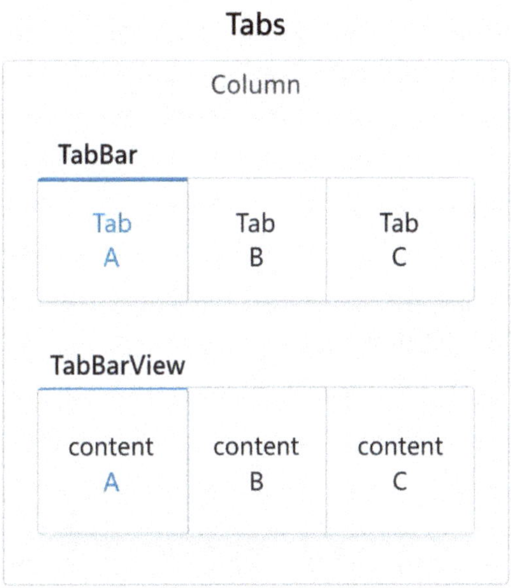

Structure of Tabs

A typical Tabs layout follows this structure:

1. Tabs contains a layout (commonly a Column) as its main content.
2. The layout includes:
    - A TabBar
    - A TabBarView
3. The TabBar contains a list of Tab items (each with a label and/or icon).
4. The TabBarView contains a list of controls (views), and the number of views must match the number of Tab items.

Properties and Methods

content = control

Defines the main layout (usually a Column) that contains both *TabBar* and *TabBarView*.

length = int

Specifies the number of tabs in the TabBar.

Tab

A Tab represents an individual selectable item inside the TabBar. Each Tab typically contains a **label**, an **icon**, or both, and corresponds to a specific view inside the TabBarView.

Method/Property	Definition *Table 3.47*
label	Label of the tab.
icon	Optional icon for the tab.
height	Defines the vertical length of the Tab
icon_margin	Margin to separate tab icon from text.

TabBar

TabBar holds the collection of Tab items. The number of Tab items in TabBar must match the number of views in TabBarView.

Method/Property	Definition *Table 3.48*
divider_color	Color of the divider line separating tab headers from content.
divider_height	Thickness of the divider line.
enable_feedback	Provides haptic or visual feedback on tab selection.
indicator	Uses UnderlineTabIndicator to style the indicator.
indicator_animation	Specifies the animation behavior of the tab indicator using TabIndicatorAnimation. Options include ELASTIC, LINEAR.
indicator_color	Color of the selection indicator (line under active tab).
indicator_size	Specifies the indicator size relative to the tab.
indicator_thickness	Thickness of the indicator line.
label_color	Text color of the active tab header.
label_padding	Padding for the tab header text.
label_text_style	TextStyle for formatting the tab header text.
mouse_cursor	Mouse cursor when hovering over tabs.

on_click	Callback triggered when a tab is clicked.
on_hover	Callback triggered when mouse hovered on Tab.
overlay_color	Background color when a tab is selected.
padding	Padding around the entire tab content.
scrollable	It allows tabs to scroll when content exceeds screen width.
secondary	When True, a secondary or nested TabBar can be created
splash_border_radius	Radius of the ripple effect for tab selection.
tab_alignment	Aligns the tabs horizontally using TabAlignment. Options of the TabAlignment include, CENTER, FILL, START, START_OFFSET
unselected_label_color	Text color of inactive tabs.
unselected_label_text_style	TextStyle for formatting inactive tab headers.

TabBarView

TabBarView contains the actual content (screens) displayed when a tab is selected. Each tab corresponds to one view.

Table 3.49

Method/Property	Definition
controls	Defines the list of views (controls) displayed for each tab.
clip_behavior	Determines how content is clipped when it overflows its boundaries.
viewport_fraction	Specifies how much of the viewport each tab view occupies (useful for custom scrolling behavior).

Example 1,

```python
import flet as ft

async def main(page: ft.Page):

    page.appbar = ft.AppBar(
        title= ft.Text("Tabs", size=25, color="white"),
        bgcolor="#0477e6"
    )


    tabs = ft.Tabs(
         length= 3,
         expand= True,
         content= ft.Column(
             controls =[
             ft.TabBar(
                 tabs = [
```

```
                    ft.Tab(label="Home"),
                    ft.Tab(label="Shop", icon= ft.Icons.SHOPIFY),
                    ft.Tab(label="Checkout", icon= ft.Image("money.png")),
                ],
                label_text_style= ft.TextStyle(size=18)
            ),#TabBar

            ft.TabBarView(
                expand=True,
                controls=[
                    ft.Container(content=ft.Text("View A",size= 25)),
                    ft.Container(content=ft.Text("View B",size= 25)),
                    ft.Container(content=ft.Text("View C",size= 25)),
                ]
            )#TabBarVie
            ]
        ) #Column
    )#Tabs

    page.add(tabs)

ft.run(main)
```

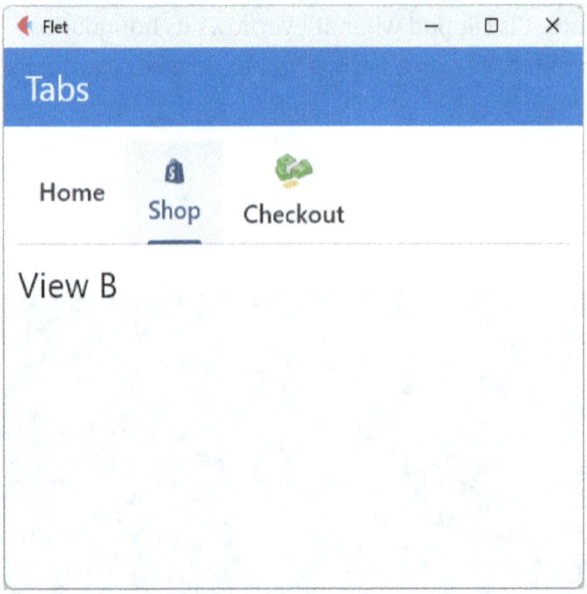

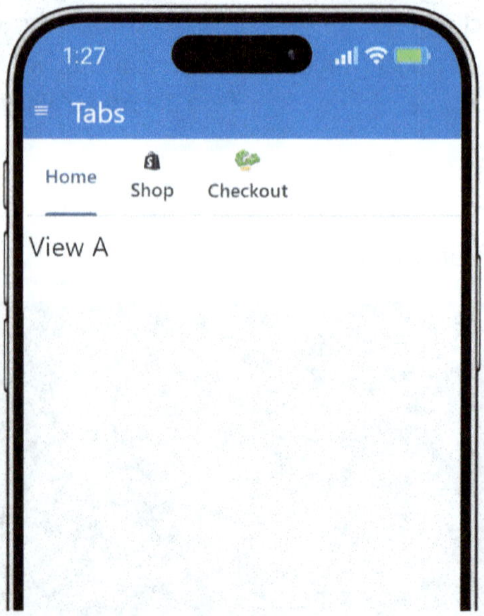

Example 2,

●●● Python

```python
import flet as ft

async def main(page: ft.Page):

    page.appbar = ft.AppBar(
        title= ft.Text("Tabs", size=25, color="white"),
        bgcolor="blue"
    )

    def Profile():
        return ft.Column(
            controls=[
                ft.ListTile(title=ft.Text("Name", size=25),
                    subtitle=ft.Text("Oleando Georgina", size=20)),
                ft.ListTile(title=ft.Text("Address", size=25),
                    subtitle=ft.Text("USA\nIllinois\nChicago", size=20)),
                ft.ListTile(title=ft.Text("Favorites",size=25),
                    subtitle=ft.Text("Gamming\nRobotics", size=20)),
            ]
        )

    def Gallery():
        return ft.GridView(
            runs_count=2,
            controls=[
                ft.Image("image1.jpg",fit=ft.BoxFit.COVER),
                ft.Image("image2.jpg",fit=ft.BoxFit.COVER),
                ft.Image("image3.jpg",fit=ft.BoxFit.COVER),
                ft.Image("image4.jpg",fit=ft.BoxFit.COVER),
            ]
        )


    tabs = ft.Tabs(
         length= 2,
         expand= True,
         content= ft.Column(
             controls =[
             ft.TabBar(
                 indicator_color= "orange",
                 indicator_size=5,
                 label_color="green",
                 label_text_style= ft.TextStyle(size=28),
                 divider_color="blue",
                 divider_height=5,
                 tab_alignment= ft.TabAlignment.CENTER,
                 tabs = [
                     ft.Tab(label="Profile"),
                     ft.Tab(label="Gallery"),
                 ],
             ),#TabBar

             ft.TabBarView(
                 expand=True,
```

```
                 controls=[
                     ft.Container(content=Profile()),
                     ft.Container(content=Gallery()),
                 ]
             )#TabBarVie
             ]
         ) #Column
    )#Tabs

    page.add(tabs)

ft.run(main)
```

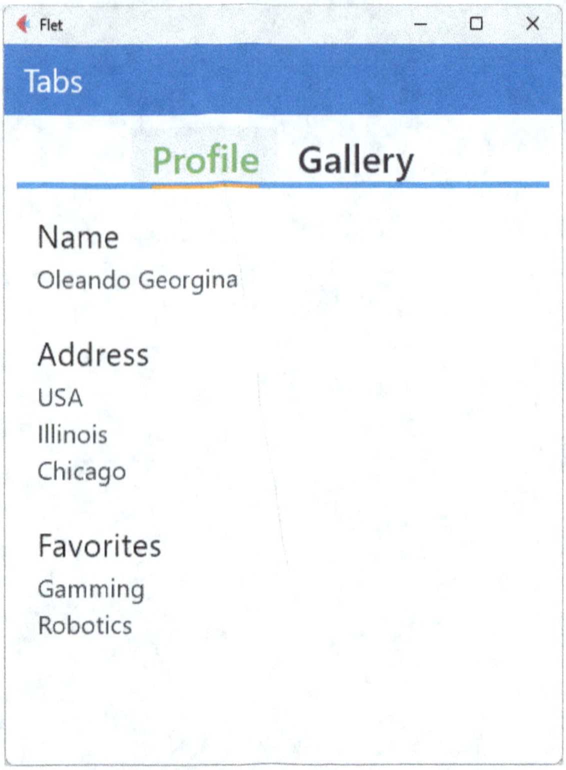

selected_index = int

Gets or sets the currently selected tab index (the active view).

animation_duration = flet.Duration

Defines how long the transition animation takes when switching tabs. *See page 406 for Duration options.*

on_change = callback

Triggered when the selected tab changes.

```python
import flet as ft

async def main(page: ft.Page):

    page.appbar = ft.AppBar(
        title= ft.Text("Flet Tabs", size=25, color="white"),
        bgcolor="blue"
    )

    def getCurrentIndex(e):
        #Actual logic goes here ...
        index = tabs.selected_index
        print(f"Current Index->{index}")


    tabs = ft.Tabs(
         on_change= getCurrentIndex,
         animation_duration= ft.Duration(seconds=3),
         length= 3,
         expand= True,
         content= ft.Column(
             controls =[
                ft.TabBar(
                 indicator= ft.UnderlineTabIndicator(
                     border_side= ft.BorderSide(width=2, color="cyan"),
                     border_radius= 5
                    ),
                 indicator_animation= ft.TabIndicatorAnimation.ELASTIC,
                 scrollable = True,
                 secondary = True,
                 unselected_label_color="grey",
                 unselected_label_text_style= ft.TextStyle(size=18),
                 label_text_style= ft.TextStyle(size=25, color="cyan"),
                 tabs = [
                     ft.Tab(label="About",
                          icon= ft.Icon(ft.Icons.DASHBOARD,color="teal")
                         ),
                     ft.Tab(label="Services", icon= ft.Icons.CALL),
                 ],
             ),#TabBar

             ft.TabBarView(
```

```
                expand=True,
                controls=[
                    ft.Container(
                        content=ft.Text("Flet + Coffee + Rain ...", size=80,
                                text_align = ft.TextAlign.CENTER,
                                weight= ft.FontWeight.BOLD, color="#F0F0F0"),
                        alignment=ft.Alignment.CENTER,
                        image=ft.DecorationImage("image.jpg", opacity=0.6)
                      ),

                    ft.Container(content=ft.Text("Services")),
                ]
            )#TabBarVie
            ]
        ) #Column
    )#Tabs

    page.add(tabs)

ft.run(main)
```

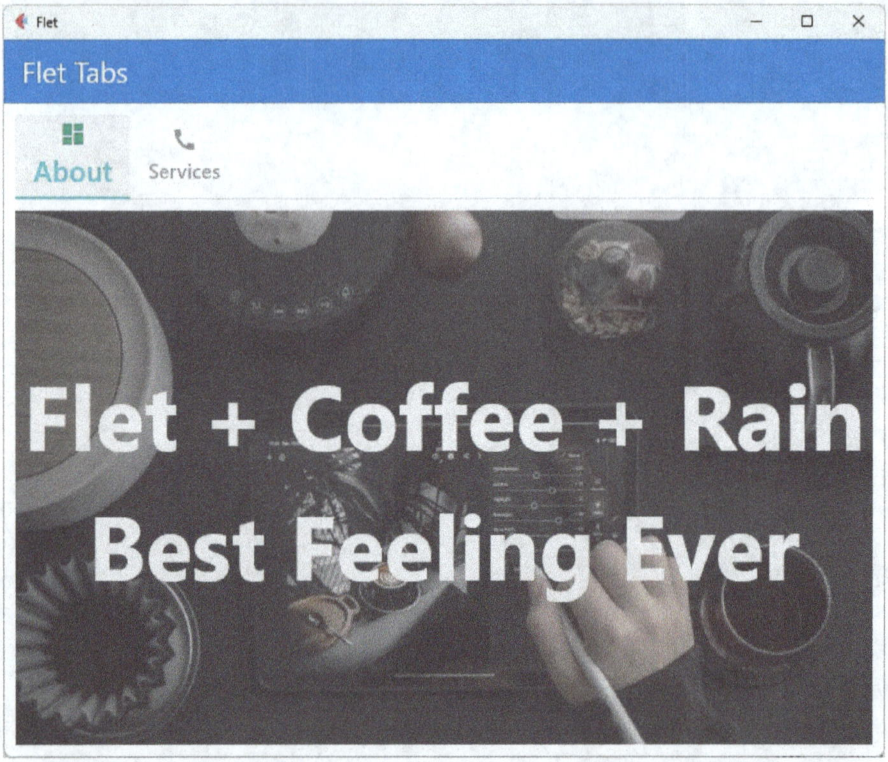

Page View

In Flet applications, the user interface is composed of **views (screens)**, with the **Page** control serving as the default screen. Screens are essential because they contain unique content whose tasks or functionality may differ from other screens.

Applications often include buttons or controls that, when clicked or tapped, switch from one screen to another. This process is called **routing**. Flet allows users to navigate back and forth between views, with each view managed by a Page and containing a unique set of controls.

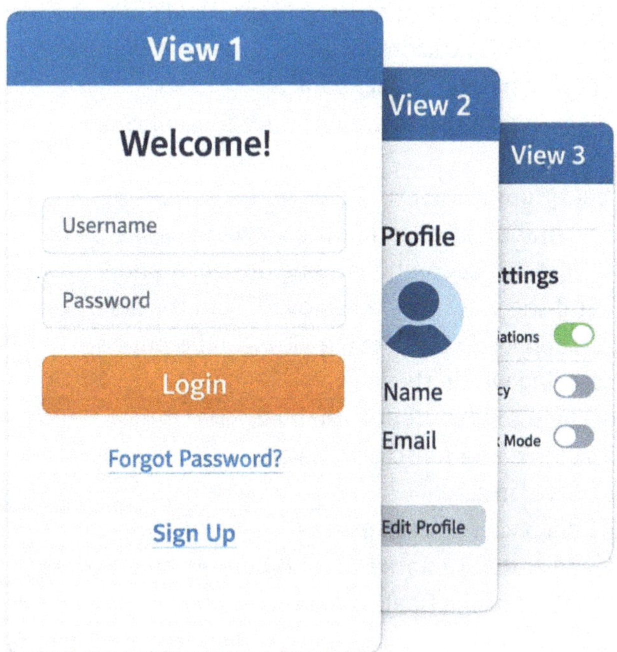

Figure 3.7 : Samples of mobile views

Creating Views

Views or screens in Flet exhibit the same properties as the **Page** control. They provide parameters for adding UI components such as **AppBar, FloatingActionButton, NavigationBar, NavigationDrawer** and other controls.

Key Properties

Method/Property	Definition *Table 3.50*
route	A unique string that identifies the view for navigation purposes.
controls	A list of child controls. The default layout is Column.
appbar	Adds an AppBar control to the view.
bottom_appbar	Adds a BottomAppBar control.
floating_action_button	Adds a FloatingActionButton.
navigation_bar	Adds a navigation bar to the view.
drawer	Adds a left-side drawer.
end_drawer	Adds a right-side drawer.
vertical_alignment	Aligns child controls vertically using MainAxisAlignment.
horizontal_alignment	Aligns child controls horizontally using CrossAxisAlignment.
spacing	Sets the spacing between child controls.
padding	Uses the Padding control to create space around child controls.
bgcolor	Sets the background color of the view.
decoration	Uses BoxDecoration to decorate the view. *See page 145*.
foreground_decoration	Applies foreground decorations using BoxDecoration.
can_pop	Determines if the view can be removed from the stack.
on_confirm_pop	Registers a callback to confirm if a view can be popped.
scroll	Enables scrolling within the view.
auto_scroll	Automatically scrolls content if enabled.
fullscreen_dialog	Displays the view as a fullscreen dialog.
scroll_interval	Sets gaps between scroll
on_scroll	Registers a callback for scroll events.
adaptive	Adjusts the layout automatically for different screen sizes.
floating_action_button_location	Sets the location of the floating action button.

Note

The **NavigationDrawer**, **AppBar**, **NavigationBar** and **FloatingActionButton** have already been discussed in the preceding chapters. Refer to those chapters for guidance on their use in an application.

Adding Views

The Page control manages views using a stack structure, where the last added view is the current view displayed. The **page.views** object provides methods to manage this stack:

Table 3.51

Method/Property	Definition
append(view)	Adds a view to the top of the stack.
insert(index, view)	Inserts a view at a specific index in the stack.
extend(list_of_views)	Adds multiple or list of views to the stack.
pop()	Removes the topmost view from the stack.
index(view)	Returns the position of a specific view.
remove(view)	Deletes a specified view from the stack.
clear()	Deletes all views from the stack.
copy()	Creates a duplicate of the stack.
count()	Returns the number of views in the stack.
reverse()	Reverses the order of views in the stack.
sort(key_function)	Sorts the views according to a key or custom function.

Routing

Routing is the process of **switching between views**. Each view has a **route** parameter that assigns a unique key for navigation. To navigate to a view:

```
asyncio.create_task(page.push_route(route))
```

Navigating Back

Views are stored in a stack, with the **last added view displayed on top**. To navigate back to the previous view, remove the current view using pop(). The previous view then becomes the topmost view:

```
page.views.pop()
```

Handling Navigation Automatically

The **Page** control provides callback methods to manage routing and navigation:

- **page.on_route_change = callback** → Fires when the route changes or a new view is displayed.
- **page.on_view_pop = callback** → Fires when a view is popped from the stack. This function can contain logic to remove the view and display the previous view as the current screen.

Example 1 – Creating a Login Page

1. The **Login page** serves as the home view and includes a **Sign Up** button at the bottom.
2. When new users click the **Sign Up** button, a new view opens displaying the Sign Up page.

```python
import flet as ft
import asyncio

async def main(page: ft.Page):

    login = ft.View(
        route="/login",

        horizontal_alignment= ft.CrossAxisAlignment.CENTER,
        vertical_alignment= ft.MainAxisAlignment.CENTER,

        appbar = ft.AppBar(
        title= ft.Text("Flet View - Login Page", size=25, color="white"),
        bgcolor="green",
        automatically_imply_leading=False
        ),
        controls= [
            ft.Text("Welcome", size=30, weight= ft.FontWeight.BOLD),
            ft.TextField(label="Username", width=300),
            ft.TextField(label="Password", width=300),
```

```
            ft.Container(height=20),
            ft.Button(content=ft.Text("Login", size=18, color="white"),
                bgcolor="orange",width=300, height=50
            ),

            ft.TextButton(content=ft.Text("Forgot Password?", size=18),
                width=300, height=50
            ),

            ft.TextButton(content=ft.Text("Sign Up", size=18),
                width=300, height=50,
                on_click= lambda _:asyncio.create_task(
                        page.push_route("/signup")
                ),
            ),
        ]
    )

    page.views.append(login)

ft.run(main)
```

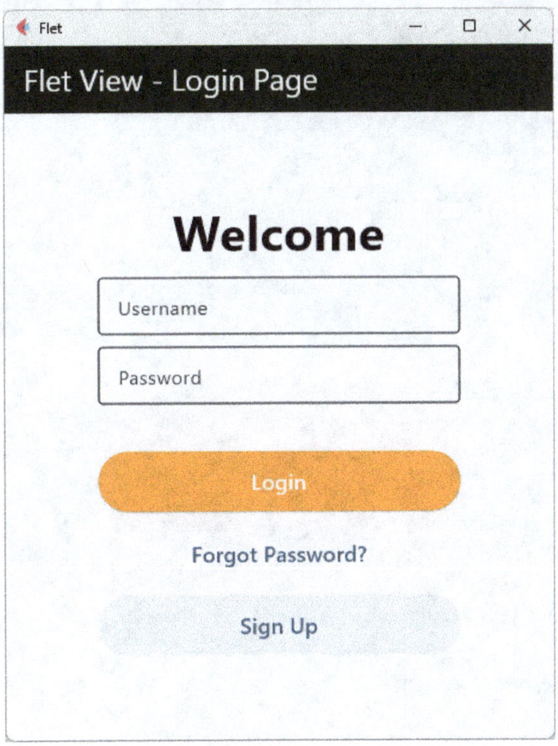

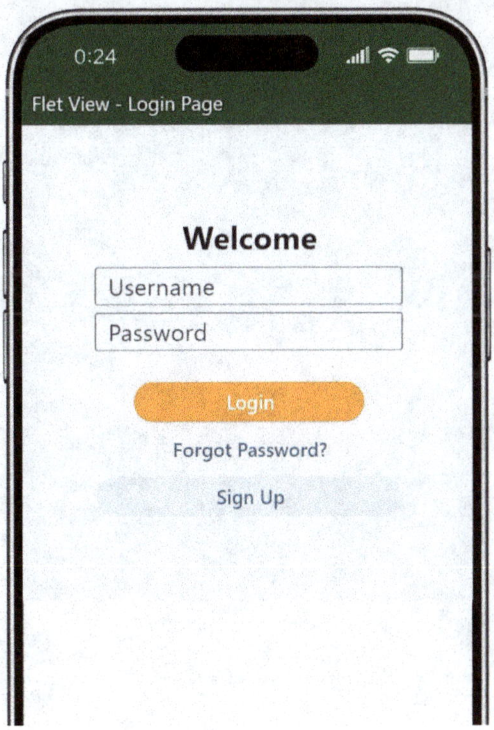

Example 2 – Creating the Sign Up Page

1. When a user clicks the **Sign Up** button on the **Login** view, the current view switches immediately to the Sign Up page.
2. The user can return to the home (Login) screen by clicking the **Back** button in the AppBar.

Python

```
import flet as ft
import asyncio

async def main(page: ft.Page):

    signup = ft.View(
        route="/signup",

        horizontal_alignment= ft.CrossAxisAlignment.CENTER,
        vertical_alignment= ft.MainAxisAlignment.CENTER,

        appbar = ft.AppBar(
        title= ft.Text("Flet View - Sign Up", size=25, color="white"),
        bgcolor="#093a18",
        leading= ft.IconButton(
            icon= ft.Icons.ARROW_BACK,
            icon_color="white",
            on_click= lambda _:asyncio.create_task(
                        page.push_route("/login")
             ),
          )
        ),

        controls= [
            ft.Text("Create account", size=40),
            ft.TextField(label="Email", width=300),
            ft.TextField(label="Password", width=300),
            ft.TextField(label="Phone", width=300),
            ft.Container(height=20),

            ft.Button(content=ft.Text("Create", size=18, color="white"),
               bgcolor="#093a18", width=300, height=40
            ),

            ft.Text("or", size=20, weight= ft.FontWeight.BOLD),

            ft.OutlinedButton(content=ft.Text("Continue with Facebook"),
                icon= ft.Icons.FACEBOOK ,width=300, height=40),
```

```
            ft.OutlinedButton(content=ft.Text("Continue with Google"),
                icon= ft.Image("google.png"),width=300, height=40
            ),

            ft.OutlinedButton(content=ft.Text("Continue with Apple"),
                icon= ft.Image("apple.png") ,width=300, height=40
            ),
        ]
    )

    page.views.append(signup)


ft.run(main)
```

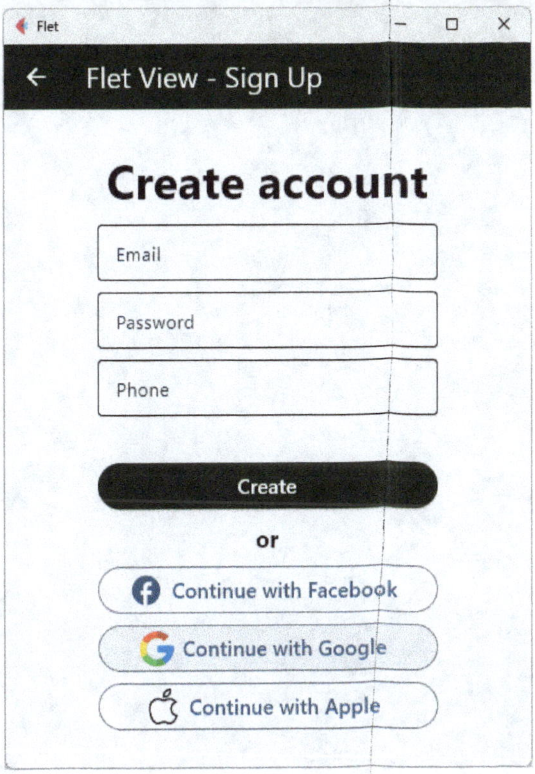

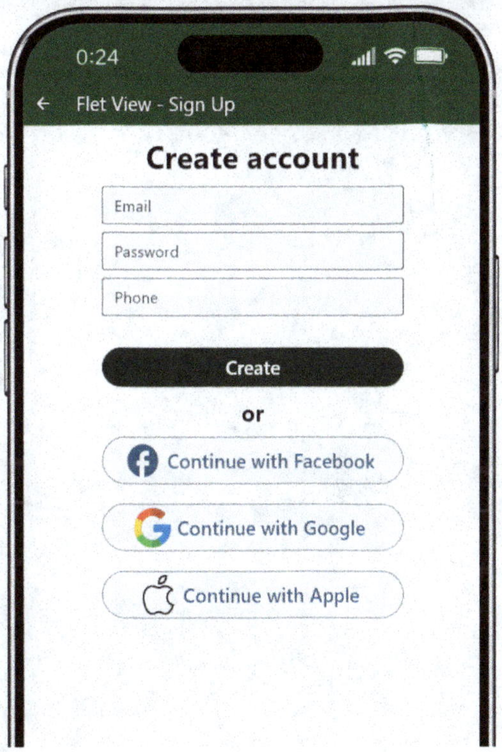

Example 3 – Adding all the views in one program.

```python
import flet as ft
import asyncio

async def main(page: ft.Page):

    #Switching views
    def appendView(route):
        page.views.clear()
        if page.route == "/signup":
           page.views.append(signup)
        else:
            page.views.append(login)
        page.update()


    #Switching to previous view(pop)
    async def view_pop(e):
        if e.view is not None:
            print("View pop:", e.view)
            page.views.remove(e.view)
            top_view = page.views[-1]
            await page.push_route(top_view.route)


    signup = ft.View(
        route="/signup",
        #Code continues below ...
    )

    login = ft.View(
        route="/login",
        #Code continues below ...
    )


    page.on_route_change = appendView
    page.on_view_pop = view_pop
    appendView(page.route)

ft.run(main)
```

Example 4

Python

```
import flet as ft
import asyncio

async def main(page: ft.Page):
    page.bgcolor = "white"

    def changeView(route):
        page.views.clear()
        if page.route == "/account":
            page.views.append(account)
        elif page.route == "/settings":
            page.views.append(settings)
        else:
            page.views.append(homepage)
        page.update()


    async def removeView(e):
        try:
            if e.view is not None:
               page.views.remove(e.view)
               top_view = page.views[-1]
               await page.push_route(top_view.route)
        except:
            page.go("/homepage")


    homepage = ft.View(
        route="/homepage",
        appbar=ft.AppBar(
            title= ft.Text("HomePage"),
            bgcolor="#0096c7",
            color="white"
        ),
        vertical_alignment= ft.MainAxisAlignment.CENTER,
        horizontal_alignment=ft.CrossAxisAlignment.CENTER,
        spacing= 20,
        controls=[
          ft.ElevatedButton(content ="Account",
            on_click= lambda _:asyncio.create_task(page.push_route("/account"))
            ),

          ft.ElevatedButton(content="Settings",
```

```
            on_click= lambda _:asyncio.create_task(page.push_route("/settings"))
            ),
        ]
        )

    settings = ft.View(
        route="/account",
        appbar=ft.AppBar(
            title= ft.Text("Settings"),
            bgcolor="#0096c7",
            color="white",
            leading= ft.IconButton(icon=ft.Icons.ARROW_BACK,
                                      on_click=removeView)),
        controls=[
            ft.Switch(label="Dark theme"),
            ft.Switch(label="Notifications")
        ],
        decoration= ft.BoxDecoration(bgcolor="white")
       )

    account = ft.View(
        route="/account",
        appbar=ft.AppBar(
            title= ft.Text("Account"),
            bgcolor="#0096c7",
            color="white",
            leading= ft.IconButton(
                     icon=ft.Icons.ARROW_BACK, on_click=removeView)
             ),
        controls=[
            ft.TextField(label="Username", width=200),
            ft.TextField(label="Country", width=200),
            ft.OutlinedButton(content="Submit")
        ],
       )

    page.on_route_change = changeView
    page.on_view_pop = removeView
    changeView(page.route)

ft.run(main)
```

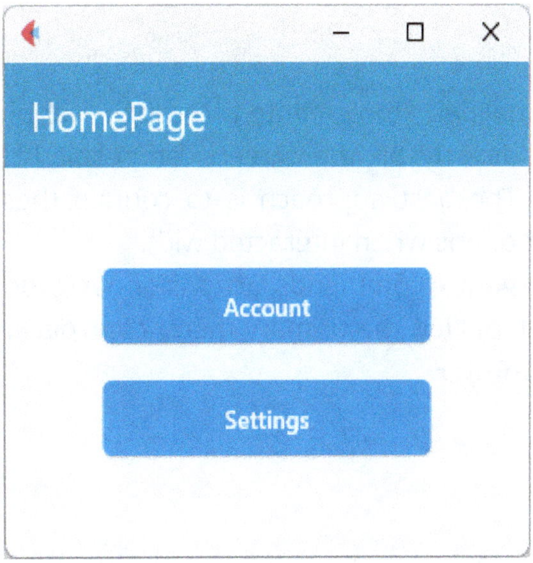
HomePage
Account
Settings

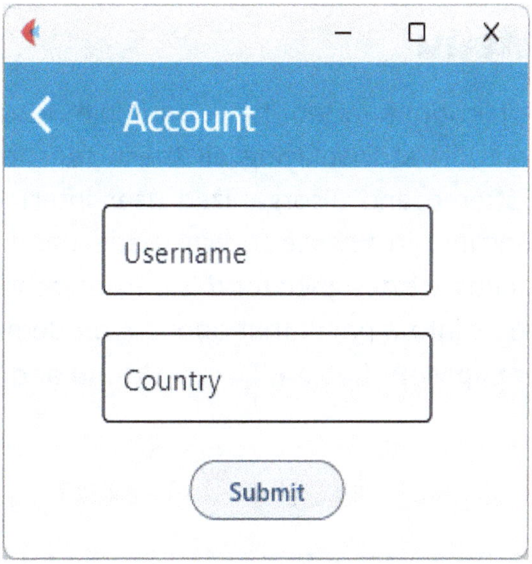
Account
Username
Country
Submit

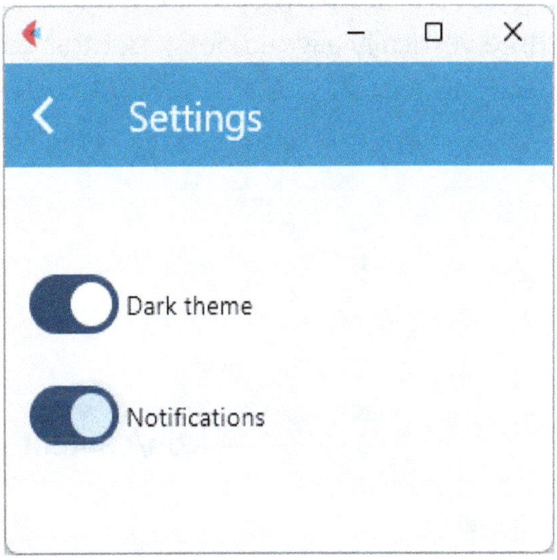
Settings
Dark theme
Notifications

Menu

Applications often have multiple functionalities implemented through various controllers. Displaying all these functions directly on the screen can result in a cluttered and disorganized user interface. The best approach is to contain these functions in a single control that expands or opens when interacted with.
Menus are designed for this purpose: they organize commands, actions or navigation items into a panel that appears on demand. In Flet, the primary menu controls are **PopupMenuButton**, **ContextMenu** and **MenuBar**.

PopupMenuButton

The **PopupMenuButton** is a material design control represented as a button. When clicked, it opens a **pop-up menu** containing several items (PopupMenuItem). By default, the button shows the "more" icon (three vertically aligned dots), but this can be customized.

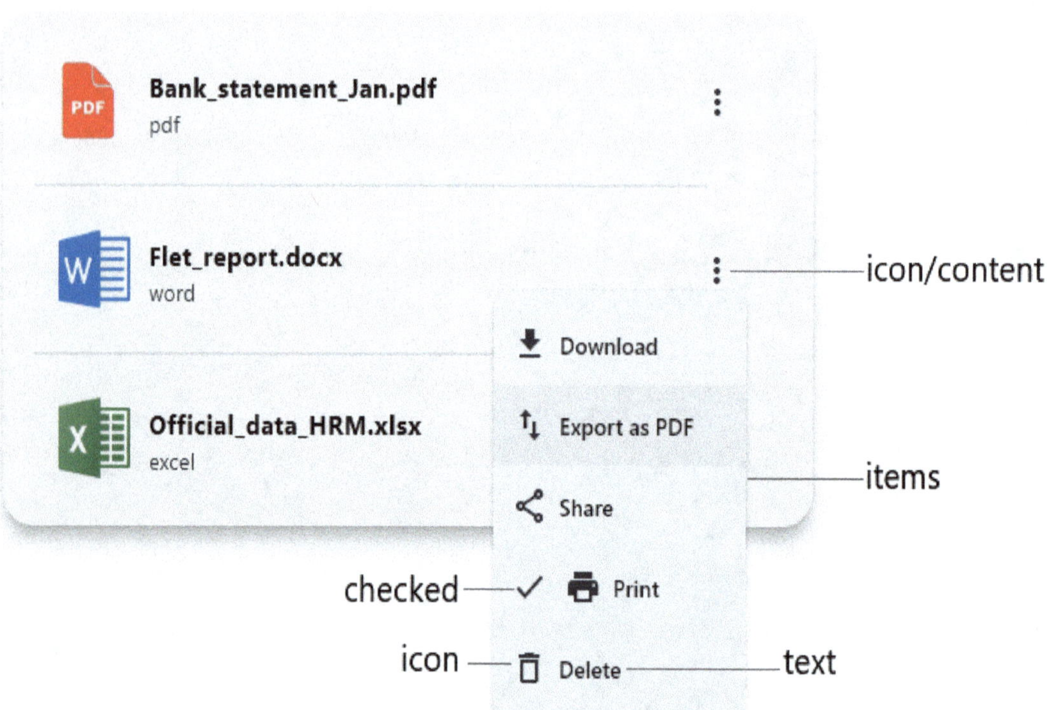

Properties and Methods

content = control

Sets a control (e.g., Text, Icon) to represent the PopupMenuButton itself, overriding the default "more" icon.

items = [flet.PopupMenuItem]

Sets a list of PopupMenuItem that defines the menu items.

PopupMenuItem

Table 3.52

Method/Property	Definition
icon	Adds an icon to the menu item.
checked	When True, displays a checkmark on the item.
content	Sets text or provides a custom control.
height	Sets the height of the menu item.
padding	Uses the Padding control to create space around the item.
mouse_cursor	Sets the type of cursor when hovering over the item.
on_click	Registers a callback function that fires when the item is clicked.

Python

```python
import flet as ft

def main(page: ft.Page):

    popup = ft.PopupMenuButton(
        content= ft.Text("Options", weight= ft.FontWeight.BOLD),
        items= [
           ft.PopupMenuItem(content="Open with",icon= ft.Icons.FILE_OPEN),
           ft.PopupMenuItem(content="Share", icon= ft.Icons.SHARE,
                                checked=True
                            ),
            ft.PopupMenuItem(content="Print", icon= ft.Icons.PRINT,
                                on_click=lambda _:print('printing')
                            ),
        ]
    )
    page.add(popup)

ft.run(main)
```

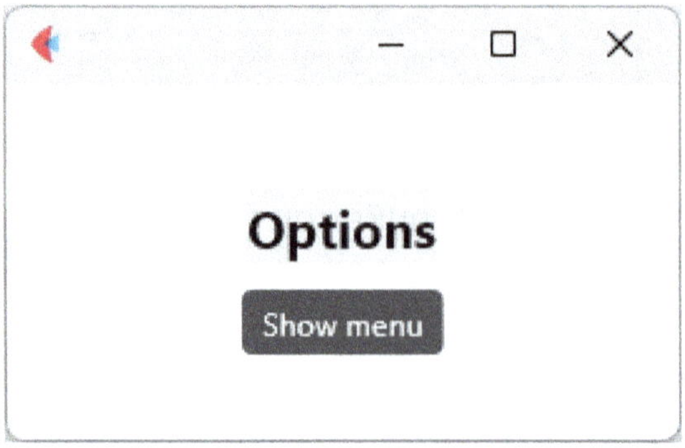

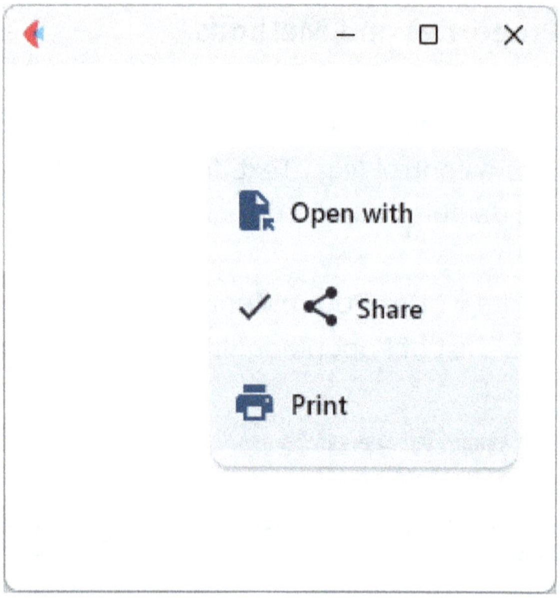

icon = icon

Overrides the default "more" icon for the PopupMenuButton.

bgcolor = color

Sets the background color of the pop-up panel.

icon_color = color

Sets the color of the PopupMenuButton icon.

elevation = number

Adds a raised effect to the PopupMenuButton.

shadow_color = color

Sets the shadow color of the pop-up panel.

icon_size = number

Sets the size of the icon.

splash_radius = number

Defines the ripple effect radius on tap.

Python

```
import flet as ft

async def main(page: ft.Page):

    def uninstall(appname):
        #Actual logic goes here
        print(f"uninstalling {appname}")

    def subscribe(appname):
        pass

    def notify(appname):
        pass

    def menu_template(appname):
        popup = ft.PopupMenuButton(
           icon= ft.Icons.MORE_VERT,
           elevation=10,
           icon_size=25,
           bgcolor="#F0F0F0",
           splash_radius=5,
           items= [
              ft.PopupMenuItem(content="Uninstall",
                    icon= ft.Icons.UNPUBLISHED_OUTLINED,
                    on_click= lambda _:uninstall(appname)
                  ),
               ft.PopupMenuItem(content="Subscribe",
                    icon= ft.Icons.PAID_OUTLINED,
                    on_click= lambda _:subscribe(appname)
                  ),
               ft.PopupMenuItem(content=ft.Switch(label="Notification",
                                label_position= ft.LabelPosition.LEFT,
                    on_change= lambda _:notify(appname))
                  ),
             ]
        )
        return popup



    col = ft.Column(
        controls=[
           ft.ListTile(leading =ft.Image("netflix.png"),
             title=ft.Text("Netflix"),
             trailing=menu_template("Netflix"),
             bgcolor="#F0F0F0"
             ),

           ft.ListTile(leading =ft.Image("Chatgpt.png"),
           title=ft.Text("ChatGPT"), trailing=menu_template("ChatGPT"),
```

```
                    bgcolor="#F0F0F0")
                ],
            )

        page.add(col)

ft.run(main)
```

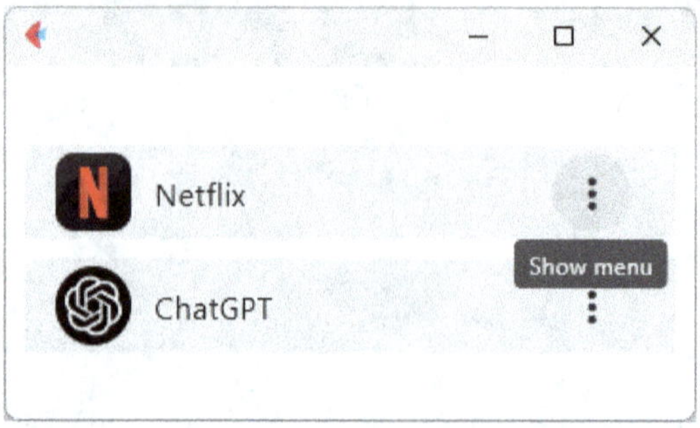

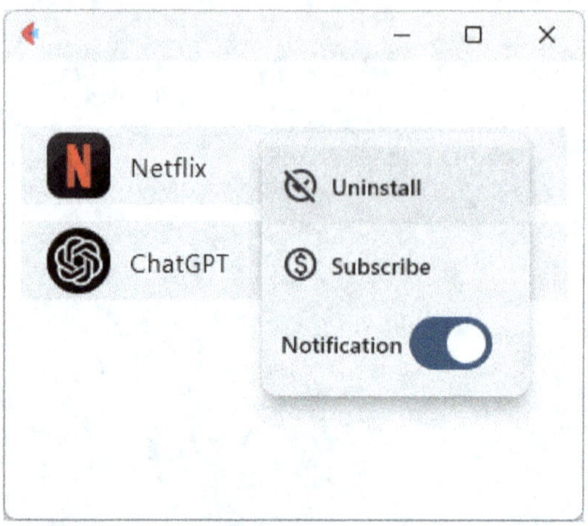

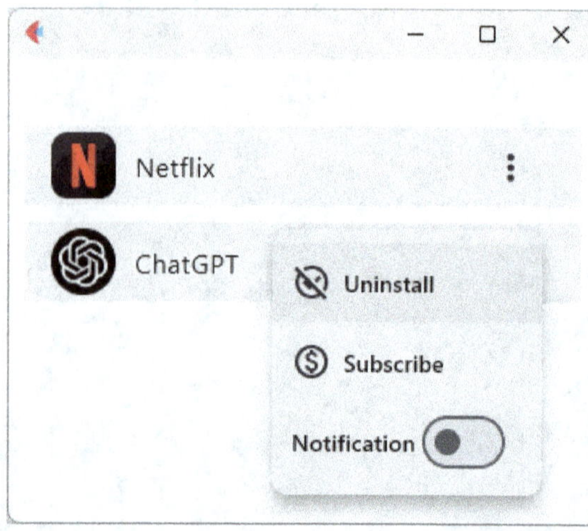


```
#Output
uninstalling Netflix
```

```
#Output
uninstalling ChatGPT
```

menu_position = flet.PopupMenuPosition

Uses PopupMenuPosition to position the panel relative to the button. Options: UNDER or OVER.

clip_behavior = flet.ClipBehavior

Defines how the pop-up content is clipped.

enable_feedback = bool
Enables or disables tactile or visual feedback on tap.

shape = shape
Defines the panel's border shape. *See page 206 for samples of shapes.*

padding = flet.Padding(left, right, top, bottom)
Pads the contents inside the pop-up panel.

menu_padding = flet.Padding(left, right, top, bottom)
Applies padding specifically around the menu items.

style = flet.ButtonStyle
Uses ButtonStyle to format or style the PopupMenuButton. *See table 3.30 for methods and properties of the ButtonStyle.*

on_open = callback
Registers a callback that fires when the menu opens.

on_cancel = callback
Fires when no item is selected and the menu closes.

on_select = callback
Registers a callback that triggers when a menu item is selected.

popup_animation_style = flet.AnimationStyle(curve, duration)
Defines the animation style when the menu opens. Animation curves include

BOUNCE_IN	EASE_IN_QUAD	EASE_OUT_QUAD	EASE_IN_OUT_CIRC
LINEAR	EASE_IN_QUART	EASE_OUT_QUART	EASE_IN_OUT_CUBIC
BOUNCE_OUT	EASE_IN_QUINT	EASE_OUT_QUINT	EASE_IN_OUT_CUBIC_EMPHASIZED
DECELERATE	EASE_IN_SINE	EASE_OUT_SINE	EASE_IN_OUT_EXPO
EASE	EASE_IN_TO_LINEAR	ELASTIC_IN	EASE_IN_OUT_QUAD
EASE_IN	EASE_OUT	ELASTIC_IN_OUT	EASE_IN_OUT_QUART
EASE_IN_BACK	EASE_OUT_BACK	ELASTIC_OUT	LINEAR_TO_EASE_OUT
EASE_IN_CIRC	EASE_OUT_CIRC	EASE_IN_OUT_QUINT	EASE_IN_OUT_SINE
EASE_IN_CUBIC	EASE_OUT_CUBIC	FAST_OUT_SLOWIN	FAST_LINEAR_TO_SLOW_EASE_IN

EASE_IN_EXPO	EASE_OUT_EXPO	EASE_IN_OUT	
SLOW_MIDDLE	BOUNCE_IN_OUT	EASE_IN_OUT_BACK	

```python
import flet as ft

def main(page: ft.Page):

    def save(e):
        #Actual logic goes here
        pass

    def export(e):
        pass


    popup = ft.PopupMenuButton(
        icon=ft.Icons.EDIT,
        elevation=10,
        icon_color="white",
        menu_position= ft.PopupMenuPosition.UNDER,
        shape= ft.RoundedRectangleBorder(radius=10),
        style=ft.ButtonStyle(bgcolor="blue"),
        on_open= lambda _:print("menu is in view"),
        on_cancel=lambda _:print("menu is closed"),
        on_select= lambda _:print("an item has been selected"),
        popup_animation_style= ft.AnimationStyle(
                   curve = ft.AnimationCurve.BOUNCE_OUT),
        items= [
               ft.PopupMenuItem(content="Save to device",
                   icon= ft.Icons.SAVE_OUTLINED, on_click= save),

               ft.PopupMenuItem(content="Export to PDF",
                     icon= ft.Icons.IMPORT_EXPORT, on_click= export),
            ]
        )

    listtile = ft.ListTile(
        bgcolor="#F0F0F0",
        leading=ft.Image("word.png", height=35, width=35),
        title= ft.Text("myfile.docx"),
        trailing=popup
    )


    page.add(listtile)

ft.run(main)
```

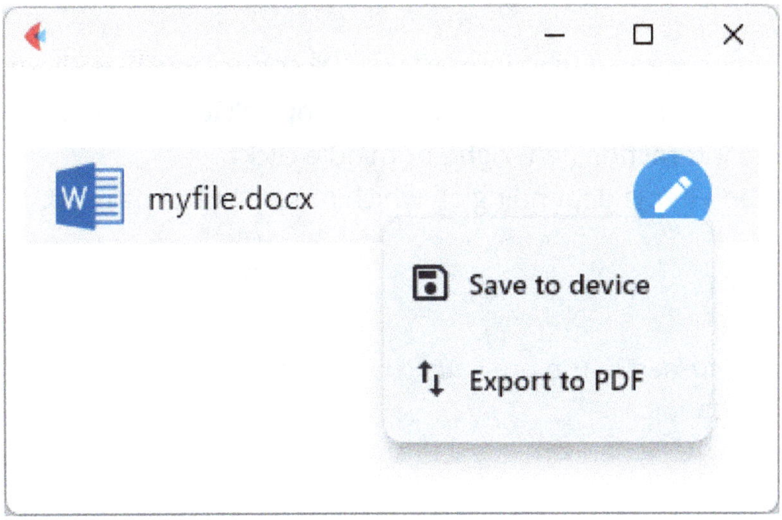

size_constraints = **flet.BoxConstraints**

Uses BoxConstraints to set minimum and maximum width and height for the pop-up panel.

ContextMenu

ContextMenu displays a menu when a user interacts with a control (such as clicking or long-pressing it). It wraps a control and shows a list of **PopupMenuItem** options based on the type of mouse interaction (left, right, or middle click).
You can define different menu items depending on which mouse button is used.

> **Note**
>
> **PopupMenuButton** was discussed in the previous chapter. Refer to it for details about its properties and methods.

Properties and Methods

content = control
The control wrapped by ContextMenu that responds to user interaction.

items = [flet.PopupMenuItem]
A list of PopupMenuItem displayed when the ***open*** method is called programmatically.

primary_items = [flet.PopupMenuItem]
A list of PopupMenuItem shown when the left mouse button is used.

secondary_items = [flet.PopupMenuItem]
A list of PopupMenuItem shown when the right mouse button is used.

tertiary_items = [flet.PopupMenuItem]
A list of PopupMenuItem shown when the middle (wheel) mouse button is used.

primary_trigger / secondary_trigger / tertiary_trigger = ContextMenuTrigger
Defines the gesture that activates the menu for each mouse button using ContextMenuTrigger.
Available options include: DOWN, LONG_PRESS.

on_dismiss = callback

Triggered when the context menu is closed.

```python
import flet as ft

async def main(page: ft.Page):

    def orderFood(e):
        pass

    banner = ft.Container(
        padding= 20, border_radius= 30,
        bgcolor= "#224766", alignment= ft.Alignment.CENTER,
        content= ft.Column(
            alignment= ft.MainAxisAlignment.CENTER,
            controls= [
                ft.Image("food.png",height=200, width=200),
                ft.Text("$25.99", color="#CC361e", size=25),
                ft.Text("Potato Beef", color="#f0f0f0", size=25)
            ]
        )
    )

    menu = ft.ContextMenu(
        content= banner,
        primary_items = [
            ft.PopupMenuItem(content="Order", on_click= orderFood),
            ft.PopupMenuItem(content="Explore",
                             on_click= lambda _:print("explore")),
            ft.PopupMenuItem(content="Compare Prices",
                             on_click= lambda _:print("prices")),
            ft.PopupMenuItem(content="Add to favorite",
                             on_click= lambda _:print("favorite"))
        ],
        primary_trigger= ft.ContextMenuTrigger.DOWN,
        width= 350, height=330
    )

    page.add(menu)

ft.run(main)
```

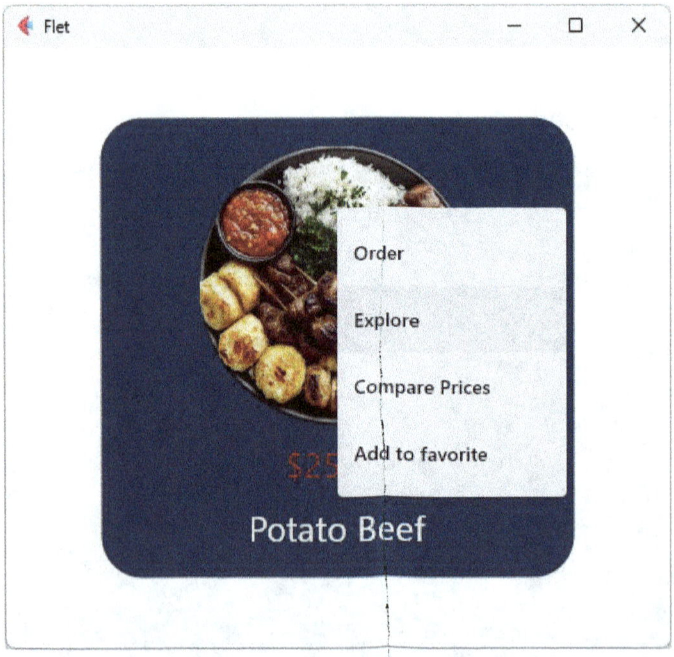

on_select = callback

Triggered when a PopupMenuItem is selected.

open()

Opens the menu programmatically.

```python
import flet as ft

async def main(page: ft.Page):

    async def openMenu(e):
        await menu.open()

    def getAction(e):
        #Actual code goes here ...
        trigger = e.item.content
        print(f"Action-> {trigger}")

    paypal = ft.ListTile(
        leading= ft.Image("paypal.png"), bgcolor="#122435",
        title= ft.Text("Paypal", color="white", size=20),
        on_click = openMenu
    )

    menu = ft.ContextMenu(
```

```
        content= paypal,
        items = [
            ft.PopupMenuItem(content="Send money",),
            ft.PopupMenuItem(content="View charges",),
            ft.PopupMenuItem(content="Recent transaction"),
        ],

        secondary_items = [
            ft.PopupMenuItem(content="Report",
                             icon= ft.Icons.FILE_DOWNLOAD),
            ft.PopupMenuItem(content="Terms and Conditions",
                             icon= ft.Icons.VERIFIED),
            ft.PopupMenuItem(content="Delete",
                             icon= ft.CupertinoIcons.DELETE ),
        ],
        secondary_trigger = ft.ContextMenuTrigger.DOWN,
        on_select = getAction,
        width= 350
    )

    page.add(menu)

ft.run(main)
```

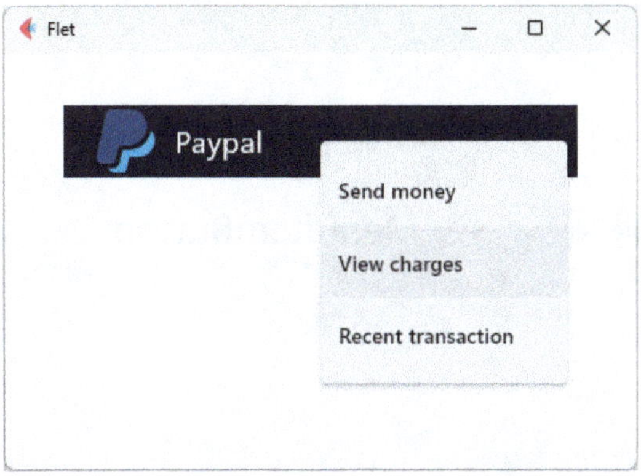

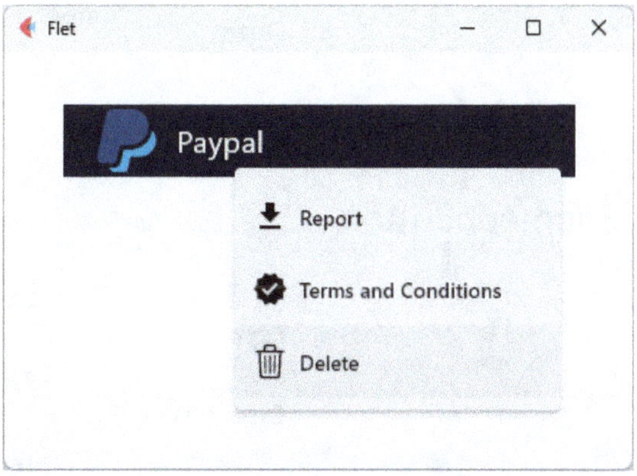


```
#Output
Action-> Terms and Conditions
Action-> View charges
```

MenuBar

The **MenuBar** is a material design control used to create menus that are typically positioned at the top of the application window. It organizes multiple menu items in a horizontal bar, allowing easy access to commands and functionalities.
Menu items in a MenuBar can be either:

- **MenuItemButton** → Triggers a direct action when clicked.
- **SubmenuButton** → Opens a panel to reveal nested menus. SubmenuButton can contain further SubMenuButton, creating a tree-like hierarchical structure of menus.

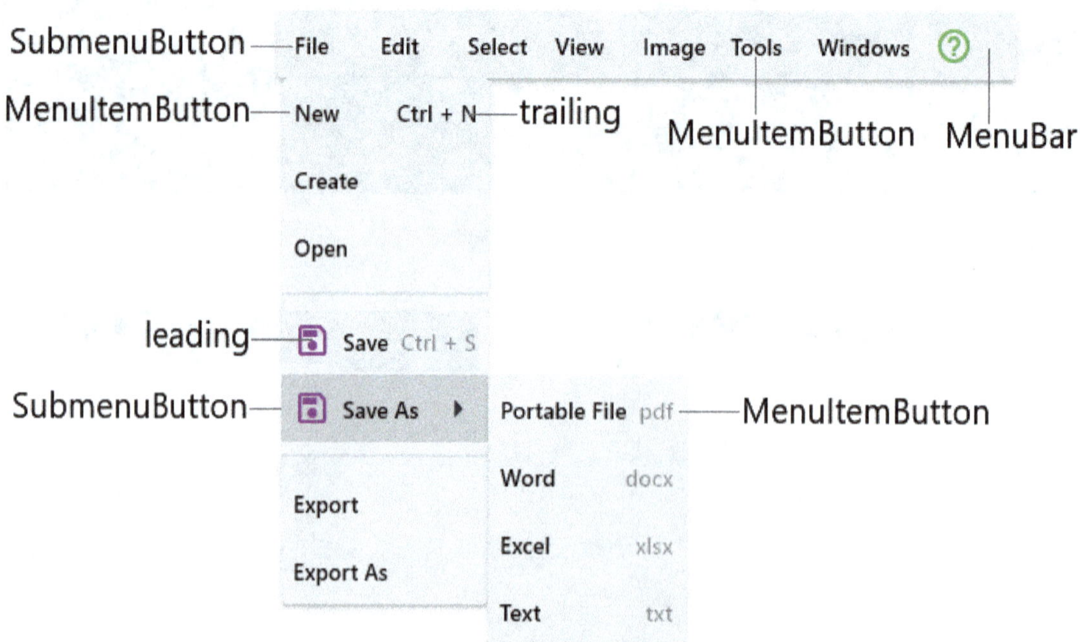

Insight

This structure is especially useful for applications with multiple functionalities, such as text editors, IDEs or data processing apps.

Properties and Methods

controls = [controls]

Sets a list of MenuItemButton or SubMenuButton objects. The list can be a mix of both types.

MenuItemButton / SubMenuButton

Table 3.53

Method/Property	Definition
content	Sets a control (e.g., Text, Icon) to represent the menu item.
close_on_click	Determines whether the menu closes automatically after clicking.
focus_on_hover	When True, the menu item gains focus as the mouse passes over it.
leading	Adds a control or icon before the menu item.
trailing	Adds a control or icon after the menu item.
clip_behavior	Determines how content is clipped within the menu item.
style	Uses ButtonStyle to format the item's appearance. *This property is only available for MenuItemButton.*
menu_style	Uses the MenuStyle to style or define the appearance of the menu. *This property is only available for SubmenuButton.*
semantic_label	Provides a label for accessibility purposes.
autofocus	Automatically focuses the menu item when set to True.
overflow_axis	Defines behavior for overflow content using Axis control. Options include HORIZONTAL, VERTICAL
on_open	Fires a callback when the SubmenuButton opens menu items.
on_close	Fires a callback when opened menu items closes.
on_click	Registers a callback that fires when the item is clicked.
on_hover	Fires a callback when the mouse moves over the item.
on_focus	Fires a callback when the item gains focus.
on_blur	Fires a callback when the item loses focus.

Example 1,

```python
import flet as ft

def main(page: ft.Page):
    page.bgcolor = "white"
    page.padding = ft.Padding.only(top=0)
```

```
    def fileFunction(e):
        pass

    def editFunction(e):
        pass

    def viewFunction(e):
        pass

    def saveFunction(e):
        pass

    menubar = ft.MenuBar(
        controls=[
            ft.MenuItemButton(content= "File", on_click= fileFunction),
            ft.MenuItemButton(content= "Edit", on_click= editFunction),
            ft.MenuItemButton(content= "View", on_click= viewFunction),
            ft.MenuItemButton(content= ft.Icon(ft.Icons.SAVE_OUTLINED),
                              on_click= saveFunction
                             ),
            ft.MenuItemButton(content= ft.Icon(ft.Icons.FOLDER_OPEN),
                              on_click= lambda _:print("Open")
                             ),
            ft.MenuItemButton(content= ft.Icon(ft.Icons.UNDO),
                              on_click= lambda _:print("Undo")
                             ),
            ft.MenuItemButton(content= ft.Icon(ft.Icons.REDO),
                              on_click= lambda _:print("Redo")
                             ),
        ]
    )

    page.add(menubar)

ft.run(main)
```

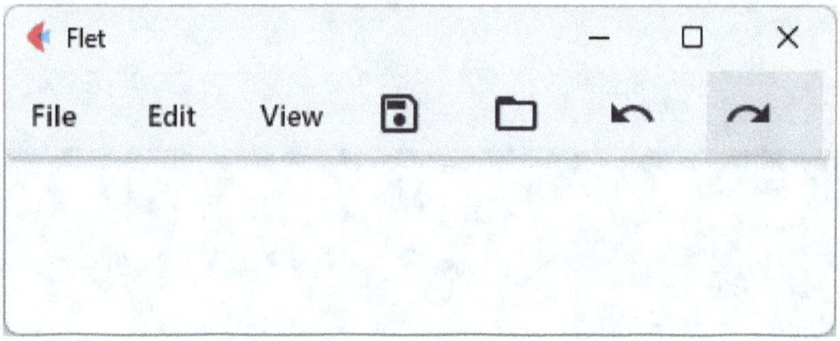

Example 2

```python
import flet as ft

def main(page: ft.Page):
    page.bgcolor = "white"
    page.padding = ft.Padding.only(top=0)

    def newFile(e):
        pass

    def openFile(e):
        pass

    def saveAsWord(e):
        pass

    filemenu = ft.SubmenuButton(
        content=ft.Text("File", color="black"),
        controls=[
            ft.MenuItemButton( content=ft.Text("New"), on_click= newFile),
            ft.MenuItemButton( content=ft.Text("Open", color="black"),
                    trailing=ft.Text("Ctrl + O"), on_click= openFile),

            ft.Divider(),
            ft.MenuItemButton( content=ft.Text("Save", color="black"),
                  leading=ft.Icon(ft.Icons.SAVE_OUTLINED,  color="purple")),

            ft.SubmenuButton( content=ft.Text("Save As", color="black"),
                leading=ft.Icon(ft.Icons.SAVE_ALT, color="blue"),
                controls=[
                    ft.MenuItemButton( content=ft.Text("Word", color="black"),
                        trailing=ft.Text('docx'), on_click=saveAsWord),
                ]),

            ft.MenuItemButton( content=ft.Text("Export", color="black")),
        ],
        tooltip= "Create, open and save file"
    )

    editmenu = ft.SubmenuButton(
        content= ft.Text("Edit", color="black"),
        controls=[
            ft.MenuItemButton( content=ft.Text("Undo", color="black"),
                               leading = ft.Icon(ft.Icons.UNDO),
                               on_click= lambda _:print("undo action")),

            ft.MenuItemButton( content=ft.Text("Copy", color="black"),
                               leading = ft.Icon(ft.Icons.COPY),
                               on_click= lambda _:print("redo redo action")),
        ]
```

```
    )

    menubar = ft.MenuBar(
        controls=[
            filemenu,
            editmenu,
            ft.MenuItemButton( content=ft.Text("View", color="black"),
                                on_click= lambda _:print("View file")),

            ft.MenuItemButton( content=ft.Icon(ft.Icons.HELP_OUTLINE_ROUNDED,
                               color="green"),on_click= lambda _:print("Help")),
        ],
    )

    page.add(menubar)

ft.run(main)
```

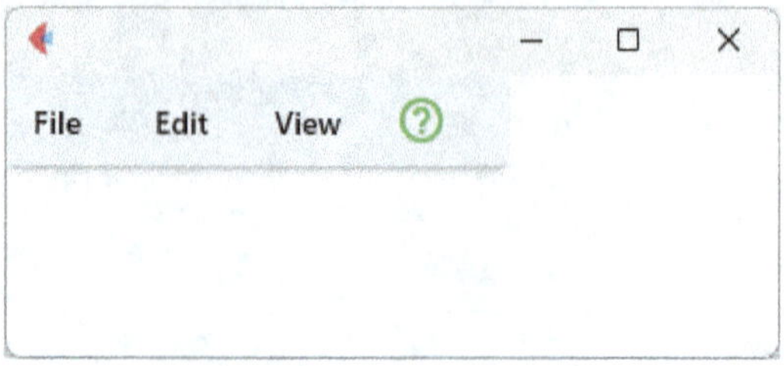

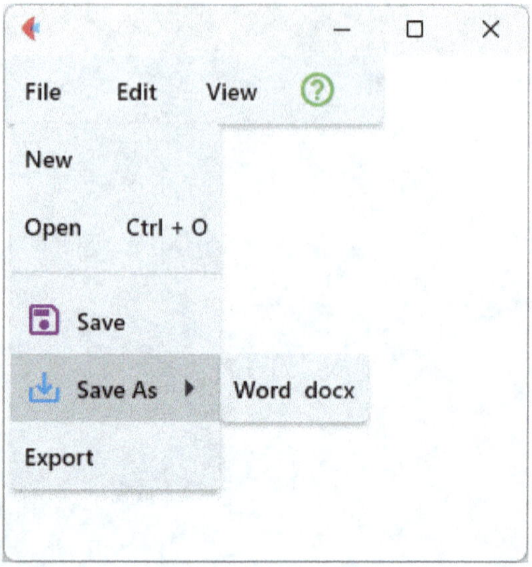

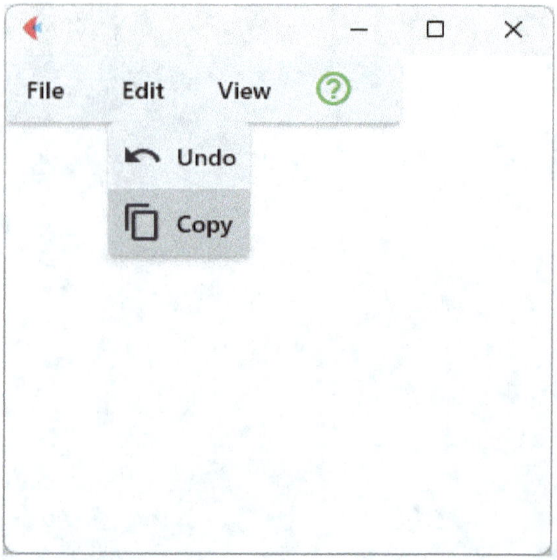

clip_behavior = flet.ClipBehavior

Defines how content in the MenuBar is clipped. *See table 3.24 for clip options.*

style = flet.MenuStyle

Implements MenuStyle to format and style the entire MenuBar.

MenuStyle

Method/Property	Definition	*Table 3.54*
alignment	Aligns menu items horizontally within the MenuBar.	
bgcolor	Sets the background color of the MenuBar.	
shadow_color	Specifies the shadow color for the MenuBar (default is grey).	
elevation	Adds a raised effect to the MenuBar.	
padding	Pads the MenuBar content.	
side	Uses BorderSide to decorate the outer edges with color and thickness.	
shape	Defines the MenuBar's shape. Options include OutlinedBorder, StadiumBorder, RoundedRectangleBorder, CircularBorder, InputBorder, BeveledRectangleBorder or ContinuousRectangleBorder.	
mouse_cursor	Sets the type of mouse cursor when hovering over the MenuBar.	
fixed_size	Specifies a constant size for the MenuBar.	
max_size/min_size	Sets the maximum and minimum size of the MenuBar.	

```
Python
import flet as ft

def main(page: ft.Page):
    page.bgcolor = "#24252B"
    page.padding = ft.Padding.only(top=0)

    def Action(e):
        #Actual logic goes ...
        task = e.control.data
        print(f"Action -> {task}")


    menubar = ft.MenuBar(
        style= ft.MenuStyle(
            bgcolor="#424349",
            alignment=ft.Alignment.CENTER,
            elevation= 10,
            padding= ft.Padding.all(2),
            shape= ft.RoundedRectangleBorder(radius=0),
            mouse_cursor= ft.MouseCursor.GRAB
        ),
```

```
        controls=[
            ft.MenuItemButton( content=ft.Icon(ft.Icons.FOLDER_OPEN,
                color="yellow"), data="open file", on_click=Action),
            ft.MenuItemButton( content=ft.Icon(ft.Icons.SAVE,
                color="purple"),data="save file", on_click= Action),
            ft.MenuItemButton( content=ft.Icon(ft.Icons.UNDO,
                color="#F0F0F0"),data="undo", on_click=Action),
            ft.MenuItemButton( content=ft.Icon(ft.Icons.REDO,
                color="#F0F0F0"),data="redo", on_click=Action),
            ft.MenuItemButton( content=ft.Icon(ft.Icons.CUT_OUTLINED,
                color="cyan"),data="cut", on_click=Action),
            ft.MenuItemButton( content=ft.Icon(ft.Icons.COPY,
                color="blue"), data="copy",on_click=Action),
            ft.MenuItemButton( content=ft.Icon(ft.Icons.PASTE_OUTLINED,
                color="orange"),data="paste",on_click=Action),
            ft.MenuItemButton( content=ft.Text("Help",color="#eeeeee"),
                data="help",on_click=Action),
        ],
    )

    page.add(menubar)

ft.run(main)
```

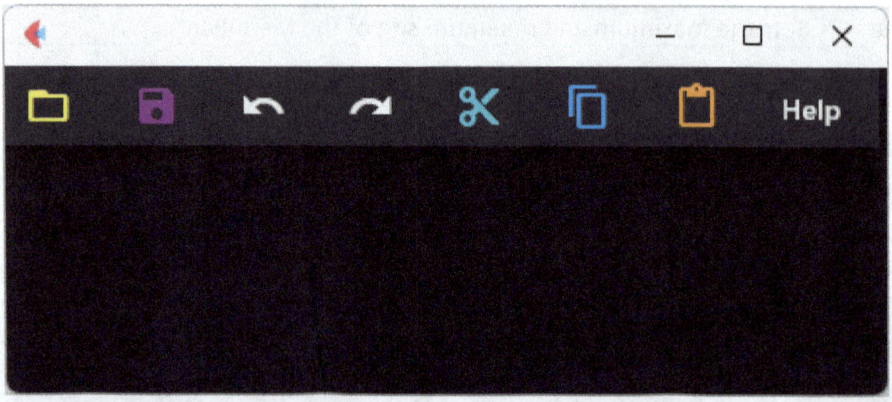


```
#Output
Action -> open file
Action -> save file
Action -> redo
Action -> paste
```

Gestures and Interactive Controls

Modern applications are no longer limited to rigid or static user interfaces. Instead, they rely heavily on gesture-based interactions to create responsive, dynamic and engaging user experiences. Flet applications are designed with this flexibility in mind, allowing user interface controls to respond naturally to user gestures and interactions.

In a Flet application, controls are not fixed in place. They can be moved, resized, expanded, zoomed in or out, dragged across the screen, swiped in different directions or dismissed entirely based on user interaction. These interactions are achieved by attaching gesture recognition logic to controls, enabling the application to detect specific gestures and execute corresponding callbacks or functions.

Gesture-driven interaction plays a critical role in a wide range of applications, including games, data visualization tools, graphic design software, simulators, educational platforms, animations, dashboards and interactive media applications. By responding to user gestures such as taps, drags, swipes and scaling, applications become more intuitive and immersive.

Flet provides several built-in controls and utilities that support gesture handling and interactive behavior, including:

Draggable	**InteractiveViewer**	**ExpansionPanelList**	**GestureDetector**
Dismissible	**ExpansionTile**	**ShakeDetector**	

Note

GestureDetector detects a wide range of gestures such as taps, double taps, long presses, drags, pans and scale gestures and maps them to callbacks.
The **GestureDetector** control has been explored in detail in the *Buttons* chapter. Refer to that chapter for an in-depth explanation of gesture callbacks and practical implementation examples.

Draggable

The **Draggable** control is a material design control that allows a child control to be moved interactively from its current position to another location within the application page. It is commonly paired with the **DragTarget** control, which detects when the Draggable is dropped within its area and triggers corresponding events. This makes Draggable ideal for drag-and-drop interfaces, reordering lists or interactive UI components.

> **Insight**
>
> The **Draggable** control is ideal for creating interactive and intuitive interfaces where users need to move items dynamically, such as in dashboards, sortable lists or drag-and-drop editors.

Properties and Methods

content = control

The child control that will be dragged. This is the main visual element of the Draggable.

group = string

Specifies a string identifier to link the Draggable with a corresponding **DragTarget**. Only targets with the same group value can accept the Draggable.

DragTarget

The **DragTarget** is a control that receives **Draggable** controls and triggers callbacks to update the application page. It acts as a designated drop area, detecting when a Draggable enters, leaves or is dropped within its region. This makes it an essential component in drag-and-drop interfaces, enabling dynamic user interactions such as sorting, moving or transferring data between containers.

Properties and Methods

Table 3.53

Method/Property	Definition
content	Sets the child control of the DragTarget, often a visual container indicating the drop area.
group	Specifies a string identifier to match with corresponding **Draggable** controls. Only Draggables with the same group value can interact with the DragTarget.
on_accept	Registers a callback that triggers when a **Draggable** is dropped onto the DragTarget.
on_leave	Registers a callback that triggers when a **Draggable** leaves the DragTarget region without being dropped.
on_move	Triggers a callback when a **Draggable** is moved over the DragTarget region.
on_will_accept	Registers a callback to determine whether the DragTarget should accept the incoming Draggable before it is dropped.

Insight

The **DragTarget** control is essential for creating interactive drag-and-drop UI experiences, allowing dynamic data placement, sorting and manipulation with visual feedback for the user.

Python

```python
import flet as ft

def main(page: ft.Page):
    page.bgcolor = "white"

    def onAccept(e):
        #Actual logic goes ...
        print("Goal...")


    drager = ft.Draggable(
        content=ft.Image("basketball.png", height=100, width=100),
        group="basketball",
    )

    target = ft.DragTarget(
        content=ft.Image("basket.png", height=150, width=150),
        group="basketball",
        on_accept=onAccept,
        on_leave = lambda _:print("Ouch!, ball has been missed"),
        on_move = lambda _:print("Target is moving within region"),
    )


    row = ft.Row(
        vertical_alignment=ft.CrossAxisAlignment.CENTER,
        alignment=ft.MainAxisAlignment.SPACE_AROUND,
        controls=[drager, target],
        width=page.width,
        height=page.height,
    )

    page.add(row)


ft.run(main)
```

```
#Output
Target is moving within region
Goal...
```

affinity = flet.Axis

Specifies the preferred drag direction affinity if any, guiding the movement of the Draggable.

axis = flet.Axis

Constrains the drag movement to a specific axis. Uses the **Axis** control with options HORIZONTAL or VERTICAL. If unspecified, the Draggable can move freely in both directions.

content_feedback = control

Specifies a control to display as a visual feedback while dragging, often a translucent version of the content.

content_when_dragging = control

Defines an alternate representation of the content during the drag operation.

max_simultaneous_drags = number

Limits the number of Draggables that can be moved at the same time.

on_drag_complete = callback

Registers a callback that executes when the drag operation is finished, either by dropping the control on a target or releasing it elsewhere.

on_drag_start = callback

Registers a callback that executes when the user begins dragging the control.

```
Python
import flet as ft

def main(page: ft.Page):
    page.bgcolor = "white"

    def onAccept(e):
        #Actual logic goes ...
        print("File has been deleted"),
        target.visible = False
        print(e.control)
        page.update()

    def onDragStart(e):
        #Actual logic goes ...
        target.visible = True
        page.update()

    def onDragComple(e):
        #Actual logic goes ...
        target.visible = False
        filename = e.control
        row.controls.remove(filename) #Deleting control
        page.update()


    file1= ft.Draggable(
        content=ft.Image("word.png", height=100, width=100),
        group="deletingfiles",
        content_when_dragging= ft.Image("word.png", opacity=0.5,height=50),
        affinity= ft.Axis.VERTICAL,
        max_simultaneous_drags=1,
        on_drag_start= onDragStart,
        on_drag_complete=onDragComple)

    file2= ft.Draggable(
        content=ft.Image("csv.png", height=100, width=100),
        group="deletingfiles",
        content_when_dragging= ft.Image("csv.png", opacity=0.5,height=50),
        on_drag_start= onDragStart,
        on_drag_complete=onDragComple)

    target = ft.DragTarget(
        content=ft.Image("recycle-bin.png", height=100, width=100),
        group="deletingfiles",
        on_accept=onAccept,
        visible= False)

    row = ft.Row( controls=[file1, file2])
```

```
    col = ft.Column(controls=[row, ft.Container(height=50),target],
        width=page.width,height=page.height)


    page.add(col)

ft.run(main)
```

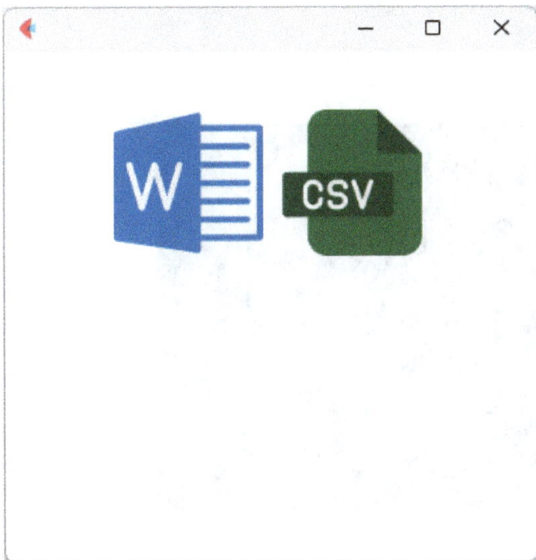

Before dragging

The Word file is dragged into the bin

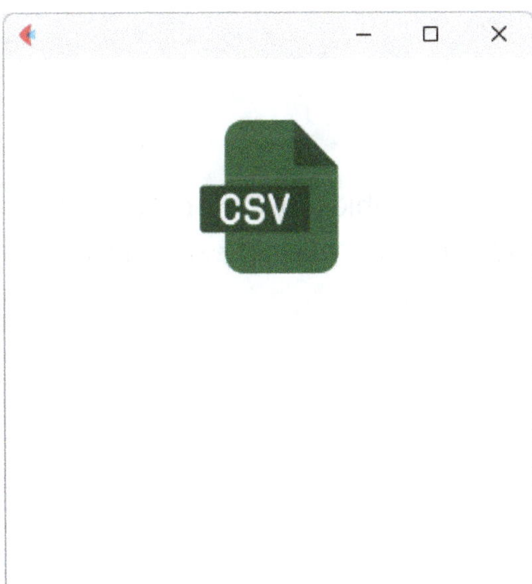

The Word file has been deleted

The CSV file is dragged into the bin

Dismissible

The **Dismissible** control provides a flexible and intuitive way to remove content from an application. It is commonly used in lists where a user can swipe a control horizontally or vertically to trigger a deletion or other action. This eliminates the need for a separate delete button elsewhere in the interface, improving usability and efficiency.

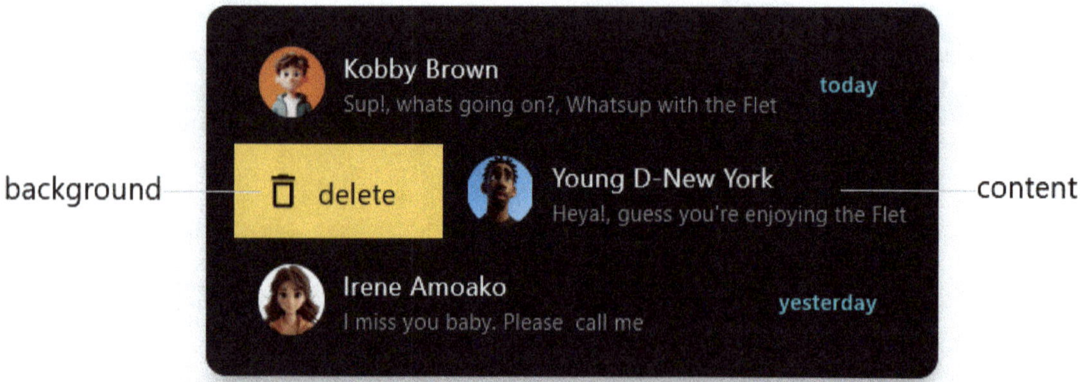

Insight

The **Dismissible** control is especially useful in lists, tables or card-based layouts where removing an item quickly and intuitively improves the user experience.

Properties and Methods

content = control

The main child control of the Dismissible. This is the content that can be swiped.

background = control

Specifies a control that appears behind the Dismissible when swiped. This is often a delete icon or alert, but can be any control.

secondary_background = control

Specifies an alternate background control, typically shown for swipe in the opposite direction.

on_dismiss = callback

Registers a callback that triggers when the Dismissible control is successfully dismissed.

```python
import flet as ft

def main(page: ft.Page):
    page.bgcolor = "white"

    def onDismiss(e):
        #Actual logic goes here ...
        item = e.control.data
        print(f"{item} is deleted")


    background = ft.Container(
        bgcolor="cyan",
        padding= ft.Padding.only(left=10),
        content=ft.Icon(ft.Icons.DELETE),
        alignment=ft.Alignment.CENTER_LEFT
    )

    secondary = ft.Container(
        bgcolor="red",
        padding= ft.Padding.only(right=10),
        content=ft.Text("Delete", size=20),
        alignment=ft.Alignment.CENTER_LEFT
    )


    def myList(title):
        return ft.ListTile(
            leading= ft.Icon(ft.Icons.CODE_OUTLINED),
            title= ft.Text(title),
            bgcolor="#F0F0F0")


    listview = ft.ListView(
```

```
        spacing=2,
        width=300,
        controls=[
            ft.Dismissible(content=myList("Python"),
                  data="Python",background=background,
                  secondary_background=secondary,on_dismiss=onDismiss),

            ft.Dismissible(content=myList("JavaScript"),
                  data="JavaScript",background=background,
                  secondary_background=secondary,on_dismiss= onDismiss),

            ft.Dismissible(content=myList("C++"),
                  data="C++",background=background,
                  secondary_background=secondary, on_dismiss=onDismiss),

            ft.Dismissible(content=myList("Java"),
                  data="Java",background=background,
                  secondary_background=secondary,on_dismiss=onDismiss),
        ],
    )

    col = ft.Column(
        controls=[ft.Text("Swipe to Delete Language"),listview])


    page.add(col)

ft.run(main)
```

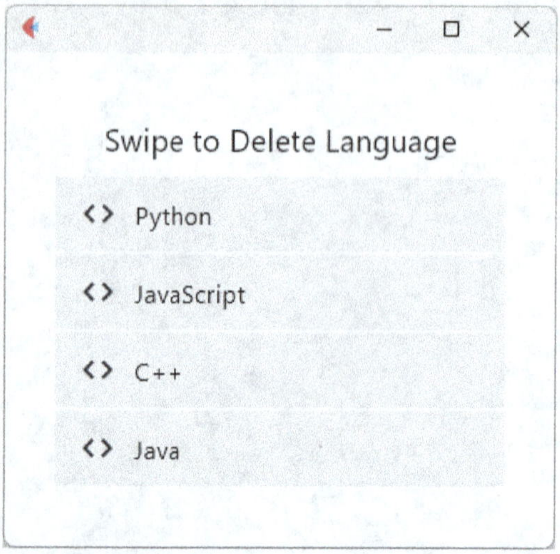

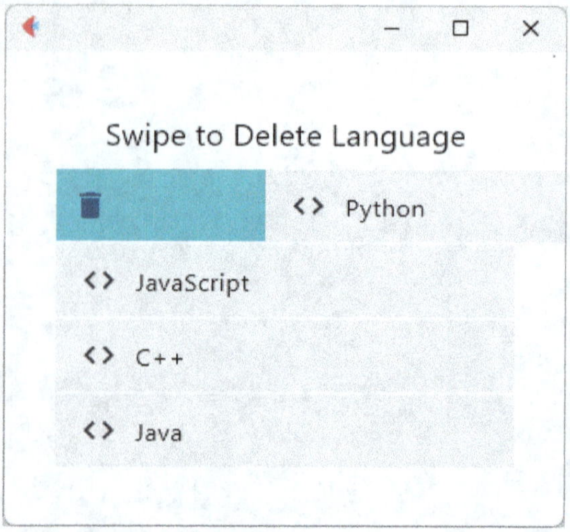

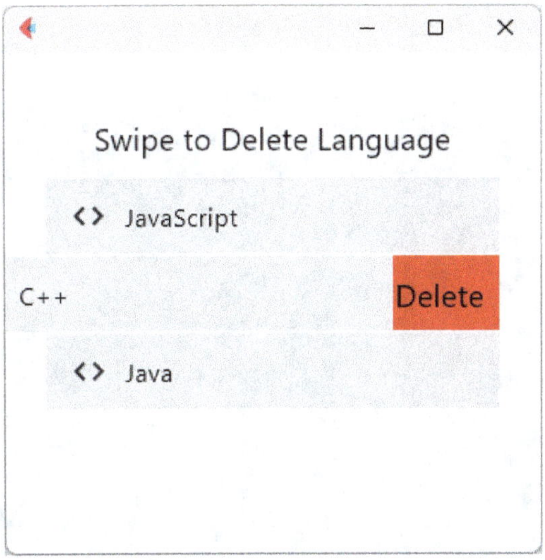

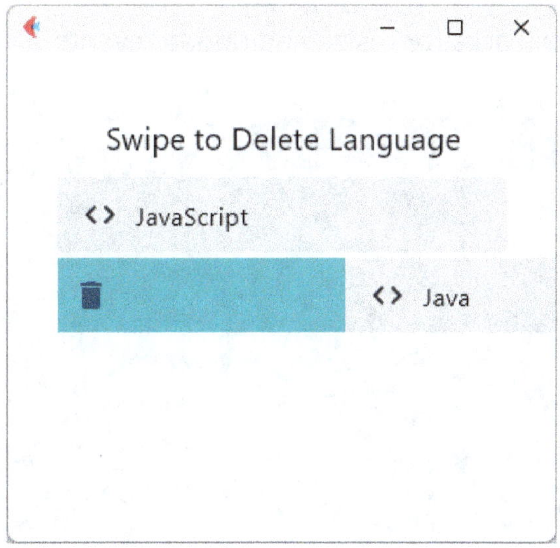

cross_axis_end_offset = number

Specifies the ending offset along the cross-axis when the swipe is complete.

dismiss_direction = flet.DismissDirection

Specifies the swipe direction(s) that trigger dismissal using the **DismissDirection** options:

- DOWN
- UP
- HORIZONTAL
- VERTICAL
- START_TO_END
- END_TO_START
- NONE

dismiss_thresholds = {DismissDirection : number}

Defines the proportion of swipe distance required to trigger a dismissal.

height = number

Specifies the height of the Dismissible control.

movement_duration = number, flet.Duration

Duration of the swipe animation in seconds. *See page 406 for Duration methods.*

on_confirm_dismiss = callback

Registers a callback that confirms whether the dismissal should proceed.

on_resize / on_update = callback

Callbacks for resize and update events.

```python
import flet as ft

def main(page: ft.Page):
    page.bgcolor = "white"
    page.vertical_alignment = ft.MainAxisAlignment.CENTER
    page.horizontal_alignment = ft.CrossAxisAlignment.CENTER

    def onConfirm(e):
        try:
            page.data = e.control
            page.show_dialog(alertdialog)
            print("hello")
        except:
            print("error")
        page.update()


    async def delete(e):
        await page.data.confirm_dismiss(True)
        page.pop_dialog()
        page.update()


    async def cancel(e):
        await page.data.confirm_dismiss(False)
        page.pop_dialog()
        page.update()



    alertdialog = ft.AlertDialog(
        title= ft.Text("Delete Contact"),
        content=ft.Text("This contact will be deleted ...."),
        actions=[ft.OutlinedButton(content="Delete", on_click=delete),
                 ft.OutlinedButton(content="Cancel", on_click= cancel),]
        )

    item1 = ft.Dismissible(
        dismiss_direction= ft.DismissDirection.END_TO_START,
        on_confirm_dismiss= onConfirm,
        movement_duration= 5,
        content=ft.ListTile(bgcolor="#076C44",
            title= ft.Text("Alice White", color="white"),)
    )
```

```
    item2 = ft.Dismissible(
        dismiss_direction= ft.DismissDirection.END_TO_START,
        dismiss_thresholds= {ft.DismissDirection.END_TO_START:0.2},
        on_confirm_dismiss= onConfirm,
        content=ft.ListTile(bgcolor="#076C44",
          title= ft.Text("George Wood", color="white"),
        )
      )

    listview = ft.ListView(spacing=2,width=300,controls=[item1, item2])

    col = ft.Column(controls=[ft.Text("Contact", size=20),listview],)

    page.add(col)

ft.run(main)
```

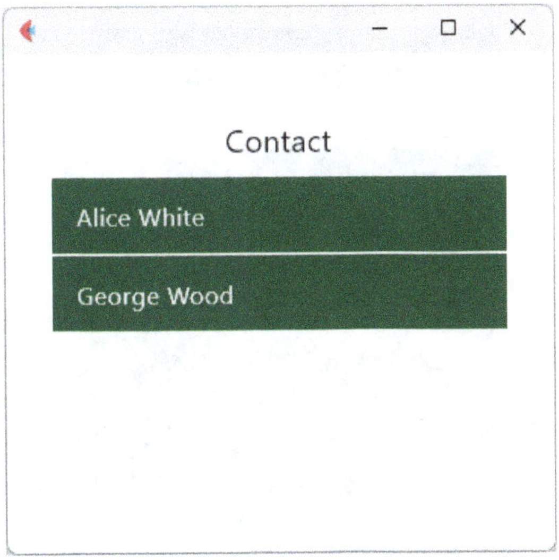

Before swiping

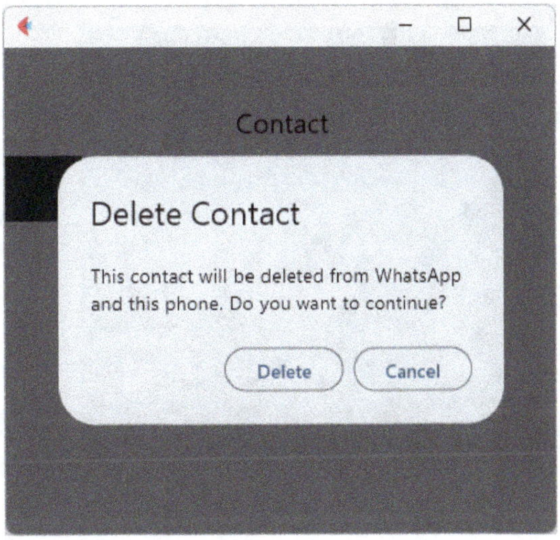

Confirmation dialog

resize_duration = number, flet.Duration

Time taken to resize the control after dismissal. *See page 406 for Duration methods.*

InteractiveViewer

The **InteractiveViewer** is a Material Design control that enables direct, gesture-based interaction with its child control. It allows users to **pan, zoom** and **scale** content dynamically, making it especially useful when displaying content that may be larger, smaller or more detailed than the available screen space.

With InteractiveViewer, users can zoom in to inspect fine details or zoom out to view the overall structure of a control. It also allows moving (panning) the control within its container after scaling. This makes the user interface more flexible, intuitive and efficient, particularly when working with rich visual content.

The InteractiveViewer can be applied to any control, including images, text, charts, diagrams, maps and custom layouts, enabling users to interactively explore content that would otherwise be difficult to view at a fixed size.

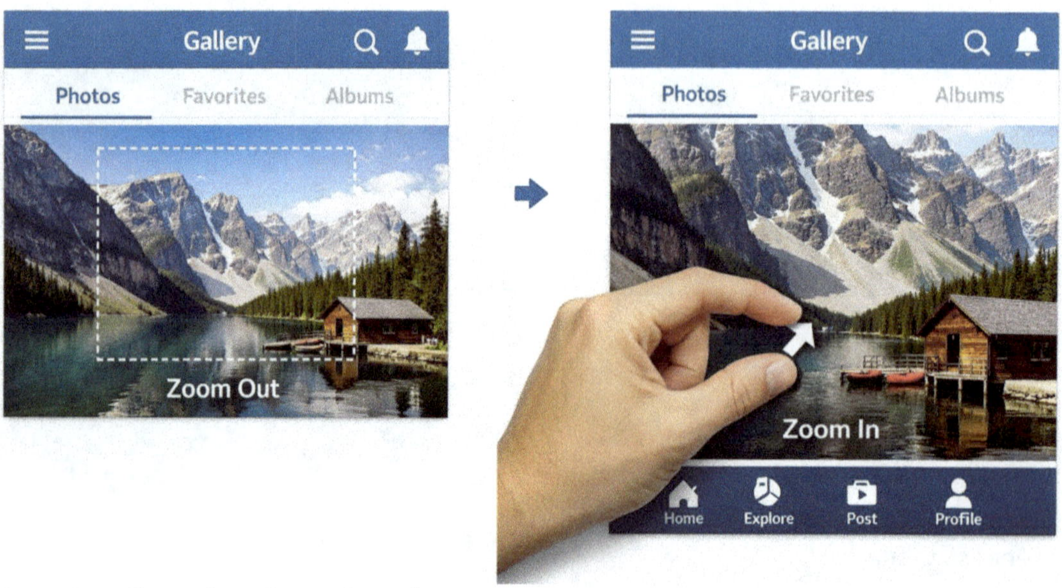

Figure 3.7: Illustration of zoom in and out

Properties and Methods

content = control

The content property sets the control to be wrapped by the InteractiveViewer. This is the element that responds to scaling, panning and gesture interactions.

pan_enabled = bool

When set to True, the user can move (pan) the content within its container after scaling. If set to False, the content remains fixed in position.

scale_enabled = bool

When set to True, the content can be zoomed in and out using pinch or scroll gestures. Disabling this property prevents scaling while still allowing other interactions if enabled.

on_interaction_start = callback

The on_interaction_start callback is triggered when the user begins an interaction with the InteractiveViewer, such as starting a pan or zoom gesture.

on_interaction_update = callback

The on_interaction_update callback fires repeatedly while the interaction is ongoing.

on_interaction_end = callback

The on_interaction_end callback is invoked when the user completes an interaction and releases the gesture.

trackpad_scroll_causes_scale = bool

When enabled, scrolling with a trackpad (commonly on desktop platforms) causes the content to scale instead of pan. This improves usability on desktop and laptop devices.

constrained = bool

When True, the content is constrained to remain within the bounds of its parent container while being panned or scaled. When set to False, the content can move freely outside its original layout boundaries.

Python

```
import flet as ft

async def main(page: ft.Page):
    page.vertical_alignment = ft.MainAxisAlignment.CENTER
    page.horizontal_alignment = ft.CrossAxisAlignment.CENTER
    page.bgcolor = "white"
```

```
    def getScale(e):
        #Actual logic goes here ...
        scale = e.control.scale_factor
        print(f"Current scale ->{scale}")

    page.appbar = ft.AppBar(
        title= ft.Text("InteractiveViewer", color="#F0F0F0"),
        bgcolor="#102a45")


    interactive = ft.InteractiveViewer(
        on_interaction_start= lambda _:print("Started zooming"),
        on_interaction_update= getScale,
        content=ft.Text(
            """Lorem ipsum dolor sit amet, consectetur adipiscing elit.
             Curabitur quis nibh vitae purus consectetur... """,size=8
        ),
        height=500, width=500,
    )

    page.add(interactive)

ft.run(main)
```

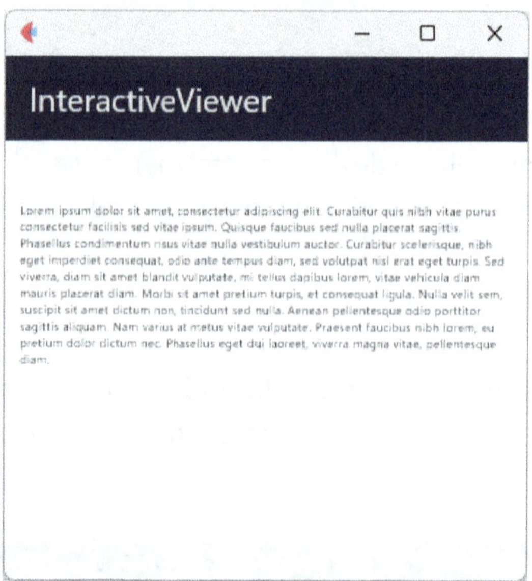

Normal view

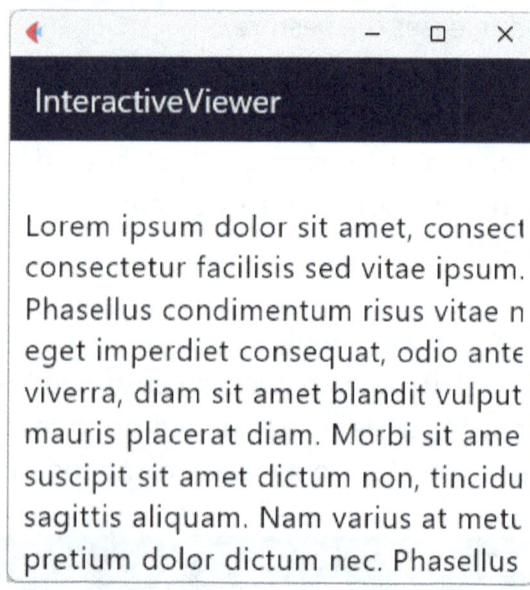

Zoomed

max_scale = number

Defines the maximum scale factor allowed when zooming in. This prevents the content from being enlarged beyond a reasonable or usable limit.

min_scale = number

Defines the minimum scale factor allowed when zooming out. This prevents the content from shrinking excessively and becoming too small to view.

interaction_end_friction_coefficient = int

Controls the friction applied when a pan or scale interaction ends. Higher values cause the motion to stop more quickly, while lower values allow smoother momentum-based movement.

scale_factor = number

Specifies the amount of scaling applied per zoom gesture step. This determines how fast or slow the zooming effect occurs during interaction.

alignment = flet.Alignment

The alignment property specifies how the content is aligned within the InteractiveViewer when it is smaller than the available space or when scaling occurs.

boundary_margin = number, flet.Margin(left, right, top, bottom)

The boundary_margin property sets the extra space outside the content's normal bounds that the user is allowed to pan into.

interaction_update_interval = int

The interaction_update_interval defines the time interval (in milliseconds) at which interaction update events are fired during an active pan or scale gesture.

```python
import flet as ft

def main(page: ft.Page):
    page.bgcolor = "white"

    page.appbar = ft.AppBar(
        title= ft.Text("InteractiveViewer", color="#F0F0F0"),
        bgcolor="#102a45")
```

```
    interactive = ft.InteractiveViewer(
        max_scale=10,
        min_scale=1,
        scale_factor=10,
        alignment= ft.Alignment.CENTER,
        boundary_margin=ft.Margin.all(10),
        interaction_update_interval=5,
        content = ft.Image("basketball_player.jpg"),
        #Code continues below ...
    )


    page.add(interactive)

ft.run(main)
```

ExpansionTile

The **ExpansionTile** is a material design control that can expand and collapse to reveal or hide a set of child controls. It is particularly useful for organizing large sets of controls, grouping related options or creating collapsible menus. The control has a title, optional subtitle, leading icon and trailing icon that indicates its expandable state.

When the trailing icon is clicked, the tile expands to display its children and collapses back when clicked again. This provides a compact and organized layout, ideal for settings, forms or hierarchical lists.

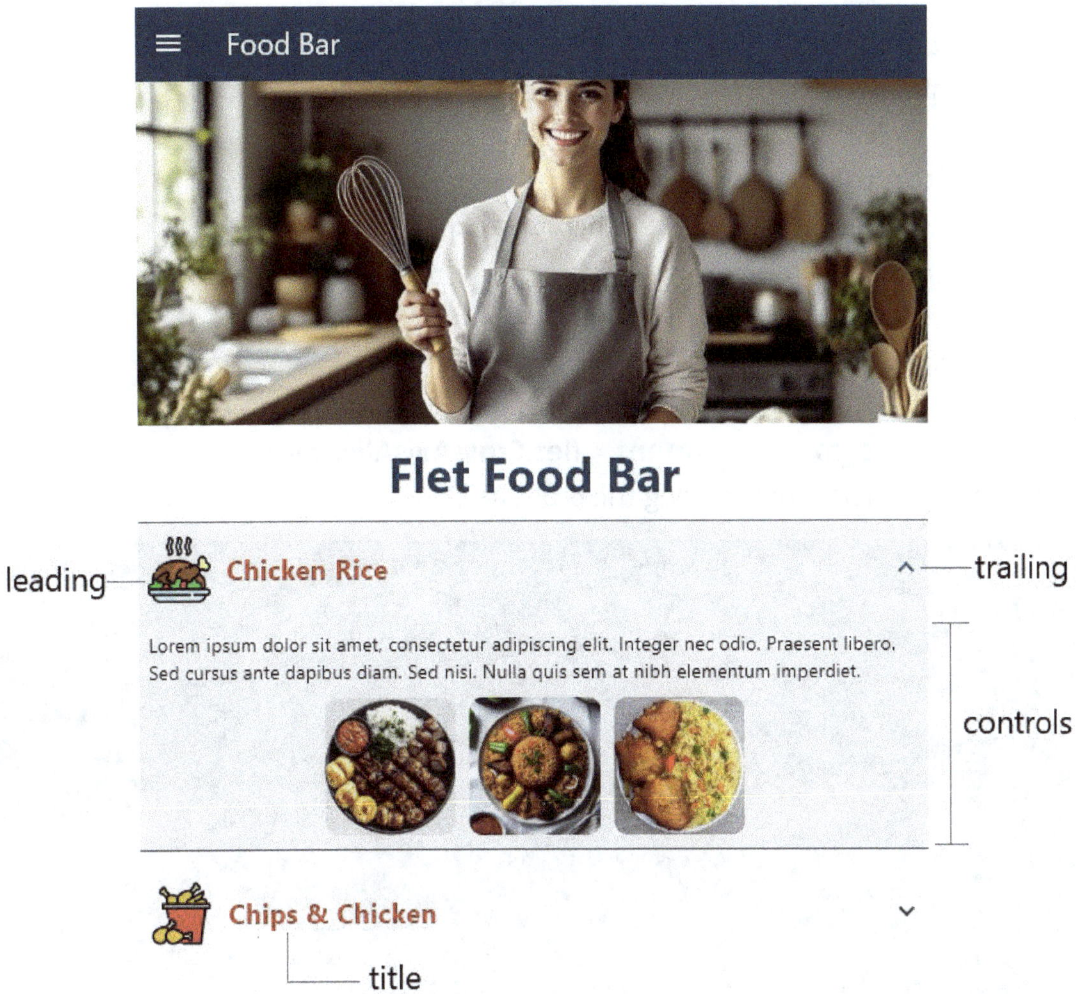

Properties and Methods

title = string/control

Main label for the ExpansionTile, typically a sting or **Text** control.

subtitle = string/control

Optional secondary label displayed below the title.

leading = icon/control

Optional icon or control displayed at the start of the tile.

trailing = icon/control

Optional control to replace the default expand/collapse icon.

controls = [controls]

List of child controls displayed when the tile is expanded.

expanded_alignment = flet.Alignment

Aligns the expanded content along the main axis.

expanded_cross_axis_alignment = flet.CrossAxisAlignment

Aligns the expanded content along the cross axis.

```python
import flet as ft

def main(page: ft.Page):
    page.bgcolor = "white"
    page.appbar = ft.AppBar(
        title= ft.Text("ExpansionTile", color="#F0F0F0"),
        bgcolor="#102a45")

    wild_animals = ft.ExpansionTile(
        leading=ft.Image(r"lion.png"),
        title=ft.Text("Wild Animals", size=15),
        subtitle= ft.Text("See examples of the wild animals"),
        expanded_cross_axis_alignment=ft.CrossAxisAlignment.START,
        controls=[
            ft.Text("1. Lion"),
            ft.Text("2. Crocodile"),
            ft.Text("3. Zebra"),
```

```
        ]
    )

    domestic_animals = ft.ExpansionTile(
        leading=ft.Image(r"hen.png"),
        title=ft.Text("Domestic Animals", size=15),
        subtitle= ft.Text("See examples of the domestic animals"),
        expanded_cross_axis_alignment=ft.CrossAxisAlignment.START,
        controls=[
            ft.Text("1. Hen"),
            ft.Text("2. Cow"),
            ft.Text("3. Dog"), ]
    )

    col = ft.Column(
        controls=[
            ft.Text("Wild animal is any animal living in a natural.."),
            wild_animals,
            ft.Text("Domestic animal is any of the various animals..."),
            domestic_animals ],
    )

    page.add(col)

ft.run(main)
```

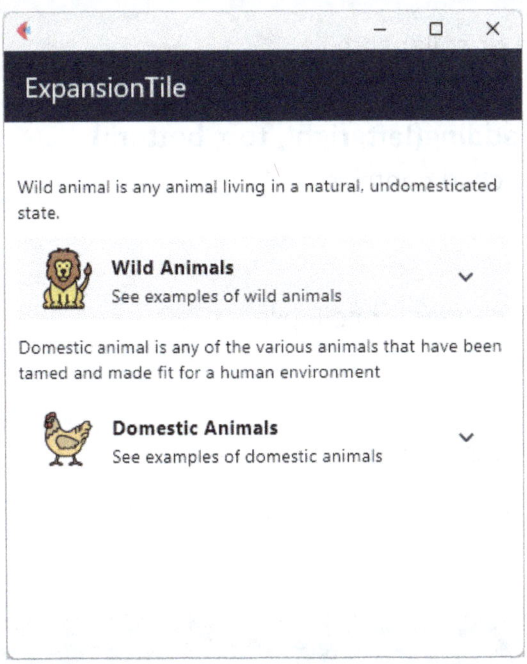

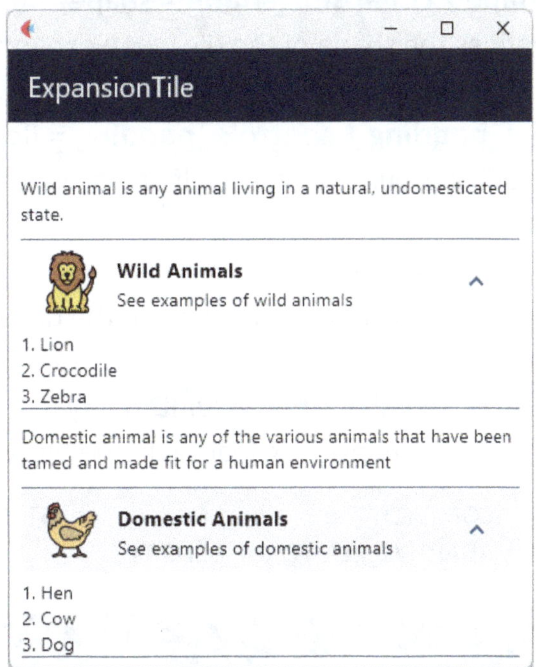

bgcolor = color
Background color of the expanded tile.

collapsed_bgcolor = color
Background color when the tile is collapsed.

collapsed_icon_color = color
Color of the trailing icon when the tile is collapsed.

collapsed_text_color = color
Color of the title and subtitle when the tile is collapsed.

text_color = color
Color of the title text when expanded.

icon_color = color
Color of the trailing icon when expanded.

shape / collapsed_shape = shape
Defines the shape of the tile when expanded or collapsed.

tile_padding / controls_padding = flet.Padding(left, right, top, bottom)
Padding around the tile itself and around the child controls.

on_change = callback
Callback function that fires when the tile is expanded or collapsed.

visual_density = flet.VisualDensity
Adjusts the density of spacing in the tile. Options include

- COMPACT
- STANDARD
- COMFORTABLE
- ADAPTIVE_PLATFORM_DENSITY

Python

```
import flet as ft

def main(page: ft.Page):
```

```
    page.bgcolor = "white"

    page.appbar = ft.AppBar(
        title= ft.Text("ExpansionTile", color="#F0F0F0"),
        bgcolor="#102a45")

    def isExpanded(e):
        #Actual logic goes here ...
        if subtitle.visible:
           subtitle.visible = False
        else:
            subtitle.visible = True
        page.update()


    subtitle = ft.Text("Expand to see profile")

    profile = ft.ExpansionTile(
        bgcolor="#102a45",
        collapsed_bgcolor= "teal",
        collapsed_text_color="white",
        collapsed_icon_color="white",
        text_color="orange",
        icon_color="orange",
        shape=ft.RoundedRectangleBorder(radius=10),
        controls_padding= ft.Padding.all(10),
        leading=ft.Image("profile_picture.jpg"),
        title=ft.Text("Olivia Jackson",size=15),
        subtitle= subtitle,
        expanded_cross_axis_alignment=ft.CrossAxisAlignment.START,
        on_change= isExpanded,
        controls=[
            ft.ListTile(leading = ft.Image("locator.png"),
              title=ft.Text("Address", color="white"),
              subtitle= ft.Text("Chicago\nIllinois\nUSA", color="white")),
            ft.Text("Profile Pictures", size=18, color="white"),
            ft.Container(height=10),
            ft.Row(controls=[
                ft.Image("image1.jpg", height= 100, width=100),
                ft.Image("image2.jpg", height= 100, width=100),
                ft.Image("image3.jpg", height= 100, width=100),
                ft.Image("image4.jpg", height= 100, width=100),
            ])
        ]
    )
    page.add(profile)

ft.run(main)
```

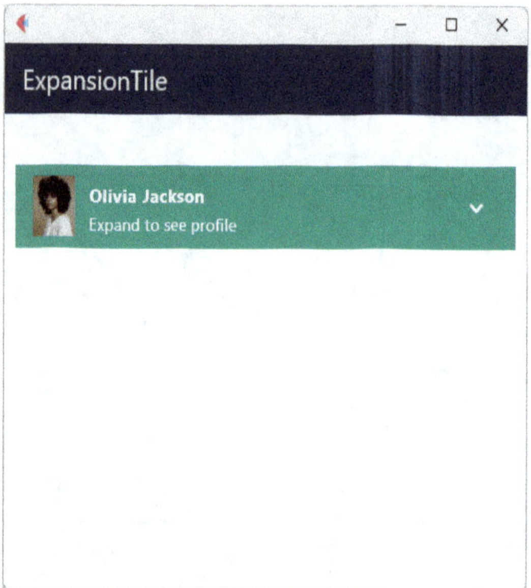

height / min_tile_height = number

Sets the height of the tile and the minimum height when collapsed.

maintain_state = bool

Preserves the state of child controls when the tile collapses.

show_trailing_icon = bool

Whether to display the trailing expand/collapse icon.

on_animation_end = callback

Triggered after the expansion or collapse animation completes.

dense = bool

Reduces the vertical height of the tile for a compact layout.

affinity = flet.TileAffinity

Determines how the tile aligns within its parent layout. Options include

- LEADING
- TRAILING
- PLATFORM

ExpansionPanelList

In UI design, displaying a long list of controls in a **ListView** can overcrowd the screen, since all controls are rendered even if not needed immediately. The **ExpansionPanelList** addresses this by allowing collapsible and expandable panels, improving readability and user interaction.

The ExpansionPanelList is a material design control that contains a list of ExpansionPanel controls. Each panel can be expanded to show its content or collapsed to hide it and the list can scroll when the content exceeds the screen.

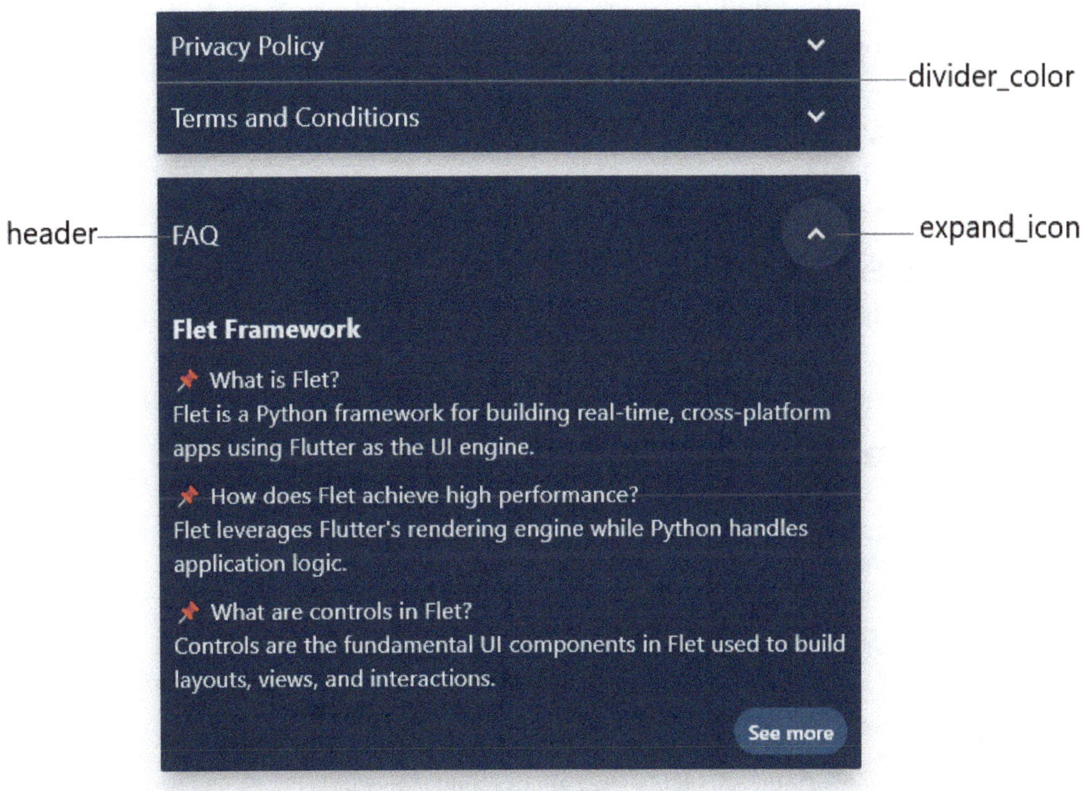

Properties and Methods

divider_color = color
Color of the divider separating each panel; grey by default.

elevation = number
Elevation of the panel to give a raised appearance.

expanded_header_padding = number, flet.Padding(left, right, top, bottom)
Padding around the header when expanded.

expand_icon_color = color
Color of the trailing icon that expands or collapses the panel.

on_change = callback
Callback function triggered when a panel expands or collapses.

controls = [flet.ExpansionPanel]
List of **ExpansionPanel** controls to display.

ExpansionPanel

Method/Property	Definition *Table 3.56*
header	Control for the panel label, usually a Text control.
content	Control(s) displayed when the panel is expanded.
bgcolor	Background color of the panel.
expanded	Boolean to programmatically expand the panel.
can_tap_header	Allows clicking the header to expand or collapse the panel.
splash_color	Color of ripple effect when panel is tapped.
highlight_color	Color of panel highlight on tap.

Python

```python
import flet as ft
```

```
def main(page: ft.Page):
    page.bgcolor = "white"
    page.appbar = ft.AppBar(
        title= ft.Text("ExpansionPanelList", color="#F0F0F0"),
        bgcolor="#102a45"
    )

    fag = ft.Column(
        alignment= ft.MainAxisAlignment.CENTER,
          controls=[
            ft.Text("Flet Framework", size=18),
            ft.Text("📌 What is Flet?\nFlet is a Python framework.."),
            ft.Text("📌 How does Flet achieve high performance?\nFlet..."),
            ft.Container(alignment= ft.Alignment.CENTER_RIGHT,
                         content=ft.FilledButton(content="See more")
                 )
            ]
        )

    expandable = ft.ExpansionPanelList(
        elevation= 15,
        on_change= lambda _:print("A panel has been expanded"),
        expanded_header_padding= ft.Padding.only(left=10, top=10,),
        controls=[
            ft.ExpansionPanel(
                expanded=True,
                header= ft.Text("Privacy Policy", size=18),
                bgcolor= "#F0F0F0",
                content= ft.Text("Privacy Policy We respect your...")
            ),

            ft.ExpansionPanel(
                header= ft.Text("Terms and Conditions", size=18),
                bgcolor= "#F0F0F0",
                content= ft.Text("By using this application, you ....."),
                can_tap_header=True,
                splash_color="grey",
                highlight_color="green"
            ),

            ft.ExpansionPanel(
                header= ft.Text("FAQ", size=18),
                bgcolor= "#F0F0F0",
                content= fag
            )
        ],

        width= 500
    )

    page.add(expandable)
```

```
ft.run(main)
```

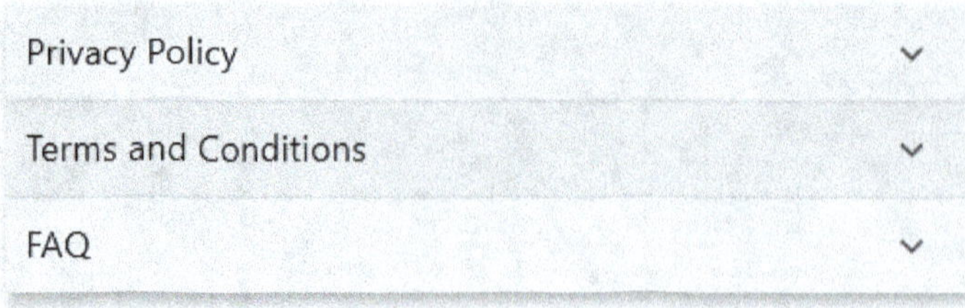

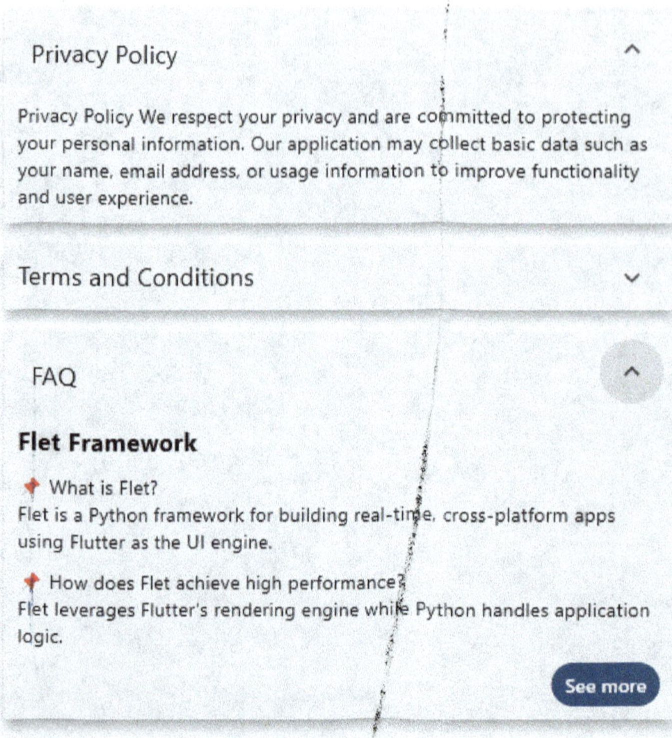

spacing = number

Space between each panel.

File Handling and Media Playback

Many modern applications rely heavily on files for tasks such as viewing, playing, editing, uploading, downloading, exporting, converting, sharing and archiving data. These files may include documents, images, audio, video and other media or data formats. To support such workflows, an application's user interface must provide mechanisms that allow users to select files and folders from device storage and save processed output to a chosen location.

In Flet, file interaction is primarily handled through **system file dialogs**, which provide a native and secure way for users to access files across supported platforms. These dialogs allow users to pick existing files or specify a destination when saving new or processed files.

Beyond file selection, many applications also require **media playback capabilities**, particularly for audio and video content. Flet provides dedicated media controls that allow applications to load and play media files selected from the device or bundled with the application assets. These controls support common playback features such as play, pause, volume control and event handling during media playback.
The core Flet controls used for file handling and media playback include:

FilePicker	**Audio**	**Video**	**Image**

Note

The **Image** control is commonly used alongside file dialogs to display or preview selected image files. It supports multiple image sources, fitting modes and rendering options.
The **Image** control has been studied in earlier chapters; refer to the relevant section to learn more about its implementation and usage.

FilePicker

Many applications are designed to process files by performing tasks such as displaying, reading, converting, editing, playing or analyzing them. These files may include images, documents, audio and video files.

The first step in processing files is often selecting and uploading a file from a storage location or ***saving*** a file to a location. In Flet, the **FilePicker** service allows users to **select, upload** or **save files**.

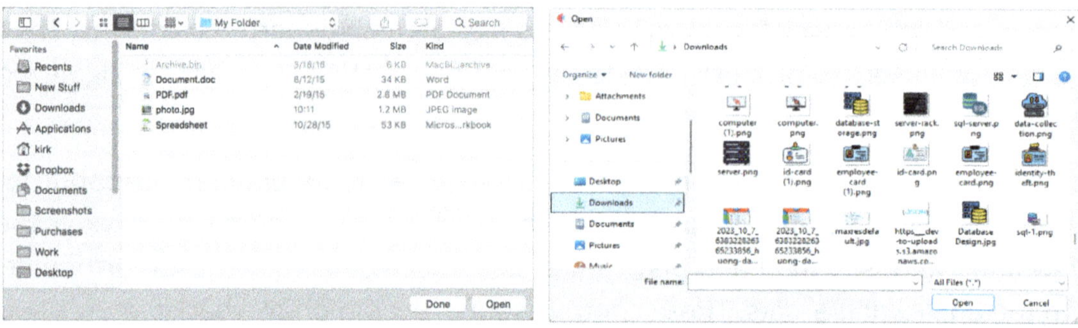

Figure 3.8 : macOS and Windows file dialog

Insight

The **FilePicker** must be opened via another control, typically a **button**, when clicked or tapped.

FilePicker relies on the platform's native dialog style; therefore, its appearance varies between Windows, macOS, Linux, iOS and Android.

Key Events

on_upload = callback

Registers a callback that fires when a file is successfully picked. The callback receives a ***FilePickerUploadEvent*** object to access the uploaded file details.

FilePicker Result

The result of FilePicker refers to the picked files and their attributes. FilePicker creates a buffer of files and each file has its own attributes.

Method/Property	Definition *Table 3.57*
files	Returns a list of picked files. Each file includes: • **name** → The file name. • **path** → Absolute path of the file. • **id** → Unique identifier for the file. • **size** → File size in kilobytes.

Modes of FilePicker

The FilePicker supports two main modes: ***Picking*** and ***Saving*** files.

Picking Files

This mode is used when the user wants to **upload a file** into the application for processing:

Method/Property	Definition *Table 3.58*
dialog_title	Title displayed in the file picker dialog.
initial_directory	Initial folder path where the picker opens.
file_type	Filters expected file type using FilePickerFileType. Options include **ANY**, **AUDIO**, **VIDEO**, **IMAGE**, **CUSTOM** and **MEDIA**.
allowed_extensions	A list of specific file extensions allowed for selection.
allow_multiple	Enables selecting multiple files if set to True.

Python

```
import flet as ft

async def main(page: ft.Page):
    page.vertical_alignment = ft.MainAxisAlignment.CENTER
    page.horizontal_alignment = ft.CrossAxisAlignment.CENTER

    page.appbar = ft.AppBar(
```

```
        title= ft.Text("FilePicker", color="#F0F0F0"),
        bgcolor="#075056"
    )

    filepicker = ft.FilePicker()

    async def openFileDialog(e):
        files = await filepicker.pick_files(
            dialog_title="Select Files",
            initial_directory="~/Desktop/Downloads",
            file_type= ft.FilePickerFileType.CUSTOM,
            allowed_extensions= ["docx", "pdf", "mp3", "png"],
            allow_multiple=True
        )

        for file in files:
            print(f"File names->{file.name}")
            print(f"File paths->{file.path}")
            print(f"File size->{file.size}")
            print(f"File id->{file.id}\n")


    upload = ft.Button(
        on_click= openFileDialog,
        content="Upload",color="white",width= 400,
        style=ft.ButtonStyle(bgcolor="#075056",
            shape=ft.RoundedRectangleBorder(radius=5),),
    )


    page.add(upload)

ft.run(main)
```

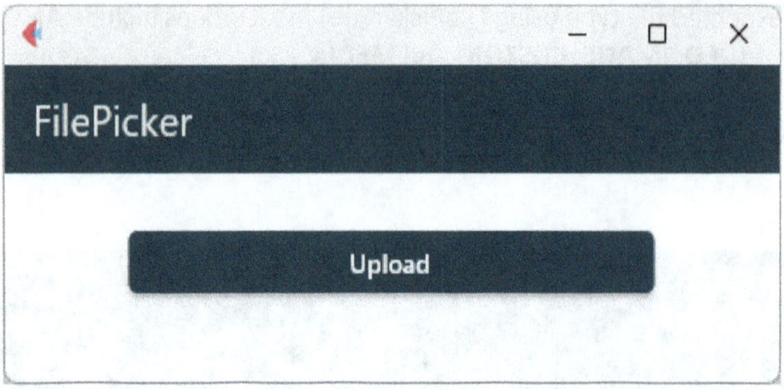

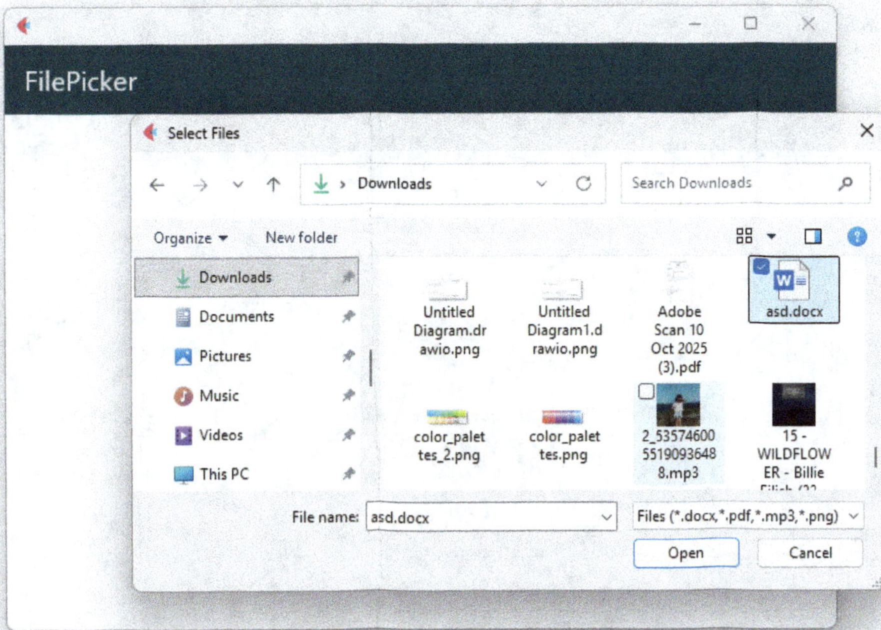


```
#Output
File names->fried-chicken.png
File paths->C:\Users\Asiedu\Downloads\fried-chicken.png
File size->28023
File id->0
```

Saving Files

This mode lets the user save a processed file to a location:

Method/Property	Definition *Table 3.59*
dialog_title	Title displayed in the save file dialog.
file_name	Initial name of the file to be saved. User can rename it.
initial_directory	Initial folder path where the file will be saved.
file_type	Filter expected file types.
allowed_extensions	List of allowed file extensions.

Python

```python
import flet as ft

async def main(page: ft.Page):
    page.vertical_alignment = ft.MainAxisAlignment.CENTER
    page.horizontal_alignment = ft.CrossAxisAlignment.CENTER

    page.appbar = ft.AppBar(
        title= ft.Text("FilePicker", color="#F0F0F0"),
        bgcolor="#967ADC" )

    filepicker = ft.FilePicker()


    async def openFileDialog(e):
        path = await  filepicker.save_file(
            dialog_title="Saving File",
            file_type= ft.FilePickerFileType.ANY,
        ),
        print(path)


    save = ft.Button(
        on_click= openFileDialog,
        content="Save",color="white", width= 300,
        style=ft.ButtonStyle(bgcolor="#967ADC",
            shape=ft.RoundedRectangleBorder(radius=5)),
    )


    page.add(save)

ft.run(main)
```

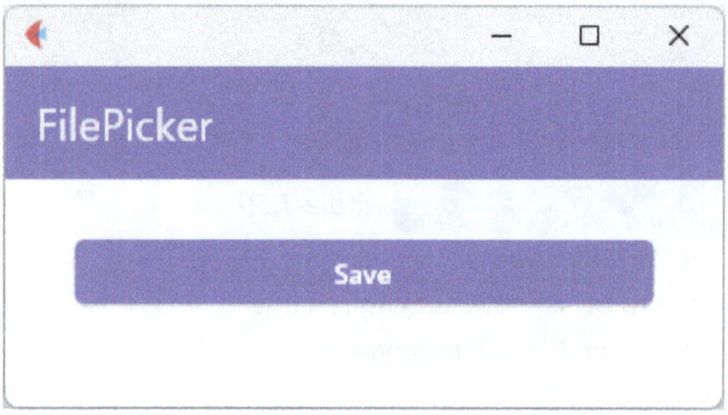

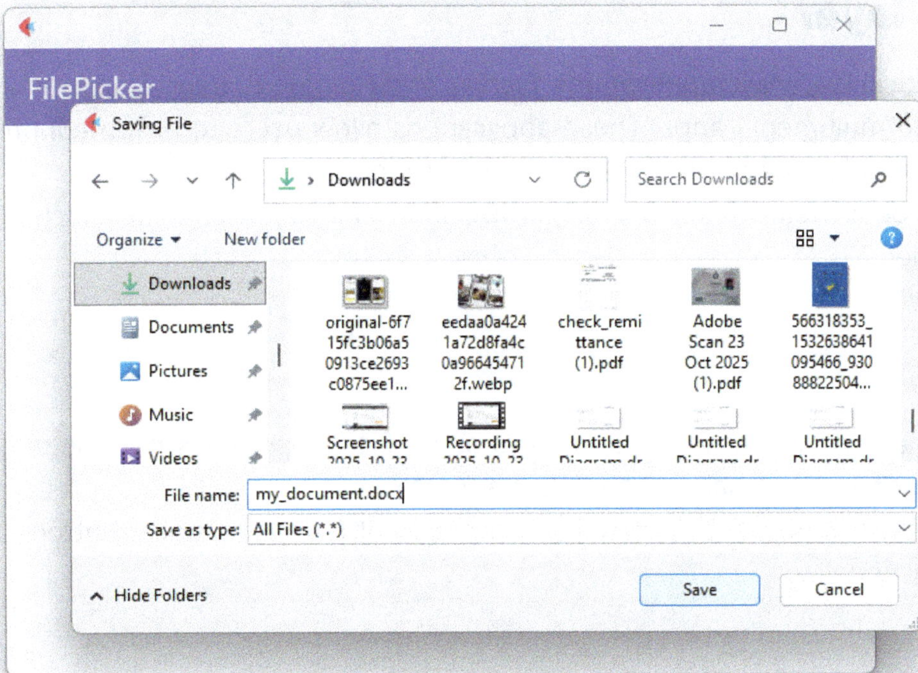
FilePicker
Saving File
Downloads
Search Downloads
Organize
New folder
Downloads
Documents
Pictures
Music
Videos
original-6f7 15fc3b06a5 0913ce2693 c0875ee1...
eedaa0a424 1a72d8fa4c 0a96645471 2f.webp
check_remi ttance (1).pdf
Adobe Scan 23 Oct 2025 (1).pdf
566318353_ 1532638641 095466_930 88822504...
Screenshot
Recording
Untitled
Untitled
Untitled
File name:
my_document.docx
Save as type:
All Files (*.*)
Hide Folders
Save
Cancel

Media Player

Media is a critical feature in applications such as entertainment, education, training, e-learning and multimedia apps. These applications allow users to pick media files which the application then processes by playing or modifying them.

Flet provides dedicated UI controls for playing and managing media files, including audio and video.

Audio

The Audio is a service that reads and plays audio files. It provides parameters to control playback, volume, balance and playback rate.

The Audio service is non-visual, meaning it requires other controls (like buttons) to trigger its functionality.

> **Note**
>
> The Audio control has been deprecated as of Flet version 0.28. Audio support is now provided through an external package, which can be installed using:
> ***pip install flet-audio***

Key Properties and Methods:

src = string(path or url)
Path to the audio file. Can be from internet URL, assets or selected via **FilePicker**.

autoplay = bool
If True, audio plays automatically when loaded.

volume = number
Controls sound intensity; range from 0.0 (mute) to 1.0 (max).

balance = **number**
Adjusts left-right audio balance.

playback_rate = **number**
Sets playback speed (e.g., 1.0 = normal speed).

release_mode = **flet_audio.ReleaseMode**
Defines what happens after playback completes. Options include STOP, RELEASE and LOOP.

on_loaded = **callback**
Callback fired when the audio is loaded.

on_duration_changed = **callback**
Callback fired when the duration of audio changes.

on_state_changed = **callback**
Callback fired when playback state changes (PLAYING, PAUSED, STOPPED).

on_position_changed = **callback**
Callback fired when the current position in the audio changes.

on_seek_complete = **callback**
Callback fired when a seek operation completes.

Audio Playback API

The Audio control in Flet provides programmatic control over audio playback, allowing applications to play, pause, resume and manage audio resources efficiently.

Table 3.60

Method/Property	Definition
play()	Starts audio playback. If the audio was previously stopped, playback begins from the start.
pause()	Temporarily suspends audio playback while preserving the current playback position.

resume()	Resumes audio playback from the position at which it was paused.
seek(position)	Moves the playback cursor to a specified position (in milliseconds) within the audio track.
release()	Releases audio resources associated with the control. Once released, the audio object must be reloaded before playback can resume.
get_current_position()	Returns the current playback position of the audio in milliseconds.
get_current_position_async()	Asynchronously returns the current playback position as a Future.
get_duration()	Returns the total duration of the audio track in milliseconds.
get_duration_async()	Asynchronously returns the total duration of the audio track as a Future.

Python
```
import flet as ft
import flet_audio as fta

def playButtons(name, icon, width, function):
    return  ft.ElevatedButton(
        on_click= function,
        content= ft.Text(name, color="white", size=16),
        icon = icon,
        icon_color="white",
        width= width,
        style= ft.ButtonStyle(shape = ft.RoundedRectangleBorder(radius=5),
                              icon_size=25, bgcolor="#1C1C1C")
    )


def main(page: ft.Page):
    page.bgcolor = "white"

    page.appbar = ft.AppBar(
        title= ft.Text("Audio", color="#F0F0F0"),
        bgcolor="#1C1C1C")

    async def Play(e):
        await audio.play()

    async def Pause(e):
        await audio.pause()

    async def Resume(e):
        await audio.resume()
```

```python
    audio = fta.Audio(src="Hillsong Worship - Q7JsK50NGaA.m4a")

    play = playButtons("Play", ft.Icons.PLAY_CIRCLE, 410, Play)
    pause = playButtons("Pause", ft.Icons.PAUSE, 200, Pause)
    resume= playButtons("Resume", ft.Icons.PLAY_CIRCLE,200, Resume)



    page.add(play, ft.Row(controls=[pause, resume]))

if __name__ == "__main__":
    ft.run(main)
```

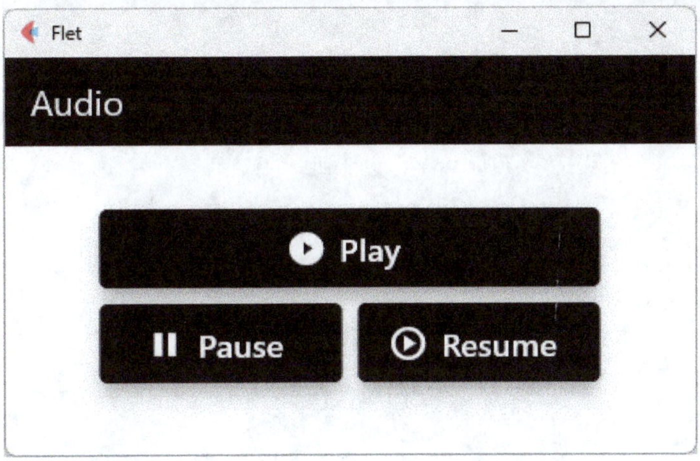

Example 2

```python
import flet as ft
import flet_audio as fta


def main(page: ft.Page):
    page.vertical_alignment = ft.MainAxisAlignment.CENTER
    page.horizontal_alignment = ft.CrossAxisAlignment.CENTER
    page.bgcolor = "white"

    page.appbar = ft.AppBar(
```

```
        title= ft.Text("Audio", color="#F0F0F0"),
        bgcolor="#1C1C1C")

    async def Pause(e):
        await audio.pause()

    async def Resume(e):
        await audio.resume()

    async def seekForward(e):
        position = await audio.get_current_position()
        position = position.seconds
        await audio.seek(ft.Duration(seconds=10 + position))

    async def seekBackward(e):
        position = await audio.get_current_position()
        position = position.seconds
        await audio.seek(ft.Duration(seconds= position-10))

    def seekCompleted(e):
        print("Audio has been seeked")

    async def positionChange(e):
        duration = await audio.get_duration()
        position = await audio.get_current_position()
        reader.value =  position.in_seconds/duration.in_seconds
        page.update()


    def stateChanged(e: fta.AudioStateChangeEvent):
        state = e.state
        print(state)


    reader = ft.ProgressBar(value=0)

    audio = fta.Audio(
        src=r"D:\Vault\temp\Phil-Collins-True-Colors-128.mp3",
        autoplay=True,
        release_mode= fta.ReleaseMode.LOOP,
        volume= 0.8,
        on_position_change= positionChange,
```

```
        on_duration_change= lambda _:print("Audio has started playing"),
        on_state_change= stateChanged,
        on_seek_complete= seekCompleted
    )

    pause = ft.IconButton(icon= ft.Icons.PAUSE, on_click= Pause)
    resume = ft.IconButton(icon= ft.Icons.PLAY_CIRCLE, on_click= Resume)

    forward = ft.IconButton(icon = ft.Image("next.png", height=20,
                                width=2), on_click= seekForward)

    backwards = ft.IconButton(icon= ft.Image(r"previous.png", height=20,
                                width=20), on_click= seekBackward)



    page.add(reader, ft.Row(controls=[backwards,pause, resume, forward]))

if __name__ == "__main__":
    ft.run(main)
```

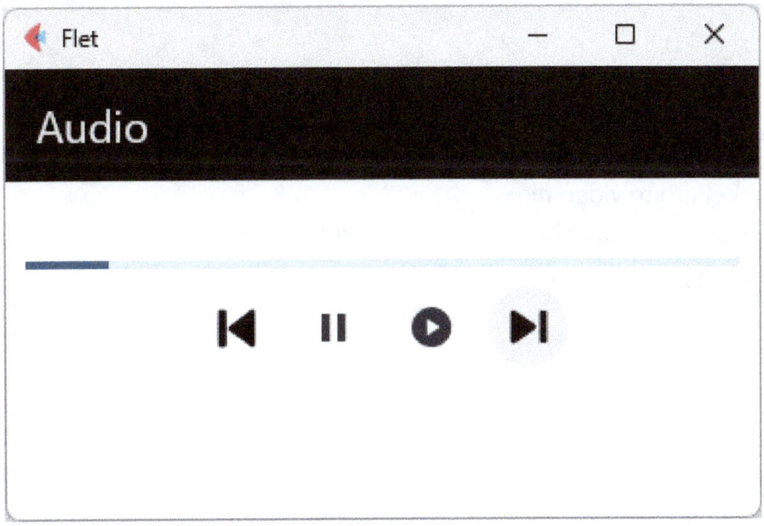

Video

The **Video** is a material design control used to play video files. It provides parameters for playback, display, playlist management and configuration.

> 📖 **Note**
>
> As of recent Flet releases, the **Video** control is no longer bundled with the core library. Video support is available through the external flet-video package, which must be installed separately using the command: ***pip install flet-video***

Key Properties and Methods:

playlist = flet_video.VideoMedia
List of videos, each as a VideoMedia object.

VideoMedia

Method/Property	Definition	*Table 3.61*
resources	(string) - Path to video file.	
http_headers	(dictionary) -Optional headers for video request.	
extras	(dictionary) - Additional configuration.	

title = string
Title of the video.

fit = flet.BoxFit
Determines how the video fits within its frame using BoxFit. The BoxFit options include COVER, CONTAIN, SCALE_DOWN, FILL, FIT_WIDTH, FIT_HEIGHT and NONE.

fill_color = color
Background color of the video frame.

wakelock = bool

Keeps screen awake during playback without going standby or sleep.

autoplay = bool

Plays the video automatically when loaded.

show_controls = bool

Shows playback controls (play, volume, seek). Default is True.

muted = bool

Plays video without sound if True. Default is False.

```python
import flet as ft
import flet_video as ftv

def main(page: ft.Page):
    page.bgcolor = "white"

    page.appbar = ft.AppBar(
        title= ft.Text("Video", color="#F0F0F0"),
        bgcolor="#29282C"
    )


    video = ftv.Video(
        playlist=[
            ftv.VideoMedia(resource=r"D:\Media\Video\Monster.mp4"),
            ftv.VideoMedia(resource=r"D:\Video\Breakingbad.mp4"),
            ],
        title= "My Video",
        autoplay= True,
        width= 500,
        height= 300,
    )

    page.add(video)

if __name__ == "__main__":
    ft.run(main)
```

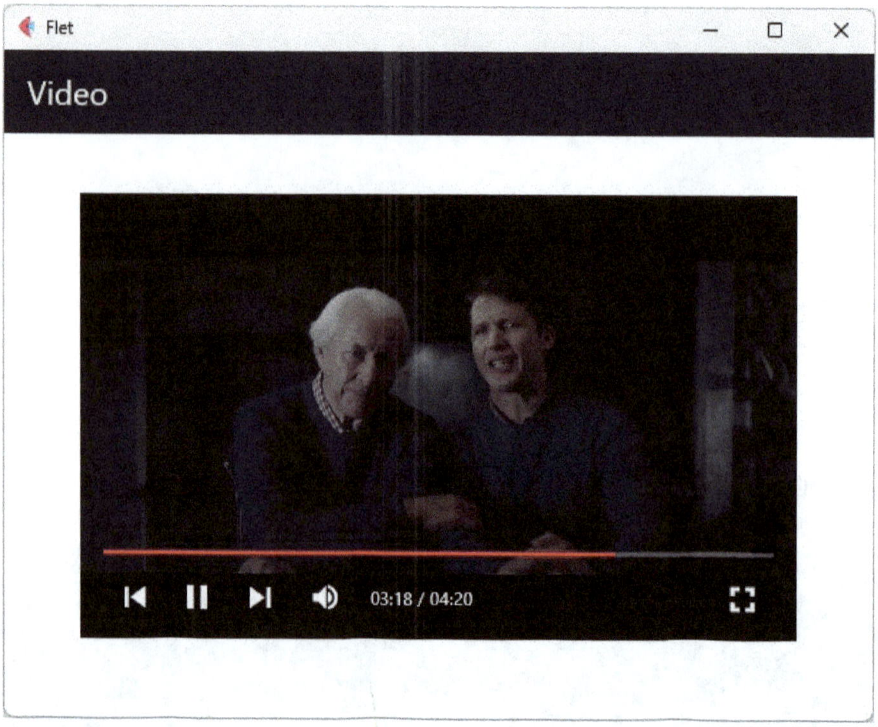

playlist_mode = **flet_video.PlaylistMode**
Defines video repeat behavior (PlaylistMode: LOOP, SINGLE and NONE).

shuffle_playlist = **bool**
Plays videos in random order if True.

volume = **number**
Sets playback volume (0.0 to 1.0).

playback_rate = **number**
Playback speed.

alignment = **flet.Alignment**
Video alignment within the frame. *See page 133 for Alignment options.*

filter_quality = **flet.FilterQuality**
Sets the quality of video rendering (FilterQuality: HIGH, MEDIUM, LOW and NONE).

pitch = number
Adjusts audio pitch.

configuration = flet_video.VideoConfiguration
Uses VideoConfiguration to set output driver, hardware decoding API and hardware acceleration.

subtitle_configuration = flet_video.VideoSubtitleConfiguration
Manages subtitle display.

on_load = callback
Fires when video is loaded.

on_exit_fullscreen = callback
Fires when video exits fullscreen.

on_completed = callback
Fires when the video completes.

on_track_changed = callback
Fires when the video track in a playlist changes.

on_error = callback
Fires when an error occurs during playback.

on_enter_fullscreen = callback
Fires when video enters fullscreen.

Video Playback API

The Video control in Flet enables playback and management of video content, including playlist support and asynchronous state tracking.

Table 3.62

Method/Property	Definition
play()	Starts video playback from the beginning or from the current position if previously paused.

pause()	Temporarily pauses video playback while retaining the current position.
play_or_pause()	Toggles playback state: plays the video if paused or pauses it if currently playing.
stop()	Stops video playback entirely and resets the playback position, releasing associated resources.
seek(position)	Jumps to a specified playback position (in milliseconds) within the video.
jump_to(index:int)	Immediately switches playback to a specific video item in the playlist.
get_current_position()	Returns the current playback position of the video in milliseconds.
get_current_position_async	Asynchronously returns the current playback position as a Future.
get_duration()	Returns the total duration of the video in milliseconds.
get_duration_async()	Asynchronously returns the total duration of the video as a Future.
playlist_add(source)	Adds a video source to the playback playlist.
playlist_remove(index)	Removes a video from the playlist at the specified index.
next()	Advances playback to the next video in the playlist.
previous()	Returns playback to the previous video in the playlist.
playlist_mode	Controls how the playlist behaves (for example, sequential or looped playback, depending on platform support).
is_playing	Returns True if the video is currently playing; otherwise, False.
is_playing_async()	Asynchronously returns the playback state as a Future.
is_completed	Returns True if the video has finished playing; otherwise, False.
is_completed_async()	Asynchronously returns the completion state as a Future.

Python

```
import flet as ft
import flet_video as ftv


def main(page: ft.Page):
    page.bgcolor = "white"

    async def playVideo(e):
        await video.play()

    async def pauseVideo(e):
        await video.stop()

    async def stopVideo(e):
```

```
        await video.stop()

    async def getStat(e):
        duration = await video.get_duration()
        position = await video.get_current_position()
        volumne = video.volume
        print(f"current_position {position.in_seconds} ")


    video = ftv.Video(
        playlist=[ftv.VideoMedia(resource=r"D:\Video\Breakingbad.mkv")],
        on_load= lambda _:print("video is loaded"),
        on_complete= lambda _:print("Video has finished playing"),
        on_track_change= lambda _:print("video track has changed"),
        configuration= ftv.VideoConfiguration(
            width=400,height=200,
            enable_hardware_acceleration=True,
            ),

        subtitle_configuration= ftv.VideoSubtitleConfiguration(
            text_style= ft.TextStyle(size= 16, color="red"),
            text_scale_factor= 2,
            text_align= ft.TextAlign.JUSTIFY
           ),
        #Code continues below ...
    )

    play = ft.IconButton(icon= ft.Image("play-button.png"),
                         on_click= playVideo
        )
    pause = ft.IconButton(icon= ft.Image("pause.png"),
                         on_click= pauseVideo
        )
    stop = ft.IconButton(icon= ft.Image("stop-button.png"),
                         on_click= stopVideo
        )
    stat = ft.IconButton(icon= ft.Icons.DASHBOARD,icon_color="black",
                         on_click= getStat)

    row = ft.Row(
        controls=[video,ft.Column(controls=[play, pause, stop, stat])],
       )

    page.add(row)

if __name__ == "__main__":
    ft.run(main)
```

pause_upon_entering_background_mode = **bool**
Pauses video when app is backgrounded.

resume_upon_entering_foreground_mode = **bool**
Resumes video when app is foregrounded.

aspect_ratio = **number**
Sets width-to-height ratio of the video.

Tables

In applications where users need to view, compare or analyze large amounts of data across different categories, tables provide an effective and structured way to present information. Tables organize data into clearly defined rows and columns, allowing each value to be placed in a specific cell for easy reading and comparison.

In Flet applications, table controls are commonly used for displaying tabular data such as records, reports, lists and summaries. Depending on the complexity of the data and the required features, Flet provides two main table controls:

1. **DataTable**
2. **DataTable2**

Each table type is designed to handle different levels of data complexity and interaction, offering flexibility in how structured data is displayed within an application.

DataTable

The **DataTable** is a Material Design control in Flet used for presenting structured data in a tabular format. It organizes content into ***columns*** and ***rows***, where the intersection of a row and column forms a ***cell*** that contains the data. **DataTable** is ideal for displaying complex datasets, supporting interactive operations like sorting, selecting and editing.

Properties and Methods

columns = **[flet.DataColumn]**

A list of **DataColumn** objects representing each column.

DataColumn

Method/Property	Definition *Table 3.63*
label	The column header (usually a Text control).
numeric	Indicates numeric content alignment.
tooltip	Text displayed when the header is hovered or focused.
heading_row_alignment	Aligns content in the column header using **MainAxisAlignment**.
on_sort	Callback triggered when the column is sorted.

rows = **[flet.DataRow]**

A list of **DataRow** objects.

DataRow

Method/Property	Definition *Table 3.64*
cells = [DataCell]	Each **DataRow** contains **DataCell** objects. Each **DataCell** can define: • **content** → Child control for the cell (text, icon, etc.). • **placeholder** → Displays the content faintly. • **show_edit_icon** → Shows a pencil icon to indicate editable data. • **on_tap, on_double_tap, on_long_press, on_tap_cancel, on_tap_down** → Event callbacks for cell interactions.
selected	Programmatically selects the row.
on_long_press	Fires a callback when row is pressed for a long duration.
on_select_change	Fires a callback when the selected row changes.
color	Row background color.

column_spacing = **number**

Defines the horizontal space between columns.

●●● Python

```
import flet as ft

def main(page: ft.Page):
    page.bgcolor = "white"

    page.appbar = ft.AppBar(
        title= ft.Text("DataTable", color="#F0F0F0"),
        bgcolor="#4A7766")

    table = ft.DataTable(
        columns=[
            ft.DataColumn(label="Name"),
            ft.DataColumn(label="Email"),
            ft.DataColumn(label="School"),
            ft.DataColumn(label="Course"),
            ft.DataColumn(label="Year")
           ],

        rows= [
            ft.DataRow(
                cells = [
                    ft.DataCell(content="Oliveth Brown"),
                    ft.DataCell(content="olive3@outlook.com"),
                    ft.DataCell(content="Harvard"),
                    ft.DataCell(content="Computer Science"),
                    ft.DataCell(content="3"),]
              ),

            ft.DataRow(
                cells = [
                    ft.DataCell(content="Daniel Bruce"),
                    ft.DataCell(content="danbru@gmail.com"),
                    ft.DataCell(content="Yale"),
                    ft.DataCell(content="Computer Engineering"),
                    ft.DataCell(content="1")]
               ),

            ft.DataRow(
                cells = [
                    ft.DataCell(content="John Walt"),
                    ft.DataCell(content="walt100@yahoo.com"),
                    ft.DataCell(content="Illinois Tech"),
                    ft.DataCell(content="Biological Science"),
                    ft.DataCell(content="4"),]
                ),
         ]
        )
```

```
    page.add(table)

ft.run(main)
```

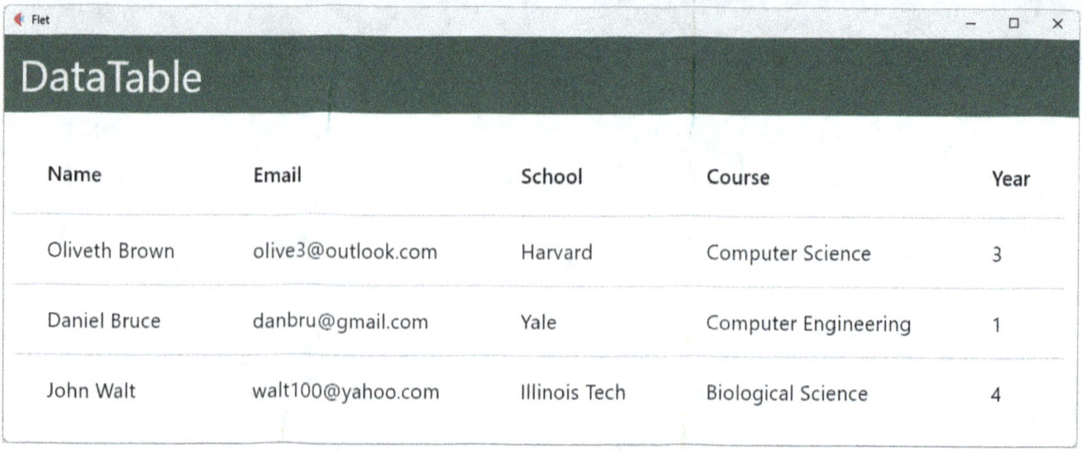

bgcolor = color

Sets the background color of the DataTable. Colors can be specified using names, hex codes or **ColorValue**.

divider_thickness = number

Defines the thickness of horizontal dividers separating rows.

show_checkbox_column = bool

If True, it displays a column of checkboxes for row selection.

checkbox_horizontal_margin = number

Specifies horizontal spacing for checkboxes when using *show_checkbox_column*.

data_row_max_height, data_row_min_height = number

Set maximum and minimum height thresholds for all table rows.

data_text_style = flet.TextStyle

Formats the text in rows using **TextStyle**.

heading_text_style = flet.TextStyle

Formats the header row text using **TextStyle**.

horizontal_line = flet.BorderSide

Uses BorderSide to decorate horizontal dividers with color and thickness. *See page 135 (Container) for BorderSide options.*

vertical_lines = flet.BorderSide

Defines the thickness and color of the vertical lines using the BorderSide.

horizontal_margin = number

Sets left and right margin for the table content.

show_bottom_border = bool

Adds a horizontal line at the bottom of the table.

```python
import flet as ft

def main(page: ft.Page):
    page.bgcolor = "white"


    table = ft.DataTable(
        bgcolor="#4A7766",
        divider_thickness=2,
        horizontal_lines= ft.BorderSide(width=1, color="white"),
        vertical_lines= ft.BorderSide(width=1, color="white"),
        data_text_style=ft.TextStyle(color="white"),
        heading_text_style= ft.TextStyle(
                            color="Orange",
                            weight= ft.FontWeight.BOLD
            ),
        #Code continues below ...
       )


    page.add(table)

ft.run(main)
```

Name	Email	School	Course	Year
Oliveth Brown	olive3@outlook.com	Harvard	Computer Science	3
Daniel Bruce	danbru@gmail.com	Yale	Computer Engineering	1
John Walt	walt100@yahoo.com	Illinois Tech	Biological Science	4

border = flet.Border

Adds a border around the table using the **Border** control. By default, DataTables have no visible border.

border_radius = number, flet.BorderRadius

Applies corner radius to the table using **BorderRadius**. You can specify the same radius for all corners or different radii per corner.

heading_row_color = color

Sets the background color of the header row.

data_row_color = color

Sets the background color for all rows except the header row.

heading_row_height = number

Sets the height of the header row.

```python
import flet as ft

def main(page: ft.Page):
    page.bgcolor = "white"


    table = ft.DataTable(
        border= ft.Border.all(width=1, color="#0096C7"),
        border_radius= ft.BorderRadius.only(
           bottom_left=15, bottom_right=15, top_left=5, top_right=5
         ),
        heading_row_color= "#0096C7",
        heading_row_height= 40,
```

```
        horizontal_margin=20,
        heading_text_style= ft.TextStyle(color="white", size=18),
        #Code continues below ...
       )

    page.add(table)

if __name__ == "__main__":
    ft.run(main)
```

Name	Email	School	Course	Year
Oliveth Brown	olive3@outlook.com	Harvard	Computer Science	3
Daniel Bruce	danbru@gmail.com	Yale	Computer Engineering	1
John Walt	walt100@yahoo.com	Illinois Tech	Biological Science	4

gradient = **Gradient**

Applies a gradient background to the table.

Insight

The usage of the **Gradient** control has been thoroughly discussed in the preceding section on the **Container** control. Refer to that section for detailed guidance on applying gradients.

on_select_all = **callback**

Callback triggered when all rows are selected.

sort_ascending = **bool** , sort_column_index = **int**

Controls sorting behavior for columns.

Graphics, Animation and Data Visualization

The appeal of an application is not determined solely by its user interface layout, but also by the quality of its visual graphics, animations and graphical representations of data such as charts, diagrams and visual indicators. These elements enhance user experience, improve clarity and make applications more engaging and intuitive.

Flet provides several ways to create, render and animate graphical content within applications. It supports custom drawing through canvas-based rendering, animated transitions between controls and the integration of rich animation assets. Beyond visual enhancement, graphical components in Flet are also widely used for data presentation and analysis, particularly through charts and visual indicators.

In Flet, the following controls are commonly used for graphics and visual rendering:

1. **Painting (Canvas and Paint)**
2. **AnimatedSwitcher**
3. **Lottie**
4. **Rive**
5. **Charts**

Painting

Designing modern applications involves more than performance and functionality—it also demands aesthetically pleasing user interfaces. Users are naturally drawn to applications with visually appealing designs. Flet provides tools for creating custom UI designs through **painting**. Using **Canvas** and **Paint** controls, developers can craft complex shapes and visuals, combining them into beautiful and interactive UI components.

Paint

The **Paint** control defines the visual properties of shapes, including color, stroke and blending styles. It specifies the tools and materials to use when rendering shapes.

Properties:

Method/Property	Definition Table 3.65
color	Sets the stroke color or fill color. Colors can be color names, hex codes or predefined ColorValues.
blend_mode	Determines how the paint blends with existing pixels. Methods of the BlendMode include : • COLOR_DODGE • DST_IN • HUE • DARKEN • DST_OUT • LIGHTEN • DIFFERENCE • DST_OVER • LUMINOSITY • DST • EXCLUSION • MODULATE • DST_A_TOP • HARD_LIGHT • MULTIPLY • OVERLAY • SOFT_LIGHT • SRC_OUT • PLUS • SRC • SRC_OVER • SATURATION • SRC_A_TOP • VALUES • SCREEN • SRC_IN • XOR
blur_image	Applies a blur effect to the paint stroke or fill.
anti_alias	Enables smoother edges on shapes by reducing jaggedness.
on_sort	Callback triggered when the column is sorted.
gradient	Applies a gradient to the stroke or fill instead of a solid color. Types of gradients: • **PaintLinearGradient** → Creates a gradient along a straight line between two points. • **PaintSweepGradient** → Creates a radial gradient that sweeps around a center point. • **PaintRadialGradient** → Creates a gradient radiating outward from a central point.
stroke_cap	Defines the shape of the stroke endings (e.g., round, square).
stroke_dash_pattern	Defines a dash pattern for stroked lines.
stroke_join	Specifies how stroke corners are joined (miter, bevel, round).
stroke_miter_limit	Sets the limit for mitered joins to avoid long spikes at sharp angles.
stroke_width	Specifies the thickness of the stroke.
style	Uses the **PaintingStyle** class to define whether the shape is filled (**FILL**) or only stroked (**STROKE**).

Canvas

The **Canvas** control implements **Paint** across various predefined shape classes to render designs in the application. A canvas can draw multiple shapes, each with its own paint properties. Shapes are combined to create rich and dynamic UI designs.

Properties and Methods

content = control
Sets a child control for the canvas.

shapes = [shapes]
Defines the list of shapes to draw on the canvas.

resize_interval = number
Sets the frequency of automatic canvas resizing.

on_resize = callback
Registers a callback that fires when the canvas is resized.

Rect

Draws a rectangle with optional rounded corners. Methods or properties include

• x	• y	• height	• width	• paint	• border_radius

```python
import flet as ft
import flet.canvas as cv

def main(page: ft.Page):
    page.bgcolor = "white"

    page.appbar = ft.AppBar(
        title= ft.Text("Rect", color="#F0F0F0"),
        bgcolor="#4A7766")


    cont = ft.Container(
        padding= ft.Padding.all(20),
        bgcolor="#1c1c1c",
        opacity= 0.6,
        width=400, height=500,
        content=ft.Text("Lorem ipsum dolor sit amet ...",color="white"),
       )

    paint1 = ft.Paint(color="cyan", style=ft.PaintingStyle.STROKE,
                      stroke_width=15)
    paint2 = ft.Paint(color= "green", style=ft.PaintingStyle.STROKE,
```

```
                        stroke_width=10)
    paint3 = ft.Paint(color="red", stroke_cap= ft.StrokeCap.ROUND)
    paint4 = ft.Paint(color="orange", style=ft.PaintingStyle.STROKE,
                        stroke_width=15)
    paint5 = ft.Paint(color="purple", )

    canvas = cv.Canvas(
        content= cont,
        shapes= [
            cv.Rect(x=100, y=100, height=150, width=150,
                    border_radius=10, paint= paint1),
            cv.Rect(x=260, y=150, height=200, width=200,
                    paint= paint2,border_radius=10,),
            cv.Rect(x=200, y=70, height=100, width=100,
                    paint= paint3,border_radius=10,),
            cv.Rect(x=150, y=300, height=150, width=150,
                    paint= paint4,border_radius=10,),
            cv.Rect(x=30, y=200, height=200, width=200,
                    paint= paint5,border_radius=10,),
        ],
    )


    page.add(canvas)

if __name__ == "__main__":
    ft.run(main)
```

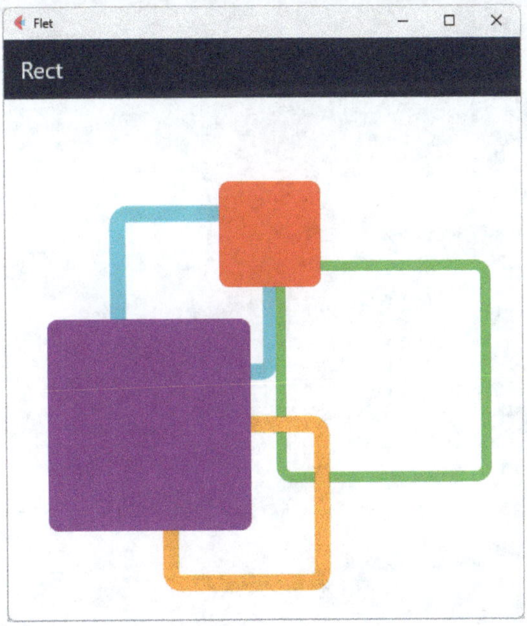

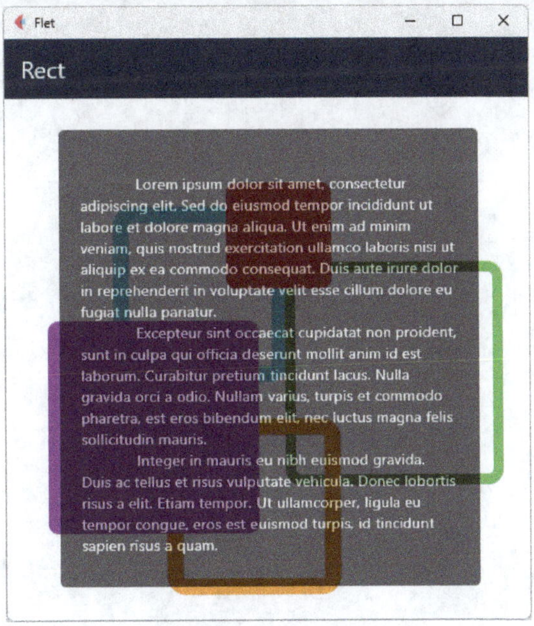

Circle

Draws a circular shape. Methods or properties include:

• x	• y	• radius	• paint

```
Python
import flet as ft
import flet.canvas as cv

def main(page: ft.Page):
    page.bgcolor = "white"

    page.appbar = ft.AppBar(
        title= ft.Text("Rect", color="#F0F0F0"),
        bgcolor="#4A7766")

    cont = ft.Container(
        padding= ft.Padding.all(20),
        bgcolor="#1c1c1c",
        opacity= 0.6,
        width=400, height=500,
        content=ft.Text("Lorem ipsum dolor sit amet ...",color="white"),
       )

    paint1 = ft.Paint(color="cyan", style=ft.PaintingStyle.STROKE,
                      stroke_width=15)
    paint2 = ft.Paint(color= "green", style=ft.PaintingStyle.STROKE,
                      stroke_width=10)
    paint3 = ft.Paint(color="red", stroke_cap= ft.StrokeCap.ROUND)
    paint4 = ft.Paint(color="orange", style=ft.PaintingStyle.STROKE,
                      stroke_width=35)
    paint5 = ft.Paint(color="purple", )

    canvas = cv.Canvas(
        content= cont,
        shapes= [
            cv.Circle(x= 10, y= 100, radius=50, paint= paint1),
            cv.Circle(x= 250, y= 200, radius=100, paint= paint2),
            cv.Circle(x= 100, y= 300, radius=80, paint= paint3),
            cv.Rect(x= 90, y=20, width=100, height=100,
                    paint= paint5, border_radius=10 ),
            cv.Circle(x= 200, y= 400, radius=120, paint= paint1),
            cv.Circle(x= 100, y= 170, radius=40, paint= paint4),
            cv.Circle(x= 400, y= 280, radius=60, paint= paint5),
        ],
    )

    page.add(canvas)

ft.run(main)
```

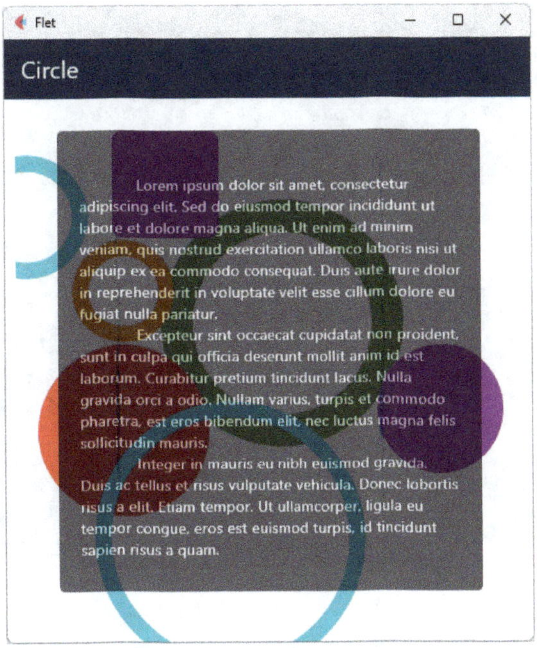

Arc

Draws an arc section of a circle. Methods or properties include:

• start_angle	• sweep_angle	• height	• width	• x	• y
• use_center					

```python
import flet as ft
import flet.canvas as cv
import math

def main(page: ft.Page):
    page.bgcolor = "white"
    page.appbar = ft.AppBar(
        title= ft.Text("Arc", color="#F0F0F0"),
        bgcolor="#00334C"
    )

    paint1 = ft.Paint(color="red", blend_mode= ft.BlendMode.DARKEN,
                      stroke_width=2, style=ft.PaintingStyle.STROKE)
    paint2 = ft.Paint(style=ft.PaintingStyle.FILL)

    canvas= cv.Canvas(
        expand=True,
```

```
        shapes=[
            cv.Circle(x=100, y=100, radius=50, paint=paint1),
            cv.Circle(x=80, y=90, radius=10, paint=paint1),
            cv.Circle(x=84, y=87, radius=5, paint=paint2),
            cv.Circle(x=120, y=90, radius=10, paint=paint1),
            cv.Circle(x=124, y=87, radius=5, paint=paint2),
            #Arc
            cv.Arc(x=70,y=95,width=60,height=40,start_angle=0,
                sweep_angle=math.pi,paint=paint1,
                ),
            ],
        )

    page.add(canvas)

if __name__ == "__main__":
    ft.run(main)
```

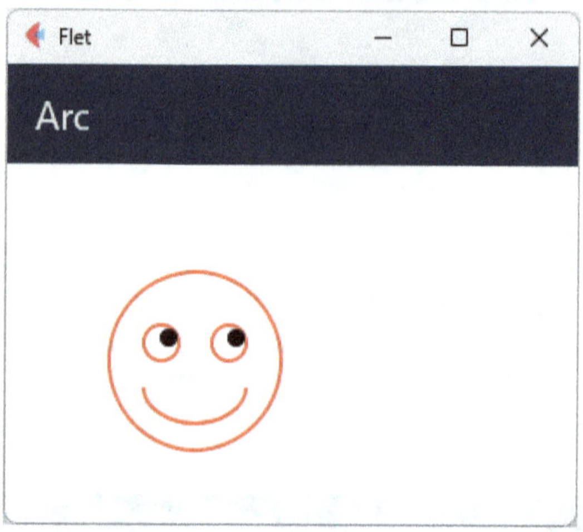

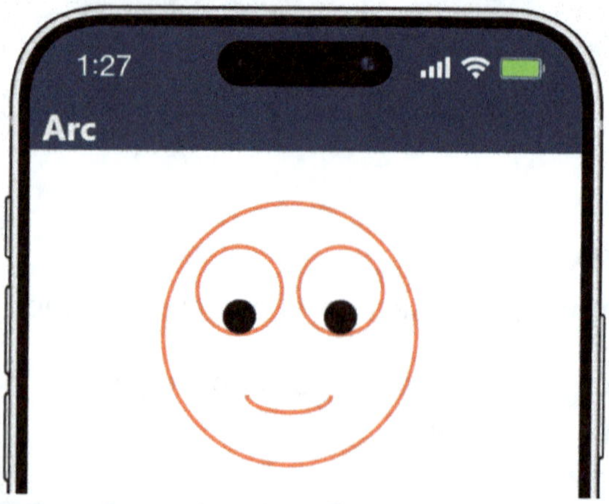

Oval

Draws an ellipse. Methods or properties include

• paint	• height	• width	• x	• y

Path

Draws a custom path using multiple points or curves. Methods or properties include

• elements	• paint	• Arc()	• ArcTo()	• CubicTo()
• LineTo()	• MoveTo()	• Oval()	• QuadraticTo()	• Rect()
• SubPath()				

●●● Python

```
import flet as ft
from flet import canvas

def main(page: ft.Page):

    page.appbar = ft.AppBar(
        title= ft.Text("Path", color="#F0F0F0"),
        bgcolor="#00334C")

    drawing = canvas.Canvas(
        [
            # ⭐ Star
            canvas.Path(
                [
                    canvas.Path.MoveTo(80, 20),
                    canvas.Path.LineTo(100, 70),
                    canvas.Path.LineTo(155, 70),
                    canvas.Path.LineTo(110, 105),
                    canvas.Path.LineTo(130, 160),
                    canvas.Path.LineTo(80, 125),
                    canvas.Path.LineTo(30, 160),
                    canvas.Path.LineTo(50, 105),
                    canvas.Path.LineTo(5, 70),
                    canvas.Path.LineTo(60, 70),
                    canvas.Path.Close(),
                ],
                paint=ft.Paint(
                    color=ft.Colors.AMBER,
                    style=ft.PaintingStyle.FILL,
                ),
            ),

            # 💚 Heart (Bezier curves)
            canvas.Path(
                [
                    canvas.Path.MoveTo(250, 70),
                    canvas.Path.CubicTo(250, 20, 330, 20, 330, 70),
                    canvas.Path.CubicTo(330, 130, 250, 160, 250, 190),
                    canvas.Path.CubicTo(250, 160, 170, 130, 170, 70),
                    canvas.Path.CubicTo(170, 20, 250, 20, 250, 70),
                    canvas.Path.Close(),
```

```
            ],
            paint=ft.Paint(
                color=ft.Colors.RED,
                style=ft.PaintingStyle.FILL,
            ),
        ),

        # ⬡ Hexagon
        canvas.Path(
            [
                canvas.Path.MoveTo(60, 220),
                canvas.Path.LineTo(110, 190),
                canvas.Path.LineTo(160, 220),
                canvas.Path.LineTo(160, 280),
                canvas.Path.LineTo(110, 310),
                canvas.Path.LineTo(60, 280),
                canvas.Path.Close(),
            ],
            paint=ft.Paint(
                color=ft.Colors.BLUE,
                style=ft.PaintingStyle.STROKE,
                stroke_width=4,
            ),
        ),

        # 🌊 Wave curve
        canvas.Path(
            [
                canvas.Path.MoveTo(200, 260),
                canvas.Path.QuadraticTo(240, 220, 280, 260),
                canvas.Path.QuadraticTo(320, 300, 360, 260),
            ],
            paint=ft.Paint(
                color=ft.Colors.GREEN,
                style=ft.PaintingStyle.STROKE,
                stroke_width=3,
            ),
        ),
    ],
    width=420,
    height=340,
)

page.add(drawing)

ft.run(main)
```

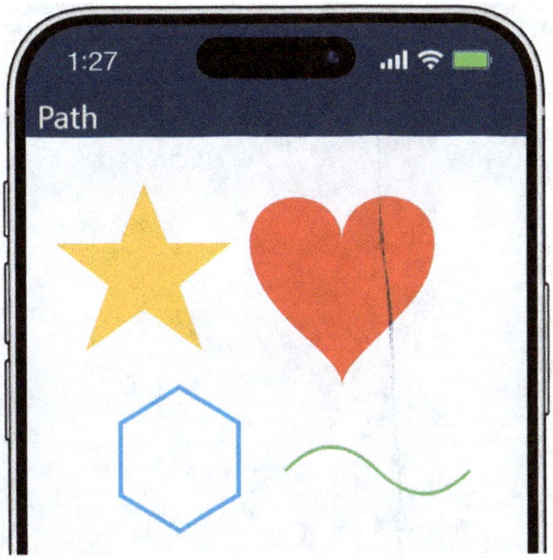

Example 2,

```python
import flet as ft
import flet.canvas as cv

def main(page: ft.Page):
    canvas = cv.Canvas(
        width=float("inf"),
        expand=True,
        shapes=[
            cv.Path(
                paint=ft.Paint(stroke_width=2, style=ft.PaintingStyle.STROKE),
                elements=[
                    cv.Path.MoveTo(x=75, y=25),
                    cv.Path.QuadraticTo(cp1x=25, cp1y=25, x=25, y=62.5),
                    cv.Path.QuadraticTo(cp1x=25, cp1y=100, x=50, y=100),
                    cv.Path.QuadraticTo(cp1x=50, cp1y=120, x=30, y=125),
                    cv.Path.QuadraticTo(cp1x=60, cp1y=120, x=65, y=100),
                    cv.Path.QuadraticTo(cp1x=125, cp1y=100, x=125, y=62.5),
                    cv.Path.QuadraticTo(cp1x=125, cp1y=25, x=75, y=25),
                ],
            ),
            cv.Path(
              elements=[
                cv.Path.SubPath(
                   x=100,y=100,
                   elements=[
                      cv.Path.MoveTo(x=75, y=40),
                      cv.Path.CubicTo(
```

```
                        cp1x=75, cp1y=37, cp2x=70, cp2y=25, x=50, y=25),
                      cv.Path.CubicTo(
                        cp1x=20, cp1y=25, cp2x=20, cp2y=62.5, x=20, y=62.5),
                      cv.Path.CubicTo(
                        cp1x=20, cp1y=80, cp2x=40, cp2y=102, x=75, y=120),
                      cv.Path.CubicTo(
                        cp1x=110, cp1y=102, cp2x=130, cp2y=80, x=130, y=62.5),
                      cv.Path.CubicTo(
                        cp1x=130, cp1y=62.5, cp2x=130, cp2y=25, x=100, y=25),
                      cv.Path.CubicTo(
                        cp1x=85, cp1y=25, cp2x=75, cp2y=37, x=75, y=40),
                        ],
                    )
                ],
                paint=ft.Paint(
                    style=ft.PaintingStyle.FILL,
                    gradient=ft.PaintRadialGradient(
                        center=ft.Offset(150, 150),
                        radius=50,
                        colors=[ft.Colors.PINK_100, ft.Colors.PINK],
                    ),
                ),
            ),
        ],
    )

    page.add(canvas)

ft.run(main)
```

Text

Renders text onto the canvas with custom paint properties. Methods or properties include

• value	• style	• spans	• alignment	• x	• y
• text_align	• max_lines	• max_width	• ellipsis	• rotate	

Python

```python
import math
import flet as ft
import flet.canvas as cv

def main(page: ft.Page):
    page.add(
        cv.Canvas(
            expand=True,
            shapes=[
                # Card
                cv.Rect(
                    x=60, y=60, width=520, height=260, border_radius=22,
                    paint=ft.Paint(
                        gradient=ft.PaintLinearGradient(
                            begin=(60, 60), end=(580, 320),
                            colors=[ft.Colors.BLUE_50, ft.Colors.WHITE],
                        )
                    ),
                ),

                # Title (outline)
                cv.Text(
                    x=95, y=95, value="FLET FEST",
                    style=ft.TextStyle(
                        size=72, weight=ft.FontWeight.W_900,
                        foreground=ft.Paint(
                            style=ft.PaintingStyle.STROKE,
                            stroke_width=10, color=ft.Colors.WHITE,
                            stroke_join=ft.StrokeJoin.ROUND,
                        ),
                    ),
                ),
                # Title (gradient fill)
                cv.Text(
                    x=95, y=95, value="FLET FEST",
                    style=ft.TextStyle(
                        size=72, weight=ft.FontWeight.W_900,
                        foreground=ft.Paint(
                            gradient=ft.PaintLinearGradient(
                                begin=(95, 95), end=(360, 190),
                                colors=[ft.Colors.PINK, ft.Colors.AMBER],
                            ),
                        ),
```

```
                ),
            ),

            # Rotated tag
            cv.Text(
                x=510, y=85, value="NEW",
                alignment=ft.Alignment.TOP_CENTER,
                rotate=math.pi * 0.10,
                style=ft.TextStyle(
                    size=22, weight=ft.FontWeight.BOLD,
                    foreground=ft.Paint(color=ft.Colors.WHITE),
                    bgcolor=ft.Colors.BLUE_600,
                ),
            ),

            # Subtitle with span
            cv.Text(
                x=100, y=200, value="Canvas text: ",
                style=ft.TextStyle(size=20, weight=ft.FontWeight.W_600),
                spans=[
                    ft.TextSpan(
                        text="outline + gradient + rotate",
                        style=ft.TextStyle(color=ft.Colors.BLUE),
                    )
                ],
            ),
        ],
    )
)

ft.run(main)
```

Line

Draws a straight line between two points. Methods or properties include

• paint	• x1	• y1	• x2	• y2

Points

Draws a collection of points. Methods or properties include

• points	• points_mode	• paint

Image

Renders an image onto the canvas. Methods or properties include

• src	• paint	• height	• width	• x	• y

```
Python

import flet as ft
import flet.canvas as cv

def main(page: ft.Page):
    page.bgcolor = "white"

    cont = ft.Container(
        bgcolor="#1c1c1c",
        opacity=0.6,
        width=400,
        height=200,
        alignment= ft.Alignment.CENTER,
        content= ft.Text("Flet Image Canvas", size= 35, color="white")
    )

    canvas = cv.Canvas(
        expand=True,
        shapes=[
            cv.Image(src="tropical_Summer_Coloring.jpg",
                x=5, y=5,
                width=400, height=500)
        ],
      content=cont,
       )


    page.add(canvas)

ft.run(main)
```

Color

Represents a color object used in paints or fills. Methods or properties include

- color
- blend_mode

Fill

Fills an area with a color or gradient. Methods or properties include

- paint

AnimatedSwitcher

Animation is an essential aspect of modern UI/UX design, as it adds motion and visual dynamics to controls, creating a more engaging and artistic experience for users. In Flet, the **AnimatedSwitcher** control is used to animate transitions between controls when they are inserted (switching in) or removed (switching out) from the UI.

Properties and Methods

content = control

Sets the child control to perform the animation on. This can be any Flet control that should appear, disappear or change during the animation.

duration = flet.Duration

Specifies the total time the animation takes. It uses the **Duration** class, which allows time to be defined in various units:

microseconds	→	Time in microseconds	minutes	→	Time in minutes
milliseconds	→	Time in milliseconds	hours	→	Time in hours
seconds	→	Time in seconds	days	→	Time in days

reverse_duration = flet.Duration

Specifies the duration for the **reverse animation** when the control is being removed or switched out. Uses the same **Duration** format.

switch_in_curve = flet.AnimationCurve

Defines the animation curve for entering (switching in) the control. Uses the **AnimationCurve** class, with options such as:

EASE	EASE_IN_QUART	EASE_IN_OUT_BACK	EASE_IN_OUT_CUBIC_EMPHASIZED
EASE_IN	EASE_IN_QUINT	EASE_IN_OUT_CIRC	FAST_LINEAR_TO_SLOW_EASE_IN
EASE_IN_BACK	EASE_IN_SINE	EASE_IN_OUT_CUBIC	LINEAR_TO_EASE_OUT
EASE_IN_CIRC	EASE_IN_TO_LINEAR	BOUNCE_IN	EASE_IN_OUT_QUAD
EASE_IN_CUBIC	SLOW_MIDDLE	BOUNCE_IN_OUT	EASE_IN_OUT_QUART
EASE_IN_EXPO	EASE_OUT_BACK	BOUNCE_OUT	EASE_IN_OUT_QUINT
EASE_IN_OUT	EASE_OUT_CIRC	DECELERATE	EASE_IN_OUT_SINE
EASE_IN_QUAD	EASE_OUT_CUBIC	EASE_OUT_EXPO	ELASTIC_IN_OUT
ELASTIC_IN	EASE_OUT_QUINT	EASE_OUT_QUAD	ELASTIC_OUT
LINEAR	EASE_OUT_SINE	EASE_OUT_QUART	FAST_OUT_SLOWIN

EASE_OUT			

switch_out_curve = flet.AnimationCurve

Defines the animation curve for exiting (switching out) the control. It uses the same **AnimationCurve** options as above.

transition = flet.AnimationSwitcherTransition

Specifies the style of transition between states, using **AnimationSwitcherTransition.** Options include:

- ROTATION → Rotates the control during the transition
- FADE → Fades the control in or out
- SCALE → Scales the control up or down during the transition

```
Python
import flet as ft

def main(page: ft.Page):
    page.bgcolor = "white"
    page.appbar = ft.AppBar(
        title= ft.Text("AnimatedSwitcher", color="#F0F0F0"),
        bgcolor="#00334C")

    def changeImage(e):
        switcher.content = image_2 if switcher.content == image_1 else image_1

        if e.control.data == "rotate":
            switcher.transition = ft.AnimatedSwitcherTransition.ROTATION
        elif e.control.data == "fade":
            switcher.transition = ft.AnimatedSwitcherTransition.FADE
        else:
            switcher.transition = ft.AnimatedSwitcherTransition.SCALE

        page.update()


    image_1= ft.Image("forest.jpg",width= page.width,height= 500,)
    image_2 = ft.Image("dev_room.jpg", width= page.width,height= 500)


    rotate = ft.Button(content= ft.Text("Rotate"), data="rotate",
                       on_click= changeImage)
    fade = ft.Button(content= ft.Text("Fade"), data = "fade",
                       on_click= changeImage)
    scale = ft.Button(content= ft.Text("Scale"), data = "scale",
                       on_click= changeImage)

    switcher = ft.AnimatedSwitcher(
        content= image_1,
```

```
        duration= ft.Duration(seconds=5),
        reverse_duration= ft.Duration(seconds=6),
        switch_in_curve= ft.AnimationCurve.BOUNCE_IN_OUT
    )

    page.add(switcher, ft.Row(controls=[rotate, fade, scale]))

ft.run(main)
```

AnimatedSwitcherTransition.ROTATION

AnimatedSwitcherTransition.FADE

AnimatedSwitcherTransition.SCALE

Charts

Some applications are data-oriented, with their core functionality revolving around processing, analyzing, evaluating and presenting data. These applications may include banking apps, financial dashboards, sales tracking tools, analytics software and monitoring systems. Data can often be complex and displaying it in a meaningful way requires intuitive and visually appealing features.
Flet provides a set of controls for graphical data visualization, including:

BarChart	PieChart	PlotlyChart	ScatterChart
LineChart	MatplotlibChart	RadarChart	CandlestickChart

Note

Chart support is not included in the core Flet package and is provided through the external flet-charts package, which can be installed using: ***pip install flet-charts***

BarChart

The **BarChart** displays data as rectangular bars along the X-axis and Y-axis. Each bar typically represents a category on the X-axis, with its height indicating the corresponding value on the Y-axis. BarCharts are ideal for comparing quantities across categories.

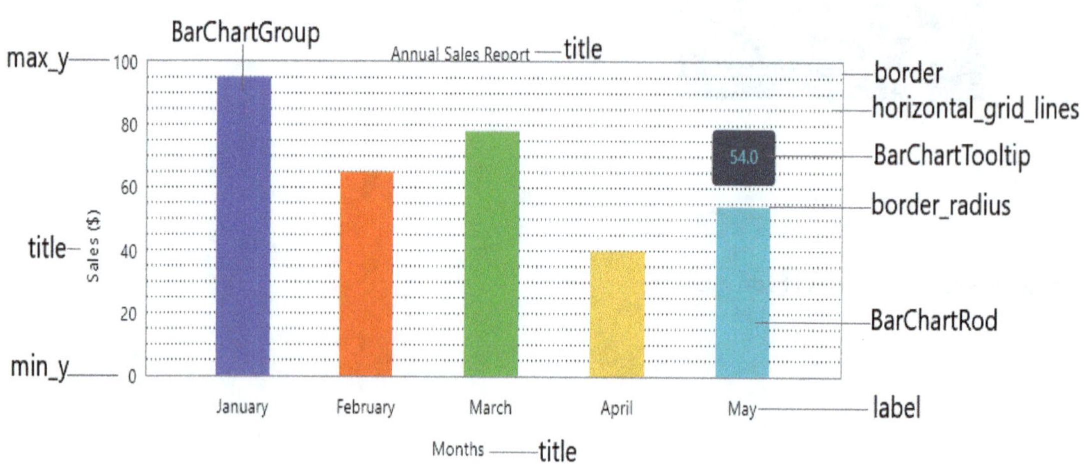

Properties and Methods

bar_groups = [flet_charts.BarChartGroup]

A list of BarChartGroup objects. Each group clusters multiple bars into a single entity.

BarChartGroup

Table 3.66

Method/Property	Definition
x	Integer specifying the X-axis position of the group.
group_vertically	Boolean specifying if bars are stacked vertically.
bar_space	Space between individual bars within the group.
bar_rods	List of **BarChartRod** objects representing the individual bars in the group. The **BarChartRod** Represents a single bar with the following attributes: • **from_y** → Starting Y-axis value of the bar (bottom). • **to_y** → Ending Y-axis value of the bar (top). • **width** → Width of the bar along the X-axis. • **color** → Fill color of the bar. • **gradient** → Optional gradient to fill the bar instead of a solid color. • **border_radius** → Curvature of the bar corners. • **border_side** → Uses BorderSide to style the bar edges. • **bg_from_y** → Starting Y value for background coloring. • **bg_to_y** → Ending Y value for background coloring. • **bg_color** → Background color for the bar. • **bg_gradient** → Background gradient instead of color. • **selected** → Highlights the bar when set to True. • **show_tooltip** → Displays a tooltip on hover or focus when True. • **tooltip** → Text or control displayed in the tooltip. • **tooltip_style** → TextStyle to format tooltip text. • **tooltip_align** → Alignment of tooltip text relative to the bar.

border = flet.Border

Border for the chart canvas using Border or BorderSide.

min_y, max_y = number

Minimum and maximum values for Y-axis.

baseline_y = number

Y-axis baseline for the chart.

groups_space = number
Space between consecutive BarChartGroups.

animate = flet.Animation(curve, duration)
Enables animation of bars when the chart loads. *See page 519 for Animation options.*

Python

```
import flet as ft
import flet_charts as charts

def main(page: ft.Page):
    page.bgcolor = "white"

    page.appbar = ft.AppBar(
        title= ft.Text("BarChart", color="#F0F0F0"),
        bgcolor="#00334C")

    bar_chart = charts.BarChart(
        groups= [
          charts.BarChartGroup(
            x = 0,
            rods= [charts.BarChartRod(from_y=0, to_y=80,width=40)]),

          charts.BarChartGroup(
            x = 0,
            rods= [charts.BarChartRod(from_y=0, to_y=40,width=40,
                 color="green")]),

          charts.BarChartGroup(
            x = 0,
            rods= [charts.BarChartRod(from_y=0, to_y=60,width=40),
                    charts.BarChartRod(from_y=0, to_y=30,width=40,
                    color="red"),])
        ],
        min_y= 10, max_y=100,
        border= ft.Border.all(width=2)
    )

    page.add(bar_chart)

ft.run(main)
```

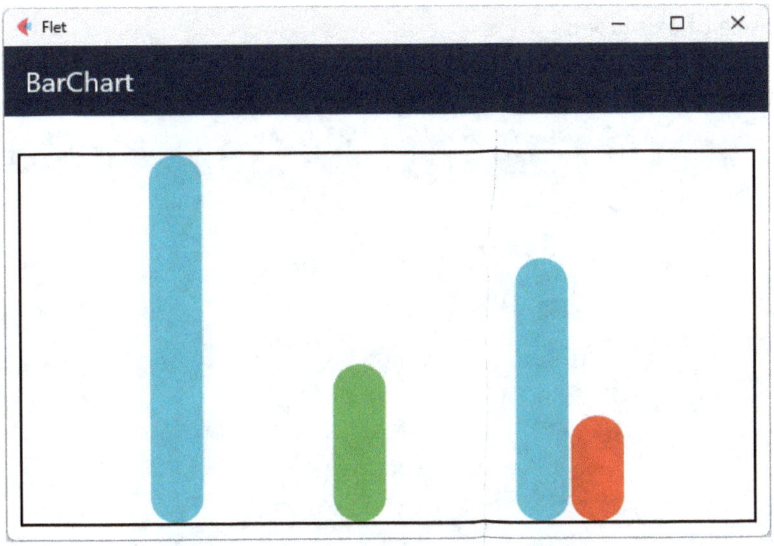

horizontal_grid_lines / vertical_grid_lines **= flet_charts.ChartGridLines**
ChartGridLines object defining horizontal or vertical lines:

ChartGridLines

Method/Property	Definition *Table 3.67*
Interval	Distance between grid lines.
color	Color of the lines.
width	Thickness of the lines.
dash_pattern	Optional pattern for dashed lines.

left_axis, right_axis, top_axis, bottom_axis **= ChartAxis**
ChartAxis objects defines each axis:

ChartAxis

Method/Property	Definition *Table 3.68*
title	Control (often Text) for the axis title.
title_size	Font size of the title.
show_labels	Show or hide axis labels.
labels	List of **ChartAxisLabel** controls for marking points on the axis.
label_interval	Interval between numeric labels.

label_size	Font size of axis labels.

●●● Python
```
import flet as ft
import flet_charts as charts

def main(page: ft.Page):
    page.bgcolor = "white"
    page.appbar = ft.AppBar(
        title= ft.Text("BarChart", color="#F0F0F0"),
        bgcolor="#00334C")

    bar_chart = charts.BarChart(
        horizontal_grid_lines= charts.ChartGridLines(
            color= "grey", interval= 5, dash_pattern=[1,3], width=1),

        left_axis= charts.ChartAxis(
              title=ft.Text("Scores(%)"),label_spacing=10,
              title_size= 40, label_size=40
            ),

        bottom_axis= charts.ChartAxis(
              title=ft.Text("Student"),
              title_size= 40, label_size=40, show_labels=True,
              labels=[
                  charts.ChartAxisLabel(value=0, label=ft.Text("John")),
                  charts.ChartAxisLabel(value=1, label=ft.Text("Alice")),
                  charts.ChartAxisLabel(value=2, label=ft.Text("Irene")),
                  charts.ChartAxisLabel(value=3, label=ft.Text("Bob")),
              ]
            ),


        groups= [
            charts.BarChartGroup(
                x = 0,
                rods= [charts.BarChartRod(from_y=0, to_y=78,width=40,
                                          color="green",border_radius=0)]
            ),

            charts.BarChartGroup(
                x = 1,
                rods= [charts.BarChartRod(from_y=0, to_y=62,width=40,
                                          color="red",border_radius=0)]
            ),

            charts.BarChartGroup(
                x = 2,
                rods= [charts.BarChartRod(from_y=0, to_y=88,width=40,
                                          color="blue",border_radius=0)]
```

```
            ),

            charts.BarChartGroup(
                x = 3,
                rods= [charts.BarChartRod(from_y=0, to_y=95,width=40,
                                          color="purple",border_radius=0)]
            ),
        ],
        min_y= 0, max_y=100,
        border= ft.Border.all(width=1)
    )

    page.add(bar_chart)

ft.run(main)
```

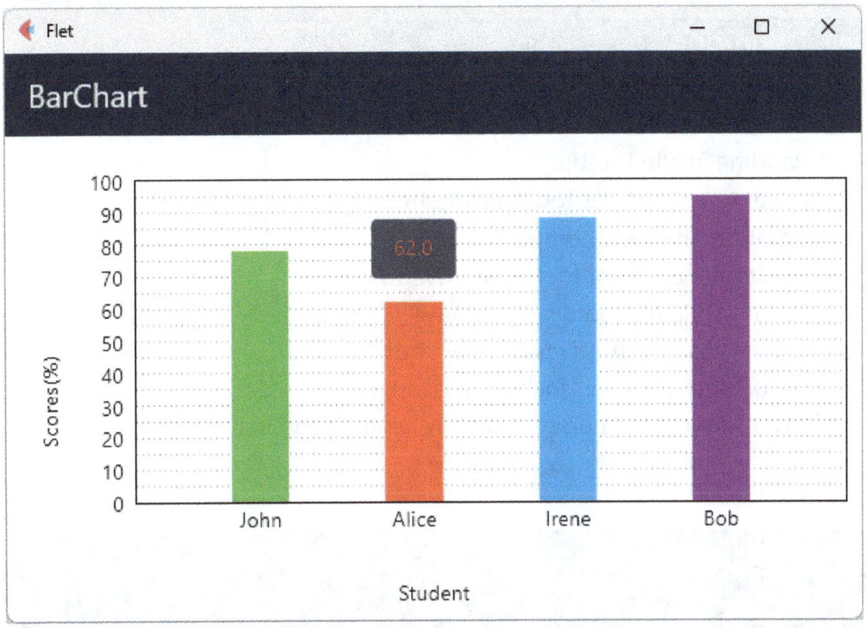

interactive = bool

When True, enables tooltips and interaction on bars.

bgcolor = color

Background color of the chart canvas.

tooltip_bgcolor = color
Background color of tooltips for each bar.

on_event = callback
Callback triggered for chart interactions, such as tapping a bar or group.

tooltip = flet_charts.BarChartTooltip
Defines a piece of message display over the bars. It uses the BarChartTooltip for customization.

BarChartTooltip

Method/Property	Definition *Table 3.69*
border_radius	Corner radius of tooltips.
margin	Margin or space around tooltip.
padding	Padding inside tooltip.
max_width	Maximum width for tooltip content.
rotation	Rotation angle of tooltip.
horizontal_offset	Horizontal offset of tooltip relative to bar.
border_side	Border style for tooltip.
fit_inside_horizontally	Ensures tooltip stays inside chart horizontally.
fit_inside_vertically	Ensures tooltip stays inside chart vertically.
direction	Orientation/direction of tooltip relative to the bar.

Python

```
import flet as ft
import flet_charts as charts

def main(page: ft.Page):
    page.bgcolor = "white"

    page.appbar = ft.AppBar(
        title= ft.Text("BarChart", color="#F0F0F0"),
        bgcolor="#00334C")

    bar_chart = charts.BarChart(
        bgcolor= "black",
        border= ft.Border.all(width=2, color="orange"),
        interactive= True,
```

```
        tooltip= charts.BarChartTooltip(
            bgcolor="#F0F0F0",
            border_radius= 20,
            border_side= ft.BorderSide(color="blue", width=2),
        ),

        #Code continues below ...
    )

    page.add(bar_chart)

ft.run(main)
```

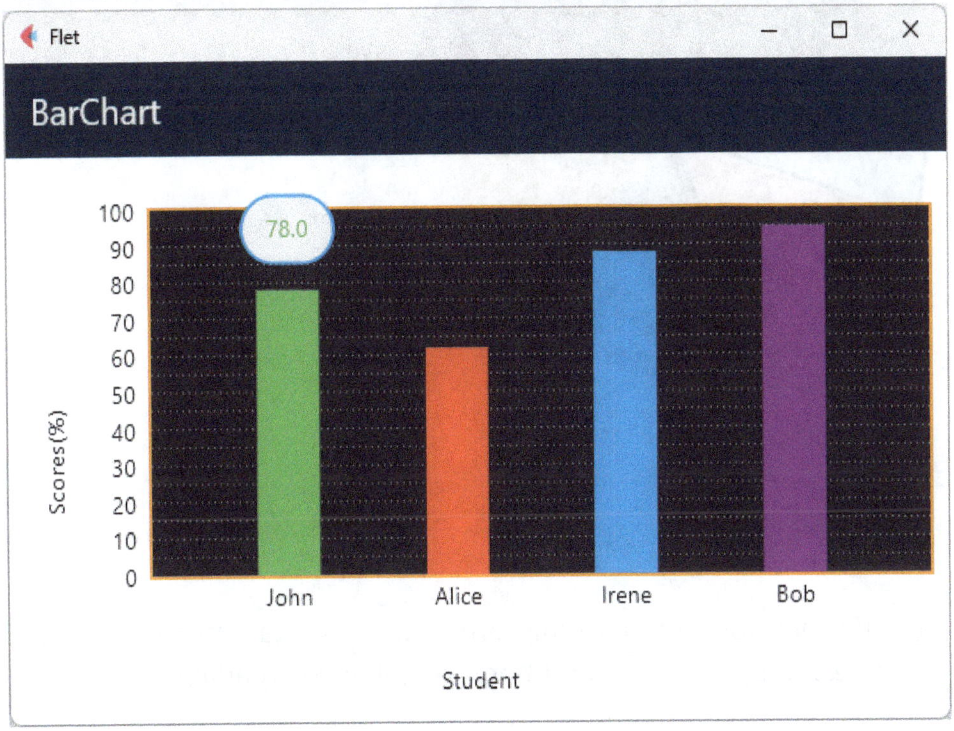

PieChart

The **PieChart** is a graphical control that presents data in a circular layout, divided into individual sections. Each section represents a percentage of the total data, making it ideal for visualizing proportions, distributions or shares. Sections are distinguished by color, labels, badges or borders, providing a clear and intuitive representation of data. PieCharts are commonly used in financial dashboards, survey results, market share analysis and performance metrics.

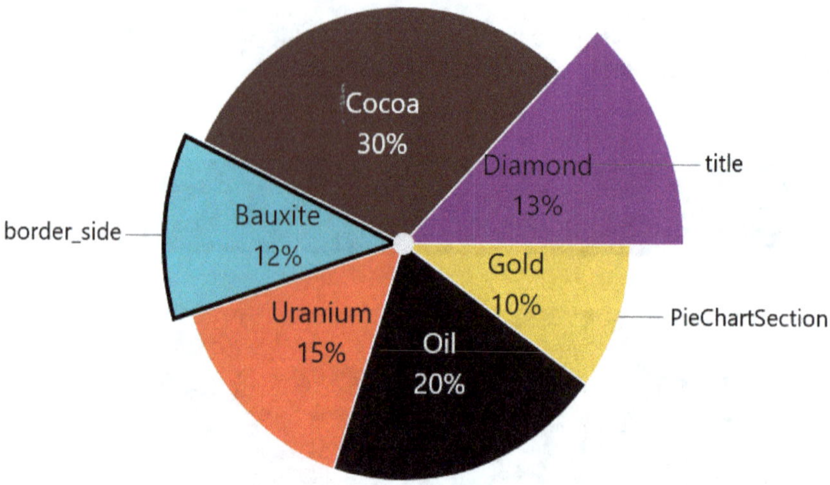

Insight

PieCharts are effective for summarizing proportional data visually and the combination of titles, badges, colors and borders enhances readability and user experience.

Properties and Methods

sections = [flet_charts.PieChartSection]

A list of PieChartSection objects defining individual sections of the chart:

PieChartSection

Method/Property	Definition	*Table 3.70*
value	The numerical value or percentage of the section relative to the total data.	
radius	The radius of the section, affecting the overall size.	
color	Background color of the section.	
border_side	Decorates the edges of the section using BorderSide. *See page 135.*	
title	Text label for the section.	
title_style	Formats the section title using TextStyle.	
title_position	Defines the relative position of the title within the section (range: 0.0 to 1.0).	
badge	Optional badge control displayed within the section.	
badge_position	Defines the position of the badge relative to the section (range: 0.0 to 1.0).	

```python
import flet as ft
import flet_charts as charts

def main(page: ft.Page):
    page.bgcolor = "white"
    page.appbar = ft.AppBar(
        title= ft.Text("PieChart", color="#F0F0F0"),
        bgcolor="#00334C")

    pie_chart = charts.PieChart(
        sections= [
            charts.PieChartSection(
                radius=150, value= 35,
                color="green", title="Food\n35%",
                title_style= ft.TextStyle(size=20, color="white"),
            ),

            charts.PieChartSection(
                radius=150, value= 30,
                color="black",title="Rent\n30%",
                title_style= ft.TextStyle(size=20, color="#F0F0F0")
            ),

            charts.PieChartSection(
                radius=150, value= 15,
                color="#FC574E", title="Transport\n15%",
                title_style= ft.TextStyle(size=20)
            ),

            charts.PieChartSection(
```

```
                radius=150, value= 20,
                color="cyan",title="Others\n20%",
                title_style= ft.TextStyle(size=20)
            ),
        ]
    )

    page.add(pie_chart)

ft.run(main)
```

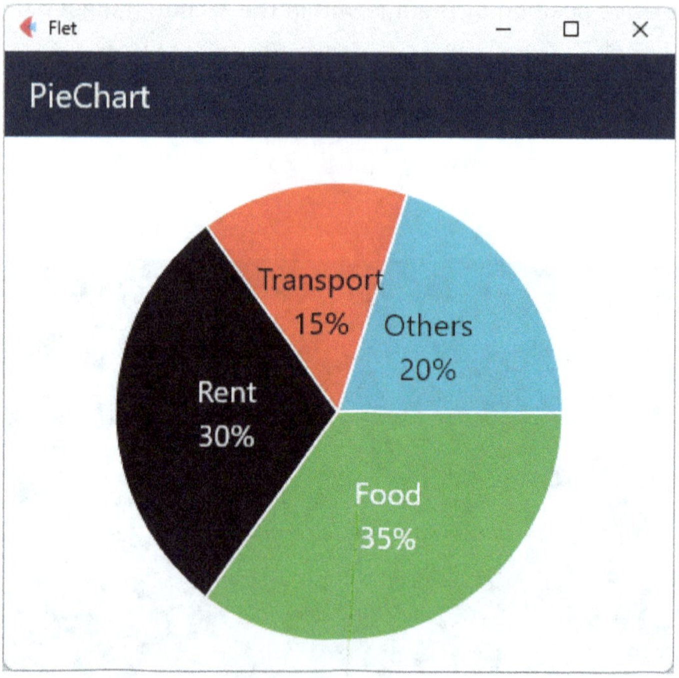

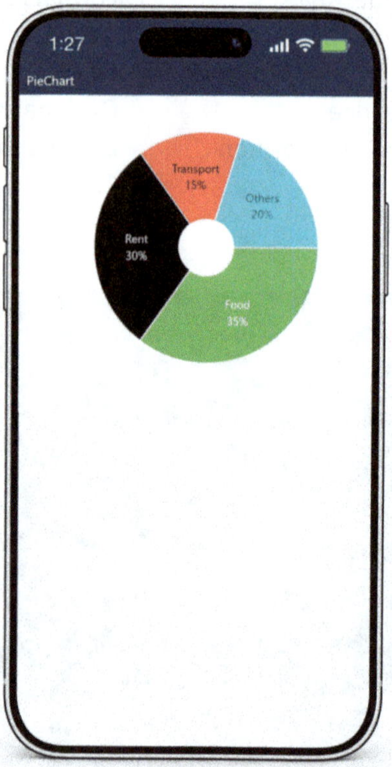

center_space_color = color
Color of the central space surrounded by the sections.

center_space_radius = number
Radius of the central space.

sections_space = number
Space between individual sections of the chart.

start_degree_offset = flet.Offset(x, y)

Rotation offset of the starting angle of the first section in degrees.

animate = flet.Animation(curve, duration)

Enables animation when the chart is rendered. *See page 519 for Animation options.*

```python
import flet as ft
import flet_charts as charts

def main(page: ft.Page):
    page.bgcolor = "white"

    page.appbar = ft.AppBar(
        title= ft.Text("PieChart", color="#F0F0F0"),
        bgcolor="#00334C")

    pie_chart = charts.PieChart(
        center_space_radius=30,
        center_space_color="#F0F0F0",
        sections= [
            charts.PieChartSection(
                radius=150, value= 30, color="green", title="A",
                title_style= ft.TextStyle(size=20, color="white")
             ),

            charts.PieChartSection(
                radius=150, value= 25, color="purple", title="B",
                title_style= ft.TextStyle(size=20, color="#F0F0F0")
             ),

            charts.PieChartSection(
                radius=200, value= 15, color="red",title="C",
                title_style= ft.TextStyle(size=20)
             ),

            charts.PieChartSection(
                radius=150, value= 10, color="orange",title="D",
                title_style= ft.TextStyle(size=20)
             ),

            charts.PieChartSection(
                radius=100, value= 20, color="cyan",title="E",
                title_style= ft.TextStyle(size=20)
             ),
        ]
    )
```

```
    page.add(pie_chart)

ft.run(main)
```

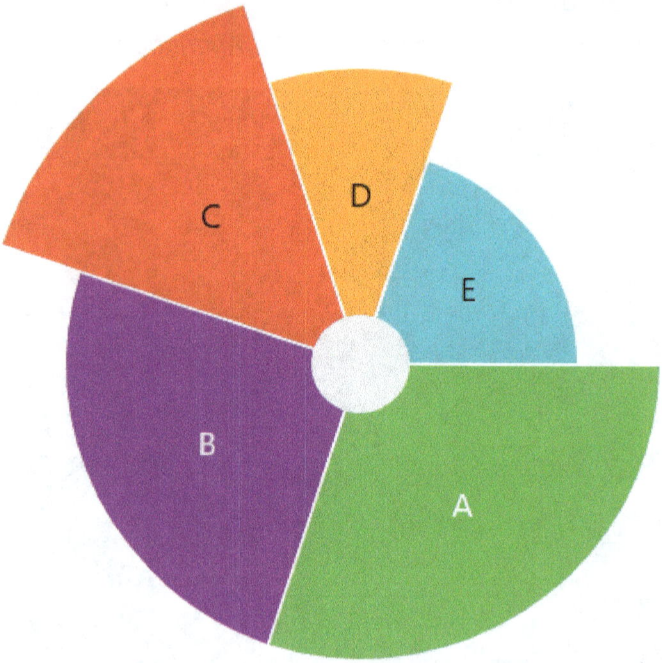

on_chart_event = callback

Callback triggered on interactions with the PieChart (e.g., tapping a section).

LineChart

The **LineChart** is a graphical control used to display data trends over a continuous range, typically across an X-axis and Y-axis. It is ideal for visualizing time series, stock prices, sensor readings, performance metrics or scientific data. Data points are connected with lines to illustrate progression, patterns or correlations, making it easier to analyze trends and compare datasets.
LineCharts can include multiple data series, interactive tooltips, gridlines, axis labels and customizable styling to provide a detailed and intuitive representation of data.

Properties and Methods

data_series = [flet_charts.LineChartData]
A list of LineChartData objects, each representing a line on the chart. Each series includes points, line style and optional markers or tooltips.

LineChartData

Method/Property	Definition *Table 3.71*
Points	A list of **LineChartDataPoint** objects that define the line plot. **LineChartDataPoint** **x: Number** → The horizontal (X-axis) value of the data point. **y: Number** → The vertical (Y-axis) value of the data point. **selected** → Indicates whether the data point is currently selected. **point** → Visual style used to draw a normal (unselected) data point. **selected_point** → Visual style applied when the data point is selected. **show_above_line** → Displays a visual indicator above the line at this point. **show_below_line** → Displays a visual indicator below the line at this point. **selected_below_line** → Shows the below-line indicator when the point is selected. **tooltip: LineChartDataPointTooltip** → Tooltip configuration displayed for the data point. **show_tooltip** → Enables or disables tooltip visibility for the point.

curved	Draws the line as a smooth curve instead of sharp segments.
color	Sets a single solid color for the line.
gradient	Applies a gradient color effect to the line stroke.
stroke_width	Defines the thickness of the line.
rounded_stroke_cap	Rounds the ends of the line stroke.
rounded_stroke_join	Rounds the joints where line segments connect.
curve_smoothness	Controls how smooth the curved line appears.
prevent_curve_over_shooting	Prevents curves from extending beyond data points.
dash_pattern	Draws the line as dashed segments based on a numeric pattern.
shadow	Adds a shadow effect beneath the line.
step_direction	Draws the line in step-like horizontal or vertical transitions.
above_line	Enables drawing a filled area above the line.
above_line_bgcolor	Background color for the area above the line.
above_line_gradient	Gradient fill for the area above the line.
above_line_cutoff_y	Y-axis value that limits how far the above-line fill extends.
below_line	Enables drawing a filled area below the line.
below_line_bgcolor	Background color for the area below the line.
below_line_gradient	Gradient fill for the area below the line.
below_line_cutoff_y	Y-axis value that limits how far the below-line fill extends.
selected_below_line	Applies below-line styling only when the line or point is selected.

min_x / max_x = number

Sets minimum and maximum values for the X-axis range.

baseline_y = number

Sets a baseline value for the Y-axis.

min_y / max_y = number

Sets minimum and maximum values for the Y-axis range.

baseline_x = number

Sets a baseline value for the X-axis.

interactive = bool

When set to True, enables tooltips and selection effects on hover or tap.

point_line_start = number

Defines the starting style for line points (markers).

point_line_end = number

Defines the ending style for line points (markers).

bgcolor = color

Sets the background color of the chart area.

```python
import flet as ft
import flet_charts as charts

def main(page: ft.Page):
    page.title = "Simple Line Chart"
    page.appbar = ft.AppBar(
        title= ft.Text("LineChart", color="#F0F0F0"),
        bgcolor="#00334C")


    # Sample data points
    points_1 = [
        charts.LineChartDataPoint(0, 3),
        charts.LineChartDataPoint(1, 5),
        charts.LineChartDataPoint(2, 4),
    ]

    points_2 = [
        charts.LineChartDataPoint(0, 6),
        charts.LineChartDataPoint(1, 4),
        charts.LineChartDataPoint(2, 7),
    ]

    # Line configuration
    line_1 = charts.LineChartData(
            points=points_1, stroke_width=3, curved=True,color="red"
    )

    line_2 = charts.LineChartData(
        points=points_2, stroke_width=3, curved=True, color="green"
    )

    # Chart widget
    chart = charts.LineChart(
        data_series= [line_1, line_2],
    )

    page.add(chart)

ft.run(main)
```

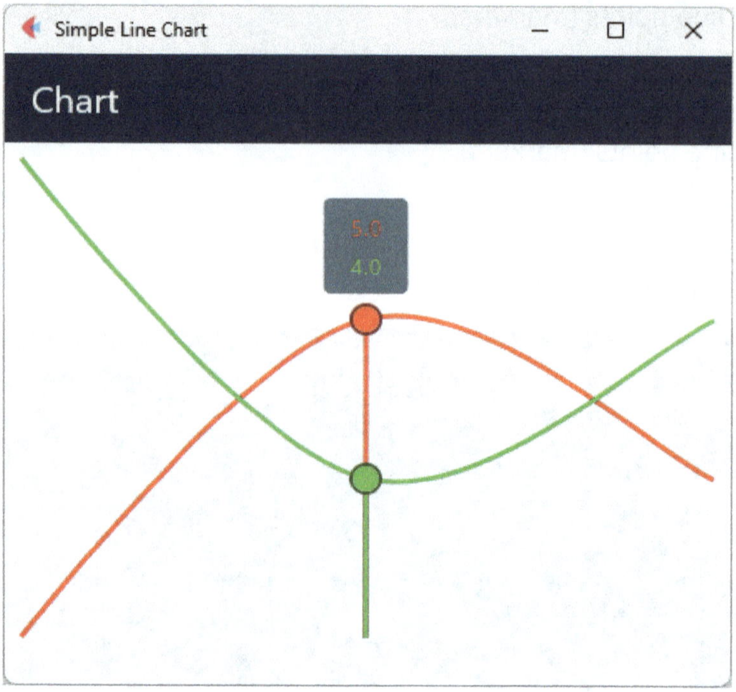

animate = **flet.Animation(curve, duration)**
Enables animation when the chart is rendered or updated.

tooltip_bgcolor = **color**
Sets the background color for tooltips displayed over points.

border = **flet.Border**
Uses the Border control to set the chart's edge styling.

horizontal_grid_lines = **flet_charts.ChartGridLines**
Defines horizontal grid lines using ChartGridLines to improve readability. Includes interval, color, width and optional dash_pattern.

vertical_grid_lines = **flet_charts.ChartGridLines**
Defines vertical grid lines using ChartGridLines. *See table 3.67* .

left_axis = flet_charts.ChartAxis

Defines the left Y-axis using ChartAxis. Includes title, labels, interval and style. *See table 3.68.*

top_axis = flet_charts.ChartAxis

Defines the top X-axis using ChartAxis. *See table 3.68.*

right_axis = flet_charts.ChartAxis

Defines the right Y-axis using ChartAxis. *See table 3.68.*

bottom_axis = flet_charts.ChartAxis

Defines the bottom X-axis using ChartAxis.

tooltip = flet_charts.LineChartTooltip

Uses the LineChartTooltip to customize the piece of message displayed when the mouse passes over the lines.

LineChartTooltip

Table 3.72

Method/Property	Definition
rounded_radius	Defines the corner radius for tooltips.
margin	Sets the space around tooltips.
padding	Sets the internal padding of tooltips content.
max_content_width	Defines the maximum width a tooltip can occupy.
rotate_angle	Rotates the tooltip by a specified angle.
horizontal_offset	Horizontally offsets the tooltip relative to the data point.
border_side	Uses BorderSide to decorate tooltip borders.
fit_inside_horizontally/ fit_inside_vertically	Ensures tooltip remains inside the chart boundaries.
show_on_top_of_chart_box_area	Determines whether the tooltip appears above the chart layer.

Python

```python
import flet as ft
import flet_charts as charts

def main(page: ft.Page):
    page.title = "Beautiful LineChart (flet-charts)"
    page.padding = 20
    page.bgcolor = ft.Colors.SURFACE

    # --- Data (e.g., monthly sales vs target) ---
    sales = charts.LineChartData(
        curved=True,
        stroke_width=5,
        rounded_stroke_cap=True,
        color=ft.Colors.CYAN,
        # soft fill under the line
        below_line_bgcolor=ft.Colors.with_opacity(0.12, ft.Colors.CYAN),
        points=[
            charts.LineChartDataPoint(1, 12), charts.LineChartDataPoint(2, 18),
            charts.LineChartDataPoint(3, 15), charts.LineChartDataPoint(4, 22),
            charts.LineChartDataPoint(5, 19), charts.LineChartDataPoint(6, 27),
            charts.LineChartDataPoint(7, 24), charts.LineChartDataPoint(8, 30),
            charts.LineChartDataPoint(9, 28), charts.LineChartDataPoint(10, 35),
            charts.LineChartDataPoint(11, 32),charts.LineChartDataPoint(12, 40),
        ],
    )

    target = charts.LineChartData(
        curved=True,
        stroke_width=4,
        rounded_stroke_cap=True,
        color=ft.Colors.AMBER,
        below_line_bgcolor=ft.Colors.with_opacity(0.0, ft.Colors.AMBER),
        points=[
            charts.LineChartDataPoint(1, 14), charts.LineChartDataPoint(2, 16),
            charts.LineChartDataPoint(3, 17), charts.LineChartDataPoint(4, 18),
            charts.LineChartDataPoint(5, 20), charts.LineChartDataPoint(6, 22),
            charts.LineChartDataPoint(7, 24), charts.LineChartDataPoint(8, 26),
            charts.LineChartDataPoint(9, 28), charts.LineChartDataPoint(10, 30),
            charts.LineChartDataPoint(11, 32),charts.LineChartDataPoint(12, 34),
        ],
    )

    # --- Axis labels ---
    month_labels = {
        1: "Jan", 2: "Feb", 3: "Mar", 4: "Apr", 5: "May", 6: "Jun",
        7: "Jul", 8: "Aug", 9: "Sep", 10: "Oct", 11: "Nov", 12: "Dec"
    }

    bottom_axis = charts.ChartAxis(
        label_size=36,
        labels=[
            charts.ChartAxisLabel(
                value=m,
                label=ft.Container(
                    margin=ft.Margin(top=10),
                    content=ft.Text(
```

```
                    month_labels[m], size=12, weight=ft.FontWeight.W_600,
                    color=ft.Colors.with_opacity(0.75, ft.Colors.ON_SURFACE),
                ),
            ),
        )
        for m in [1, 3, 5, 7, 9, 11, 12]
    ],
)

left_axis = charts.ChartAxis(
    label_size=44,
    labels=[
        charts.ChartAxisLabel(
            value=v,
            label=ft.Text(
                f"{v}k",
                size=12,weight=ft.FontWeight.W_600,
                color=ft.Colors.with_opacity(0.75, ft.Colors.ON_SURFACE),
            ),
        )
        for v in [10, 20, 30, 40]
    ],
)

chart = charts.LineChart(
    data_series=[sales, target],
    min_x=1,max_x=12, min_y=10,max_y=42,interactive=True,
    tooltip=charts.LineChartTooltip(
        bgcolor=ft.Colors.with_opacity(0.85, ft.Colors.BLUE_GREY)
    ),
    border=ft.Border.all(2, ft.Colors.with_opacity(0.18, ft.Colors.ON_SURFACE)),
    horizontal_grid_lines=charts.ChartGridLines(
        interval=5,width=1,
        color=ft.Colors.with_opacity(0.15, ft.Colors.ON_SURFACE),
    ),
    vertical_grid_lines=charts.ChartGridLines(
        interval=1,width=1,
        color=ft.Colors.with_opacity(0.06, ft.Colors.ON_SURFACE),
    ),
    left_axis=left_axis,
    bottom_axis=bottom_axis,
    right_axis=charts.ChartAxis(show_labels=False),
    top_axis=charts.ChartAxis(show_labels=False),
    expand=True,
)
# --- Card layout around the chart ---
card = ft.Container(
    padding=20,
    border_radius=18,
    bgcolor=ft.Colors.with_opacity(0.04, ft.Colors.ON_SURFACE),
    content=ft.Column(
        spacing=12,
        controls=[
            ft.Row(
                alignment=ft.MainAxisAlignment.SPACE_BETWEEN,
                controls=[
                    ft.Column(
```

```
                                spacing=2,
                                controls=[
                                    ft.Text("Performance", size=18,
                                            weight=ft.FontWeight.BOLD),
                                    ft.Text("Sales vs Target (monthly)", size=12,
                                            color=ft.Colors.OUTLINE),
                                ],
                            ),
                            ft.Row(
                                spacing=10,
                                controls=[
                                    ft.Container(width=10, height=10,
                                       bgcolor=ft.Colors.CYAN, border_radius=10),
                                    ft.Text("Sales", size=12),
                                    ft.Container(width=10, height=10,
                                       bgcolor=ft.Colors.AMBER, border_radius=10),
                                    ft.Text("Target", size=12),
                                ],
                            ),
                        ],
                    ),
                    ft.Container(height=320, content=chart),
                ],
            ),
    )

    page.add(card)

ft.run(main)
```

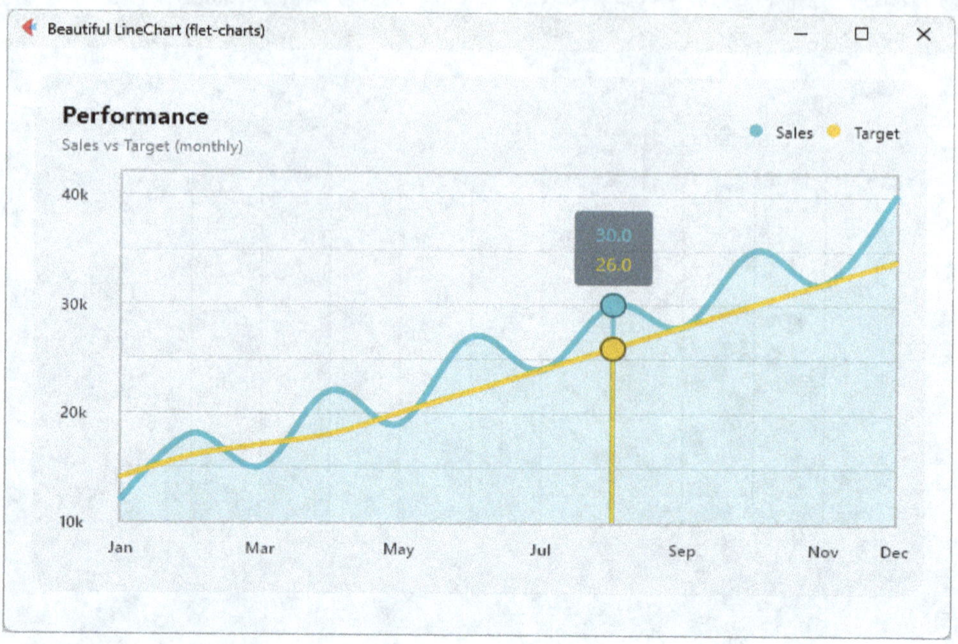

on_event = callback

Callback triggered when the chart is interacted with, such as clicking or hovering over points.

> 📖 **Note**
>
> The remaining chart types, particularly **PlotlyChart** and **MatplotlibChart**, require advanced knowledge for effective use and the installation of additional libraries.
>
> For example, the PlotlyChart control depends on the *plotly* and *kaleido* Python packages, while the MatplotlibChart control requires the *matplotlib* library to be installed.
>
> To learn more about the documentation, methods and properties of the various chart controls, consult the official Python module documentation or use the built-in **help()** and **dir()** functions.

WebView

The **WebView** control allows applications to display web content directly inside the app by opening a specified URL. Essentially, it creates a web browser embedded within the application, enabling users to view and interact with web pages without leaving the app. This is particularly useful for apps that need to show online content, documentation or web-based tools.

> 📖 **Note**
>
> **WebView** is not part of the standard Flet core package and must be installed separately using the following command: ***pip install flet-webview***
>
> At the time of writing this book, the WebView control is supported only on iOS android, web and macOS platforms.

Properties and Methods

url = string

Specifies the URL of the webpage to be loaded. This can be any valid HTTP or HTTPS link.

enable_javascript = bool

When True, allows the execution of JavaScript on the loaded webpage, enabling interactive web content.

prevent_link = bool

When True, prevents navigation to other links within the WebView, keeping the user on the current page.

bgcolor = color

Sets the background color of the WebView area in the application.

on_page_started / on_page_ended = callback

Registers a callback that fires when the page begins or finishes loading. Useful for showing loading indicators.

on_web_resource_error = callback

Fires when a web resource fails to load, providing details for error handling.

on_progress = callback

Fires during page loading to report the loading progress as a percentage.

on_url_change = callback

Fires when the WebView URL changes, allowing the app to respond or update navigation controls.

on_scroll = callback

Fires when the user scrolls within the WebView content.

```python
import flet_webview as wv
import flet as ft

def main(page: ft.Page):
    page.add(
        wv.WebView(
          url="https://google.com",
          on_page_started=lambda _: print("Page has started"),
          on_page_ended=lambda _: print("Page has ended"),
          on_web_resource_error=lambda e: print("WebView error:"),
          expand=True,
        )
    )

ft.run(main)
```

on_console_message = callback

Registers a callback to capture JavaScript console messages for debugging.

on_javascript_alert_dialog = callback

Fires when the webpage triggers a JavaScript alert dialog, allowing the app to handle it.

Services

In the new architecture of the **Flet framework**, non-visual controls are classified as **services**. Services do not render UI elements directly; instead, they provide access to device features and system-level functionality that can be used by other controls within an application.

Some services are shipped as part of the core Flet package, while others must be installed separately using the Python ***pip*** command and then imported into the application. Services are typically accessed through the page object and interact with the underlying platform APIs.

Flet provides a wide range of services that enable applications to access hardware sensors, device capabilities, storage and operating system features.

> 📖 Note
>
> **Platform Support Note**
>
> Some Flet services are platform-specific, meaning they may not be available on all platforms such as Windows, Linux, macOS, Android and iOS. For example, the **Flashlight** service is typically unavailable on desktop platforms due to hardware limitations.
>
> Other services, such as Clipboard, FilePicker and SharedPreferences, are supported across multiple platforms.
>
> This book focuses primarily on cross-platform services, while also highlighting platform-specific services where applicable.

Common Flet Services

Below is a brief explanation of commonly available Flet services.

Clipboard

The Clipboard provides access to the system clipboard for copying and pasting text or other supported content. It exposes methods(set() and get()) for setting clipboard data and reading previously copied content.

set(value)

Used to place text or supported data onto the system clipboard.

get()

Retrieves the current content stored in the clipboard for use within the application.

```python
import flet as ft

def main(page: ft.Page):

    clipboard = ft.Clipboard()

    async def getClipboard(e):
        #Actual code goes here ...
        value = await clipboard.get()
        print(value)


    async def setClipboard(e):
        #Actual code goes here ...
        await clipboard.set("Hi Pythonist!")


    from_clip = ft.TextButton(
                content= "Get clipboard",
                on_click=getClipboard
        )

    to_clip = ft.TextButton(
                content= "Set clipboard",
                on_click=setClipboard
        )


    page.add(from_clip, to_clip)

ft.run(main)
```

AudioRecorder

The **AudioRecorder** is a service in Flet used to capture and record audio from the device's microphone. This control is essential in applications that require voice input, audio notes, podcasts or sound sampling, such as education apps, voice messaging, multimedia and recording utilities.

> **Note**
>
> To use the **AudioRecorder** service, install the flet-audio-recorder package by running the following command: ***pip install flet-audio-recorder***

Table 3.73

Method/Property	Definition
cancel_recording	Terminates the current recording session and discards any recorded audio.
get_input_devices	Returns a list of available audio input devices that can be used for recording.
has_permission	Verifies whether the application has the required permission to record audio.
is_paused	Indicates whether the audio recorder is currently in a paused state.
is_recording	Indicates whether an audio recording session is currently active.
is_supported_encoder	Determines whether a specified audio encoder is supported by the recorder.
pause_recording	Temporarily halts an ongoing audio recording without ending the session.
resume_recording	Continues an audio recording that was previously paused.
start_recording	Initiates audio recording and saves the output to the specified file path.
stop_recording	Ends the audio recording session and optionally returns the path of the saved audio file.

Python

```
import flet as ft
import flet_audio_recorder as far

def main(page: ft.Page):
```

```python
path = "test-audio-file.wav"

def show_snackbar(message):
    page.show_dialog(ft.SnackBar(ft.Text(message)))

async def handle_recording_start(e: ft.Event[ft.Button]):
    show_snackbar("Starting recording...")
    await recorder.start_recording(output_path=path)

async def handle_recording_stop(e: ft.Event[ft.Button]):
    output_path = await recorder.stop_recording()
    show_snackbar(f"Stopped recording. Output Path: {output_path}")
    if page.web and output_path is not None:
        await page.launch_url(output_path)

async def handle_list_devices(e: ft.Event[ft.Button]):
    o = await recorder.get_input_devices()
    show_snackbar(
        f"Input Devices: {', '.join([f'{d.id}:{d.label}' for d in o])}")

async def handle_has_permission(e: ft.Event[ft.Button]):
    try:
        status = await recorder.has_permission()
        show_snackbar(f"Audio Recording Permission status: {status}")
    except Exception as e:
        show_snackbar(f"Error checking permission: {e}")

async def handle_pause(e: ft.Event[ft.Button]):
    print(f"isRecording: {await recorder.is_recording()}")
    if await recorder.is_recording():
        await recorder.pause_recording()

async def handle_resume(e: ft.Event[ft.Button]):
    print(f"isPaused: {await recorder.is_paused()}")
    if await recorder.is_paused():
        await recorder.resume_recording()

async def handle_audio_encoder_test(e: ft.Event[ft.Button]):
    print(await recorder.is_supported_encoder(far.AudioEncoder.WAV))

recorder = far.AudioRecorder(
    configuration=far.AudioRecorderConfiguration(
    encoder=far.AudioEncoder.WAV),
    on_state_change=lambda e: print(f"State Changed: {e.data}"),
)

page.add(
    ft.Button(content="Start Audio Recorder",
              on_click=handle_recording_start),
    ft.Button(content="Stop Audio Recorder",
             on_click=handle_recording_stop),
    ft.Button(content="List Devices", on_click=handle_list_devices),
    ft.Button(content="Pause Recording", on_click=handle_pause),
```

```
        ft.Button(content="Resume Recording", on_click=handle_resume),
        ft.Button(content="WAV Encoder Support",
                  on_click=handle_audio_encoder_test),
        ft.Button(
            content="Get Audio Recording Permission Status",
            on_click=handle_has_permission,
        ),
    )

ft.run(main)
```

Geolocator

Provides access to the device's geographical location.

Gyroscope

Reads rotational movement data from the device's gyroscope sensor.

HapticFeedback

Triggers vibration or haptic feedback on supported devices.

ScreenBrightness

Allows reading or adjusting the device screen brightness.

Connectivity

Detects the network connection status of the device (online or offline).

Table 3.74

Method/Property	Definition
on_change	Registers a callback that triggers when connectivity changes.
get_connectivity()	Returns the current connectivity type

Python

```python
import flet as ft

async def main(page: ft.Page):
    connectivity = ft.Connectivity()
```

```python
    status = ft.Text()
    changes = ft.Text()

    async def refresh(_=None):
        results = await connectivity.get_connectivity()
        status.value = "Connectivity: " + ", ".join(r.value for r in results)

    async def on_change(e: ft.ConnectivityChangeEvent):
        changes.value = "Connectivity changed: " + ", ".join(
            r.value for r in e.connectivity
        )
        await refresh()

    connectivity.on_change = on_change

    await refresh()

    page.add(
        ft.Column(
            [
                status,
                ft.Button("Refresh connectivity", on_click=refresh),
                changes,
            ],
        )
    )

ft.run(main)
```

Accelerometer

Provides access to the device's accelerometer sensor, allowing detection of motion and orientation changes.

Barometer

Provides atmospheric pressure data from supported devices.

BrowserContextMenu

Controls the browser's context menu behavior in web-based Flet applications.

Share

Enables sharing of text or files with other applications installed on the device.

Method/Property	Definition *Table 3.75*
share_text	Share plain text with optional subject, title and thumbnail. Parameters include **text** → The text to share. **title** → Optional title for the share sheet. **subject** → Optional subject for the shared text. **preview_thumbnail** → Optional thumbnail file to show in the share sheet. **share_position_origin** → Optional position origin for the share sheet. **download_fallback_enabled** → Whether to enable download fallback. **mail_to_fallback_enabled** → Whether to enable mailto fallback. **excluded_cupertino_activities** → Optional list of iOS/macOS activities to exclude.
share_file	Share one or more files with optional text/metadata. Parameters include **files** → List of ShareFile instances to share. **title** → Optional title for the share sheet. **text** → Optional text to accompany the files. **subject** → Optional subject for the shared files. **preview_thumbnail** → Optional thumbnail file to show in the share sheet. **share_position_origin** → Optional position origin for the share sheet. **download_fallback_enabled** → Whether to enable download fallback. **mail_to_fallback_enabled** → Whether to enable mailto fallback. **excluded_cupertino_activities** → Optional list of iOS/macOS activities to exclude.
share_uri	Share a link or URI. Parameters include **uri** → The URI to share. **share_position_origin** → Optional position origin for the share sheet. **excluded_cupertino_activities** → Optional list of iOS/macOS activities to exclude.

```python
import os
import flet as ft

class Sender:
    def __init__(self, page: ft.Page):
        self.page = page
        self._share = ft.Share()

    async def text(self, msg, *, subject="", title=""):
```

```
        return await self._share.share_text(msg, subject=subject,
                                            title=title)

    async def link(self, url):
        return await self._share.share_uri(url)

    async def file_bytes(self, data: bytes, *, name, mime, text=""):
        f = ft.ShareFile.from_bytes(data, mime_type=mime, name=name)
        return await self._share.share_files([f], text=text)

    async def file_temp(self, *, name, content: bytes, text=""):
        if self.page.web:
            return None
        temp = await ft.StoragePaths().get_temporary_directory()
        path = os.path.join(temp, name)
        with open(path, "wb") as f:
            f.write(content)
        return await self._share.share_files(
            [ft.ShareFile.from_path(path)], text=text
        )


async def main(page: ft.Page):
    send = Sender(page)
    status = ft.Text()

    async def send_text(_):
        r = await send.text("Hello 👋", subject="Hi", title="Send hello")
        status.value = f"{r.status}"
        page.update()

    page.add(
        ft.Button("Send text", on_click=send_text),
        status,
    )

ft.run(main)
```

UrlLauncher

The **UrlLauncher** utility in Flet enables applications to open external URLs using system browsers, in-app web views or popup windows. It also provides methods to check device compatibility and supported launch behaviors.

Table 3.76

Method/Property	Definition
can_launch_url	Determines whether the specified URL can be handled by any application installed on the device.
close_in_app_web_view	Closes the currently open in-app web view, if one exists.
launch_url	Opens a URL using a web browser or an in-app web view, depending on the selected launch mode and platform. **Parameters:** **url** →The URL to be opened. **mode** → The preferred launch mode for opening the URL. **web_view_configuration** → Optional settings for configuring in-app web views. **browser_configuration** → Optional settings for configuring in-app browser views. **web_only_window_name** → Specifies the window name for web-only launches.
open_window	Opens a popup browser window in web environments. **Parameters:** **url** → The URL to open in the popup window. **title** → The title displayed on the popup window. **width** → The desired width of the popup window in logical pixels. **height** → The desired height of the popup window in logical pixels.
supports_close_for_launch_mode	Checks whether the close_in_app_web_view operation is supported for a given launch mode.
supports_launch_mode	Verifies whether the specified launch mode is supported on the current platform.

Python

```
import flet as ft


async def main(page: ft.Page):
```

```
url_launcher = ft.UrlLauncher()

url = ft.TextField(label="URL to open", value="https://flet.dev",
                   expand=True)
status = ft.Text()

async def can_launch():
    can = await url_launcher.can_launch_url(url.value)
    status.value = f"Can launch: {can}"

async def launch_default():
    await url_launcher.launch_url(url.value)

async def launch_in_app_webview():
    await url_launcher.launch_url(
        url.value,
        mode=ft.LaunchMode.IN_APP_WEB_VIEW,
        web_view_configuration=ft.WebViewConfiguration(
            enable_javascript=True, enable_dom_storage=True
        ),
    )

async def launch_in_app_browser_view():
    await url_launcher.launch_url(
        url.value,
        mode=ft.LaunchMode.IN_APP_BROWSER_VIEW,
        browser_configuration=ft.BrowserConfiguration(show_title=True),
    )

async def launch_external():
    await url_launcher.launch_url(
        url.value,
        mode=ft.LaunchMode.EXTERNAL_APPLICATION,
        web_only_window_name="_blank",
    )

async def launch_popup():
    await url_launcher.open_window(
        url.value, title="Flet popup", width=480, height=640
    )

async def close_webview(_):
    supported = await url_launcher.supports_close_for_launch_mode(
        ft.LaunchMode.IN_APP_WEB_VIEW
    )
    if supported:
        await url_launcher.close_in_app_web_view()
    else:
        status.value = "Web view not supported on this platform"


page.add(
    ft.Column(
        [
```

```
                url,
                ft.Row(
                    [
                    ft.Button("Launch URL", on_click=launch_default),
                    ft.Button(
                        "Launch in-app webview", on_click=launch_in_app_webview
                            ),
                    ft.Button(
                        "Launch in-app browser view",
                                on_click=launch_in_app_browser_view,
                        ),
                        ft.Button("Launch external/new tab",
                                on_click=launch_external),
                        ft.Button("Open popup window (web)",
                                on_click=launch_popup),
                        ft.Button("Can launch?", on_click=can_launch),
                        ft.Button("Close in-app webview", on_click=close_webview),
                        ],
                        wrap=True,
                    ),
                    status,
                ],
            )
        )


ft.run(main)
```

Wakelock

Prevents the device from entering sleep mode while the application is running.

Table 3.77

Method/Property	Definition
enable	Keeps the device awake.
disable()	Allows the device to sleep normally again.
is_enabled()	Returns True if wakelock is currently active.

Flashlight

The Flashlight service provides access to the device's flashlight (torch). It allows you to turn the flashlight on or off programmatically. (supported mainly on mobile devices).

> 📖 **Note**
>
> Flashlight is not part of the core Flet package. It must be installed separately:
> ***pip install flet-flashlight***

Table 3.78

Method/Property	Definition
is_available()	Checks whether the device has a flashlight.
on()	Turns the flashlight on.
off()	Turns the flashlight off.

Python

```python
import flet as ft
import flet_flashlight as ffl

def main(page: ft.Page):
    async def turn_on_flashlight():
        await ffl.Flashlight().on()

    async def turn_off_flashlight():
        await ffl.Flashlight().off()

    page.add(
        ft.Button("Turn On", on_click=turn_on_flashlight),
        ft.Button("Turn Off", on_click=turn_off_flashlight),
    )


ft.run(main)
```

SecureStorage

Provides encrypted storage for sensitive data such as tokens or credentials.

StoragePath

StoragePath provides access to important directories on the device for storing files such as cache, documents, temporary files, and external storage.

Table 3.79

Method/Property	Definition
get_application_cache_directory()	Returns the path to the app-specific cache directory.
get_application_documents_directory()	Returns the path to the directory for user-generated files.
get_application_support_directory()	Returns the path used for internal application support files.
get_console_log_filename()	Returns the path to the console.log file used for debugging.
get_downloads_directory()	Returns the path to the device's downloads directory.
get_external_cache_directories()	Returns a list of external cache directory paths.
get_external_storage_directories()	Returns a list of available external storage directory paths.
get_external_storage_directory()	Returns the path to the main external storage directory.
get_library_directory()	Returns the path to the library directory (primarily used on iOS/macOS).
get_temporary_directory()	Returns the path to a temporary storage directory.

Battery

The Battery service provides information about the device's battery level and state.

Table 3.80

Method/Property	Definition
get_battery_level()	Returns the current battery level (0–100%).
get_battery_state()	Returns the current battery status (charging, discharging, full, or unknown).
is_in_battery_save_mode()	Returns True if battery saver mode is enabled.

on_state_change	Triggered when the battery state changes (e.g., charging to full).

Python

```
import flet as ft

async def main(page: ft.Page):
    page.vertical_alignment = ft.MainAxisAlignment.CENTER
    page.horizontal_alignment = ft.CrossAxisAlignment.CENTER

    async def refresh_info(e: ft.Event[ft.Button] = None):
        level = await battery.get_battery_level()
        state = await battery.get_battery_state()
        save_mode = await battery.is_in_battery_save_mode()
        info.value = (
            f"Battery level: {level}% \n"
            f"Battery state: {state.name} \n"
            f"Battery saver: {'ON' if save_mode else 'OFF'}"
        )

    async def on_state_change(e: ft.BatteryStateChangeEvent):
        print(f"State changed: {e.state}")
        await refresh_info()

    battery = ft.Battery(on_state_change=on_state_change)
    page.services.append(battery)

    page.add(
        ft.SafeArea(
            content=ft.Column(
                horizontal_alignment=ft.CrossAxisAlignment.CENTER,
                controls=[
                    info := ft.Text(),
                    ft.Button("Battery info", on_click=refresh_info),
                ],
            )
        )
    )
    await refresh_info()


ft.run(main)
```

Magnetometer

Measures magnetic field strength using the device's magnetic sensor.

PermissionHandler

Manages runtime permissions required to access certain device features.

ShakeDetector

ShakeDetector detects when the device is physically shaken.

Method/Property	Definition *Table 3.81*
minimum_shake_count(int)	Number of shakes required before detection is triggered.
shake_count_reset_time_ms(int)	Time (in milliseconds) before the shake counter resets.
shake_slop_time_ms(int)	Minimum time between individual shakes.
shake_threshold_gravity(number)	Sensitivity threshold for shake detection (measured in G-force).
on_shake	Triggered when the required shake pattern is detected.

UserAccelerometer

Measures acceleration applied to the device by the user, excluding gravity.

SemanticsService

Improves accessibility by providing semantic information for assistive technologies.

Chapter 4

Publishing and Deployment

Learning Objectives

Upon completing this chapter, you will be able to:

- Package applications into standalone distributable formats.
- Understand and configure the pyproject.toml file.
- Build and package Android applications for deployment.
- Build and package iOS applications for deployment.

Publishing and Deployment

Publishing

Publishing is the final stage of the development process. It begins after your application has been thoroughly tested and debugged to ensure there are no errors, crashes, or unexpected behavior.

At this stage, your application source code and associated files are bundled into a standalone package. This package can then be:

- Distributed through app marketplaces such as:
    - Apple App Store
    - Google Play Store
    - Microsoft Store
    - Snap Store (Linux)
    - Direct web hosting (for web apps)
- Or used for personal and internal distribution.

Flutter SDK Requirement

Flet is built on the Flutter engine, and its UI is rendered using the Flutter SDK.

To package a Flet application, a minimum compatible version of the Flutter SDK is required.

- If Flutter is not available in your system PATH, Flet automatically downloads and installs it the first time you run a ***build*** command.
- It is installed in $HOME/flutter/{version}

> **Note**
>
> An active internet connection is required during the first build process.

The build Command

The ***flet build*** command is used to package your application into a standalone executable or installable file.
Before running the build command, your project must follow this structure:

```
README.md
pyproject.toml
📁 src
├──── 📁 assets
│     └──── icon.png
└──── main.py
```

📖 **Note**

📌 If this structure does not exist, you can create it using:
flet create <project_name>
📌 Internet access is required for this operation.

To build your app, navigate to the project directory and run:

```
flet build <target_platform>
```

Target Platforms

Flet applications can be packaged for multiple platforms. However, some platforms can only build certain targets.

Windows (.exe)

```
flet build windows
```

Can be built on ***Windows*** only.

macOS (.app)

```
flet build macos
```

Can be built on ***macOS*** only.

Linux

```
flet build linux
```

Can be built on ***Linux*** and ***Windows***.

Android (.apk / .aab)

```
flet build apk
flet build aab
```

Can be built on ***Linux*** ,***Windows*** and ***macOS***.

iOS (.ipa)

```
flet build ipa
```

Can be built on ***macOS*** only

Web

```
flet build web
```

Can be built on ***Linux***, ***Windows*** and ***macOS***.

pyproject.toml

The pyproject.toml file is automatically generated when you create a Flet project using ***flet create <project_name>***

The pyproject.toml contains project settings, dependencies, flet version, build configurations and metadata for packaging.

pyproject.toml

```
[project]
name = "comdev"
version = "0.1.0"
description = ""
readme = "README.md"
requires-python = ">=3.10"
authors = [
  { name = "Flet developer", email = "you@example.com" }
]
dependencies = [
  "flet>=0.80.5"
]

[dependency-groups]
dev = [
  "flet-cli>=0.80.5",
  "flet-desktop-light>=0.80.5",
  "flet-web>=0.80.5",
]

[tool.flet]
org = "com.mycompany"
product = "comdev"
company = "Flet"
copyright = "Copyright (C) 2023-2026 by Flet"

[tool.flet.app]
path = "src"
```

You can configure build settings either:

- Directly in pyproject.toml, or
- Via command-line arguments when running *flet build*.

Important Build Configuration Settings

Output Directory

Specifies where the build output will be saved. If the directory already exists, it is deleted and recreated during each build.

flet build

```
flet build <target> --output <path/to/dir>
```

Project Name

The internal identifier of your project. It must be lowercase, no spaces. For example: flet_app, my_application etc. This forms part of the Bundle ID.

flet build

```
flet build <target> --project my_app
```

pyproject.toml

```
[project]
name = "my_app"
```

Product Name

The display name shown in window titles, app launchers and about dialogs.

flet build

```
flet build <target> --product "My First App"
```

pyproject.toml

```
[tool.flet]
product = "My First App"
```

Artifact Name

The filename of the generated executable or app bundle. It determines .exe name on Windows and sets .app name on macOS.
It does **not** affect the Bundle ID.

flet build

pyproject.toml

```
flet build <target> --artifact "My First App"
```

```
[tool.flet]
artifact = "My First App"
```

Organization Name

A reverse-domain identifier used as a prefix for the Bundle ID.
For example com.company.

flet build

```
flet build <target> --org com.company
```

pyproject.toml

```
[tool.flet]
org = "com.company"
```

Bundle ID

The unique identifier of your application. For example, com.mycompany.my_app.
If not specified, it is generated from Organization name and Project name.

flet build

```
flet build <target> --bundle-id com.company.myapp
```

pyproject.toml

```
[tool.flet]
bundle_id = "com.company.myapp"
```

Company Name

Displayed in about dialogs and Application metadata (especially on desktop platforms)

flet build

```
flet build <target> --company "My Company"
```

pyproject.toml

```
[tool.flet]
company = "My Company"
```

Copyright

Copyright text displayed in about dialogs and application metadata

flet build

```
flet build <target> --copyright "Copyright © 2027 My Company"
```

pyproject.toml

```
[tool.flet]
copyright = "Copyright © 2027 My Company"
```

Build Number

This is the build number (integer) that increases with every build. It is used by app stores to differentiate builds. Example: 1, 2 and 3.

flet build

```
flet build <target> --build-number 1
```

pyproject.toml

```
[tool.flet]
build_number = 1
```

Build Version

User-facing version in x.y.z format. Example:1.0.0, 1.1.0 and 2.0.0 .
Increment this for every public release.

flet build

```
flet build <target> --build-version 1.0.0
```

pyproject.toml

```
[project]
version = "1.0.0"
```

Adding Dependencies

Any external Python package your application depends on must be added to pyproject.toml.
Without declaring dependencies, they will not be packaged into the final build.

pyproject.toml

```
[project]
dependencies = [
    "flet",
    "requests",
```

```
    "flet_charts",
    "flet_audio",
    "ffmpeg",
]
```

Icons

You can customize your application icon (except Linux) by placing: icon.png inside the *assets* directory.

Splash Screen

A splash screen appears when the app launches, usually showing a logo while the app loads. To customize this, place splash.png in the *assets* directory. It is supported on iOS, Android and Web only.

Splash Background Colors

You can define:

- **Splash Color** → Background for light mode
- **Splash Dark Color** → Background for dark mode

flet build

```
flet build <target> --splash-color #f0f0f0 -splash-dark-color #eeeeee
```

pyproject.toml

```
[tool.flet.splash]
color = "#ffffff"
dark_color = "#24252B"
```

Boot Screen

The boot screen appears after the splash screen while the packaged archive (app.zip) is being extracted, typically on first launch.

It is **disabled by default** and should be enabled only if extraction time is noticeable.

pyproject.toml

```
[tool.flet.app.boot_screen]
```

```
show = true
message = "App will launch very soon"
```

Startup Screen

The startup screen appears after the boot screen while the Python runtime and dependencies are loading. It is **disabled by default**.

pyproject.toml

```
[tool.flet.app.startup_screen]
show = true
message = "Starting up the app"
```

Permissions

Different platforms restrict access to device hardware such as Camera, Microphone, Storage, Location, Notifications, Bluetooth etc.

To use these features, you must declare the required permissions in pyproject.toml. Without proper permission declarations, the app may:

- Fail to access hardware
- Be rejected during app store review

📌 location

pyproject.toml

```
# iOS
[tool.flet.ios.info]
NSLocationWhenInUseUsageDescription = "This app uses location service when in use."
NSLocationAlwaysAndWhenInUseUsageDescription = "This app uses location service."

# macOS
[tool.flet.macos.info]
NSLocationWhenInUseUsageDescription = "This app uses location service when in use."
NSLocationAlwaysAndWhenInUseUsageDescription = "This app uses location service."

[tool.flet.macos.entitlement]
"com.apple.security.personal-information.location" = true

# Android
[tool.flet.android.permission]
"android.permission.ACCESS_FINE_LOCATION" = true
"android.permission.ACCESS_COARSE_LOCATION" = true
"android.permission.ACCESS_BACKGROUND_LOCATION" = true
```

```
[tool.flet.android.feature]
"android.hardware.location.network" = false
"android.hardware.location.gps" = false
```

📌 microphone

pyproject.toml

```
# iOS
[tool.flet.ios.info]
NSMicrophoneUsageDescription = "This app uses microphone to record sounds."

# macOS
[tool.flet.macos.info]
NSMicrophoneUsageDescription = "This app uses microphone to record sounds."

[tool.flet.macos.entitlement]
"com.apple.security.device.audio-input" = true

# Android
[tool.flet.android.permission]
"android.permission.RECORD_AUDIO" = true
"android.permission.WRITE_EXTERNAL_STORAGE" = true
"android.permission.READ_EXTERNAL_STORAGE" = true
```

📌 camera

pyproject.toml

```
# iOS
[tool.flet.ios.info]
NSCameraUsageDescription = "This app uses the camera to capture photos and videos."

# macOS
[tool.flet.macos.info]
NSCameraUsageDescription = "This app uses the camera to capture photos and videos."

[tool.flet.macos.entitlement]
"com.apple.security.device.camera" = true

# Android
[tool.flet.android.permission]
"android.permission.CAMERA" = true

[tool.flet.android.feature]
"android.hardware.camera" = false
"android.hardware.camera.any" = false
"android.hardware.camera.front" = false
```

```
"android.hardware.camera.external" = false
"android.hardware.camera.autofocus" = false
```

photo_library

pyproject.toml

```
# iOS
[tool.flet.ios.info]
NSPhotoLibraryUsageDescription = "This app saves photos to the photo library."

# macOS
[tool.flet.macos.info]
NSPhotoLibraryUsageDescription = "This app saves photos to the photo library."

[tool.flet.macos.entitlement]
"com.apple.security.personal-information.photos-library" = true

# Android
[tool.flet.android.permission]
"android.permission.READ_MEDIA_VISUAL_USER_SELECTED" = true
```

flet build

```
flet build <target> --permission location camera microphone
```

pyproject.toml

```
[tool.flet]
permissions = ["location", "microphone"]
```

Android Packaging for Deployment

Flet allows you to package your application into an **APK** or **AAB (Android App Bundle)** using the *flet build* command. While this may be sufficient for testing, deploying to the Google Play Store requires additional steps such as signing and proper configuration.

Android SDK Requirements

Building for Android requires:

- **Java Development Kit (JDK 17)**
- **Android SDK**

If either is missing or incompatible, Flet automatically installs the required tools the first time you *run flet build*.

Installation Locations

JDK

$HOME/java/<version>

Android SDK (if Android Studio is installed)

- macOS: ~/Library/Android/sdk
- Windows: %LOCALAPPDATA%\Android\Sdk
- Linux: ~/Android/Sdk

If Android Studio is NOT installed

- macOS/Linux: ~/Android/sdk
- Windows: %USERPROFILE%\Android\sdk

Flet also respects the following environment variables if already configured:

- ANDROID_HOME
- ANDROID_SDK_ROOT

Building Android Packages

Build APK

flet build apk

This generates a **release APK**. Release builds are optimized for production and are suitable for app store distribution

Build Android App Bundle (Recommended)

flet build aab

The AAB format is recommended for Google Play Store because:

- It reduces app download size
- Google Play generates optimized APKs per device
- It improves installation efficiency

Split APK per ABI (Optional Optimization)

Android devices use different CPU architectures (ABIs), such as:

- arm64-v8a
- armeabi-v7a
- x86
- x86_64

By default, Flet builds a **fat APK** containing binaries for all supported ABIs. This ensures maximum compatibility but increases file size.
Enabling ABI split:

- Generates one APK per architecture
- Reduces file size
- Requires distributing the correct APK for each device

flet build

```
flet build apk -split-per-abi
```

pyproject.toml

```
[tool.flet]
split_per_abi = true
```

For Play Store deployment, using **AAB is preferred** instead of manual ABI splits.

Signing for Google Play Store

Android requires all apps to be digitally signed before installation or publishing. When deploying to Google Play:

- You upload an **AAB or APK signed with an Upload Key**
- Google Play re-signs the app using the **App Signing Key**
- Users download the version signed by Google

If you do not provide an upload keystore, Flet signs the app with a debug key. Debug-signed apps cannot be uploaded to the Play Store.

Creating an Upload Keystore

If you do not already have a keystore, create one using:

macOS / Linux

```
keytool -genkey -v -keystore ~/upload-keystore.jks -keyalg RSA \
-keysize 2048 -validity 10000 -alias upload
```

Windows (PowerShell)

```
keytool -genkey -v -keystore $env:USERPROFILE\upload-keystore.jks `
-storetype JKS -keyalg RSA -keysize 2048 -validity 10000 `
-alias upload
```

You will be prompted to enter:

- Keystore password
- Key alias
- Key password
- Organization details

A file named **upload-keystore.jks** will be created in your home directory (or the specified location).

Keep this file secure. Losing it may prevent you from updating your app.

Key Alias

The unique name assigned to the key inside the keystore.

flet build

```
flet build aab --android-signing-key-alias value
```

pyproject.toml

```
[tool.flet.android.signing]
key_alias = "value"
```

Keystore

The .jks file that stores your signing keys.

flet build

```
flet build aab --android-signing-key-store path/to/store.jks
```

pyproject.toml

```
[tool.flet.android.signing]
key_store = "path/to/store.jks"
```

Keystore Password

Password used to unlock the keystore file.

flet build

```
flet build aab --android-signing-store-password value
```

Key Password

Password used to access the private key within the keystore.

flet build

```
flet build aab --android-signing-key-password value
```

Minimum SDK version

The minimum Android API level your app can be installed on.

pyproject.toml

```
[tool.flet.android]
min_sdk_version = 24
```

Target SDK version

The Android API level your app targets for runtime behavior and compatibility.

pyproject.toml

```
[tool.flet.android]
target_sdk_version = 35
```

Meta-Data (Android Manifest)

Meta-data is additional information you can attach to your Android application. It is stored as a name–value pair and is usually used to pass configuration details to the Android system or other components.

Each meta-data item contains:

- **name** → A unique identifier (usually written in Java-style format). Example: com.sample.project.activity.fred
- **value** → The value assigned to the name.

You can define Android meta-data inside your pyproject.toml file or use in *flet build* like this:

flet build

```
flet build apk --android-meta-data name_1=value_1 name_2=value_2
```

pyproject.toml

```
[tool.flet.android.meta_data]
"name_1" = "value_1"
"name_2" = "value_2"
```

During the build process, Flet automatically converts this into the appropriate entries inside AndroidManifest.xml:

AndroidManifest.xml

```
<application>
    <meta-data android:name="name_1" android:value="value_1" />
    <meta-data android:name="name_2" android:value="value_2" />
</application>
```

Permissions (Android)

Permissions allow your app to access protected device features such as storage, camera, location, etc. Whenever possible, use Flet's **cross-platform permissions.** If a permission is specific to Android, you can declare it in pyproject.toml.

Adding Android Permissions

flet build

```
flet build apk --android-permissions
android.permission.READ_EXTERNAL_STORAGE=True
android.permission.WRITE_EXTERNAL_STORAGE=True
```

pyproject.toml

```
[tool.flet.android.permission]
"android.permission.READ_EXTERNAL_STORAGE" = true
"android.permission.WRITE_EXTERNAL_STORAGE" = true
```

This will automatically be added to AndroidManifest.xml as:

AndroidManifest.xml

```
<manifest>
  <uses-permission android:name="android.permission.READ_EXTERNAL_STORAGE" />
  <uses-permission android:name="android.permission.WRITE_EXTERNAL_STORAGE" />
</manifest>
```

iOS Packaging for Deployment

Packaging an iOS application is more restrictive than other platforms because Apple requires code signing and official developer credentials before an app can be distributed. To generate a certified **.ipa** file for App Store submission, several tools and configurations are required.

Prerequisites

Rosetta 2

A translation layer required on Apple Silicon Macs when certain Flutter or CocoaPods components still use Intel binaries. Install it if prompted by running:
sudo softwareupdate --install-rosetta --agree-to-license

Xcode (version 15 or later)

Apple's official development environment used to compile and sign iOS applications. After installation, open Xcode once to accept the license agreement and install additional components.

CocoaPods (1.16 or later)

A dependency manager required to build and integrate Flutter plugins into the iOS project.

Building an IPA File

To build an iOS archive: *flet build ipa*

This command creates an .xcarchive file and, when signing is properly configured, exports a distributable .ipa file suitable for testing or uploading to App Store Connect. To successfully generate a production-ready .ipa, you must have:

- An active Apple Developer Program subscription
- A registered App ID
- A Bundle ID that matches your Flet configuration
- A valid signing certificate
- A provisioning profile

Building for iOS Simulator

For testing without signing: *flet build ios-simulator*

This command (macOS only) builds an unsigned .app file for use in the iOS Simulator. It does not require a developer account, signing certificate, or provisioning profile.

Application Identifier (App ID)

An App ID uniquely identifies your app within Apple's ecosystem. It is required for signing and enabling services like push notifications, iCloud, or in-app purchases.
An App ID consists of:

- **Team ID** – A 10-character string assigned to your Apple Developer account.
- **Bundle ID** – A reverse-domain identifier such as com.company.myapp.

Example:
Team ID → ABCDEF1234
Bundle ID → com.company.myapp
App ID → ABCDEF1234.com.company.myapp

The Bundle ID defined in your Flet configuration must exactly match the one registered in your Apple Developer account.

Team ID

The Team ID identifies your Apple Developer organization. It can be found in your Apple Developer account dashboard and must be included during the export and signing process.

flet build

```
flet build ipa --ios-team-id ABCDEFE234
```

pyproject.toml

```
[tool.flet.ios]
team_id = "ABCDEFE234"
```

Signing Certificate

A signing certificate verifies your identity as a developer and allows Apple to trust your application.

You may use either a specific certificate (by name or SHA-1 hash) or allow Xcode to automatically select one. Common automatic selectors include:

- Apple Development
- Apple Distribution
- iOS Developer
- iOS Distribution
- Developer ID Application
- Mac Developer
- Mac App Distribution

For App Store submission, you typically use **Apple Distribution**.

flet build

```
flet build ipa --ios-signing-certificate "Apple Distribution"
```

pyproject.toml

```
[tool.flet.ios]
signing_certificate = "Apple Distribution"
```

Permissions on iOS

iOS permissions are defined in the **Info.plist** file using privacy usage descriptions. These entries explain to users why your app requires access to resources such as the camera, microphone, or location.

Flet allows you to:

- Use cross-platform permission bundles
- Add or override iOS-specific entries

flet build

```
flet build ipa --info-plist NSLocationWhenInUseUsageDescription="This app
uses location service when in use."
```

pyproject.toml

```
[tool.flet.ios.info]
NSCameraUsageDescription = "This app will access the camera ..."
```

Index

Author's Remarks

I am truly delighted that you chose to read this book. In a world filled with countless learning resources, your decision to invest your time and attention here means a great deal. Writing this book has been a journey of passion, research, testing, and refinement, and knowing that it is now in your hands is both humbling and exciting.
My sincere hope is that this book becomes more than just a guide—it becomes a stepping stone in your development journey. Whether you are a beginner taking your first steps into application development or an experienced programmer expanding your skills, I hope the knowledge shared here equips you with clarity, confidence, and the courage to build meaningful projects.

Technology continues to evolve rapidly. Frameworks improve, tools change, and new opportunities emerge every day. However, one thing remains constant: the value of continuous learning. By choosing to study and improve your skills, you are already positioning yourself for growth and success. I encourage you not only to read but to practice. Build small projects. Experiment with ideas. Break things and fix them again. That is how true mastery is developed.
This book was written with the intention of making complex ideas simple and practical. Every explanation, code sample, and illustration was carefully structured to help you move from understanding concepts to applying them confidently. If at any point you feel challenged, remember that learning is a process. Take your time, revisit sections when necessary, and most importantly, stay consistent.

Ouereila Publishing is a growing firm committed to producing practical, accessible, and high-quality technical resources. Growth, however, is a shared effort. We improve through constructive criticism, thoughtful feedback, and the experiences of our readers. Your suggestions, observations, and insights are invaluable to us.
If you have questions, feedback, corrections, or recommendations, please do not hesitate to reach out. We genuinely appreciate hearing from our readers. You can contact us via email at: ouereila@gmail.com
Your feedback helps us refine future editions and create even better learning materials for developers around the world.
Thank you once again for your trust, your time, and your commitment to learning. I wish you success, creativity, and excellence in your journey as a developer.

Warm regards,
The Author

Acknowledgments

This book would not have been possible without the support, encouragement, and contributions of several remarkable individuals.
First, I extend my heartfelt gratitude to my dear friend, Anokyewaa Theresa, whose encouragement and thoughtful support throughout this journey meant more than words can express. Your belief in this project gave me strength during both the exciting and challenging moments of writing.

To my family, especially my beautiful sisters, Alice and Vero, thank you for your constant love, patience, and motivation. Your support has always been a source of inspiration, and I am truly grateful to have you in my life.
I would also like to sincerely thank every member of the Ouereila Team for their dedication, careful review, constructive feedback, and incredible support. Your commitment to excellence helped refine this work and bring it to its final form.

To everyone who contributed in any way—through encouragement, technical insight, proofreading, or simple words of motivation—please accept my deepest appreciation.
This book is not just the result of one person's effort; it is the outcome of collective support and shared belief. Thank you all.

About the Author

Williams Asiedu is a computer engineer, author, and philanthropist with a deep passion for technology and social impact. He earned his Ph.D. from the Illinois Institute of Technology in Chicago, USA, and currently works as a Data Analyst, applying advanced computational and analytical techniques to solve real-world problems.

Beyond his professional career in technology, Williams is a dedicated writer who has authored several books, including programming guides and works of fiction. His writing reflects both technical expertise and a commitment to making knowledge accessible to learners at all levels. Through clear explanations and practical examples, he aims to empower readers to develop skills that can transform their careers and communities.

Williams is also actively engaged in philanthropic efforts. Through his publications and personal initiatives, he supports individuals and communities in the fight against poverty, discrimination, and abuse—particularly in parts of Africa. He strongly believes that social responsibility is a collective obligation and that meaningful change happens when individuals contribute in their own unique ways.

Mr. Asiedu maintains that knowledge, opportunity, and compassion are powerful tools for transformation. He encourages readers not only to pursue professional excellence but also to use their skills and resources to uplift others.

Through both technology and service, Williams Asiedu remains committed to building solutions that improve lives and inspire hope.

6 9 0 2 9 7 *